Dedicated to the memory of my father,
the late Newton James, and to the
memory of Darius Simon,
a philosopher and a scholar.

CONTENTS IN BRIEF

a problem-solving approach

MicroECONOMICS

fifth edition

a problem-solving approach

MicroECONOMICS

fifth edition

Elijah M. James

Dawson College and Concordia University

Prentice Hall Canada Inc., Scarborough, Ontario

Canadian Cataloguing in Publication Data

James, Elijah M.
   Microeconomics: a problem-solving approach

5th ed.
Includes index.
ISBN 0-13-011615-7

1. Microeconomics. I. Title.

HB172.J35 2000   338.5   C99-930056-3

Prentice-Hall, Inc., Upper Saddle River, New Jersey
Prentice-Hall International (UK) Limited, London
Prentice-Hall of Australia, Pty. Limited, Sydney
Prentice-Hall Hispanoamericana, S.A., Mexico City
Prentice-Hall of India Private Limited, New Delhi
Prentice-Hall of Japan, Inc., Tokyo
Simon & Schuster Southeast Asia Private Limited, Singapore
Editora Prentice-Hall do Brasil, Ltda., Rio de Janeiro

ISBN 0-13-011615-7

Publisher: Pat Ferrier
Acquisitions Editor: Sarah Kimball
Associate Editor: Laurie Goebel
Senior Marketing Manager: Ann Byford
Copy Editor: Laurel Sparrow
Production Editor: Sarah Dann
Production Coordinator: Jane Schell
Permissions/Photo Research: Susan Wallace-Cox
Art Director: Mary Opper
Cover Design: Lisa LaPointe
Cover Image: Glenn Ryan
Page Layout: Nelson Gonzalez

2 3 4 5   04 03 02 01 00

Printed and bound in Canada.

Visit the Prentice Hall Canada Web site! Send us your comments, browse our catalogues, and more at **www.phcanada.com**. Or reach us through e-mail at **phcinfo_pubcanada@prenhall.com**.

DETAILED CONTENTS

CHAPTER 3   THE ECONOMIC PROBLEM: THE PROBLEM OF SCARCITY   33

CHAPTER 4   ELEMENTS OF DEMAND AND SUPPLY   54

PART II   MICROECONOMICS

CHAPTER 5   ELASTICITY   83

CHAPTER 6   THE THEORY OF CONSUMER BEHAVIOUR   103

CHAPTER 7   BUSINESS ORGANIZATION, SPECIALIZATION, AND INDUSTRIAL LOCATION   118

CHAPTER 8   THEORY OF PRODUCTION   132

CHAPTER 12   IMPERFECT COMPETITION: MONOPOLISTIC COMPETITION AND OLIGOPOLY   208

PART IV   CURRENT ECONOMIC PROBLEMS

CHAPTER 20   TARIFFS AND TRADE POLICY ISSUES   335

SPECIAL FEATURES

GLOBAL PERSPECTIVE

APPLICATIONS

PREFACE

Economic times are changing, and economics textbooks should reflect these changes. Few of us teach economics the way we did 20 or even 15 years ago. Not only have the topics selected for inclusion in our courses undergone considerable change, but so has the degree of emphasis placed on various topics. Moreover, students have changed. Technology has placed certain resources at their disposal, like computers, the Internet, VCRs, and the World Wide Web. Economics textbooks should keep up-to-date with these developments.

Amidst all of these changes, the fundamental purpose of the fifth edition of *Economics: A Problem-Solving Approach* has remained the same as for the previous editions: to present introductory economics to students clearly and lucidly, so that they can understand basic economic concepts, theories, and relationships and apply these to their day-to-day lives, and be able to make sense of economic events that are happening in the world around them.

One cannot claim that the fifth edition of *Economics: A Problem-Solving Approach* is an entirely new book, but it is more than just another edition. It builds on the strengths of the fourth edition and introduces several new features. Revisions, additions, extensions, and deletions have been made in order to bring the book up to date. Some important changes have been made to the organizational structure of the book, and the author believes that these are improvements that will help students to better understand how our economic system works.

A focus of this fifth edition is "readability," which has been a hallmark of this text through all its revisions. The author has gone to great lengths and has taken great pains to ensure that students continue to find this book easy to read and understand. The fifth edition of *Economics: A Problem-Solving Approach* reflects the author's philosophy that a good introductory textbook in economics should make this abstract subject comprehensible without avoiding difficult concepts and issues. Here is a truly student-friendly textbook, designed to facilitate students' understanding of economic principles and their use of economic tools to solve real-world economic problems. This has been one of the major objectives of this book.

SUBSTANTIVE CHANGES IN THE FIFTH EDITION

Naturally, the statistics have been updated. In addition, numerous changes have been made throughout, in both the microeconomic and the macroeconomic parts of the book.

Changes to Microeconomics

1. The material in Chapters 1, 2, and 3 of the fourth edition is now contained in Chapters 1 and 3. The material covered under "Some Useful Tools" in Appendix 1A of the fourth edition has been expanded and is now contained in a new Chapter 2.

2. The appendices to Chapters 6 and 8 have been deleted.

3. Chapter 16 has been substantially rewritten and re-worked with new emphasis on pollution.

4. Chapter 17 has been expanded and now includes a discussion of the agri-food industry in Canada.

5. Chapter 20 on Tariffs now contains a more detailed discussion of NAFTA.

Changes to <u>Macroeconomics</u>

1. Chapter 24 now contains a more detailed discussion of aggregate demand and aggregate supply shifters.

2. Chapter 29 on the Foreign Sector has been eliminated and much of the material is now contained in Chapter 36 on Economic Policy in an Open Economy.

3. The material in Chapters 31 to 34 of the fourth edition has been re-arranged into three chapters (Chapters 30, 31, and 32).

4. Chapter 35 of the fourth edition has been dropped and the Rational Expectations Hypothesis is now contained in Chapter 33, with expanded treatment of the natural rate of unemployment and the NAIRU.

5. Chapter 34 on Deficits, Surpluses and the National Debt contains an expanded treatment of surpluses to reflect the Canadian reality.

SPECIAL PEDAGOGICAL AND OTHER FEATURES

1. The fifth edition of *Economics: A Problem-Solving Approach* contains a series of Web sites and Internet exercises that provide an opportunity for students to access information on economics and related topics.

2. Seven new video cases have been written for this fifth edition. They are designed to be used in conjunction with seven specially selected CBC video segments.

3. The surplus has occupied the spot once held by the deficit as a hot macroeconomic issue. It receives greater attention in this fifth edition. The public debt and unemployment continue to receive due emphasis.

4. The international economic environment and global issues continue to exert significant influence on the Canadian economy. New *Global Perspectives* have been written for this fifth edition.

5. The *Applications* feature has been retained, and new applications have been added.

6. The use of practical examples and real statistical data help to make economics come alive, as students are able to relate the theories to their own life experiences. This useful pedagogical feature is retained in this edition.

7. The fifth edition continues to engage the students by using the investigative approach and by appealing to their sense of intuition.

8. Marginal notes and definitions, the highlighting of important terms and concepts throughout the text, Chapter Summaries, and the listing of important terms at the end of each chapter are all important pedagogical devices retained in the fifth edition.

9. The Questions for Review and Discussion provide opportunities for students to test their understanding of the material, and the Problems and Exercises allow students to actually *do* economic analysis.

10. A new feature of the fifth edition is the inclusion of questions for class discussion or group work. This gives students an opportunity to actually practise economics and to discuss issues among themselves.

11. The glossary continues to be one of the most extensive glossaries of any introductory economics text.

12. As in the fourth edition, the judicious use of colour in this fifth edition enhances graphical presentations and emphasizes important points.

13. The tradition of using tabular and graphical analyses to reinforce each other in the presentation of the material continues in this edition.

14. The statistical tables in Appendix I have been updated. Students and instructors both should find this to be very useful and convenient.

TO THE INSTRUCTOR

For instructional purposes, the text is arranged so that any sequence of chapters may be followed. The following outlines are suggestions only. It is expected that instructors will adapt the text according to their own particular needs and preferences.

OUTLINE FOR A ONE-SEMESTER COURSE IN MICROECONOMICS

Chapter	Title
1.	The Nature of Economics
2.	Some Useful Tools
3.	The Economic Problem: The Problem of Scarcity
4.	Elements of Demand and Supply
5.	Elasticity
6.	The Theory of Consumer Behaviour
8.	Theory of Production
9.	The Costs of Production
10.	The Purely Competitive Firm
11.	The Theory of Monopoly
12.	Imperfect Competition: Monopolistic Competition and Oligopoly
Note:	Chapters or sections of chapters may be added or deleted according to the instructor's needs. For example, given the importance of international trade to the Canadian economy, instructors may want to include material from Chapters 19 and 20.

OUTLINE FOR A ONE-SEMESTER COURSE IN MACROECONOMICS

Chapter	Title
1.	The Nature of Economics
2.	Some Useful Tools
3.	The Economic Problem: The Problem of Scarcity
4.	Elements of Demand and Supply
21.	An Overview of Macroeconomics
22.	National Income and Product Accounts
23.	Unemployment and Inflation
24.	Aggregate Demand and Aggregate Supply
25.	Equilibrium in the Product Market
26.	Changes in Income and the Multiplier
28.	Fiscal Policy
29.	Business Fluctuations
30.	Money: Its Nature and Functions
32.	Monetary Theory and Policy
33.	Inflation and Anti-Inflation Policies

34.	Deficits, Surpluses, and the National Debt
35.	Balance of Payments and Exchange rates
Note:	Chapters or sections of chapters may be added or deleted according to the instructor's needs.

OUTLINE FOR A ONE-SEMESTER COURSE COVERING BOTH MICRO AND MACRO

Chapter	**Title**
1.	The Nature of Economics
2.	Some Useful Tools
3.	The Economic Problem: The Problem of Scarcity
4.	Elements of Demand and Supply

Micro

5.	Elasticity
6.	The Theory of Consumer Behaviour
8.	Theory of Production
9.	The Costs of Production
10.	The Purely Competitive Firm
11.	The Theory of Monopoly
12.	Imperfect Competition: Monopolistic Competition and Oligopoly
19.	International Trade

Macro

21.	An Overview of Macroeconomics
22.	National Income and Product Accounts
23.	Unemployment and Inflation
24.	Aggregate Demand and Aggregate Supply
25.	Equilibrium in the Product Market
26.	Changes in Income and the Multiplier
28.	Fiscal Policy
30.	Money: Its Nature and Functions
32.	Monetary Theory and Policy
34.	Deficits, Surpluses, and the National Debt
35.	Balance of Payments and Exchange Rates

Note: The instructor may wish to substitute certain chapters for different emphasis or to omit sections of some chapters.

SUPPLEMENTARY MATERIALS

Video segments, a study guide, an instructor's manual, a test bank, transparency masters, and a website have been prepared to accompany *Economics: A Problem-Solving Approach*, Fifth Edition.

Study Guides

A Programmed Learning Guide for each of *Microeconomics* and *Macroeconomics* takes students through a series of programs and exercises designed to enhance their understanding of economics.

Instructor's Manual

The instructor's manual is designed to help the instructor make the best possible use of his or her limited time. It outlines the objectives of each chapter, and provides answers to the questions at the end of the chapters.

Transparency Masters

These are clear and enlarged reproductions of tables, graphs, and charts presented in the text. Instructors using a projector will find these of immense value.

Test Item File

A test item file containing a wide selection of multiple-choice and true or false questions based on *Economics: A Problem-Solving Approach* has been prepared for instructors using the text. The questions have been carefully selected with economic comprehension as the central consideration.

PH Test Manager

The test item file is also available electronically in Windows.

Videos

Seven new video segments have been selected for use with the cases in the fifth edition of the text.

Companion Website

For the fifth edition, we have added a website to our list of supplements. This site contains an online study guide as well as other valuable resources for students and instructors. Visit the site at **www.prenticehall.ca/james**.

ACKNOWLEDGEMENTS

One of the more pleasurable tasks in writing a book is that the author gets an opportunity to acknowledge the contributions of the many people who have helped to make the book a reality, and to thank them for their part in the project. So, as has been my tradition, I wish to thank the many individuals who have helped to make possible the fifth edition of *Economics: A Problem-Solving Approach*.

I am indebted to my colleagues at Dawson College, John Abbott College, Concordia University, and in colleges and universities across Canada and elsewhere. I thank them for their generosity in sharing their wisdom, experience, and insight with me. Matlub Hussain, Voyo Kovalski, and Mohammed Islam of Dawson College deserve credit for much of the improvement in the fifth edition. I owe a debt of gratitude to Dan Otchere and Alan Hochstein of Concordia University, Charles Reid, June Riley, and Cheryl Jenkins of John Abbott College, Izhar Mirza and Alaka Ganguli of Dawson College, and Sadat Kazi of Vanier College.

I acknowledge, with pleasure, the reviewers of this edition. I am appreciative of the constructive comments and suggestions made by Rene H. Blaise of Southern Alberta Institute of Technology, Tom Chambers of Canadore College, John Farrugia of Mohawk College, James Hnatchuk and John Saba of Champlain Regional College, and Peter Peters of University College of the Cariboo. Many of their suggestions have been incorporated in this fifth edition of the book. My students at Dawson College, John Abbott College, and Concordia University have again forced me to "come clear." I thank them for helping me to make the book easy to read and student-friendly.

I wish again to acknowledge the great debt that I owe to the Prentice Hall team who worked on this project. Their contributions must be registered. I thank Sarah Kimball, Acquisitions Editor; Laurie Goebel, Associate Editor; and Melanie Meharchand and Sarah Dann, Production Editors.

Ms. Constance Patricia Simon has once more demonstrated her unselfishness by sacrificing her time which was particularly scarce during the preparation of this edition. She provided expert secretarial services, and I owe her a tremendous debt of gratitude. Thanks Pat, you are wonderful. I must also thank my dear friend, Veronica Martin, for providing much-needed inspiration while I was working on the manuscript. Veronica, your contribution is much appreciated.

Finally, I must thank my children Ted and Andrea, whose support and encouragement have been forever with me, and my parents for their sacrifice and their love. In a very real sense, they started it all.

Elijah M. James

ABBREVIATIONS

AC	Average cost		LP	Liquidity preference
AD	Aggregate demand		LRAC	Long-run average cost
AE	Aggregate expenditure		M	Imports
AFL-CIO	American Federation of Labour and Congress of Industrial Organization		MC	Marginal cost
			MEI	Marginal efficiency of investment
AO	Aggregate output		M(P)P	Marginal (physical) product
A(P)P	Average (physical) product		MPC	Marginal propensity to consume
APC	Average propensity to consume		MPS	Marginal propensity to save
APS	Average propensity to save		MPW	Marginal propensity to withdraw
AR	Average revenue		MR	Marginal revenue
AS	Aggregate supply		MRP	Marginal revenue product
AFC	Average fixed cost		MTR	Marginal tax rate
ATC	Average total cost		NDI	Net domestic income
AVC	Average variable cost		NI	National income
C	Consumption (personal expenditure on consumer goods and services)		OECD	Organization for Economic Cooperation and Development
CCU	Confederation of Canadian Unions		OPEC	Organization of Petroleum Exporting Countries
CDIC	Canada Deposit Insurance Corporation			
CFL	Canadian Federation of Labour		P	Price or price level
CLC	Canadian Labour Congress		PI	Personal income
CNTU	Confederation of National Trade Unions		Q	Quantity (output)
CPI	Consumer price index		r	Rate of interest
CSD	Centrale des syndicats democratiques		S	Saving
DI	Disposable income		T	Taxes
EB	External balance		TC	Total cost
EC	European Community		TFC	Total fixed cost
G	Government purchases of goods and services		TVC	Total variable cost
			TR	Total revenue
GDP	Gross domestic product		V	Velocity of circulation (of money)
GNP	Gross national product		WHO	World Health Organization
I	Investment		X	Exports
IB	Internal balance		(X–M)	Net exports
K	Capital		Y	Income (output)

CHAPTER 1

THE NATURE OF ECONOMICS

Learning Objectives

After studying this chapter, you should be able to:

1 formulate an adequate definition of economics

2 discuss the subject matter of economics

3 discuss the importance of economics

4 explain what economists do in terms of employment

5 discuss the nature of scientific inquiry

6 explain economic methodology

7 distinguish between positive and normative economics

8 explain why economists sometimes disagree

9 understand relations among variables

10 explain the meaning of economic policy

11 distinguish between microeconomics and macroeconomics

I believe economic understanding is to be gained through an understanding of the central core of economics that dominates all economics situations and issues.

Ben W. Lewis, *"Economic Understanding: Why and What."*

INTRODUCTION

The Supreme Court of Canada recently handed down its decision regarding the unity issue in Canada. This has given rise to a new round of debate over the issue of the "Quebec question." Is this a purely political issue, or does it have economic implications? What will be the impact of Quebec's secession on the economy of Canada? Does the mere threat of separation pose a problem for the Canadian economy? These are important issues.

When the fourth edition of this book was being prepared, the deficit and the debt were major economic concerns. Now, the federal government's budget has shifted from a deficit to a surplus position. At the end of 1997, the value of the Canadian dollar, in terms of the U.S. dollar, was $0.7222. By the end of August 1998, the value of the dollar had fallen to just over $0.63. Some claim that this fall in value is good for the Canadian economy, while others say that it is a disaster. Can there be elements of truth in both views?

The government claims that not much can be done about the falling dollar because its decline is caused by external forces, that is, economic events in Russia and Asia. It seems as if we have been more successful in controlling inflation than in reducing unemployment. Youth unemployment is still high, and many graduates are experiencing considerable difficulty in finding suitable jobs. For many, job prospects are less than optimistic. Whereas inflation has virtually disappeared from the Canadian economy, the unemployment rate is still hovering above eight percent. Why is this so? Listen to the radio, watch television, or pick up a newspaper, and you are bound to see or hear some news relating to the economy. Indeed, economic events are all around us, reminding us of the importance of understanding economics.

A knowledge of economics will help us to understand many of the issues which confront us daily.

There can be little doubt that economic issues occupy a key position in the political arena. Governments are frequently judged by their economic performances, and their chances of reelection are closely correlated with the effects of their economic policies. Clearly then, it is to our benefit to understand economics.

THE SUBJECT MATTER OF ECONOMICS

Consumers, businesses, the various levels of government, and all types of other organizations are always making choices. These choices determine how society uses its resources. If people choose to purchase huge quantities of personal computers and microwave ovens, society's resources will be used to produce these items. If a government chooses to upgrade its highway system and to improve the education and health of its citizens, then resources will be allocated to roads and to education and health services. How do individuals, firms, governments, and other organizations make decisions about the use of society's resources? This question is at the heart of economics.

Economics is the social science that studies how people cope with the ever-present problem of scarcity.

Economists concern themselves with the behaviour of human beings engaged in the activity of using scarce resources to satisfy their unlimited wants. As a science that studies human behaviour, economics belongs in the same category as social psychology, anthropology, sociology, and political science. For our purposes, let us adopt the following definition of economics:

Learning Objective 1: formulate a definition of economics

Social science studies aspects of behaviour of human society.

Economics is the social science that studies how people use scarce resources to satisfy their unlimited wants.

Let us examine certain aspects of this definition. First, note that we have defined economics as a **social science**. This means that it deals with certain aspects of human behaviour within a social framework. Second, the resources with which we are concerned are *scarce* or *limited*, and third, the wants that we seek to satisfy are unlimited. If society had an *unlimited* amount of all resources, and if human wants were limited, we would have a utopia, indeed. But let us return to reality. **Scarcity** of resources is a fact of life, and this is one of the facts with which society must cope.

SCARCITY AND CHOICE

Economics is the study of scarcity.

Economics is concerned with the fact that the means or resources for satisfying human wants are limited. Most of us want more than what we currently have, and collectively, we want more than we can produce with our limited resources. The economist is interested in the use of these scarce resources in a manner that will result in the satisfaction of the most important wants. If resources were unlimited, there would be no need to use them economically. Not much practical point would exist, therefore, for studying economics. But economic problems arise out of the fact that resources are scarce or limited, while wants are unlimited. And the economist must try to find solutions for these problems. We could therefore, as an alternative, define economics as the study of how people cope with the ever-present problem of scarcity.

Learning Objective 2: discuss the subject matter of economics

Because resources are both desirable and scarce, we must choose how we will allocate them among various uses. We will always have to choose between one thing and another when we do not have the means to obtain both. If you won $20 million in a lottery (good luck), and you wanted to buy a car and take a vacation in Europe, you could do both. You would not have to choose either one or the other. So too, if a society could produce all of the goods and services that each member wants, then the problem of choice would not exist. **Choice**, therefore, is a direct result of scarcity. Economics is the study of choice.

Economics is the study of choice.

PROBLEM SOLVING 1-1

Is scarcity a problem for an enormously wealthy woman who can have anything that she wants?

THE IMPORTANCE OF ECONOMICS

Learning Objective 3: discuss the importance of economics

Why should we study economics? The study of economics is important for several reasons, some of which are discussed below.

UNDERSTANDING THE ECONOMY AND SOCIETY

Economics helps us to understand society.

Understanding the operation of our economic system enables us to improve its performance and helps us to deal with many of the problems that face our country. The economy is such an important part of society that it is impossible to understand society without a basic knowledge of economics. Our relationships with one another, our environment, the manner in which our collective wealth is distributed, and the types of work we do are all related to our economic system. Our lives are shaped by the myriad economic decisions that have been made by our ancestors and that are being made today by our contemporaries. A decision to build more war planes instead of spending more money on education and health will affect us not only today, but also for a long time in the future.

The better our understanding of our economy and our society, the better the control that we are likely to have over our destiny. It has been suggested that our grandparents could have avoided the economic catastrophe of the Great Depression of the 1930s if they had had a more thorough understanding of the economic forces at work.

UNDERSTANDING WORLD AFFAIRS

Economics helps us to understand world affairs.

Rapid changes are occurring in the world. Just pick up a newspaper or turn on the radio or television and you will get an idea of the many important changes that are taking place. The Soviet Union no longer exists, the unification of Germany is a reality, there is continuing tension in the Middle East, and the face of Europe has been transformed. The European Community has moved toward a relatively high level of economic integration, and here in Canada, the possible separation of Quebec from the Canadian federation remains an issue of considerable debate and uneasiness. These issues all have economic causes or economic consequences; therefore, an understanding of economics will enhance our understanding of these and other world affairs.

BEING AN INFORMED CITIZEN

Economics helps us to be informed citizens.

As consumers, it is important for us to know how to spend our income so that we can derive maximum satisfaction from our purchases. It is also important for us to use our labour services and other resources wisely. Not only should people be wise consumers, but as citizens in a democracy, they must be able to visualize and evaluate the consequences of different courses of action in order to determine which ones are most likely to lead to improvements in economic and social well-being.

During the federal election of 1988, the dominant issue was the Canada–U.S. free trade agreement — clearly an economic issue. During the 1993 campaign, the issues were NAFTA, unemployment, and the deficit. What should be done about unemployment? What policies should be adopted to deal with the huge deficit? Should Canada pursue a policy of protectionism as a means of supporting its domestic industries? Can subsidies to farmers be justified on economic grounds? In an election, citizens are frequently asked to vote for a party on the basis of its political platform, which, to a significant degree, contains issues and intended policies that are essentially economic in nature. A knowledge of economics allows us to replace emotional judgment with reasoned analysis in the decision-making process.

THINKING LOGICALLY

Economics helps us to think logically.

One of the most important reasons for studying economics is that it develops a particular way of thinking and making decisions. Good decision-making requires a careful evaluation of the benefits (advantages) and costs (disadvantages) associated with the decision or the choice that we make. Actually, economic analysis is, to a large extent, an exercise in logic and thus helps to sharpen our common sense.

GETTING PERSONAL SATISFACTION

Economics gives personal satisfaction.

There may be a more personal, selfish reason for studying economics. Because the study of economics can be intellectually exciting and stimulating, it yields great personal satisfaction. If you happen to become a great economist, you could end up being the president or chief executive officer of a corporation, or an economic consultant to one of our levels of government, with an annual salary in the six-figure range. In the 1940s, economists worked mainly on the campuses of universities. Today, professional economists work in practically every aspect of business and government.

PROBLEM SOLVING 1-2
Economics does not teach one how to earn a living, so it does not have much practical value. Do you agree?

WHERE ECONOMISTS WORK AND WHAT THEY DO

Learning Objective 4:
explain what economists do

Economists work in many aspects of business and government. You will find economists

- working in private firms such as insurance companies, large manufacturing companies, banks, unions, service associations, telephone companies, etc.

- teaching in high schools, colleges, and universities

- working in different departments of government and government agencies

- employed as researchers in various research institutions

- working for a variety of non-profit organizations

- working for themselves as consultants

- working for international organizations and agencies such as the United Nations, the World Bank, and the International Monetary Fund.

You have a good idea of what your economics instructor does. But what other kinds of jobs do economists do? A large corporation such as General Motors or your telephone company might hire economists to estimate the demand for its products or to figure out what effects a change in price will have on its profits. A bank might employ economists to forecast interest rates or the demand for loans. The federal government or a provincial government might hire economists to determine the effects of certain taxes on the government's revenue and on the level of economic activity. Finally, a union might employ economists to study matters relating to wages and employment. Economists serve as presidents, vice-presidents, general managers, and executives of a wide variety of organizations.

THE SCIENTIFIC METHOD

Learning Objective 5:
the nature of scientific inquiry

There is a certain appeal to anything that is said to be "scientific." This is perhaps due to the fact that we are living in a scientific age. In our definition of economics, we used the term science, but is economics really a science? We shall answer this question in this section.

Before we can determine whether or not economics is a science, we must understand the meaning of science and the scientific method. Everyone knows that economics is not a science like physics or chemistry are sciences. Physicists and chemists can conduct controlled laboratory experiments, while economists and other social scientists cannot. Science refers to a particular method of inquiry: **the scientific approach** or **method** is the systematic investigation and observation of phenomena and the formulation of general laws or tendencies therefrom, after testing and verification of hypotheses. We can discuss the main elements of the scientific approach under the headings of observation and measurement, formulation of hypotheses, and verification.

Scientific investigation comprises observation and measurement, the formulation of hypotheses, and verification.

OBSERVATION AND MEASUREMENT

Empirical: descriptive; as in observed, measured and recorded.

One of the basic tasks of scientists is to observe, measure, and record facts about what they are investigating. This is the descriptive or **empirical** aspect of science. In order to facilitate this aspect of their work, scientists use certain technical terms which have very precise meanings. The development of such a particularized vocabulary is an important step in the development of any field of scientific inquiry. Scientists must also exercise judgment in gathering information or facts relevant to the phenomenon that they are trying to explain.

HYPOTHESES

Hypothesis: an expression of the relation among variables.

The next task of scientists is to specify some relations among the variables that have been selected for investigation. Such specifications are called **hypotheses**. A hypothesis is not a statement about some fact that has been observed, but a statement about something that is observable. For example, the statement "Sixty students passed the economics examination" is not a hypothesis, but a statement about a fact that has been observed. On the other hand, the statement "If two extra review classes are given, at least sixty students will pass their economics examination" is a hypothesis. Student performance in an examination following review classes is observable. Note that the latter statement (the hypothesis) can be tested by giving (or not giving) two extra review classes and then observing the results. The statement "Review classes should be given before a final examination" is not expressed in a testable manner, because it does not express any specific relationship. A hypothesis must be stated in a testable (verifiable) manner so that it can be confirmed or disproved.

VERIFICATION

Once scientists have formulated their hypotheses, they proceed to test these hypotheses to see the extent to which they are supported by empirical evidence. Relating questions to evidence sets scientific inquiry apart from other types of inquiry.

ECONOMIC METHODOLOGY

We have now examined the basic components of the scientific method. Our next task is to see how economists follow the scientific approach in their attempt to explain economic phenomena. The factors involved in real-world economic events are often quite complex. The scientific economist comes to grips with these complexities by constructing models. Simply stated, a **model** or theory is an abstraction from the real world and consists of the factors that appear to pertain most to what is being studied. Details that do not pertain directly to the question that is being studied are simply stripped away in the model. The principle of stripping away irrelevant detail is often referred to as the principle of Occam's razor, named after the fourteenth-century philosopher William Occam.

Model: A simplified version of reality that facilitates our understanding of complex economic relations.

Economists use models in much the same way that engineers use them. An engineer who has the job of building a bridge would, most likely, design a model before building the real thing. The model allows the engineer to study certain aspects of the bridge before it actually exists. For example, the model bridge could give information about how the actual bridge would look, how it would accommodate traffic, and what modifications might be necessary to make it safe. Similarly, economists construct and use economic models to understand how the real economy works.

Learning Objective 6: how economists study the economy

The following example will help to illustrate how economists use models. People can travel from point A to point B either by air, which takes 50 minutes, or by car, which takes 4 hours. Let us assume that people are alike in terms of their preference for air travel and car travel, and that, except for the time factor, one mode of transportation is just as good as the other. What kind of people will be likely to fly, and what kind will be likely to travel by car? One of the factors that would influence a decision to travel by air or by car would be the cost involved. But here we are not talking only about the price of the plane ticket, or the price of gas and oil, and wear and tear on the car. We must consider also the cost of time. To a passenger who earns $50.00 an hour, the cost of his or her time is estimated at $50.00 an hour. To a passenger who earns $10.00 an hour, the cost of his or her time is estimated at $10.00 an hour. The greater the cost of your time, the less time you will want to spend travelling. The model predicts that the more you earn, the more likely it is that you will fly. On this basis, a decision could be made to start a plane service from A to B if there were many high-income earners travelling between points A and B.

An economic model or theory may be expressed verbally, mathematically, or graphically. Whatever form an economic model takes, it has the following components: a set of definitions, a set of assumptions, one or more hypotheses, and one or more predictions or generalizations. Let us briefly discuss each component in turn.

Definitions

Definitions, assumptions, hypotheses, and predictions are important aspects of a model.

Definitions identify the model's variables.

The various terms and phrases that economists use must be clearly defined. Economists have developed an impressive number of terms and concepts that form a part of the specialized language or jargon of the discipline. As you work through this book, many of the terms and concepts that are a part of the economist's vocabulary will become familiar to you. The main purpose of the set of **definitions** is to identify the variables of the model so that measurement can be facilitated. For example, it would be extremely difficult to measure the amount of consumer spending in an economy if that variable were not clearly defined.

Assumptions

Assumptions describe the model's operating conditions.

Assumptions are statements about the conditions under which the model operates. Basically, we usually make two types of assumptions in economic theory. One type of assumption relates to what motivates economic behaviour – for example, the objectives of consumers and producers. It is assumed that consumers try to maximize satisfaction, whereas firms try to maximize profit. Another type of assumption made in economic theory is aimed at simplifying the task of economists. For example, if economists are not currently concerned with an economy's external trade relations, they may simplify their analyses by assuming that the country does not engage in trade with the rest of the world. Abstractions of this nature are necessary because of the complexities of the real economy. An assumption of particular importance in economic theory is the idea of ***ceteris paribus***, which means *other things being equal*. By assuming that other things are equal, economists keep all other factors constant while investigating a particular relation. We shall look at this assumption more fully in a later section.

Ceteris paribus: other things being equal.

Hypotheses

We have already briefly discussed hypotheses. Recall that hypotheses specify the relations between variables. Economists have formulated a number of important hypotheses, many of which will be introduced throughout this book.

Predictions

An economic prediction is general while an economic forecast is more specific.

We formulate theories so that we can make predictions with them. Economic predictions usually take the form, "If you do this, then such and such will result." Economic prediction should not be confused with economic forecasting. Economic forecasting assigns future values to certain economic variables on the basis of known relations. An **economic prediction** is a statement about the general direction of events resulting from fulfillment of certain conditions, while an **economic forecast** gives us the specific value expected for a particular variable. The following examples help to illustrate the difference between a prediction and a forecast.

> *Prediction:* If the rate of interest increases, the level of investment spending will fall, other things being equal.

> *Forecast:* By the end of the year, the rate of unemployment will rise to 15%.

Economists, in attempting to explain economic events, follow the scientific procedure outlined above. They gather information, analyze it, and select what they consider to be most relevant. They formulate and test hypotheses and thus arrive at general statements or laws concerning economic phenomena. Economics, therefore, has a legitimate claim to be considered a science.

THE GOODNESS OF A MODEL

When is an economic model or theory considered to be "good"? The whole purpose of an economic model is to explain some aspect of economic reality and to predict certain outcomes. A model that does this well is a good model. If model A explains and predicts economic phenomena better than model B does, then model A is judged to be better than model B. If a model fails to explain what we observe (that is, reality), then it may be rejected.

The goodness of a model depends on how well it explains and predicts reality.

The use of computers has enabled economists to manipulate huge amounts of data in an incredibly short time. Thus, it is relatively easy to test economic theories against observed phenomena. The branch of economics that deals with the use of statistics to test economic theories is called **econometrics**. This has become such an important branch of economics that most schools require their economics majors to take at least one course in economic statistics or econometrics.

Econometricians use statistics to test economic theories.

POSITIVE AND NORMATIVE ECONOMICS

Learning Objective 7:
the difference between positive and normative economics

Before we continue, we must make sure that we understand the difference between positive and normative statements. This will help us to distinguish between positive and normative economics. Economists conduct both positive and normative analyses. **Positive statements** are about *what is*. A positive statement is a statement about some fact, and is therefore conceptually verifiable. The statement that the student population of your school is 5000 is a positive statement, even if your school has only 3000 students. The point is, it is a statement about some fact – the student population. The statement can be verified (or disproved) by the simple process of counting. Note that a positive statement may be true or false. Since a positive statement relates to facts, it can be verified (or disproved) by examining the facts. A statement such as "an increase in the money supply will lead to a higher rate of inflation" is an example of a positive statement in economics.

Positive statements are statements of facts expressed in a testable (verifiable) manner.

On the other hand, **normative statements** are value judgements or statements of opinion about *what ought to be*. Normative statements cannot be verified by examining the facts. A statement such as "the money supply should be reduced" is a normative statement. Try to compose examples of your own to illustrate the distinction between positive statements and normative statements.

Normative statements are value judgements about what ought to be.

Obviously, normative statements are not scientific because they cannot be subjected to empirical testing. This does not suggest that the scientific economist is never concerned with normative issues. In fact, concern with the normative aspect of economics is a major focus for disagreement among economists. Most economists, for example, would agree on the effects of a tax on textbooks, but would likely disagree on whether a tax *should* be imposed. Value judgements, though not scientific, are therefore important. Economists should indicate, however, when they are dealing with positive statements and when they are dealing with matters of opinion.

This discussion of positive and normative statements should help us to understand the difference between positive and normative economics. **Positive economics** deals with the behaviour of economic units and with the operation of the economic system. Positive economics attempts to explain what will happen under certain conditions, but does not

Positive economics is the study of the state of the economy.

explain what the economic situation ought to be. It does not seek to make any judgments about whether the result of any economic action is good or bad. The concern of positive economics is to describe the economic system as it is and how it actually works. What causes the prices of television sets to rise? What are the effects of the GST? How has the Canada-U.S. trade agreement affected employment in Canada? These types of questions fall within the subject of positive economics.

Normative economics suggests what the economy should be.

Normative economics is concerned with what the economic situation ought to be. It attempts to judge whether economic outcomes are good or bad, and to what extent they can be improved. Should the Government of Canada invest public funds in an airline company to keep it in business? Should the government sell some of its property? Should farmers be subsidized? Should the price of milk be set by government? Should there be a ceiling on the amount of profits that foreign firms are allowed to take out of Canada? Normative economics deals with answers to such questions. Note that the issues of normative economics are policy-oriented.

Obviously, normative economics often relies heavily on positive economics. Let us consider the following normative economic issue: Should Canada remain a part of the North American Free Trade Agreement? One could conceivably answer this question on the basis of emotion, but an answer based on an economic analysis of the situation would probably be preferable. What are the likely benefits of this agreement? What are the costs? Answers to these positive questions will help to answer the normative question about the trade agreement.

DISAGREEMENT AMONG ECONOMISTS

Learning Objective 8: the reasons for disagreement among economists

It is probably normal to expect economists to disagree about normative economic issues. They have different values, and they judge economic situations and events differently. When economists are asked to make judgments about some economic action, they may try to be objective, but their objectivity might be coloured by their own sense of what is right and what is wrong. One economist might argue that cigarette smoking is bad for your health, hence a heavy tax should be imposed on cigarettes in order to discourage smoking. Another economist might take the position that there are other products that are also dangerous — why single out cigarettes? The same economist might argue, moreover, that if people want to smoke cigarettes, it is their business and that the government has no right to interfere with a person's lifestyle.

It is not only on normative issues, however, that economists disagree. They also disagree over the positive, scientific aspects as well. Often, there are different explanations of how the economy operates, and it is not always clear which explanation is best. In other words, economists may disagree over the appropriate model of the economy. One would think that it should be easy to settle the disagreement simply by confronting the theory with the data. Unfortunately, the available data might not be such as to allow definitive conclusions.

Economists disagree because they have different values, and because they use different models.

Economists may disagree even though they use the same economic model. They may agree over the qualitative aspects, but disagree over the quantitative aspects. Two economists might agree that a fall in interest rates will increase investment. They might disagree, however, over the magnitude of the increase, one claiming that it will rise only slightly, the other claiming that the increase will be significant. Again, this type of disagreement may be prolonged because of the lack of relevant data.

Economists may also disagree about quantities, even when they use the same model.

 PROBLEM SOLVING 1-3

If economics is so scientific, why is there so much disagreement among economists?

VARIABLES

A variable can vary, but a constant does not vary.

We have seen that economists construct economic models to facilitate their understanding of economic phenomena. An economic model is a system of relations among economic variables. In general terms, a **variable** is anything that can assume different values under different circumstances. We call anything that does not vary a **constant**. Whether or not we consider something to be a variable or a constant depends on what we are investigating. The following are some economic variables that we shall encounter as we progress through this book: price, income, consumer spending, interest rates, demand for money, investment spending, exports, imports, taxes, and government spending.

Endogenous variable: value determined within the model.

Exogenous variable: value is predetermined.

When economists construct models to explain real world phenomena, some variables will be explained within the models, while others will be determined by factors outside the models. Those variables that are explained within a model are called **endogenous variables**. Those variables that are determined by factors outside a model are called **exogenous variables**. It is a serious mistake to assume that the exogenous variables whose values are predetermined are not important. In fact, they are extremely important. Exogenous variables affect endogenous variables.

Economists do not have a set of variables that they label endogenous and another set that they label exogenous at all times and under all circumstances. Whether a particular variable is endogenous or exogenous depends on the problem being studied. It is important to note also that we cannot determine whether or not a particular variable is endogenous or exogenous without the model.

PROBLEM SOLVING 1-4

You are constructing a model to explain consumption of goods and services in Canada. You specify that consumption depends on income and on the rate of interest. You believe, however, that changes in wealth and income distribution will have some effect on consumption. Identify the endogenous and exogenous variables.

STOCK VARIABLES AND FLOW VARIABLES

Stock variables have no time dimension. Flow variables do.

Before we proceed, we should understand the difference between **stock variables** (or stocks) and **flow variables** (or flows). A **stock** is a quantity existing *at a particular time*. A **flow**, on the other hand, is a measure of the change in a variable *per unit of time*. The number of books on the shelves of a college or university library on May 10, 1999 (that is, at a particular time) is a stock. The number of books taken out of the library each day is a flow. Note that a flow is a rate and has a time dimension (per day, per month, per year, etc.). A stock has no time dimension. Examples of economic flow variables are: income, consumption, and the interest that you earn on your savings account. Examples of economic stock variables are: the amount of equipment owned by a company, the number of dollars in circulation in Canada at 11:00 a.m. yesterday, and the amount of money in your bank account.

CAUSE-EFFECT RELATIONS

Learning Objective 9: relations among variables

Economists study economic variables to discover causes and effects. One must be careful, however, not to confuse correlation with causation. Two variables may be correlated, that is, they change together, even though a change in one does not cause a change in the other. A change could be a chance occurrence, or it could be the effect of a third variable. If it can be determined that a change in one variable causes a change in another, then we know that by changing one, the other will change. This conclusion may not hold if there is only a correlation between the variables. We must remember the age-old warning that correlation does not imply causation.

The post hoc fallacy

Post hoc, ergo propter hoc: the error in thinking that A causes B because A precedes B.

The discussion above is closely related to a common fallacy. When two events happen in sequence, one is tempted to conclude that the first event caused the second to occur. This, of course, may not be the case. This error is referred to as the **post hoc, ergo propter hoc** fallacy, which means "after this, therefore because of this." Let us assume that you began to read your economics textbook and then it began to rain. If you concluded that it rained because you started to read your textbook, then you would have fallen into the post hoc ergo propter hoc fallacy.

THE CETERIS PARIBUS ASSUMPTION

Economists concern themselves with the effects of changes in economic variables. How does a change in income affect consumption? How does a change in the price of a product affect the quantity that will be purchased? Do changes in the quantity of money affect the rate of interest? Do changes in interest rates affect other variables? Can certain policies be instituted to control certain economic variables? These are some of the questions for which the economist tries to find answers.

Suppose we are interested in finding out the effect of a fall in the price of apples on the quantity of apples that we will purchase. Obviously, factors other than the price of apples will affect the quantity that will be purchased. Some of these factors include our preferences for apples over other kinds of fruit, our incomes, and the prices of other fruit. We can hypothesize that if the price of apples falls, we will buy a greater quantity. If we observe that a fall in the price of apples is accompanied by an increase in the quantity purchased, can we conclude that the increase in quantity purchased results from the fall in price? Is it not possible that the increase in quantity purchased may result from an increase in income or some other exogenous factor?

The ceteris paribus assumption allows us to isolate the effects of changes in variables.

In order to determine how a change in one variable affects other variables, the economist must find some way of isolating the effects of other variables. In the above example, we must isolate income, preference (taste), and all other factors (except the price of apples) that may affect the quantity of apples that we will purchase. We can (almost magically) accomplish this task by making use of the ceteris paribus assumption. *Ceteris paribus*, a Latin phrase, means *other things being equal*. This assumption allows us to keep other factors constant while we examine the effects of the variable that currently interests us. Thus, we can investigate how a change in price affects the quantity purchased by assuming that income, taste, and all other factors except the price of apples remain unchanged throughout the process of investigation. We may emerge with a statement such as "If the price of a product falls, *other things being equal*, the quantity purchased will increase."

PROBLEM SOLVING 1-5

Why do economists put so much emphasis on the ceteris paribus assumption when it is well known that other things are not equal?

ECONOMIC POLICY

Learning Objective 10: the meaning of economic policy

A great deal of physical and human resources have been and are being devoted to the development and improvement of economic theory. These theories help us to understand how the economy functions and enable us to solve real-world economic problems. We

Economic policy is any action taken to achieve some desired economic goal.

can define **economic policy** as a course of action designed to achieve some specific economic objective. Every society usually agrees upon a number of economic objectives that it considers to be desirable. The following are among the economic objectives that most people in our society would like our policymakers to pursue: price stability; full employment; economic growth; an equitable distribution of income; economic freedom (freedom for consumers, workers, and businesses to pursue their own economic interests); economic security; and a satisfactory balance of payments equilibrium.

We should realize that some measure of conflict will occur among these goals. For example, a policy designed to reduce the rate of inflation (to achieve relative price stability) may increase the rate of unemployment. The objectives of price stability and full employment will then conflict. Similarly, the objective of an equitable distribution of income may conflict with the goal of a higher rate of economic growth. When such conflicts arise, choices must be made.

Not all of these objectives assume the same importance at any one time. Furthermore, the importance of each goal relative to other goals is likely to change from time to time. In a situation of severe unemployment, for example, it may be necessary to sacrifice another goal such as price stability. Priorities must be established, but the ranking of our priorities will change as circumstances change. For example, we are much more concerned with the environment today than we were twenty years ago, and inflation ranked higher in importance in 1975 than it does today.

MICROECONOMICS AND MACROECONOMICS

Learning Objective 11: distinguish between microeconomics and macroeconomics

Microeconomics, or price theory, deals with the behaviour of individual economic units.

Macroeconomics, or income and employment theory, concerns itself with the behaviour of economic aggregates.

The two major branches into which economics has been divided are microeconomics and macroeconomics. **Microeconomics** examines the behaviour of individual economic units and focuses on the allocation of resources. It concerns itself with what determines the composition of total output, and analyzes topics such as the behaviour of consumers and firms, the determination of relative prices, and the distribution of the economy's output among various groups. Microeconomics is sometimes called **price theory**.

Macroeconomics examines the economy as a whole rather than the individual units — the whole flock, so to speak, rather than the individual sheep comprising that flock. Macroeconomics concerns itself with the combined or aggregate behaviour of consumers and producers, and analyzes such topics as inflation, unemployment, and economic growth. Macroeconomics is sometimes called **income and employment theory**. A thorough understanding of the operation of the economic system requires knowledge of both microeconomics and macroeconomics.

CHAPTER SUMMARY

1. Economics is a social science because it is a scientific study of certain aspects of human behaviour.
2. Economics may be defined as the study of how people use scarce resources to satisfy their unlimited wants.
3. Scarcity forces us to choose. Economics is fundamentally concerned with scarcity and choice.
4. Some advantages of knowing economics are that it helps us to improve the performance of the economy and thus increases our well-being, and that it helps to sharpen our common sense.

5. Economists are employed in almost every facet of economic life. They are employed in industries, by various levels of government and different organizations, some are self-employed as economic consultants, and some teach.

6. The main elements of the scientific method are observation and measurement, the formation of hypotheses and generalizations, and testing and verification.

7. Economists employ the scientific method in describing and predicting economic phenomena. Hence, economics has a legitimate claim to be considered a science.

8. Positive economics concerns itself with explaining how an economy functions. Normative economics, on the other hand, concerns itself with opinions or value judgments about how the economy ought to function.

9. Economists disagree about normative economics because they have different values. They disagree about positive economics because they may use different models. They may also disagree over quantitative aspects.

10. A variable is anything that assumes changing values. An endogenous variable is explained within the model or theory while an exogenous variable is determined by factors outside the model.

11. What distinguishes a flow from a stock is that a flow has a time dimension while a stock does not.

12. Correlation between two variables does not establish a cause-effect relationship between them.

13. The *post hoc, ergo propter hoc* fallacy is the error of concluding that one event caused another because it preceded the other.

14. The *ceteris paribus* (other things being equal) assumption allows the investigator to study how changes in one variable affect other variables.

15. Economic policy may be defined as a course of action designed to achieve a specific objective. Economic objectives may conflict. When they do, choices must be made. The economic objectives of a society are not of equal importance or urgency at any one time. Priorities are established, and they change from time to time.

16. The two main branches into which economics is divided are microeconomics and macroeconomics. Microeconomics concerns itself with individual economic units while macroeconomics concerns itself with broad economic aggregates.

TERMS FOR REVIEW

social science (2)
scarcity (3)
choice (3
scientific method (5)
empirical (5)
hypothesis (6)
model (theory) (6)
definitions (7)
assumptions (7)
ceteris paribus (7)
economic prediction (7)
economic forecast (7)
econometrics (8)
positive statement (8)
normative statement (8)

positive economics (8)
normative economics (9)
variable (10)
constant (10)
endogenous variable (10)
exogenous variable (10)
stock variable (10)
flow variable (10)
post hoc, ergo propter hoc (11)
economic policy (12)
microeconomics (12)
price theory (12)
macroeconomics (12)
income and employment theory (12)

QUESTIONS FOR REVIEW AND DISCUSSION

1. Why do individuals, firms, and governments have to make choices? (L.O. 2)

2. Is there any relationship between choices and resource use? (L.O. 2)

3. Economics is the study of scarcity and choice. Do you consider this to be an adequate definition of economics? (L.O. 1)

4. Explain to one of your friends who is not taking economics why economics is important. (L.O. 3)

5. How can economics help you to become a better informed citizen? (L.O. 3)

6. What opportunities exist for economics graduates? (L.O. 4)

7. In what sense is economics a science? In what ways are economists different from physicists as scientists? (L.O. 5, 6)

8. What are the fundamental elements in scientific inquiry? (L.O. 5)

9. What is an economic model? Why do economists find it useful to construct models? (L.O. 6)

10. What is the difference between positive economics and normative economics? Do you agree with the statement that normative propositions have no place in scientific economics? Give reasons for your opinion. (L.O. 7)

11. Economists disagree over normative economics, but not over positive economics. Is this statement true or false? Explain. (L.O. 8)

12. Give an example of the post hoc, ergo propter hoc fallacy. (L.O. 9)

13. Give an example of an economic policy. Give reasons why such a policy might be put into effect. (L.O. 9)

14. State what the differences are between the following pairs of concepts: (L.O. 9)

    (a) stocks and flows;

    (b) endogenous variable and exogenous variable;

    (c) correlation and causation.

15. What is the difference between microeconomics and macroeconomics? Why should we study both microeconomics and macroeconomics? (L.O. 10)

PROBLEMS AND EXERCISES

1. Look through a newspaper and select three news items that are in some way related to economics and the economy. (L.O. 2, 3)

    (a) In what way are these items related to economics? (Do they have economic causes or consequences?)

    (b) Explain how a knowledge of economics might help us to understand or find solutions to issues that may have been raised in the news items.

2. Write a short dialogue in which you are trying to convince a friend of the importance of studying economics. (L.O. 3)

3. Categorize each of the following as either positive or normative statements. (L.O. 7)

    (a) An increase in price will reduce the quantity purchased.

    (b) The price of gasoline should be stabilized at its current level.

    (c) Economics is so important that it ought to be compulsory for every secondary school, college or university student.

(d) A tax imposed on cigarettes will reduce the supply of cigarettes.

(e) High interest rates tend to reduce the level of investment spending, therefore, interest rates should always be kept as low as possible.

4. Decide whether each of the following falls under the heading of positive economics or normative economics: (L.O. 7)

    (a) a study of the effect of an increase in investment on the level of income;

    (b) an evaluation of the outcome of a ban on the importation of alcohol to determine whether the ban is good or bad;

    (c) a description of how higher interest rates affect the economy;

    (d) the compilation of data with the aim of describing certain economic facts;

    (e) a program designed to make people better off based on assumptions about what is in their best interest;

    (f) the elimination of the deficit by the federal government because it is believed that it will make Canadians better off;

    (g) a study of the effect of a reduction in the money supply on interest rates;

    (h) the notion that taxing the wealthy in order to give welfare payments to the poor is unfair;

    (i) a detailed study of the relationship between consumer spending and economic performance.

5. Identify which of the following are economic predictions and which are economic forecasts. (L.O. 6)

    (a) If the level of income rises, people will buy more consumer goods.

    (b) If the money supply increases, the rate of inflation will rise.

    (c) The output of goods and services in Canada will grow by 3.2% in the year 2001.

    (d) If interest rates rise, the growth rate of output will decline.

    (e) By the end of the year, the unemployment rate will be 8.2%.

    (f) An increase in government spending will put upward pressure on interest rates.

    (g) By the year 2004, government purchases of goods and services will account for 35% of total spending.

6. List each of the following variables as stocks or flows: (L.O. 9)

    (a) the number of pairs of jeans in a Zellers department store;

    (b) the number of pairs of jeans sold by Zellers in one month;

    (c) the number of cars produced by an automobile manufacturer in a year;

    (d) the amount of office space available for rent on September 3, 1999;

    (e) the amount of equipment owned by the High Tech Company;

    (f) the amount deposited in your bank account each month;

    (g) the unpaid balance on your student loan as of January 15, 1999;

    (h) the annual interest payable on a bank loan.

7. Formulate two examples of: (L.O. 6)

    (a) economic prediction;

    (b) economic forecast.

8. Write up a list of five social, economic, or political problems or issues facing Canada today. For each problem or issue, discuss its economic aspects (if any). What role can economics play in helping us to understand the problem or issue, or in finding solutions? (L.O. 2,3)

9. Indicate whether each of the following falls under the category of microeconomics or macroeconomics: (L.O.11)

    (a) an explanation of what causes the price of wheat to increase;

    (b) an explanation of the factors that affect the total amount of spending by consumers;

    (c) an explanation of how the level of investment spending affects aggregate employment;

    (d) an explanation of how the price of your textbook is determined;

    (e) a theory which attempts to predict changes in the average level of income and employment in an economy;

    (f) a theory that leads to a prediction of the rate of growth of the economy's output of goods and services;

    (g) an explanation of how a firm can maximize its profits;

    (h) a theory that explains why the prices of home computers have fallen over the past few years.

Internet Site

http://economics.miningco.com

This site serves as a search engine for economics-related resources on the Internet. The site also features weekly articles on economics, and chat facilities.

INTERNET EXERCISE

1. Use the Mining Co. site listed above to find information on *Adam Smith*. He was the founder of economics as a discipline. Write a short paragraph about his theories.

2. Locate the following site:

http://macweb.acs.usm.maine.edu/economics/what.HTML

Read about economists and what they do. List three tasks performed by economists.

2

SOME USEFUL TOOLS

Learning Objectives

After studying this chapter, you should be able to:

1 use symbols and the functional notation to express relationships among variables

2 distinguish between dependent and independent variables

3 use graphs to represent certain relationships

4 explain and calculate slopes

If mathematics is a language, then economics is one place where we use it.

E. M. James

INTRODUCTION

Economists use a number of devices to help them to understand economic relationships. The purpose of this chapter is to provide an elementary but useful introduction to some of the basic tools used by economists in attempting to understand and explain economic events. These tools help economists to express ideas clearly and precisely. You may wish to thumb through this chapter before reading it in order to determine whether or not you are already familiar with the material it contains.

The chapter begins with a brief introduction to the use of symbols and the functional notation. Next, we will see how to use graphs to illustrate certain relations. Finally, the concept of a slope is introduced and we will see how to measure the slopes of linear and non-linear curves at given points.

THE USE OF SYMBOLS AND THE FUNCTIONAL NOTATION

Learning Objective 1:
the use of symbols

Functional notation is a mathematical tool for relating one variable to another.

A function expresses a relation between variables.

Economists and students of economics are constantly studying relations among economic variables. In expressing these relations, we can make use of a very convenient mathematical tool called the **functional notation**. A **function** expresses a relationship between two or more variables. Actually, it is quite easy to express relations among variables as functions. Consider the following statement: "The quantity of apples that people will buy depends on the price of apples." An alternative way of expressing this same idea is as follows: "The quantity of apples that people will buy is a function of the price of apples." Both statements mean exactly the same thing — namely, if the price of apples changes, the quantity that people will buy will change (other things being equal, of course). By using the functional notation, we can express this idea very concisely.

Learning Objective 1:
the functional notation

Learning Objective 2:
dependent and independent variables

To do this, let us begin by using symbols. Let us use Q to denote the quantity of apples that people will buy, and P to denote the price of apples. Note that the use of these symbols has already simplified our task of expressing the relations between the variables with which we are concerned. For, instead of writing quantity, we simply write Q, and instead of writing price, we simply write P. The idea that the quantity that will be purchased depends on price can now be expressed as

$$Q = f(P)$$

and is read "Quantity depends on price" or "Quantity is a function of price."

The dependent variable is the variable to be explained.

The independent variable (or explanatory variable) is the variable that explains.

In this example, the quantity that people will buy depends upon the price. Hence, in the above function, Q is called the **dependent variable**. The variable upon which it depends is called the **independent variable** or the **explanatory variable**. The dependent variable, then, is the variable that we are trying to explain, and the independent variable is the one which provides the explanation. In economics, it is customary to modify the form of the above functional notation. Instead of using f, we replace it with the dependent variable. The above function would therefore appear as

$$Q = Q(P)$$

Sometimes it is desirable to express the idea that one variable depends on two or more other variables. For example, suppose we want to express the idea that the quantity that people will buy depends not only on price but also on their incomes. Using P for price and Q for quantity as before, and using Y to symbolize income, we can express the idea as

$$Q = Q(P,Y)$$

Note that the independent variables P and Y are separated by a comma.

PROBLEM SOLVING 2-1

Use the functional notation to express each of the following ideas:

1. **The grade (g) you obtain on a test depends on how many hours (h) you spend preparing for the test.**

2. **The higher the proportion of the population over 65 years (a), the greater the amount spent on health services (H).**

3. **Changes in the incomes of Canadians (Y) will cause changes in imports (M) from the United States.**

4. **Higher interest rates (r) and greater income (Y) will cause you to put more money in the bank (S).**

THE USE OF GRAPHS

Graphs are effective tools for showing the relation between variables.

The saying goes that a picture is worth a thousand words. The same applies to graphs. But we should consider the following modification: "A graph that is well understood is worth more than a thousand words." **Graphs** are, indeed, an effective way of showing relations among variables. We must recognize, however, that they do not really speak for themselves. Instead, they add clarity to ideas that we try to express — they actually *show* the changes that take place.

The axes intersect at the origin from which all distances are measured.

Learning Objective 3: how to use graphs

This section provides a general introduction to the use of graphs. Consider the diagram shown as Figure 2.1. The two lines (called axes) intersect at a 90-degree angle. The point where the two lines intersect is called the **origin**. We give this point a value of 0 and from it measure all distances. Note that the two intersecting lines divide the plane into four quadrants, numbered as shown in Figure 2.1. In quadrant II, the x is negative in value, in quadrant III, both x and y are negative, and in quadrant IV, the y is negative in value.

FIGURE 2.1

Axes, origin, quadrants, and a point on a graph.

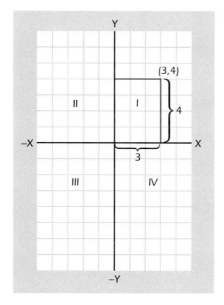

PLOTTING POINTS

Suppose we want to plot the point for the values x = 3 and y = 4, usually indicated as (3,4). First we locate the value 3 along the X-axis. Then, we move vertically up to the value 4 measured along the Y-axis. This locates the desired point (3,4). Now, consider Table 2.1, which gives values of X and Y. We can plot these values on a graph such as

Figure 2.2. Note that points will appear in quadrants II, III, and IV only when a negative value is involved.

In general, economic variables have either positive values or a value of zero. For most of our graphs, therefore, we will need only the first quadrant. Most graphs will appear without the negative parts of the axes.

TABLE 2.1	X Values	Y Values
Values of X and Y.	1	−3
	2	4
	−3	2
	4	1

FIGURE 2.2

Points plotted on a graph.

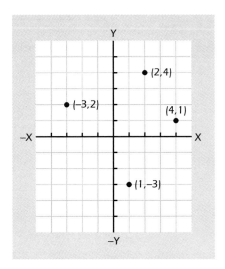

Suppose we have the information shown in Table 2.2 for the Bangalore Ice Cream Store regarding weekly ice cream sales and the number of sunny days for a six-week period.

TABLE 2.2	Week no.	Sunny days	Ice cream sales
Relationship between ice cream sales and sunny days.	1	2	$400
	2	5	900
	3	1	200
	4	3	500
	5	4	700
	6	5	800

From this table, we can see that the volume of sales increases with the number of sunny days. However, although the table does contain the information, we cannot quite see it at a glance. It would be helpful if we could display the information contained in Table 2.2 in a way that allowed us to see the relation at a glance. Figure 2.3 does this. From the graph, we can easily see that the volume of ice cream sales increases with the number of sunny days.

FIGURE 2.3

Graphic representation of the relation between ice cream sales and the number of sunny days.

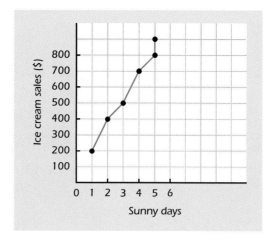

TYPICAL GRAPHS USED IN ECONOMICS

Consider the following statement: "As the rate of interest falls, the level of investment increases." Investment here refers to expenditure on plant, equipment, buildings, etc. — real capital investment. This statement deals with the relation between two variables — the rate of interest and the level of investment. We can get a very clear picture of this relation by using a graph. Note that the two variables move in opposite directions. In other words, there is an *inverse* relation between the rate of interest and the level of investment. This inverse relation is illustrated graphically by the falling curve shown in Figure 2.4. This figure shows clearly that, as the rate of interest falls from 12% to 9%, the level of investment increases from $20 million to $30 million.

FIGURE 2.4

Inverse relation between two variables.

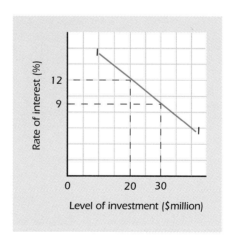

A declining curve shows an inverse relation between two variables.

Now, let us consider a case in which two variables move in the same direction. Specifically, consider this statement: "When income increases, so does consumer spending." Again, the relation between these two variables (income and consumer spending) can be clearly illustrated on a graph. In this case, there is a **direct relation** between income and consumer spending. Figure 2.5 illustrates this relation graphically by a

Direct relation: the relation that exists between variables that increase or decrease together.

FIGURE 2.5

Direct relation
between two
variables.

An upward rising curve
shows a direct relation
between two variables.

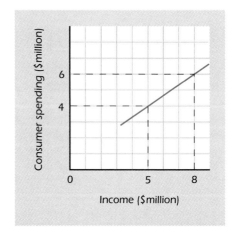

rising curve. As the level of income increases from $5 million to $8 million, consumer spending increases from $4 million to $6 million.

A graph might show a relationship starting at zero, rising to a maximum, and then falling to zero. Such might be the case between tax revenue and tax rates as shown in Figure 2.6.

FIGURE 2.6

Relation between tax
rate and tax revenue.

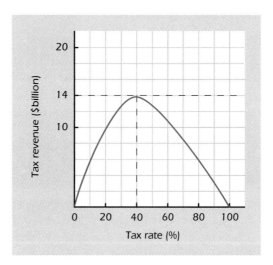

When the tax rate is zero, the government receives no tax revenue. As the tax rate increases, tax revenue rises, reaching a maximum of $14 billion at a tax rate of 40%. But as the tax rate continues to rise, it may be that the incentive to earn extra income decreases so that tax revenue falls. If the tax rate increases to 100%, no one will earn any income because any income earned will be all taxed away. The government's revenue will be zero if no one earns any income.

Economists also encounter relationships that start at a certain point, fall to a minimum, and then rise. An example of such a relationship is the cost of making photocopies shown in Figure 2.7.

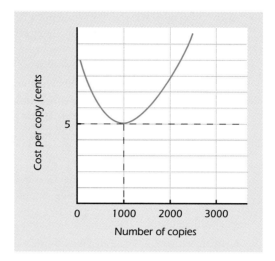

As the number of copies increases from zero, the cost per copy falls. At a volume of 1000 copies per day, the cost per copy is minimized at $0.05 per copy. But as the volume increases beyond 1000 copies per day, the cost per copy rises, due perhaps to pushing the photocopy machine beyond its most efficient operating capacity.

Quite often, it may be necessary to graph data that are unrelated. For example, there is no relation between inflation and the distance you travel per day. Such a situation is shown in Figure 2.8.

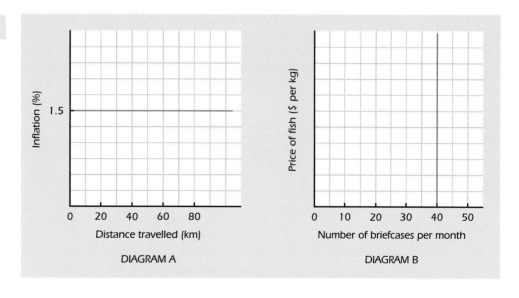

In Diagram A of Figure 2.8, the rate of inflation is 1.5% whether the distance travelled is 20, 40, 60 or 80 km per day. The graph is therefore a horizontal straight line. Consider now the situation shown in Diagram B. The price of fish in Canada has no effect on the number of briefcases sold in an Australian department store per month. When the price of fish changes, the sale of briefcases remains the same, namely, 40. There is no relationship between the two variables, so the graph is a vertical line.

PROBLEM SOLVING 2-2

Show the following relationship on a graph:

> **As a wheat farmer hires more and more workers, the output of wheat increases up to a point. But as increasingly more workers are hired, the output of wheat declines.**

PROBLEM SOLVING 2-3

When interest rates are low, people tend to borrow more money from banks than when interest rates are high. Show this information on a graph.

Clearly then, the economist can make good use of graphs in presenting certain economic relations. Despite their great advantage, however, the use of graphs is limited to cases with very few variables. As the number of variables increases, our ability to graph relations among them decreases. How would you graph the idea that consumption varies with current income, the rate of interest, and consumer expectations? This is indeed a formidable, if not impossible, exercise. Models that involve relations among several variables are usually presented verbally or algebraically rather than geometrically or graphically.

THE SLOPE: CONCEPT AND MEASUREMENT

The slope is a measure of how fast a curve or line rises or falls.

In your study of economics, you will find the concept of a **slope** and its measurement of the utmost importance. Economists are interested in knowing the rates at which the curves they draw rise or fall. Measuring the slopes of these curves provides the answer. Suppose you observe or believe that as people's incomes rise, they respond by spending more money on consumer goods and services. You could show this relationship on a graph as depicted in Figure 2.9.

FIGURE 2.9

Relation between income and consumption.

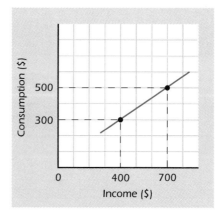

Consumption is measured along the vertical axis while income is measured along the horizontal axis. The curve in the diagram shows that as income rises, consumption also rises. The economist, however, would be also interested in knowing the degree to which

Learning Objective 4:
the concept of slope

consumers respond to changes in income. We could say, for example, that a $300 increase in income results in a $200 increase in consumption. The slope of the line gives us that information. The slope provides information on the steepness or flatness of the curve and is defined as the ratio of the vertical distance (rise) to the horizontal distance (run).

FIGURE 2.10

Slope of a straight line.

A linear curve has a constant slope.

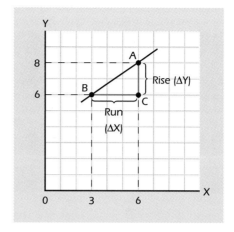

Consider Figure 2.10. Since the curve is a linear curve (that is, a straight line), it has the same slope at every point. The slope of the line in Figure 2.10 is:

$$\text{Slope} = \frac{\text{vertical distance}}{\text{horizontal distance}} = \frac{AC}{BC}$$

The slope then, is the change in the Y value over the change in the X value when Y is on the vertical axis and X is on the horizontal axis. The change in the Y value may be written as ΔY, while the change in the X value may be written as ΔX. The symbol Δ is the Greek letter *delta*, used here to mean "a change in." Thus,

$$\text{Slope} = \frac{\Delta Y}{\Delta X} = \frac{\text{rise}}{\text{run}}$$

FIGURE 2.11

Linear curves with negative and positive slopes.

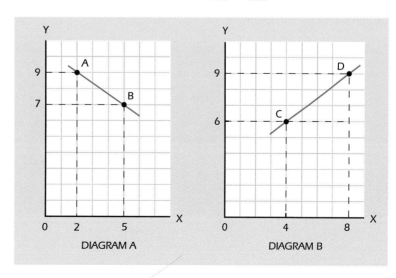

Let us calculate the slope of each of the lines shown in Figure 2.11. First, consider Diagram A. If we move from A to B, Y falls from 9 to 7. Hence, $\Delta Y = -2$. At the same time, X rises from 2 to 5; so $\Delta X = 3$. Therefore:

$$\text{Slope} = \frac{\Delta Y}{\Delta X} = \frac{-2}{3} = -\frac{2}{3}$$

If we move from B to A, Y rises from 7 to 9. Hence, $\Delta Y = 2$. But X falls from 5 to 2; so $\Delta X = -3$. Therefore

$$\text{Slope} = \frac{\Delta Y}{\Delta X} = \frac{2}{-3} = -\frac{2}{3}$$

A declining curve has a negative slope.

Let us now consider Diagram B. If we move from C to D, Y rises from 6 to 9. Hence, $\Delta Y = 3$. At the same time, X rises from 4 to 8; so $\Delta X = 4$. Therefore

$$\text{Slope} = \frac{\Delta Y}{\Delta X} = \frac{3}{4}$$

If we move from D to C, Y falls from 9 to 6 ($\Delta Y = -3$), while X falls from 8 to 4 ($\Delta X = -4$). Therefore

$$\text{Slope} = \frac{\Delta Y}{\Delta X} = \frac{-3}{-4} = \frac{3}{4}$$

A rising curve has a positive slope.

STRAIGHT LINES THROUGH THE ORIGIN

Figure 2.12 shows three straight lines passing through the origin. First, consider the line 0B which is a 45° line from the origin. The slope of 0B is

$$\frac{\Delta Y}{\Delta X} = \frac{3}{3} = 1$$

A 45° line through the origin has a slope equal to 1.

Now, let us consider the line 0A. Its slope is

$$\frac{\Delta Y}{\Delta X} = \frac{2}{1} = 2$$

For any line through the origin above the 45° line, its slope is greater than 1 ($\Delta Y > \Delta X$).

Finally, let us consider the line 0C. Its slope is

$$\frac{\Delta Y}{\Delta X} = \frac{1}{2}$$

For any line through the origin below the 45° line, its slope is less than 1 ($\Delta Y < \Delta X$).

FIGURE 2.12

Slopes of straight lines through the origin.

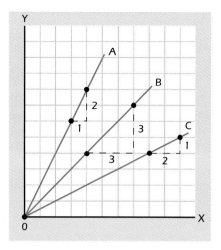

SLOPES OF NON-LINEAR CURVES

So far, we have looked at slopes of linear curves. But what if the curve is not linear? For non-linear curves, the slope is different at every point on the curve.

> **The slope of a non-linear curve at a particular point is the slope of the straight line drawn tangent to the curve at that particular point.**

Figure 2.13 shows a non-linear curve. Tangent lines are drawn at points A and B on the curve. The slope of the curve at A is the slope of the tangent line at A which is

$$\frac{\Delta Y}{\Delta X} = -\frac{2}{2} = -1$$

The slope of the curve at B is the slope of the tangent line at B, which is

$$\frac{\Delta Y}{\Delta X} = \frac{2}{1} = 2$$

FIGURE 2.13

Slope of a non-linear curve at a point.

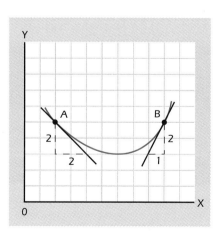

CHAPTER SUMMARY

1. If changes in A cause changes in B, then B is said to be a function of A, and is written as B = B(A).

2. By using graphs, we can depict relations between economic variables clearly and vividly, so that the relations can be seen at a glance. A rising curve shows a direct relation. A declining curve shows an inverse relation.

3. We can measure the slope of a linear curve at a point by finding the ratio of the vertical distance (rise) to the horizontal distance (run). A linear curve has a constant slope throughout.

4. A rising curve has a positive slope. A declining curve has a negative slope.

5. A 45° line through the origin has a slope of 1.

6. We can measure the slope of a non-linear curve at a point by finding the slope of the tangent line at that point. The slope varies as we move from point to point on a non-linear curve.

TERMS FOR REVIEW

functional notation (20)
function (20)
dependent variable (20)
independent (explanatory) variable
 (20)
graphs (21)

origin (21)
direct relation (23)
slope (26)
negative slope (28)
positive slope (28)
slope of a non-linear curve (29)

QUESTIONS FOR REVIEW AND DISCUSSION

1. What is the difference between: (L.O.1,2)

   (a) dependent and independent variables;

   (b) direct and inverse relations?

2. In each of the following relations, indicate the dependent and independent variables. (L.O.2)

   (a) If the price (P) of a product changes, the quantity (Q) that will be bought will also change.

   (b) Changes in the quantity (Q) that people will buy are due to changes in price (P) and income (Y).

   (c) An increase in the average income (Y) of Canadians will result in an increase in imported goods (M).

   (d) Changes in income (Y) and the rate of interest (r) will cause the level of investment (I) to change.

3. Why are graphs important in economics? (L.O.3)

4. Use the functional notation to express each of the following relations. (L.O.1)

   (a) The rate of interest (r) depends on the money supply (MS).

   (b) If the quantity produced (Q) changes, then the total cost of production (TC) will also change.

   (c) Consumer spending (C) depends on the rate of interest (r) and on the level of income (Y).

5. Explain how each of the following is measured: (L.O.4)

    (a) the slope of a linear curve;

    (b) the slope of a non-linear curve at a point.

PROBLEMS AND EXERCISES

1. Construct tables with hypothetical values to show the relations you would expect to find between: (L.O.3)

    (a) population and the number of schools;

    (b) the number of candles sold and the number of power failures in Shawinigan during a period of time;

    (c) the number of chairs and the number of desks that a carpenter can make in a given week.

2. Draw graphs to illustrate each of the relations in Question 1 above. (L.O.3)

3. Graph the relations shown in Tables 2.3 and 2.4. On the graph drawn from Table 2.3, put income on the horizontal axis and consumer spending on the vertical axis. For the graph drawn from Table 2.4, put price on the vertical axis and quantity on the horizontal axis. (L.O.3)

TABLE 2.3	Income	Expenditure on consumer goods
Relationship between income and expenditure.	40	50
	60	60
	80	70
	100	80
	120	90
	140	100

TABLE 2.4	Price of coffee	Quantity of coffee bought
Relationship between price and quantity purchased.	$7.00	15
	6.50	16
	6.00	17
	5.50	19
	5.00	21
	4.50	23
	4.00	26

4. Given that $S = S(Y)$, where S = saving, and Y = income: (L.O.1)

    (a) What is the meaning of this expression?

    (b) Which is the dependent variable?

    (c) Which is the independent variable?

5. Given that $I = I(r,E)$, where I = investment, r = rate of interest, and E = expectations: (L.O.1)

    (a) What does the expression tell you?

    (b) Identify the dependent and independent variables.

6. With price on the vertical axis and quantity on the horizontal axis: (L.O.3,4)

(a) Plot the curve from Table 2.5.

(b) Calculate the slope of this curve.

(c) Compare the slope of this curve with that of a 45° line drawn through the origin.

TABLE 2.5	P	Q
Relationship between price and quantity.	10	15
	20	20
	30	25
	40	30
	50	35

7. With reference to Figure 2.14, calculate the slope of the curve at points A and B. (L.O.4)

FIGURE 2.14

Slope calculation exercise.

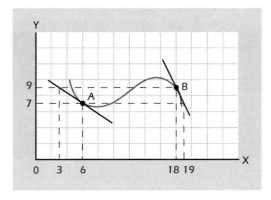

CHAPTER 3

THE ECONOMIC PROBLEM: THE PROBLEM OF SCARCITY

Learning Objectives

After studying this chapter, you should be able to:

1 identify and classify the resources of the economy

2 discuss the incomes derived from various resources

3 establish a relationship between scarcity, choice and opportunity cost

4 explain and use the concepts of production possibility schedules and production possibility curves

5 describe economic systems and their functions

6 explain the role of government in a market economy

7 discuss the basic sectors of the economy

Every act which involves time and scarce means for the achievement of one end involves the relinquishment of their use for the achievement of another. It has an economic aspect.

Lionel Robbins, *The Nature and Significance of Economic Science*

INTRODUCTION

There are numerous economic problems (for example, unemployment, an unstable dollar, inflation, low productivity, economic instability, etc.), but the fundamental economic problem is the problem of scarcity, that is, limited resources in the face of unlimited wants. Regardless of how an economic system is organized, it has to address this fundamental economic problem.

In this chapter, we focus our attention on the economy's resources, and on how different economic systems deal with the ever-present problem of scarcity. We will also discuss the roles of government, consumers, and producers in a market economy.

THE RESOURCES OF THE ECONOMY

Learning Objective 1:
classify the economy's resources

Resources (or factors of production) are the various things that can be used to produce goods and services.

Land refers to all natural resources.

Labour refers to human effort.

Capital refers to produced means of production.

Real capital includes buildings, tools, and equipment.

Human capital includes the education, skills, and health of the labour force.

Entrepreneurship refers to organizational and innovative skills.

Take another look at our definition of economics and you will see that the efficient use of resources is of crucial importance. What exactly are these resources, and how can they be classified? **Resources** are the various things (tangible and intangible) that can be used to produce goods and services. An economy has numerous different resources (or **factors of production** as they are sometimes called). There are lakes, rivers, forests, minerals, fertile land, highways, plants and equipment, warehouses, and human labour. But these resources can all be classified into four broad categories: land, labour, capital, and entrepreneurship (entrepreneurial services).

Land refers to those resources which have been given by nature and which can be used to produce goods and services to satisfy human wants. The concept is much broader than the ordinary notion of the solid portion of the earth. Economists consider any non-human resource which is made available by nature to be land. Thus, minerals embedded in the earth, fish in the sea, oxygen in the air, the sea, rivers, and lakes — even the space within which economic activity takes place — are all classified as land. The term **natural resources** is often used as a synonym for land.

Labour refers to the physical and mental efforts that people can contribute to the production processes. It is not difficult to visualize the labour expended by a craftsperson, or a farmer in the field, or an individual engaged in the production of some manufactured good. But the services rendered by sales representatives, lawyers, teachers, doctors, musicians, and actors are also classified under the heading of labour. So next time you turn on the radio and you hear one of your favourite tunes, remember that the disc jockey is providing labour services.

Capital is any manufactured good which can be used for the production of other goods and services. Buildings, roads, plants, equipment, and tools are examples of capital goods. These are sometimes called **real capital**. It is important to note that our definition of capital differs from the everyday concept which is often equated with money. To the economist, capital refers to productive agents produced by people to be used in conjunction with other productive factors to produce goods and services. The distinction between real capital and money capital is an important one in economics. The concept of human capital as distinct from physical or non-human capital has crept into the economist's vocabulary. **Human capital** refers to education, health, and individual skills.

Entrepreneurship or entrepreneural services encompasses managerial and decision-making skills. The production of goods and services requires not only the existence of land, labour, and capital, but also that these factors be brought together and organized into production. The ability to organize land, labour, and capital into production, and to innovate is called entrepreneurship. The individual who engages in these organizational and innovative activities is called an *entrepreneur*. Innovation and the organization of land, labour, and capital into the production process with the expectation of earning a profit are entrepreneurial services that involve some element of risk. The entrepreneur therefore is a risk-taker, but the rewards for innovation and creative ability can be substantial.

This discussion of resources can be summarized as shown below. Each boxed item represents a variety of resources with common characteristics.

Land	All natural resources
Labour	Human resources
Capital	Manufactured resources
Entrepreneurship	Organizational and decision-making skills

PROBLEM SOLVING 3-1

Is a car a capital good?

FACTOR PAYMENTS

Learning Objective 2: discuss the incomes derived from various resources

The factors of production must be rewarded for the services which they provide. Economists have devised special terms for the payment received for the use of these factors of production. Table 3.1 lists groups of factors of production and the compensation associated with each group. Compensation may be in monetary form, or in the form of goods and services, or partly in money and partly in goods and services. In our economic system, payment is nearly always entirely in the form of money.

TABLE 3.1	Factors	Compensation
Factors and their compensation.	Land	Rent
	Labour	Wages and salaries
	Capital	Interest and dividends
	Entrepreneurship	Profits

Rent, wages and salaries, interest and dividends, and profits are the rewards for land, labour, capital, and entrepreneurship respectively.

Land owners receive payment for the use of their land. The term **rent** is applied for such payment. Labour is compensated by the payment of **wages and salaries**. The owners of money capital receive **interest** and the owners of real capital (shareholders) receive payments called **dividends**. Entrepreneurship is rewarded by **profits**. We should keep in mind that, in modern corporations, one aspect of the entrepreneurial function (organization and direction) is carried out by hired managers, boards of directors, and other executives who receive salaries for their services. The other aspect of the entrepreneurial function (the risk-bearing function) is performed by the owners of the corporation, who receive a share of the profits as a reward for risk-taking.

PROBLEM SOLVING 3-2

Can you think of any income the source of which is not a resource? What about government welfare payments?

SCARCITY, CHOICE AND OPPORTUNITY COST

Learning Objective 3:
establish a relationship between scarcity, choice, and opportunity cost

Scarcity of resources requires a choice between wants.

Opportunity cost (or alternative cost) refers to the alternative that is sacrificed when a choice is made.

Scarcity and choice are facts of economic life. The simple truth is that there are not enough resources to enable society to produce all of the goods and services that would be required to satisfy everyone's wants. If resources were not scarce, we would satisfy all our wants and there would be no need to give up anything. Scarcity forces us to choose.

Every act of choosing requires a sacrifice. If I choose to attend a Whitney Houston concert on Saturday evening, then I am sacrificing something else that I could have done — such as watching a baseball game between the Toronto Blue Jays and the Boston Red Sox. By choosing to attend the concert, I give up the baseball game. Economists use the term **opportunity cost** or **alternative cost** to refer to alternatives or opportunities that are sacrificed.

If a city decides to build a school instead of adding a wing to a hospital, then the opportunity cost of the school is the additional hospital facilities that the city could have had instead.

PROBLEM SOLVING 3-3

1. **On the night before your final examination in economics, the Montreal Canadiens are to play against the New York Rangers for the Stanley Cup. You can either study your economics or watch the game, but you cannot do both. Use the concept of opportunity cost to decide whether you should study economics or watch the hockey game.**

2. **If Canada decided to engage in the production of anti-pollution equipment to combat acid rain, what would be the opportunity cost?**

PRODUCTION POSSIBILITIES

The economic problem of allocating resources in a situation of scarcity can be illustrated by examining the production possibility curve of an economy. Let us assume that an economy devotes all of its resources to the production of only two goods: houses and automobiles. Several possible combinations of houses and automobiles are illustrated in the **production possibility schedule** (Table 3.2).

TABLE 3.2	Possibilities	Number of houses	Number of automobiles
Production possibilities (constant cost).	1	0	8 000 000
	2	100 000	7 000 000
	3	200 000	6 000 000
Production possibility schedule: a table showing various combinations of goods that an economy can produce if it uses all of its resources.	4	300 000	5 000 000
	5	400 000	4 000 000
	6	500 000	3 000 000
	7	600 000	2 000 000
	8	700 000	1 000 000
	9	800 000	0

If this hypothetical economy uses all of its resources to produce automobiles, it can produce a maximum of 8 000 000 automobiles and no houses (possibility 1). If it uses all of its resources to produce houses, it can produce a maximum of 800 000 houses and no automobiles (possibility 9). Between these two extreme cases, Table 3.2 shows many other possibilities. For example, the economy can produce 100 000 houses and 7 000 000 automobiles (possibility 2). Or it can produce 500 000 houses and 3 000 000 automobiles (possibility 6). Note that for every 100 000 houses, the economy sacrifices 1 000 000

Production possibility (transformation) curve: a curve showing the various combinations of commodities that can be produced if all resources are fully employed and technology is constant.

A linear production possibility curve illustrates constant opportunity cost.

automobiles. Thus the opportunity cost of 100 000 houses is 1 000 000 automobiles. That is, in order to produce one house, this economy must sacrifice 10 automobiles. In this example, the opportunity cost remains constant throughout.

The relations in Table 3.2 can also be shown on a graph known as the **production possibility curve** or the **transformation curve**. This curve (represented in Figure 3.1) shows the maximum number of houses and the maximum number of automobiles that this particular economy can produce with given technology at a particular time. Let us keep in mind that, in drawing the production possibility curve, we assume that the economy has a given amount of resources and that technology is constant. The curve in Figure 3.1 is linear (a straight line) because we assume that in this case, opportunity cost is constant. In other words, automobiles could be traded off for houses at a fixed rate.

FIGURE 3.1

Production possibility curve showing constant opportunity cost.

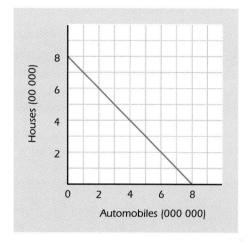

Increasing opportunity cost occurs because resources are not all equally efficient in all uses.

In the real world, however, we may seldom encounter situations of constant opportunity cost. Resources are not all equally efficient in all lines of production. Some resources will produce houses more efficiently than they will automobiles. And some will produce automobiles more efficiently than they will houses. As we continue to shift resources from the automobile industry to the housing industry, we are likely to experience increasing cost. This is so because these resources are likely to be less efficient in the housing industry. For example, it may be relatively easy at first to shift automobile workers from the automobile industry to the housing industry. As the process continues, however, it will become increasingly difficult to find automobile workers who are efficient construction workers. After all, there is a limited number of automobile workers who can work efficiently in the construction industry.

Table 3.3 is a production possibility schedule (p-p schedule for short) illustrating increasing opportunity cost. The first 100 000 houses can be obtained by giving up 1 000 000 automobiles. (The number of automobiles falls from 10 000 000 to 9 000 000.) The second 100 000 houses can be obtained by sacrificing an additional 2 000 000 automobiles. The third 100 000 houses can be obtained at an additional cost of 3 000 000 automobiles, and the fourth 100 000 houses will involve a sacrifice of 4 000 000 automobiles. Thus, each increase in the number of units of houses requires the quantities of automobiles sacrificed to increase by an increasing amount. This is the meaning of increasing opportunity cost.

	Possibilities	Number of houses	Number of automobiles	No. of automobiles given up per 100 000 houses
TABLE 3.3 Production possibilities (increasing cost).	1	0	10 000 000	1 000 000
	2	100 000	9 000 000	2 000 000
	3	200 000	7 000 000	3 000 000
	4	300 000	4 000 000	4 000 000
	5	400 000	0	

Figure 3.2 helps to explain this point. Note that the vertical segments CG, BR, and AP are all equal, representing equal increases in units of houses. The horizontal segments DG, CR, and BP represent the units of automobiles that must be sacrificed in order to obtain the additional units of houses. Thus, to obtain the first increase in houses (CG), the society gives up DG units of automobiles. To obtain the second increase in houses (BR), the society sacrifices CR units of automobiles. And to obtain the third increase in houses (AP), the society gives up BP units of automobiles. Note that BP > RC > DG. Thus, the opportunity cost of each additional increase in houses increases. Production possibility curves illustrating increasing opportunity cost will be concave to the origin as in Figure 3.2.

A concave p-p curve illustrates increasing opportunity cost.

FIGURE 3.2

Production possibility curve showing increasing opportunity cost.

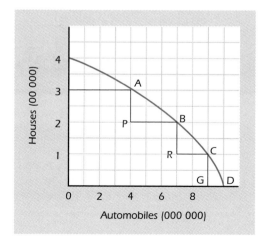

It is important to distinguish between a **production possibility point** and a production possibility curve. A production possibility point represents a combination of goods or services that an economy can produce, whereas a production possibility curve represents all production possibility points resulting from full utilization of resources.

A production possibility point represents a combination of goods or services that an economy can produce.

Let us now study the production possibility diagram shown in Figure 3.3. All points on the p-p curve such as A, B, and C represent combinations of houses and automobiles that can be produced with full employment of all available resources. A point such as U, which lies below the p-p curve, represents unemployment of resources. If the economy is operating at a point such as U, it can move to a point on the curve such as A and obtain more houses or automobiles without giving up anything else. Since the increased output associated with the move from U to A does not involve sacrificing any products, we can conclude that the opportunity cost of idle (unemployed) resources is zero.

The opportunity cost of idle resources is zero.

FIGURE 3.3

Production possibility
diagram.

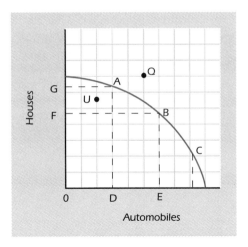

Once resources are fully employed, the output of houses can increase only if the output of automobiles decreases. A movement along the p-p curve from point B to point A, for example, implies that the production of houses increases from 0F to 0G and the production of automobiles decreases from 0E to 0D. Thus, the opportunity cost of FG houses is DE automobiles.

PROBLEM SOLVING 3-4

Antigonish Construction employs 40 previously unemployed carpenters at $80 a day. What is the opportunity cost to society of employing them for a week (5 days)?

Learning Objective 4:
explain and use the
concepts of production
possibility schedules and
curves

Refer again to Figure 3.3. Point Q is not a production possibility point because it represents a combination of houses and automobiles that is unattainable by this economy. Should technology advance or should resources increase, then the economy could produce more houses and more automobiles. This would result in a new production possibility curve lying to the right of the original curve as shown in Figure 3.4. The outward shift of the p-p curve in Figure 3.4 represents the increase in the economy's productive capac-

FIGURE 3.4

An outward shift of the
production possibility
curve.

Technological advance or
an increase in resources will
shift the production possibility curve outward.

A parallel shift in the p-p
curve implies that both
industries are affected
equally.

Economic growth is an
increase in output.

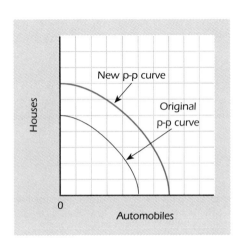

Economic growth: an increase in real per capita output.

ity. Economists sometimes call this increase in productive capacity **economic growth**. Note that this new curve consists of a whole new set of production possibility points.

In Figure 3.4, the new p-p curve runs parallel to the original curve. This implies that the increase in technology or the increase in resources has affected both industries to the same extent. If the growth occurred primarily in the housing industry, the p-p curve would shift out, but in a non-parallel manner as shown in Figure 3.5A. On the other hand, if the growth occurred primarily in the automobile industry, the p-p curve would appear as indicated in Figure 3.5B.

FIGURE 3.5

Diagram A shows growth primarily in the housing industry. Diagram B shows growth primarily in the automobile industry.

A non-parallel shift in the p-p curve implies that both industries are not affected equally.

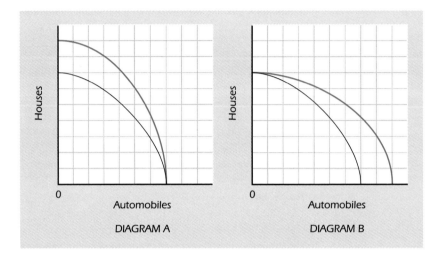

DIAGRAM A   DIAGRAM B

Note that the p-p curve will shift only if there is a change (increase or decrease) in the economy's resources, or if there is a change in technology. A shift in the p-p curve means that the economy's productive capacity has changed. Note also that there is a difference between an increase in actual production and an increase in the capacity to produce. For example, if existing resources that were not utilized are now used, actual production will likely increase, but there would be no increase in the economy's productive capacity, so the p-p curve would not shift. The capacity to produce was there, but it was not used.

Every economy has to decide on its level of economic activity, thus determining a point either on or below its p-p curve. Then, it has to decide on the most desirable combination of output, thus determining the specific point in relation to the curve. Finally, an economy must decide on its rate of economic growth, thus determining the rate at which its p-p curve shifts outward.

PROBLEM SOLVING 3-5
Would the employment of a group of previously unemployed computer programmers cause the p-p curve to shift?

ECONOMIC SYSTEMS

Learning Objective 5:
economic systems

The economic system: the system through which the functions of production and exchange are accomplished.

An **economic system** is a set of mechanisms — laws, institutions, and customs — by means of which a society accomplishes the task of producing goods and services to satisfy its wants. Such a system comprises a number of economic units which make decisions regarding the use of resources. We can classify these decision-making units as consumers or households, producers or firms, and government authorities. The way that choices are made about the use of resources (and the importance of each decision-making unit) depends on the type of economic system.

Although it is possible to classify economic systems in a variety of ways, we shall adopt a two-way classification: the **free enterprise system** (also known as **capitalism**), and the **socialistic system**. We must point out that there are many differences among the economies classified as free enterprise, just as there are differences among those classified as socialistic. In all free enterprise economic systems, however, most of the resources or factors of production are owned privately. In socialistic economies, by contrast, most of the factors of production are owned or controlled by the state. Economies such as those of Canada and the United States are basically free enterprise economies. The economies of Hungary and the former nations of Czechoslovakia, East Germany, and the Soviet Union, on the other hand, were basically socialistic economies. Socialistic economies are also known as centrally planned or command economies. The economies of the People's Republic of China and Cuba are two of the few remaining examples of centrally planned economies.

THE FREE ENTERPRISE SYSTEM

The basis of a free enterprise system is the right of private persons and private groups to own things. This principle is often referred to as the **institution of private property**. In this type of economic system, people are free to own resources and to use them in whatever way that they choose, subject to certain legal limitations designed to safeguard society. In a free enterprise economic system, individuals enjoy freedom of choice. Consumers are free, within certain legal and social constraints, to use their income to purchase the goods and services that maximize their satisfaction. They are also free to use the resources at their disposal to maximize their income. Producers also have freedom of choice. They are free to use their resources in such a way as to maximize their profits.

It is sometimes suggested that the freedom of choice that is characteristic of the free enterprise system results in a lack of order. This conclusion is erroneous, however. Consumers and producers in a free enterprise system will tend to act in such a manner as to promote their own self-interest. Consumers will buy the goods and services that give them the greatest satisfaction, and these are the very goods and services that will be most profitable to produce. Thus, freedom of choice and the pursuit of self-interest bring order rather than chaos into the free enterprise system. The system ensures that the goods and services that consumers want are those that are produced.

Advantages of a free enterprise system

One of the most important advantages of a free enterprise system is the freedom of choice that individuals enjoy. Because individuals and groups are free to use their resources to maximize their income, a free enterprise system provides initiative and incentive for people to pursue their economic objectives and improve their economic well-being. Under a free enterprise system, every individual has an opportunity to use his or her talents and resources for his or her own benefit.

Another major advantage of a free enterprise system is that the goods and services that consumers want are produced without any deliberate coordinated decision-making. The system works automatically and is therefore relatively efficient. Did you arrange with a bakery to supply you with bread tomorrow? The answer is most certainly no; yet you are quite confident that you will be able to obtain bread easily for breakfast tomorrow. You do not even need to know who bakes the bread. All you need to know is where you can buy it. One of the advantages of a free enterprise economic system is that it does not require a great deal of coordination for the economy to produce the goods and services that consumers want.

Free enterprise (capitalism): individual ownership and control of resources, and freedom of choice.

A socialistic system (command economy): state ownership and control of the economy's resources.

The institution of private property means the right of individuals to own things.

Individuals enjoy freedom of choice under a free enterprise system.

A free enterprise system is relatively efficient.

Weaknesses of a free enterprise system

Despite the great advantages of a free enterprise system, it does not work perfectly, and you often hear vicious attacks on the system. Indeed, some people blame almost every economic and social problem on the free enterprise system.

A free enterprise system may produce economic instability.

One of the major weaknesses of a free enterprise economic system is that it does not guarantee full employment. There are many people who genuinely want to work but are unable to find jobs. After you have completed your studies, there is a good chance that you will find a job where you can use the training and skills that you have developed, but the system does not guarantee it. Associated with the problem of unemployment is the problem of economic instability. A free enterprise economic system is susceptible to wide fluctuations in economic activity, sometimes with serious economic consequences.

A free enterprise system may not favour the production of public goods.

Another weakness of a pure free enterprise economic system is that certain goods and services may not be produced, or may be produced only in vastly inadequate quantities. A free enterprise system produces goods and services wanted by those individuals who can pay for them. Some goods and services, such as sanitation and defence, which benefit the entire community, may not be produced by private firms since it is difficult for private firms to exact a payment from all members of the community. Such goods, known as public goods, are better provided collectively through the government.

A free enterprise system may not adequately protect the environment.

Also, a free enterprise system, with its emphasis on private property, may not provide adequate protection to the environment. Resources such as rivers, lakes, and the air are common property, owned by everyone but by no one in particular. Often, no price is charged for the use of common property with the result that the environment becomes a dumping ground for all types of pollutants. This is a serious weakness of free enterprise systems.

A free enterprise system may not distribute income equitably.

In addition, the promotion of self-interest, a feature of a free enterprise system, may result in a very inequitable distribution of income, which may be socially unacceptable. Critics of the free enterprise system often charge that under this system, the rich get richer and the poor get poorer. When this occurs, government intervention may be necessary to deal with the problem.

Finally, a free enterprise economic system does not guarantee the competition that is necessary to ensure the efficient allocation of resources by the market system. Production of certain goods may be controlled by one seller or a few sellers who may take advantage of the opportunity to exploit other members of the society.

A SOCIALISTIC SYSTEM

You must remember that socialistic economic systems are not a homogeneous group of economies. In fact, socialistic systems can take many different forms. Some, such as those of the former Soviet Union and Czechoslovakia, relied more on central planning to make decisions about the use of resources than do others. On the other hand, others (the former Yugoslavia, for example) made greater use of the market mechanism to organize production than do some other socialistic economies. The discussion that follows focuses heavily on the Soviet-type socialistic system.

Fundamental to a socialistic economic system is government or state ownership or control of the resources of the economy. Whereas a system of markets and prices guides economic activity and the use of resources in free enterprise systems, government planning directs economic activity and the use of resources in socialistic economies. The state decides what goods and services are to be produced and establishes state-owned industries to produce them. The managers of the state-owned enterprises are given production targets, and they and the workers obtain bonuses if they exceed these targets.

Whereas individual self-interest is supreme in free enterprise systems, the interests of the society as a whole supersede individual self-interest in socialistic systems. Consequently, the government in a socialistic system will employ economic resources to meet the objectives of the society as a whole as set by the state, even at the expense of individual freedom.

In a socialistic system, individuals may not have freedom of choice in determining the occupations they will enter. The government may decide that a young student must study engineering rather than medicine, depending on the number of doctors and engineers the government wants to produce. Freedom of movement is also limited in a socialistic system. Workers with special skills may be prevented from moving away from areas where such skills are needed.

Advantages of a socialistic system

A socialistic system has the great advantage that it can maintain full employment. You will recall that inability to maintain full employment was one of the weaknesses of a free enterprise system. Another advantage of a socialistic system is the relative ease with which it can shift resources from one use to another. For example, it is relatively easy for a socialistic economy to divert resources from the production of consumer goods to its space program.

Weaknesses of a socialistic system

A major problem with a socialistic system is that individual freedom is severely limited. Individuals are not free to establish firms to produce the goods and services that consumers want, and neither are they free to pursue the occupations and professions of their own choice. Economic rewards are given at the discretion of government authorities; hence, the system does not provide much automatic incentive.

Another weakness of a socialist system is the enormous cost of planning. Since most decisions are made by central planning rather than by the market, a significant amount of resources must be devoted to the planning process.

Finally, socialistic economic systems tend to produce a smaller variety of products than do free enterprise economies. Moreover, competition among private producers in a free enterprise system forces them to produce goods of high quality. This may not be the case in a socialistic system where producers may try to achieve their physical production targets by producing goods of poor quality.

A TOUCH OF REALISM

A free enterprise economic system is essentially a **market economy** because, in such a system, a system of prices and markets coordinates the allocation of resources and the determination of the composition of output. By contrast, a socialistic economic system such as that used in the former U.S.S.R. is essentially a **command economy** since government dictates the use of resources. In the real world, neither total free enterprise nor total central planning has ever existed. Instead, all real-world economies have been **mixed economies** with elements of free enterprise *and* government intervention.

The economic system of the United States has been regarded as the most prominent example of a free enterprise economic system. Yet there is a certain amount of government (centralized) decision-making in the American economy. In the former Soviet Union, on the other hand, professional persons including lawyers and doctors and certain skilled craftspeople may engage in private practice and self-employment. Certain producers may sell their products on the free market, and some economic activities take place for private profit. Generally speaking though, inasmuch as all real-world economies are

A socialistic system is able to maintain full employment.

A socialistic system severely limits individual freedom.

A socialistic system may lead to production of goods of poor quality.

In a market economy, the market forces of demand and supply play a prominent role.

In a command economy, the government directs economic activity.

In practice, all economies are mixed economies with varying degrees of government intervention.

The market mechanism is the network of markets and prices found in most western countries.

A mixed private enterprise economy is a free enterprise economic system with government intervention

mixed economies, the classification of economic systems on the basis of the way in which economic decisions are made remains valid.

In Canada, most economic decisions are made by households and firms acting in a complicated network of markets and prices that we call the **market mechanism**. The government, however, owns some resources and conducts a significant amount of economic activity. The Canadian economy, then, is a mixed economy. A free enterprise economic system with government intervention is often called a **mixed private enterprise economy**.

PROBLEM SOLVING 3-6

Of the economic systems that we have discussed, which one would you expect businesses in Canada to favour?

THE BASIC FUNCTIONS OF AN ECONOMIC SYSTEM

Learning Objective 5: the functions of an economic system

In a market economy, questions about what, how, and for whom to produce are answered through the price system.

Any economic system, regardless of how it is organized, must deal with the fundamental economic problem of finding a way to allocate scarce resources among alternative uses. The economic system must determine what goods and services are to be produced and in what quantities, how they are to be produced, and how to distribute them among the members of the community. This fundamental economic problem is usually cast in terms of *what, how,* and *for whom.* Different economic systems deal with these questions in different ways. We shall examine briefly how these basic economic decisions are made in a market economy such as the Canadian economy. In a market economy, questions about what to produce, how to produce, and for whom to produce are answered through the mechanism of the **price system**.

WHAT TO PRODUCE

Firms in a free enterprise economic system engage in production because they hope to make a profit by selling the product at a price that exceeds the cost of production. It follows, then, that firms will produce what consumers want to buy. Consumers express their wants by their behaviour in the market. Firms respond by producing those goods that receive the highest number of dollar votes. Suppose the Kinski Company decides to produce a certain product called Super X, and then finds that consumers are unwilling to spend their money on that particular product. The firm will discover that the production of Super X is not profitable and will put its resources into some other venture. By their decision not to purchase Super X, consumers have communicated to the producers that they do not want Super X produced. The idea that consumers have the power to determine ultimately what is produced has been termed **consumer sovereignty**.

Consumer sovereignty means that consumers decide what to buy and hence what is produced in the economy.

Producer sovereignty means that producers decide what to produce and then convince consumers to buy it.

The concept of consumer sovereignty has come under attack from various quarters. Economist John Kenneth Galbraith, in particular, has argued that the concept of consumer sovereignty should be abandoned and replaced by the concept of **producer sovereignty**. He argues that firms produce the products that will help them to achieve their goals for the security of the organization and its growth, convenience, prestige, and profits. Then they use high-power advertising and hard selling to persuade consumers to purchase the products. In this way, the producer creates and manipulates the consumers' tastes and preferences. In this text, although we will not ignore the effect of persuasive advertising on consumers' behaviour, we will not discard the concept of consumer sovereignty.

HOW TO PRODUCE

The economic system must have a method of organizing its productive resources in order to provide the members of the community with appropriate quantities of goods and services. A mechanism must exist for shifting resources away from uses that contribute less to consumers' satisfaction and toward uses that contribute more to consumers' satisfaction.

In a free enterprise system, individual producers decide on the methods of production, but their decisions are guided by the system of prices and markets. If the goal of a producer is to earn as large a profit as possible, then that producer will use the method of production with the lowest cost; that is, the producer will use an efficient method of production. If a producer chooses an inefficient high-cost method of production, competition from more efficient producers will force that producer out of the market.

FOR WHOM TO PRODUCE

The economic system must also have some means of distributing its output of goods and services among the various members of the community. In a free enterprise economy, this task is accomplished mainly through the market system. The share of the total output that individuals receive depends mainly on their abilities to purchase goods and services. The ability of any individual to purchase goods and services depends on that individual's income, which in turn depends on the quantity and quality of human and physical resources over which that individual has control. If the market places a high value on particular resources, their owners will receive large payments for their use and will be able to obtain a large share of the total output of goods and services. Individuals who own very few resources that are poorly employed will receive low incomes and consequently, only small portions of the total output. Thus, the distribution of the economy's output in a free enterprise economic system depends largely on the distribution of income, which in turn depends on the distribution of resources among the members of the community.

PROBLEM SOLVING 3-7

In Canada at present, there are no laws forcing authors to write books; yet when you register for your courses, you are confident that there will be textbooks in the bookstores for your courses. Why?

ADDITIONAL FUNCTIONS OF AN ECONOMIC SYSTEM

Learning Objective 5:
the functions of an economic system

An economic system is expected to provide economic stability, economic security, and economic growth.

In addition to the basic functions of allocation and distribution (what, how, and for whom to produce), the economic system is expected to provide economic stability, which we define as full employment without inflation. We generally consider it to be undesirable to have resources (human or physical) lying idle. Inflation, moreover, is a threat to the proper functioning of the economy and to the well-being of citizens. Later, we will discuss measures that aim at achieving full employment without inflation — an important macroeconomic issue.

The provision of economic security is another task which most modern economic systems are expected to perform. The performance of this task has found expression in programs such as unemployment insurance, old age pensions, minimum wage laws, guaranteed income, and medicare. Finally, the economic system is expected to provide for an increase in the productive capacity of the economy. Economic growth is an important objective of most nations because it determines the society's standard of living.

THE ROLE OF GOVERNMENT IN A MARKET ECONOMY

Government intervention may be necessary to protect individual freedom, to protect property rights, to enforce contracts, and to regulate economic activity.

Learning Objective 6:
the role of government in a market economy

It would be a mistake for us to believe that the automatic price mechanism works perfectly. Although most economic decisions are left to private individuals acting in response to the market forces of demand and supply, the market system does not perform some tasks satisfactorily. The government therefore enters the market to assist the system in operating satisfactorily and in producing results in accord with the goals of the society.

Consideration of the weaknesses of a free enterprise system discussed above provides some guidelines as to how government intervention might improve the operation of the system. For instance, the government should ensure that conditions exist for the proper functioning of the market mechanism. One of the essentials of the market system is that individuals be free to pursue their own interests. The government should therefore enter the system to protect individual freedom.

The market mechanism functions on the basis of private ownership of property. Owners of resources need to feel secure that their properties are protected. The government must provide this security by protecting property rights. Also, individuals in a free enterprise system need to feel assured that agreements made with other individuals or groups of individuals will be honoured. The government should therefore enter the system to enforce such contracts.

There is a tendency for monopolies to develop in the market. A monopolistic situation exists when a single seller controls the supply of a product. Monopolistic elements can interfere with the proper functioning of the economic system; hence, the government must take measures to encourage competition. In some cases, however, it may be more efficient to produce certain commodities under conditions of monopoly. The government should intervene to modify and regulate such situations to prevent abuse of monopoly power.

The market economy is subject to periods of inflation and unemployment. If the rate of spending in an economy exceeds the rate of increase in the goods and services that the economy produces, then prices will tend to rise. If the rate of spending falls short of the rate of increase in the total output of goods and services of the economy, then unemployment is likely to result. Economic instability can impose severe hardships on individuals in the society. The government should therefore act to prevent such instability. The quantity of money, the rate of interest, the level of government spending, and taxation have now become important government tools to regulate spending in the economy.

Without government intervention, serious social problems may arise from unjust income distribution.

The market system, if left unregulated, may distribute the total output of goods and services among the members of the society in an unsatisfactory manner. For example, individuals who own large quantities of valuable resources and who employ them where they make great contributions to the economy's output will receive large incomes, while those individuals who happen to be in less fortunate circumstances may hardly be able to afford the bare necessities of life. The government should intervene to achieve an equitable distribution of income among individuals in the society.

Government intervention may be necessary to deal with divergencies between private and social benefits and costs.

Finally, the market system considers only private costs and private benefits. It does not take social costs and social benefits into account. For example, a firm that freely dumps waste into the environment does not include environmental damage in its cost of production. The society bears the cost of destroyed wildlife, fish, and vegetation, and decreased aesthetic value. Now, on the benefit side, if I decide to turn on my floodlights at night, I must think that the benefit I derive compensates for the increased cost of electricity — and the market will measure these benefits in terms of greater payments for electricity. But although other people may also derive benefits from my floodlights, they do not help to pay my electricity bill and I cannot force them to pay, so the market will not take this social benefit into account. In some cases, even though a good or service may produce great social benefits, individuals acting independently may choose not to produce it because the immediate benefits to these individuals may be too small to justify the cost. When such divergencies occur between private and social benefits and costs, government intervention is desirable to attempt some reconciliation.

PROBLEM SOLVING 3-8
Can you defend the provision of free elementary and secondary education by the government?

THE BASIC SECTORS OF THE ECONOMY

Learning Objective 7:
the basic sectors of the economy

The basic sectors of the economy are the household sector, the business sector, and the government sector.

For purposes of economic analysis, we may divide the economy into three **basic sectors**: the consumer sector (households), the business sector (producers or firms), and the government sector. Consumers enter the market in two main ways: they hire out or sell resources over which they have control, and they use the proceeds to purchase goods and services to satisfy their wants. The business sector purchases resources from consumers and other firms and uses these resources to produce goods and services to sell to other firms and consumers. The government sector engages in production and consumption. It provides goods and services through the activities of various government departments at the federal, provincial, and municipal levels, government agencies, and crown corporations. It also regulates economic activity by enacting laws that govern

GLOBAL PERSPECTIVE

Russia's Economic Woes

Economic reform in Russia began some six or seven years ago when Gorbachev introduced capitalism into the then-Soviet economic system. Russia began the movement toward a market economy by allowing the price system to dictate the allocation of resources, and by dismantling the institutions and instruments of central planning. The Russian society was one that was unaccustomed to the workings of the "invisible hand." It is therefore understandable that the Russian people would have difficulty understanding how their well-being could be assured when no one was directly ordering the flow of resources into specific economic activities.

It did not take long for the "makeshift" market system in Russia to begin to fall apart. The International Monetary Fund hailed 1997 as a year of achievement for the Russian economy. Inflation was on the decline, there was a surplus in the balance of payments, and there was growth, though small, in the Russian economy for the first time in five years. Then came the economic woes.

In August 1998, the ruble (the Russian currency unit) tumbled and the Russian people tried to get their money out of Russian banks. The confidence that is so necessary for the proper functioning of a country's financial system was undermined. Capital flight (the swift movement of money out of the country) has become a major problem for the Russian economy. Other major problems include unpaid salaries of government workers, increasing international indebtedness, huge amounts of unpaid taxes, and a hopelessly uncompetitive industrial infrastructure.

The causes of Russia's economic woes are legion, and it would be a Herculean task to analyze them. Suffice it to say that Russia's economic woes do not necessarily reflect a failure of the market mechanism. Perhaps it does, however, teach a lesson or two about injecting capitalism into a system without first ensuring the existence of a structure that is appropriate for the operation of a free market system.

certain aspects of production and consumption, and by conducting economic policies. The government also acts as a consumer when it purchases such items as military aircraft, ships, computers, paper, and uniforms.

Note that although the foreign sector is extremely important, we do not treat it as a basic sector. It consists of consumers, producers, and government engaged in transactions with foreigners. It is thus a particular grouping of members of the basic sectors, so we treat it as a subsector.

CHAPTER SUMMARY

1. The resources of the economy may be classified as land (natural resources), labour (human resources), capital (produced means of production), and entrepreneurship (managerial and organizational skills, decision making, risk-taking). The payments for these resources are rent, wages and salaries, interest and dividends, and profits.

2. Because of scarcity, society has to choose. When we choose, we sacrifice something. Opportunity cost or alternative cost refers to the opportunity or alternative that is sacrificed or given up when a choice is made.

3. The production possibility curve or transformation curve shows the maximum output of two goods (or classes of goods) that an economy can produce if it uses all of its resources. In drawing the curve, we assume that technology is constant.

4. A straight line (linear) production possibility curve implies constant opportunity cost, while a concave production possibility curve implies increasing opportunity cost.

5. The production possibility curve will shift only if the economy's productive capacity changes. This could be caused only by a change in resources or a change in technology.

6. The economic system is a set of laws, institutions, and customs through which a society accomplishes the task of producing and distributing goods and services to satisfy its wants.

7. Economic systems may be classified broadly into two categories: free enterprise systems, and socialistic systems or command economies.

8. The foundation of a free enterprise system is the principle of the institution of private property. This means that it is the right of private individuals to own things.

9. Advantages of the free enterprise system include individual freedom of choice, low cost of operation, and the ability of the system to produce what consumers want. Weaknesses of this system include its inability to guarantee full enployment, lack of incentive to produce public goods, inadequate protection of the environment, and an inequitable distribution of income.

10. Government or state ownership or control of the resources of the economy is fundamental to command economies. Central planning directs economic activity and the use of resources.

11. Advantages of command economies include their ability to maintain full employment and to divert resources from one use to another. Weaknesses of these economies include limited individual freedom, high cost of planning economic activity, a limited variety of products, and a tendency to produce goods of poor quality.

12. In practice, all economies are mixed economies with a greater or lesser degree of government intervention in directing and controlling economic activities.

13. Every economic system must deal with the basic problem of deciding what to produce, how to produce, and for whom to produce. In addition, an economic system is expected to provide economic stability, economic security, and economic growth.

14. The role of government in a market economy is to ensure that the system operates in a satisfactory manner and that it gives results that are in accordance with the objectives of the society.

15. The economy may be divided into three basic sectors: the household sector, the business sector, and the government sector.

TERMS FOR REVIEW

resources (factors of production) (34)
land (natural resources) (34)
labour (human resources) (34)
capital (34)
real capital (34)
human capital (34)
entrepreneurship (34)
rent (35)
wages and salaries (35)
interest (35)
dividents (35)
profits (35)
scarcity and choice (36)
opportunity cost (alternative cost) (36)
production possibility schedule (36)
production possibility
  (transformation) curve (37)
production possibility point (38)

economic growth (40)
economic system (40)
free enterprise system (capitalism) (41)
socialistic system (command
  economy) (41)
institution of private property (41)
market economy (43)
command economy (43)
mixed economy (43)
market mechanism (44)
mixed private enterprise economy (44)
price system (44)
consumer sovereignty (44)
producer sovereignty (44)
household sector (47)
business sector (47)
government sector (47)

QUESTIONS FOR REVIEW AND DISCUSSION

1. The fundamental economic problem is scarcity of resources. What are these resources and how can they be classified? (L.O.1)

2. Give two examples each of land, labour, capital, and entrepreneurship. (L.O.1)

3. "The income derived from capital is profit because firms use money and machines to make profits." Is this statement true or false? Explain. (L.O.2)

4. Make a connection between scarcity, choice and opportunity cost. (L.O.3)

5. What is opportunity cost? Give two examples to demonstrate your understanding of opportunity cost. (L.O.3)

6. Distinguish between a production possibility point and a production possibility curve. (L.O.4)

7. Will a fall in prices shift an economy's production possibility curve? Why or why not? (L.O.4)

8. Give three examples of events that would cause Canada's p-p curve to shift to the right. (L.O.4)

9. Discuss the main features of: (L.O.5)

    (a) a free enterprise economic system;

    (b) a command economy.

10. What are the main advantages and weaknesses of a free enterprise economic system? (L.O.5)

11. What are the main advantages and disadvantages of a command economy? (L.O.5)

12. Discuss the role of prices in a free enterprise economic system. (L.O.5)

13. Discuss the role of government in a market economy. Do you think that our federal government should play a more active role in our economy? Why or why not? (L.O.6)

14. Explain how a free enterprise economic system decides what to produce, how to produce, and for whom to produce. (L.O.5)

PROBLEMS AND EXERCISES

1. Indicate whether each of the following is land (T), labour (L), capital (K), or entrepreneurial services (entrepreneurship) (Es): (L.O.1)

    (a) a personal computer in the office of a travel agency;

    (b) oil deposits off the coast of Newfoundland;

    (c) a camping ground in Parc Gatineau, Quebec;

    (d) flour bought by Good Dough Bakers from Fine Flour Mill;

    (e) the services rendered by the operator of Jacob's Corner Grocery Store;

    (f) the work performed by the cashiers in the Low Price supermarket;

    (g) Snipe Lake, Alberta;

    (h) the work done by a construction worker;

    (i) anti-pollution equipment bought by Lambertus Pharmaceuticals in North Bay, Ontario;

    (j) the work performed in establishing a large chain such as Holiday Inn.

2. Indicate whether each of the following types of income is rent (R), wages and salaries (W), interest and dividend (D), or profit (P): (L.O.2)

    (a) money paid to your economics professor for his or her services;

    (b) money you receive from your part-time job;

    (c) the annual payments made by Bell to its shareholders;

    (d) the money paid to the owner of a piece of land used as a parking lot;

    (e) the net amount received by the operator of the U-Gain Retail Outlet;

    (f) the money paid to the mayor of your city for his or her services;

    (g) the money charged by the owner of Piccolo Pond for fishing privileges.

3. Makeba Electronics produces radios and TV sets. The company finds that on any given day, it can produce any of the combinations of radios and TV sets shown in Table 3.4. (L.O.4)

TABLE 3.4	Radios	TV sets
Production for Makeba Electronics.	20	0
	16	1
	12	2
	8	3
	4	4
	0	5

(a) Using this information, draw the production possibility curve for Makeba Electronics.

(b) Why is the production possibility curve for Makeba Electronics a straight line?

(c) What is the opportunity cost of a TV set in terms of radios?

4. During periods of high unemployment when it is difficult to find jobs, enrollment in colleges and universities usually increases. Use the concept of opportunity cost to explain this phenomenon. (L.O.3)

5. Show the effect of each of the following events on a country's production possibility curve. Put oil production (in barrels) on the X-axis and all other goods on the Y-axis. (L.O.4)

(a) the discovery of new oil fields;

(b) an increase in the rate of extraction of oil from existing oil fields;

(c) technological advances in the extraction of oil;

(d) a fall in unemployment due to the hiring of more workers by all firms;

(e) an increase in the number of refugees coming to Canada and being unable to find jobs;

(f) an increase in the number of refugees coming to Canada and finding jobs.

6. The Nu-Trend Office Supply Company observed that by allocating its fixed production budget between word processors and electronic calculators, it can produce per day any of the combinations of calculators and word processors shown in Table 3.5. (L.O.4)

TABLE 3.5	Number of word processors	Number of calculators
Production for Nu-Trend Office Supply Company.	0	15
	1	14
	2	12
	3	9
	4	5
	5	0

(a) Plot the production possibility curve for Nu-Trend.

(b) What is the opportunity cost of:

(i)   the first word processor;

(ii) the second word processor;

   (iii) the first two word processors;

   (iv) the third word processor;

   (v) the first three word processors?

  (c) What do you notice about the opportunity cost of word processors as more and more of them are produced?

  (d) What is the shape of the production possibility curve plotted in part (a)?

7. Referring to Nu-Trend in Question 6, suppose the company receives an increase in its production budget so that it can now produce more word processors and more calculators. (L.O.4)

  (a) Show on a graph what the new production possibility curve might look like.

  (b) If the firm dismisses some of its employees, how will the production possibility curve be affected?

  (c) What will happen to the production possibility curve if employees are shifted from the word processor section to the calculator section?

8. Under the free enterprise system, individuals enjoy freedom of choice. Does this mean that economics professors can choose not to show up for their classes any time they do not feel like teaching? (L.O.5)

9. Make a case in support of (L.O.5)

  (a) consumer sovereignty;

  (b) producer sovereignty.

10. Take a sheet of paper and draw a vertical line down the middle. On the left side, list the strengths of the market system, and on the right side, list the weaknesses. (L.O.1)

11. Repeat Exercise 10, but for a planned economy. (L.O.1)

12. (a) Compile a list of all costs involved in attending college or university for one year, then add the cost of all items to arrive at the *total cost* of attending college or university. Where costs differ among individuals, use an average. You may, for example, begin with the cost of textbooks and supplies as follows:

Items	Cost for one year
Textbooks	$_____
School supplies (pens, notebooks, etc)	$_____

  (b) Having determined the total cost of attending college or university, what should be your attitude toward college or university? (How will the information affect your behaviour?)

Internet Site

http://www.imf.org
This site is the home page of the International Monetary Fund.

INTERNET EXERCISE

1. Go to the IMF home page listed above.
2. Click on *Site Map*.
3. Click on *What is the IMF?*
4. Click on *Recent Activities?*
5. Besides Russia, in what areas of the world has the IMF been active during the 1990s?

CHAPTER 4

ELEMENTS OF DEMAND AND SUPPLY

Learning Objectives

After studying this chapter, you should be able to:

1 define demand

2 distinguish between demand and quantity demanded

3 identify the factors affecting quantity demanded

4 define supply

5 distinguish between supply and quantity supplied

6 identify the factors affecting quantity supplied

7 explain market price determination

8 use demand-supply analysis to solve simple economic problems

When demand and supply are in stable equilibrium, if any accident should move the scale of production from its equilibrium position, there will be instantly brought into play forces tending to push it back to that position; just as, if a stone hanging by a string is displaced from its equilibrium position, the force of gravity will at once tend to bring it back to its equilibrium position.

Alfred Marshall, *Principles of Economics*

INTRODUCTION

The term *demand and supply* has been used so extensively both by economists and non-economists in relation to economic matters that the term has almost become synonymous with economics. How often have you heard this statement: "It's all economics, you know — demand and supply." As someone once remarked, if the only requirement for understanding economics was the ability to repeat the phrase *demand and supply,* one could successfully teach economics to a parrot. Although economics cannot be summed up in the term *demand and supply,* a good knowledge of these two important economic concepts will enable us to understand a great deal about the operation of our economic system. Of course, economics consists of much more than just simple demand and supply, but a thorough understanding of these terms and the way that they work is absolutely essential if we are to understand many economic issues and make wise economic decisions. In this chapter, we shall study the elements of demand and supply, and how these market forces work to determine the price of a good or service. We shall also consider some applications of demand-supply analysis.

The explanation of how demand and supply work to determine the price of a good or service is presented as a model. This model assumes a free enterprise system in which economic decisions are made through the market mechanism. In this model, there is no intervention to prevent the free play of the market forces of demand and supply. It is important to note also that in this discussion, we are considering the total or market demand and supply for a particular product as opposed to a household's demand or a firm's (seller's) supply. The market consists of all buyers and all sellers of the product.

THE NATURE OF DEMAND

Learning Objective 1:
define demand

Demand: the various quantities that buyers are willing and able to buy at various prices during a period of time.

One of my economics professors once said to me, "Demand is not what you think it is." He was right. Many people use the term *demand* to mean many different things. To the economist, however, demand has a very specific meaning. **Demand** refers to the various quantities of a good or service that people will be willing and able to purchase at various prices during a period of time. It is important to note that demand refers not only to the desire for a good or service, but also to the ability to purchase the good or service. Both ingredients must be present for effective demand. It is important to note also that demand does not refer to the specific quantity that will be purchased at some particular price, but rather to a series of quantities and their associated prices.

Suppose we have information on the various quantities of apples that people will be willing and able to buy at various prices. The information may be set out in a table such as Table 4.1.

TABLE 4.1

Hypothetical demand schedule for apples.

Price of apples ($)	Quantity demanded per week (000)
0.50	100
0.45	110
0.40	120
0.35	130
0.30	140
0.25	150
0.20	160
0.15	170
0.10	180
0.05	190

Demand schedule:
a tabular representation of
demand.

A table containing this type of information is called a **demand schedule** and may be defined as a table that shows various quantities of a good or service that people will buy at various possible prices during some specified period. Note the importance of the time period. For example, to say that the quantity of apples demanded at a price of $0.35 is 130 000 is somewhat unclear. To say that the quantity of apples demanded at a price of $0.35 is 130 000 a week is more precise. Buying 130 000 apples at $0.35 each during a week is certainly not the same as buying the same quantity at the same price during a year. The quantities demanded at various prices must have some time dimension.

THE LAW OF DEMAND

The inverse relation
between price and quantity
demanded is called the law
of demand.

You will notice from Table 4.1 that as the price of apples falls, a greater quantity is demanded. This fundamental characteristic of demand is called the **law of demand**, and may be stated as follows:

> **As the price of a product falls, other things being equal, the quantity demanded increases; or alternatively, as the price of a product rises, other things being equal, the quantity demanded decreases.**

In other words, there is an inverse relation between the price of a product and the quantity demanded. Note that the law of demand assumes that all things other than price remain constant.

The market size effect:
demand increases when
the market size increases.

Let us examine the reasons for this inverse relation between price and quantity demanded. Why do people buy more as the price falls? First, as the price of apples falls, a greater number of buyers will be able to afford to buy apples. In other words, the size of the market increases, thus the quantity of apples demanded increases. We can refer to this effect as the **market size effect**. Second, those people who were buying apples before the increase in price can afford to buy more apples now that the price has fallen. In other words, a fall in price increases the buyers' purchasing power or real income, so the quantity demanded increases. This increase in quantity demanded resulting from an increase in the buyers' purchasing power or real income is often referred to as the **income effect**. Third, when the price of apples falls, some people will switch from other goods (perhaps grapes or oranges) that they were previously purchasing but that have now become relatively more expensive. That is, some people will substitute the cheaper apples for some other fruit. This change in quantity demanded resulting from substituting one good for another is often referred to as the **substitution effect**. For all of these reasons then, we might reasonably expect buyers to purchase a greater quantity of a product as its price falls, or alternatively, to buy less as the price rises.

The income effect:
demand increases as
incomes increase.

The substitution effect:
demand changes as one
good is substituted for
another.

THE DEMAND CURVE

Demand curve:
a graphical representation
of demand.

The advantage of graphical representation of information is well known: a graph enables us to see much more clearly than a table the relation between two variables. The relation between the price of apples and the quantity demanded shown in Table 4.1 may be presented in the form of a graph. It has become common practice in economics to measure price on the vertical axis and quantity demanded per unit of time on the horizontal axis. Let us see what happens if we plot the information in Table 4.1 on a graph. The result is Figure 4.1, which is called a **demand curve** and which we can define as follows:

> **The demand curve is a graph showing the various quantities of a good or service that people will be willing and able to buy at various possible prices.**

Note that because of the inverse relationship between price and quantity demanded (the law of demand), the demand curve slopes downward and to the right as shown by DD in Figure 4.1.

FIGURE 4.1

Demand curve for apples.

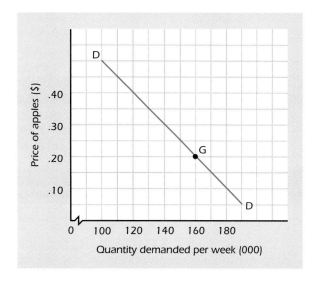

Learning Objective 2:
distinguish between demand and quantity demanded

Let us examine the demand schedule and the demand curve. At a price of $0.20, people are willing and able to buy 160 000 apples per week. This is represented by a point (point G) on the demand curve. It would be wrong to say that at a price of $0.20, the demand is 160 000. The correct way to put it is that at a price of $0.20, the *quantity demanded* (not the demand) is 160 000. In other words, the entire demand curve represents demand while a point on the demand curve represents quantity demanded at some specific price.

You will notice that the demand curve in Figure 4.1 and the demand schedule of Table 4.1 express a linear relationship between the price and the quantity demanded. It must be pointed out, however, that there is no suggestion here that demand curves (or demand schedules) are always linear. We use a linear relationship for convenience only.

PROBLEM SOLVING 4-1

Roisin Ferin, who sells roses on Confederation Square, wants to sell her entire stock by the end of the day. She begins by charging $5 a bouquet. As the day advances, she notices that her roses are moving very slowly. It seems that she will sell only half of her stock by the end of the day. What should Roisin do to rectify the situation?

FACTORS AFFECTING DEMAND

Learning Objective 3:
identify the factors affecting quantity demanded

We have seen that the price of a product affects the *quantity demanded* of that product. What are the factors that affect the *demand* for a product? Income, prices of related goods, tastes and preferences, expectations, and population: all are likely to affect the demand for a product. Since these are factors other than the price of the product under consideration, we sometimes refer to them as *non-price determinants*. Note that if we are referring to the price of another product as a determinant of demand, we still list it as a non-price determinant. Let us see how each of these non-price determinants can affect the demand for a product.

INCOME

An increase in income causes an increase in the demand for normal goods.

If their incomes increase, consumers will tend to buy more goods and services than they did before the increase in income. Let us assume that the Kurtz family was buying three kilograms of steak each week. If their income increases, the Kurtzes may find that they can now afford to purchase five kilograms of steak per week without buying less of anything else. At the same time, the Marlowe family, may be unable to buy steaks because of a low family income. If their income increases, they may decide to enter the steak market. As income increases, then, it seems likely that more of a given product will be purchased at any given price. This is the case for most goods and services; hence, economists refer to goods whose quantity demanded varies directly with income as **normal goods**.

A good is said to be a normal good if more of it is bought as income rises.

A good is said to be an inferior good if a smaller quantity of the good is purchased as income rises.

An increase in income causes a decrease in the demand for inferior goods.

Although most commodities are normal goods, there are cases when consumers may not buy more as their incomes rise. Instead, they may buy less. Let us consider regular ground beef. At a certain price of ground beef, and at a given level of income, people will buy a certain amount per week. If these people's incomes increase, they may actually reduce their purchases of regular ground beef and buy steaks or lean ground beef instead. Thus, as income rises, people may buy less, not more, regular ground beef. The same may be true of potatoes, and drink mixes such as Kool-aid. Economists refer to such goods as **inferior goods**.

It is more accurate to think of the terms *normal* and *inferior* as descriptions of consumers' behaviour or reaction to a change in income rather than as descriptions of the goods per se.

PRICES OF RELATED GOODS

Substitute goods are used to replace each other; complementary goods are used jointly.

Goods and services may be related to each other in two main ways: they may be substitutes or they may be complements. One good is said to be a **substitute** for a second good if it can be used in place of the second good. Examples of goods that are substitutes for each other are: lemons and limes, sugar and honey, butter and margarine, and tea and coffee. Two goods are said to be **complements** if one is used in conjunction with the other. Complementary goods are demanded jointly. Examples of complementary goods are: automobiles and gasoline, stereo sets and audio tapes, word processors and floppy disks, and cameras and films.

A change in the prices of related goods affects quantity demanded at each and every price.

Think about substitutable goods. If the price of limes were to increase, consumers would tend to switch to a substitute (lemons, for example). Hence, the demand for lemons would increase. In general, if the price of a substitutable commodity increases, consumers will tend to increase their purchases of the substitute in question.

Now, let us consider the case of complementary goods. As noted above, these are goods that are used together. If the price of word processors falls, people will buy more word processors and, as a consequence, the demand for floppy disks will also tend to increase. In general, if the price of a complement falls, consumers will tend to increase their purchases of the commodity in question.

The demands for independent goods are not related.

We should note, in passing, that not all goods are related. Some goods are neither substitute goods nor complementary goods. For example, we would not expect any relationship between cars and milk, radios and picture frames, computers and apple juice, or telephones and microwave ovens. Goods such as those just listed, which are not at all related, are said to be **independent goods**. If the price of radios falls, for example, we can hardly expect it to have any effect on the demand for picture frames.

TASTES AND PREFERENCES

Tastes and preferences affect demand.

The quantity of a commodity that people will buy will be affected by their tastes and preferences. If tastes in Manitoba change from meat to vegetable diets, then it is obvious that more vegetables and less meat will be demanded there. Companies spend millions of dollars in advertising in an attempt to influence consumers' tastes in favour of their products. By so doing, they are trying to increase the demand for their products.

EXPECTATIONS

Expectations affect demand.

The expectations of consumers regarding prices in the future will affect present purchases of goods and services. If consumers expect the price of a product to increase in the future, they are likely to increase their purchases now to stock up on the product and thus postpone paying the ensuing higher price for as long as possible. Conversely, if the price is expected to fall in the future, consumers will attempt to delay their purchases now in order to take advantage of the lower future price.

The expectations of consumers about future changes in income will also affect present purchases of goods and services. If people expect substantial raises in their salaries sometime in the near future, they are likely to buy more goods and services even before the increase in income materializes. If people expect decreases in income (resulting from loss of employment, for example), they are likely to buy fewer goods and services. A good example of how expected future income affects present purchases of goods and services is provided by students of law and medicine in their final year of law school or medical school. Such students usually adopt higher standards of living than individuals with similar current incomes who entertain no hope of substantial increases in their future incomes.

POPULATION

The number of buyers in the market affects the quantity that people will purchase at each and every price.

The quantity of a commodity that people will buy depends on the number of buyers in the market for that particular commodity. Other things being equal, we would expect the quantity of oranges that people will buy in Toronto, Ontario, to be significantly higher than the quantity that people will buy in Corner Brook, Newfoundland, since the population of Toronto is so much greater than that of Corner Brook. If population increases, we expect the demand for most goods and services to increase as a consequence.

PROBLEM SOLVING 4-2

1. **Petit Prince Bookstore sells crayons and colouring books. Guernica Art Supplies has just offered it a large quantity of crayons at a fraction of the regular cost. How might the bookstore use its inexpensive crayons to boost its sales of colouring books?**

2. **Sometimes when the price of gold rises, we notice that people buy more, not less. Is this a refutation of the law of demand?**

A CHANGE IN DEMAND VERSUS A CHANGE IN QUANTITY DEMANDED

Learning Objective 2: *distinguish between demand and quantity demanded*

The distinction between a change in demand and a change in quantity demanded is an important one, and we should avoid confusing these concepts. When we speak of demand, we refer to the entire demand curve or schedule. It follows then, that if demand changes, the entire curve will shift. Suppose the demand for apples in Pointe Claire was as shown in the first two columns of Table 4.2, but that now there is an increase in demand for apples (perhaps research by a team of doctors has revealed that a sufficiently large intake of apples over a certain period of time will protect the body from a wide variety of illnesses). As a consequence of this announcement, we will obtain a new demand schedule showing that a greater quantity of apples will be purchased *at each price*. The new quantities are shown in the right hand column of Table 4.2.

TABLE 4.2

Demand schedule showing an increase in demand.

Price of apples ($)	Original quantity demanded per week (000)	New quantity demanded per week (000)
0.50	100	130
0.45	110	140
0.40	120	150
0.35	130	160
0.30	140	170
0.25	150	180
0.20	160	190
0.15	170	200
0.10	180	210
0.05	190	220

We can plot these two demand curves on the same graph to illustrate the shift in demand brought about by the announcement. Figure 4.2 shows this. DD is the original demand curve; D_1D_1 is the new demand curve. The increase in demand is shown by shifting the entire demand curve to the right. The location of the curve has now changed. Note that at *any given price*, a greater quantity is purchased. A decrease in demand would mean that at *any given price* a smaller quantity would be purchased, and this would be represented by a leftward shift in the demand curve as shown in Figure 4.3.

A change in quantity demanded refers to the change in the quantity that would be bought as a result of a change in price. Let us examine the demand curve shown in Figure 4.4. At a price of $2, the quantity demanded is 48 000 per week. If the price falls

FIGURE 4.2

Increase in demand.

An increase in demand is shown by a shift in the demand curve to the right.

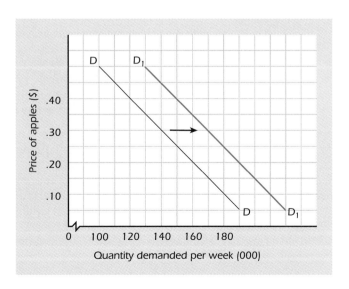

FIGURE 4.3

Decrease in demand.

A decrease in demand is shown by a leftward shift in the demand curve.

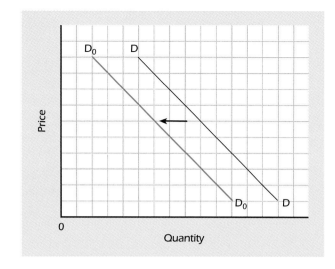

FIGURE 4.4

A change in quantity demanded.

A change in quantity demanded caused by a change in price is shown by a movement along the demand curve.

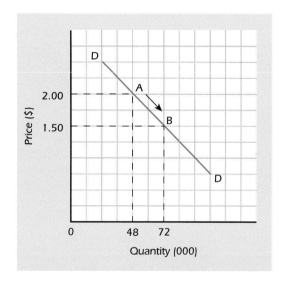

to $1.50, a quantity of 72 000 units per week will be demanded. This change in quantity demanded is represented by a movement along the same demand curve from point A to point B in Figure 4.4.

A change in the price of the commodity under consideration will not cause a change in demand, it will cause a change in quantity demanded. Only a change in a non-price determinant can cause a change in the demand for that commodity. Factors such as a change in income, a change in taste, a change in population, a change in the price of a related good, or a change in expectations will cause a change in demand — that is, cause the entire demand curve to shift.

A change in a non-price determinant causes the demand curve to shift.

Table 4.3 presents a convenient reference list of the major factors that cause the demand curve to shift. These non-price determinants are often referred to as **demand shifters.**

TABLE 4.3	Demand shifters	Illustrative examples
Demand shifters: non-price determinants that change the location of the demand curve.	1. A change in income	An increase in income increases purchasing power. The demand for most goods (normal goods) will increase, but the demand for inferior goods (used tires, for example) will decrease.
	2. A change in the prices of related goods	An increase in the price of Coke will increase the demand for Pepsi because they are substitute goods. A decrease in the price of personal computers will increase the demand for floppy disks because they are complementary goods.
	3. A change in tastes and preferences	A successful advertising campaign for eggs increases the demand for eggs because it changes buyers' tastes in favour of eggs. (Get cracking!)
	4. A change in expectations	The announcement of the imposition of a tax on video cassettes produces expectations of higher future prices and thus increases the current demand for video cassettes.
	5. A change in population	An increase in the number of immigrants into Canada increases the demand for furniture.

PROBLEM SOLVING 4-3

In January, the number of typewriters bought in Jonquière was 600. In February, the quantity bought was 750, and in March, the quantity had grown to 875. Vinud Anwar, an investor seeing these figures, decided that the demand for typewriters in Jonquière was increasing and that it was a good idea to open a store to sell typewriters. What mistake might Vinud be making?

THE NATURE OF SUPPLY

Learning Objective 4: define supply

Supply: the various quantities that sellers are willing to offer for sale at various possible prices during a period of time.

Supply schedule: a tabular presentation of supply.

A market consists of both buyers and sellers. In order to understand market behaviour, we must consider both buyers and sellers. We have looked at the demand side (the buyers' side) of the market for a product. Let us now look at the supply side (the sellers' side) of the market. **Supply** refers to the various quantities of a good or service that sellers will be willing and able to offer for sale at various prices during a period of time. As in the case of demand, supply refers not to a specific quantity that will be sold at some particular price, but to a series of quantities and a range of associated prices.

Suppose we have information on the various quantities of apples that sellers are willing and able to offer for sale at various prices. We may set this information out in a table such as Table 4.4.

A table such as Table 4.4 is called a **supply schedule** and may be defined as a table that shows various quantities of a good or service that sellers are willing and able to offer for sale at various possible prices during some specified period.

TABLE 4.4	Price of apples ($)	Quantity supplied per week (000)
Hypothetical supply schedule for apples.	0.05	40
	0.10	60
	0.15	80
	0.20	100
	0.25	120
	0.30	140
	0.35	160
	0.40	180
	0.45	200
	0.50	220

THE LAW OF SUPPLY

The direct relation between price and quantity supplied is called the law of supply.

Table 4.4 shows that as the price of apples rises, a greater quantity is offered for sale. As the price falls, a smaller quantity is offered for sale. This fundamental relationship between price and quantity offered for sale is called the **law of supply**, and may be stated as follows:

> **As the price of a product falls, other things being equal, the quantity offered for sale decreases; or alternatively, as the price of a product rises, other things being equal, the quantity supplied increases.**

There is therefore a direct relationship between the price of a product and the quantity supplied.

Why is there a direct relationship between price and quantity supplied? The main reason is that higher prices serve as an incentive for sellers to offer a greater quantity for sale. The suggestion is that sellers (or producers) can be induced by higher prices to produce and offer for sale a greater quantity of goods. Moreover, increases in price may entice new suppliers into the market.

The following example will help to explain how sellers respond to an increase in price. Suppose farmers have a certain amount of land on which they produce wheat and corn. If the price of wheat increases, farmers will find it profitable to shift land out of corn production and into wheat production. Also, it is conceivable that some farmers who were not previously producing wheat will now become wheat farmers. Hence the output of wheat increases.

THE SUPPLY CURVE

Supply curve: a graphical representation of supply.

It is advantageous to present the information contained in Table 4.4 graphically as we did in the case of demand. Plotting the data in Table 4.4 on a graph results in Figure 4.5, which is called a **supply curve** and which we can define as follows:

> **The supply curve is a graph showing the various quantities of a good or service that sellers are willing and able to offer for sale at various possible prices.**

Learning Objective 5: distinguish between supply and quantity supplied

Note that because of the direct relationship between price and quantity supplied (price and quantity supplied move in the same direction), the supply curve slopes upward as shown by SS in Figure 4.5.

FIGURE 4.5

Supply curve for apples.

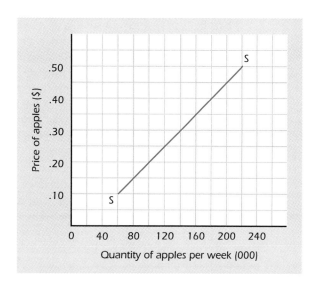

Note again that the entire supply curve represents supply while a point on the supply curve represents quantity supplied at some specific price. Also, as in the case of demand, we have assumed a linear relationship between price and quantity supplied for convenience only. There is no suggestion that supply curves are always linear.

FACTORS AFFECTING SUPPLY

Learning Objective 6:
identify the factors affecting quantity supplied

You have seen that the quantity of a good or service that sellers are willing and able to offer for sale depends on the price of the good or service. In other words, the price of a product affects the *quantity supplied*. Non-price factors, such as the number of producers (sellers), the prices of related products, technology, expectations, and input prices, are likely to affect the *supply* of a product. Let us see how each of these non-price determinants is likely to affect supply.

THE NUMBER OF PRODUCERS

The number of sellers affects quantity supplied at each and every price.

The number of sellers in the market will obviously have some effect on total market supply. This is so because the market supply of a good or service is the sum of the quantities offered for sale by all of the individual sellers in the market. We can expect market supply to increase as the number of sellers increases, and to decrease as the number of sellers decreases. If, however, the average output of producers increases significantly, the total market supply can increase even if the number of producers decreases.

PRICES OF RELATED PRODUCTS

Production substitutes and production complements affect supply.

Substitutes in production are alternatives to each other.

Complements in production, or joint products, are produced together. One may be a byproduct of the other.

You will recall our discussion of substitutes and complements on the demand side. A similar situation exists on the supply side. Goods can be substitutes or complements in production. Goods are **substitutes in production** (or production substitutes) if they are produced as alternatives to each other. Examples of substitutes in production are lettuce and tomatoes (a farmer can produce one or the other on the same piece of land), and leather bags and belts (both can be produced with the same type of resources). Goods are **complements in production** (or production complements) if they are produced together; the production of one implies the production of the other. Complements in production are also called **joint products**. Beef and hides are a classic example of goods that are complements in production.

Consider the case of substitutes in production. If the price of lettuce increases, the supply of tomatoes will decrease as producers shift from tomato production to lettuce production. In general, if the price of a substitutable product increases, sellers will tend to reduce the supply of the substitute in question.

Now consider complements in production. As noted above, these are joint products. If the price of beef rises, the quantity of beef supplied will rise, but so will the quantity of hides as more cattle are slaughtered. In general, if the price of a complement in production falls, the supply of the good in question will also fall.

TECHNOLOGY

Technology affects quantity supplied at each and every price.

Producers use inputs (factors of production) to produce goods and services. An increase in technology makes existing factors (inputs) more productive, and introduces new types of inputs that are more efficient than older types. Hence, an increase in technology causes an increase in supply. Of course, the decision to adopt new technology is based on cost considerations. If the new technology does not reduce cost, producers are unlikely to adopt it.

EXPECTATIONS

Expectations affect quantity supplied at each and every price.

If producers expect prices to rise in the future, they might begin now to expand their productive capacity and thus increase their present output levels. This is particularly so in the case of products that cannot be stored easily. However, it is entirely possible that expectations of higher future prices may lead producers into building up stocks now so that they will have a larger quantity to sell at the future higher prices. Such action will, of course, reduce current supply. Therefore, generalizations should not be made about the effect of expected price changes on supply.

PRICES OF INPUTS

Prices of inputs (production costs) affect quantity supplied at each and every price.

An increase in production costs will result in a reduction in the supply of a product. Payment for factor inputs represents a significant part of production costs. The higher the prices of these inputs, the greater the costs of production will be, and hence the less will be the supply. A reduction in input prices will, of course, cause the supply to increase.

PROBLEM SOLVING 4-4
How will an increase in wages in the shoe industry affect the supply of shoes?

A CHANGE IN SUPPLY VERSUS A CHANGE IN QUANTITY SUPPLIED

A change in supply is shown by a shift in the entire supply curve.

You will recall the distinction made earlier between a change in demand and a change in quantity demanded. A similar distinction must be made between a change in supply and a change in quantity supplied. When we speak of supply, we refer to the entire supply curve or schedule. It follows then, that if supply changes, the entire curve will shift. Suppose the supply of apples in Pointe Claire was as shown in the first two columns of Table 4.5, but that now there is an increase in the supply of apples because of technological advances in apple production. We will obtain a new supply schedule showing that a greater quantity of apples will be supplied at each price. The new quantities supplied are shown in the right column of Table 4.5.

TABLE 4.5

An increase in supply.

Price of apples ($)	Original quantity supplied (000)	New quantity supplied (000)
0.05	40	80
0.10	60	100
0.15	80	120
0.20	100	140
0.25	120	160
0.30	140	180
0.35	160	200
0.40	180	220
0.45	200	240
0.50	220	260

Let us plot these two supply curves on the same graph to illustrate the shift in supply brought about by the increase in technology. The result is Figure 4.6.

SS is the original supply curve; S_1S_1 is the new supply curve. The increase in supply is shown by shifting the entire supply curve to the right. The location of the curve has now changed. Notice that *at any given price*, a greater quantity is supplied. A decrease in supply would mean that *at any given price*, a smaller quantity would be supplied, and would be represented by a leftward shift in the supply curve as shown in Figure 4.7.

FIGURE 4.6

An increase in supply.

An increase in supply is
represented by a shift of
the supply curve to the
right or down.

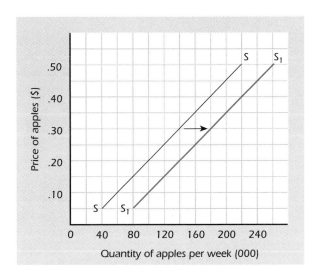

FIGURE 4.7

A decrease in supply.

A decrease in supply is
shown by a shift of the
supply curve upward or to
the left.

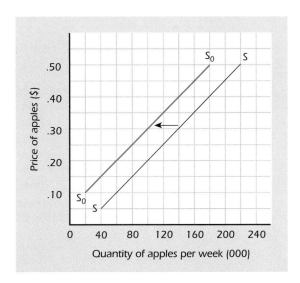

A change in quantity supplied refers to the change in quantity that would be offered for sale as a result of a change in price. Let us examine the supply curve in Figure 4.8. At a price of $3, the quantity supplied is 12 000 per week. If the price rises to $4, a quantity of 20 000 units per week will be supplied. This change in quantity supplied is represented by a movement along the same supply curve from point C to point D in Figure 4.8.

Learning Objective 5:
distinguish between
supply and quantity
supplied

A change in a non-price
determinant causes the
supply curve to shift.

A change in the price of the commodity under consideration will not cause a change in supply; it will cause a change in quantity supplied. Only a change in a non-price determinant can cause a change in the supply of that commodity. Factors such as a change in the number of producers, a change in the price of a related good, a change in technology, a change in expectations, or a change in input prices will cause a change in supply — that is, they will cause the entire supply curve to shift.

The major factors that cause the supply curve to shift are conveniently collected in a reference list in Table 4.6. These non-price determinants are sometimes referred to as **supply shifters.**

FIGURE 4.8

A movement along the supply curve caused by a change in price.

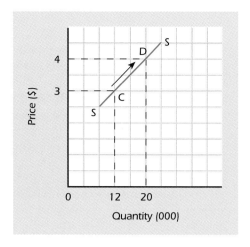

TABLE 4.6

Supply shifters: non-price determinants that change the location of the supply curve.

Supply shifters	Illustrative examples
1. A change in the number of producers	An increase in the number of manufacturers of video cassette recorders (VCRs) increases the supply of VCRs. If many of the firms producing blue jeans go out of business, the supply of blue jeans falls.
2. A change in the prices of related products	An increase in the price of lettuce reduces the supply of turnips; they are production substitutes. An increase in the price of refined cane sugar increases the supply of molasses; they are joint products.
3. A change in technology	The invention of high-speed computers increases the output (supply) of computational services.
4. A change in expectations	Suppliers expect an increase in the price of coffee so they reduce present supplies with the intention of selling at the higher price in the future.
5. A change in the price of inputs	A substantial increase in the price of steel reduces the supply of chairs with steel frames.

DETERMINATION OF EQUILIBRIUM PRICE

Learning Objective 7: explain market price determination

So far in this chapter, we have looked at demand and supply separately. It is now time to bring them together to see how market forces determine the price of a product. To help with the explanation, Table 4.7 reproduces the hypothetical demand and supply schedules shown in Tables 4.1 and 4.4 respectively.

TABLE 4.7

Hypothetical demand and supply schedules for apples.

Price of apples ($)	Quantity demanded (000)	Quantity supplied (000)
0.50	100	220
0.45	110	200
0.40	120	180
0.35	130	160
0.30	140	140
0.25	150	120
0.20	160	100
0.15	170	80
0.10	180	60
0.05	190	40

Let us first consider the situation when the price is $0.15. At this price, buyers are willing and able to purchase 170 000 apples a week, but sellers are willing and able to offer only 80 000 for sale. There will therefore be a shortage of 90 000 apples. At a price of $0.45, buyers are willing and able to purchase only 110 000 apples a week while sellers are willing to offer 200 000 apples. There will therefore be a surplus of 90 000 apples on the market. Let us now consider a price of $0.30. At this price, buyers are willing to purchase 140 000 apples a week, and sellers are willing to offer 140 000 apples for sale. At this price, there is neither a surplus nor a shortage.

At any price other than $0.30, market forces are set in motion to raise or lower the price. Consider a price of $0.40. At this price, as the supply schedule shows, sellers are willing to put 180 000 apples on the market, but buyers are willing to take only 120 000. A **surplus** or **excess quantity supplied** of apples will result. Sellers will then attempt to dispose of this surplus by lowering the price. As the price falls, a greater quantity will be demanded. The price will settle at $0.30 because, at this price, the market will be cleared.

If, on the other hand, the price happens to be $0.20, buyers will be willing to purchase 160 000 apples a week, but sellers will be willing to offer only 100 000. Pricing the apples at $0.20 will result in a **shortage** or **excess quantity demanded**. Unhappy with the shortage and wanting more apples, customers will bid up the price. Sellers, then, will offer a greater quantity at the higher prices. The price will again settle at $0.30 because, at this price, the quantity demanded equals exactly the quantity supplied. Note that the price of $0.30 is the only price that will prevail in the market. There will be no tendency for this price to change. Such a price is referred to as the **equilibrium price**, and the quantity traded (exchanged) at this price is called the **equilibrium quantity**. The market for a product is said to be in equilibrium when the quantity of the product demanded equals the quantity supplied at a specific price.

The market equilibrium condition is illustrated graphically in Diagram A of Figure 4.9. The demand curve DD and the supply curve SS are drawn from the schedules in Table 4.7.

The two curves intersect at E to give an equilibrium price of $0.30, and an equilibrium quantity of 140 000. At a price of $0.40, the quantity demanded is 120 000 and the quantity supplied is 180 000. The surplus of 60 000 is indicated on Diagram B. This surplus causes the price to fall back to the equilibrium level of $0.30. At a price of $0.25, the quantity demanded is 150 000 but the quantity supplied is 120 000. The shortage of 30 000 is indicated on the Diagram C. This shortage causes the price to rise to its equilibrium level of $0.30.

EFFECT OF A CHANGE IN DEMAND

Suppose there is an increase in the demand for apples because people have come to believe that an apple a day keeps the doctor away. What effect will such a change have on equilibrium price and quantity? Let us analyze this situation with the help of Figure 4.10.

The original demand and supply curves in this figure are DD and SS, respectively; the initial equilibrium price and quantity are $0.30 and 140 000, respectively. An increase in demand is shown by a shift in the demand curve from DD to D_1D_1. With this new higher demand, and with the initial price of $0.30, there is excess quantity demanded of 30 000 apples. This shortage will cause the price of apples to be bid up. The market establishes a new equilibrium price of $0.35 and a new equilibrium quantity of 160 000 units. The result may be stated by the following proposition:

A surplus occurs when quantity supplied exceeds quantity demanded at a given price.

A shortage occurs when quantity demanded exceeds quantity supplied at a given price.

The equilibrium price is that price which equates quantity demanded and quantity supplied, and the quantity traded at this price is the equilibrium quantity.

Learning Objective 7: explain market price determination

An increase in demand increases both price and quantity. A decrease in demand reduces both price and quantity.

FIGURE 4.9

Equilibrium price and quantity.

The intersection of the demand and supply curves determines the equilibrium price and quantity.

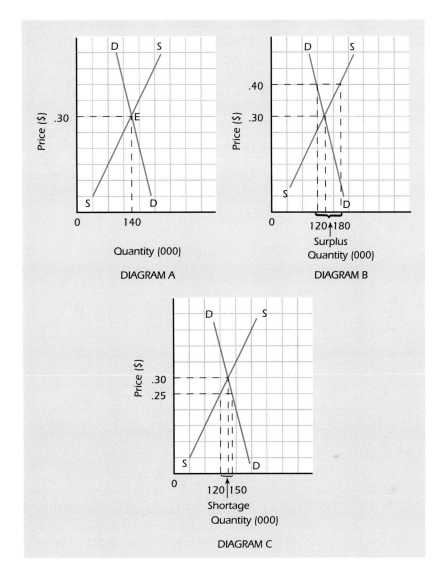

DIAGRAM A

DIAGRAM B

DIAGRAM C

FIGURE 4.10

Effect of an increase in demand.

An increase in demand results in a higher price and a greater quantity.

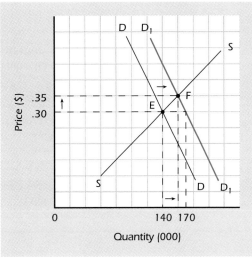

An increase in demand, other things being equal, will cause the price of the product to increase and the quantity traded to increase.

Note that although there is an increase in quantity bought and sold, there is no increase in supply; the location of the supply curve remains the same. There is, however, a movement along the supply curve from point E to point F. The effect of a decrease in demand is left as an exercise for you to work out.

EFFECT OF A CHANGE IN SUPPLY

Now suppose the supply of coffee falls because of an increase in the prices of resources used to produce coffee. Let us analyze this situation with the help of Figure 4.11.

FIGURE 4.11

Effect of a decrease in supply.

A decrease in supply results in a higher price and a smaller quantity.

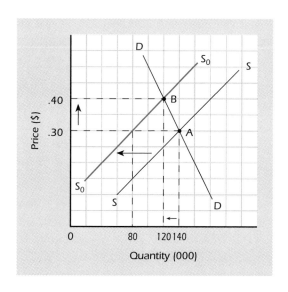

The initial demand and supply curves are DD and SS respectively. A decrease in supply is shown by an upward (leftward) shift of the supply curve from SS to S_0S_0. At the initial price of $0.30, the new quantity supplied is only 80 000 cups of coffee. There is therefore a shortage (excess quantity demanded) of 60 000 cups. Competition among buyers for coffee will cause the price to be bid up. The market establishes a new equilibrium price of $0.40, and a new equilibrium quantity of 120 000 cups. We may now state the following proposition:

An increase in supply reduces the price and increases the quantity. A fall in supply raises the price and reduces the quantity.

A decrease in supply, other things being equal, will cause the price of the product to increase and the quantity traded to decrease.

Note again that although the quantity demanded has fallen, there is no fall in demand; the location of the demand curve has not changed. Instead, there has been a movement along the demand curve from point A to point B. The effect of an increase in supply is left as an exercise for you to work out.

PROBLEM SOLVING 4-5

When the price of gold rises considerably, the price of silver also tends to rise. How might this occurrence be explained?

SOME APPLICATIONS OF DEMAND AND SUPPLY ANALYSIS

Learning Objective 8:
use demand-supply
analysis to solve simple
economic problems

Simple demand and supply analysis can help to clarify our thinking on a number of important economic issues. In this section, we will apply the demand and supply analysis developed in this chapter to some economic issues. In an economy such as the Canadian economy, the government often intervenes in the market system to produce results other than those that would be given by the market. You will see how demand and supply analysis can help us to understand the effects of such interventions.

THE EFFECT OF PRICE FLOORS

Price floor: a point beyond
which price is not allowed
to fall. A price floor is effective only if set above the
equilibrium price.

The federal government has attempted to improve the condition of egg producers in Canada by preventing the price of eggs from falling below a certain level. The minimum level to which the price is allowed to fall is called a **price floor**. If the minimum price is set below the market equilibrium price, then the market price will prevail, and the minimum price will have no effect. If, however, the minimum price is set above the equilibrium price, it is the minimum price that will prevail, and, as you will see shortly, it will have some effect. Figure 4.12 will help us to analyze the effect of setting a price floor.

FIGURE 4.12

Effect of a price floor.

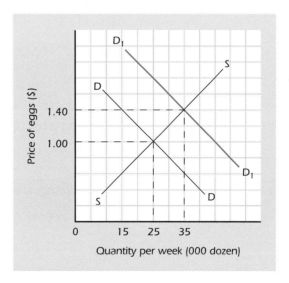

The demand and supply curves are shown by DD and SS respectively. The equilibrium price of eggs determined by the market is $1.00 a dozen. If the government sets a minimum price of $1.40 a dozen, buyers are willing to purchase only 15 000 dozen a week at that price, while producers are willing to offer 35 000 dozen for sale. A surplus of 20 000 dozen eggs results. The government will have to enter the market and purchase the surplus, thus shifting the demand curve upward to D_1D_1. The total amount received by the egg producers will be ($1.40 \times 35\ 000$) = $49 000. The government will incur a cost of ($1.40 \times 20\ 000$) = $28 000.

THE EFFECT OF PRICE CEILINGS

Learning Objective 8:
use demand-supply
analysis to solve simple
economic problems

In an attempt to protect the interest of consumers, a government may pass legislation forbidding the sale of a product above a certain price. For example, many cities set a limit on the prices that landlords may charge for apartment rentals (i.e., they impose rent control). Such control is often referred to as a **price ceiling**. Obviously, if the maximum price permissible is above the equilibrium price, then the law will be ineffective, since there will be no conflict between the market equilibrium price and the maximum price prescribed by law.

Suppose, however, that the maximum price permissible is set below the equilibrium price. Figure 4.13 illustrates the effect that setting a price ceiling would have in this case. The demand curve is DD, the supply curve is SS, and the equilibrium price is $500 per month. Assume that a price ceiling of $400 a month is established by the government; landlords may not charge more than $400 a month for their apartments. At this price, landlords are willing to offer only 40 000 units for rent, while tenants are willing to rent 60 000 units. A shortage of 20 000 units results, and this produces a tendency for the rent to rise above the legal maximum. When a shortage exists, some form of rationing must be instituted, if not by the government, then by the market. Quite often, a **black market**, in which the product is sold at a price above that prescribed by law, is the result of maximum price legislation.

> Price ceiling: a point beyond which a price is not allowed to rise. A price ceiling is effective only if the ceiling is set below the equilibrium price.

> Black market: a market in which products are sold illegally above the price prescribed by law.

FIGURE 4.13

Effect of a price ceiling.

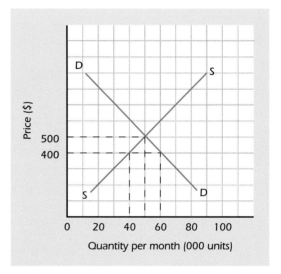

THE EFFECT OF EXCISE TAXES

> An excise tax will increase the price of the commodity upon which it is imposed, and reduce the quantity bought.

An **excise tax** is a tax imposed on a domestically produced good. It is actually a type of sales tax. Suppose a specific tax of $4.00 is imposed on each bottle of wine sold in Canada. We can analyze the effect of such a tax with the help of Figure 4.14. The demand and supply curves before the imposition of the tax are shown by DD and SS, and the equilibrium price is $10.00. The imposition of the tax causes production costs to rise by $4.00 per bottle, and thus reduces supply. This reduction is shown by an upward shift of the supply curve from SS to S_0S_0. The supply curve shifts up by the amount of the tax, so the vertical distance between SS and S_0S_0 represents the tax. Note that the new equilibrium price is not $14.00 but $12.25. The increase in price is less than the tax. This is because at the higher price, the quantity demanded is lower. The quantity traded falls from 10 000 bottles of wine to 9000 bottles. The government's revenue from the tax is ($4.00 × 9000) = $36 000.00 The consumer's share of the tax is $2.25 while the producer's share is $1.75 per bottle.

> **Learning Objective 8:** use demand-supply analysis to solve simple economic problems

FIGURE 4.14

Effect of an excise tax.

An excise tax reduces
supply and increases price

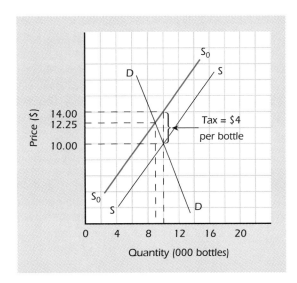

A SPECIAL APPLICATION

In January 1998, much of Quebec and Eastern Ontario was caught in the grip of an ice storm that saw vast regions literally in the dark, and hundreds of thousands of residents in the cold for a considerable period of time, as trees fell and electrical lines were broken. Economic activity as we know it came to a halt. The demand for candles skyrocketed, as did the demand for firewood, flashlights, and batteries. Naturally, the prices of these commodities rose as quantities dwindled, and, in some cases, disappeared. Some suppliers were accused of price gouging, and talks of investigations into price hikes became quite common.

 GLOBAL PERSPECTIVE

Demand and Supply Globally Contemplated

Demand and supply analysis can be used to explain the prices of certain commodities that are traded on the world market. In this capsule, we will see how decisions made in a few countries can affect the world price of a specific commodity.

A group of 13 countries, most of which are in the Middle East, accounts for a significant amount of the world's supply of oil. In 1973, this group of countries, known as the Organization of Petroleum Exporting Countries (OPEC), decided to embark on an oil embargo. The supply of oil to the West was greatly curtailed, and consequently, the price of oil rose dramatically. This rapid increase in the price of oil caused the demand for other forms of energy to increase, and led to an increase in the prices of substitutes such as electricity. Thus we see

that the laws of supply and demand apply even across international boundaries.

In the winter of 1997-98, the price of crude oil plunged to its lowest level in about nine years. In an attempt to boost sagging oil prices in the early months of 1998, OPEC promised to reduce oil production. At about the same time, Norway, the world's second largest oil exporter after Saudi Arabia (but not a member of OPEC), said that it would cut its output of oil. With Norway's help, the total supply of oil on the world market would fall significantly. With no appreciable change in demand, the demand-supply model would predict an increase in the world price of oil. The predicted price increase did, in fact, occur.

An analysis of the situation is quite simple, using the tools of demand and supply. An increase in demand followed by a fall in market supply was the fundamental cause of the price increase. Suppliers saw an opportunity and seized it. The market rationed the limited supplies and, as prices rose, there was an incentive to quickly replenish stocks. Many people complained that to increase prices was heartless and cruel, since most people were already in desperate situations. But the profit motive gave suppliers an incentive to offer commodities that were in greater demand. When quantities supplied were increased and there were no further increases in demand, prices decreased.

CHAPTER SUMMARY

1. Demand refers to the various quantities of a good or service that buyers are willing and able to purchase at various possible prices during a period of time. A demand schedule is a tabular presentation of demand, whereas a demand curve is a graphical presentation of demand.

2. The law of demand states that, other things being equal, a decrease in price will cause quantity demanded to increase, and an increase in price will cause quantity demanded to fall.

3. Non-price determinants of quantity demanded include the incomes of consumers, prices of substitutes and complements, tastes, expectations, and population.

4. A change in the price of a product will cause quantity demanded to change, and is illustrated by a movement along the demand curve. A change in a non-price determinant will cause demand to change — this is illustrated by a shift in the entire demand curve.

5. Supply refers to the various quantities of a good or service that sellers (or producers) are willing and able to offer for sale at various possible prices during a period of time.

6. The law of supply is the hypothesis that, other things being equal, an increase in the price of a product will cause quantity offered for sale to increase.

7. Non-price determinants of quantity supplied include the number of sellers in the market, prices of production substitutes and production complements, expectations, technology, and the prices of factor inputs.

8. Equilibrium price is the price at which quantity demanded equals quantity supplied. This is shown graphically by the intersection of the demand curve and the supply curve.

9. A shortage exists when, at a certain price, quantity demanded exceeds quantity supplied. If a shortage exists, economic forces will be set in motion to move the price toward the equilibrium level. A surplus exists when, at a certain price, quantity supplied exceeds quantity demanded. In a surplus situation, economic forces will be set in motion to move the price toward the equilibrium level.

10. A change in demand, other things being equal, will cause price and quantity to change in the same direction as the change in demand. A change in supply will cause price to change in the opposite direction — and quantity to change in the same direction — as the change in supply.

11. A price floor is a minimum price established for a product, while a price ceiling is a maximum price established for a product. Price ceilings usually result in black markets where products are sold at prices above the legal maximum price.

12. An excise tax of a specific amount levied on a product will reduce the supply and increase the price of the product. The quantity demanded will fall.

TERMS FOR REVIEW

demand (55)
demand schedule (56)
law of demand (56)
market size effect (56)
income effect (56)
substitution effect (56)
demand curve (56)
normal goods (58)
inferior goods (58)
substitute & complementary goods (58)
independent goods (58)
demand shifters (61)
supply (62)
supply schedule (62)
law of supply (63)

supply curve (63)
substitutes in production (64)
complements in production
 (joint products) (64)
supply shifters (66)
surplus (excess quantity supplied) (68)
shortage (excess quantity
 demanded) (68)
equilibrium price (68)
equilibrium quantity (68)
price floor (71)
price ceiling (72)
black market (72)
excise tax (72)

QUESTIONS FOR REVIEW AND DISCUSSION

1. Is there a difference between demand and want? Explain. (L.O.1)

2. Use diagrams to illustrate the difference between demand and quantity demanded. (L.O.2)

3. Explain why you would expect the demand curve for home movies to be downward sloping from left to right. (L.O.1,2)

4. What are the factors likely to affect the quantity of restaurant meals bought by Edmonton families in any given month? (L.O.3)

5. "A fall in the price of television sets will result in an increase in the quantity demanded. This increase in demand resulting from the fall in price will send the price up again." Can you detect any error in this statement? If so, name it and explain. (L.O.2)

6. Which side of the market for the specified good or service will be affected by the events shown in Table 4.8? (L.O.3,6)

TABLE 4.8	Event	Good or service
Events and commodities.	(a) A fall in the price of gasoline	Cars
	(b) A sharp increase in fares for public transportation	Gasoline
	(c) An improvement in road construction technology	Roads
	(d) An increase in enrollment in colleges and universities	Textbooks

7. What is the difference between substitutes and complements in consumption? What effect will an increase in the price of coffee have on the market for tea? (L.O.3,8)

8. Explain why a surplus of a particular product will likely reduce the price of the product. (L.O.7,8)

9. Define each of the following terms: (General)

    (a) inferior good;

    (b) joint products;

    (c) price floor;

    (d) price ceiling;

(e) black market;

(f) excise tax.

PROBLEMS AND EXERCISES

1. Construct a hypothetical demand schedule for pizza in Canada. Show how this schedule will be affected by a rapid movement of Canadians to the United States. (L.O.1,3)

2. Plot a graph of the data contained in your schedule for Question 1, then show how the movement of Canadians to the United States will affect the demand curve. (L.O.1,3)

3. Use diagrams to illustrate each of the following: (L.O.3)

    (a) the effect of an increase in the price of apple juice on the demand for orange juice;

    (b) the effect of an increase in incomes on the demand for airline tickets;

    (c) the effect of an increase in the price of steel on the demand for chairs with steel frames;

    (d) the effect of a fall in the price of home computers on the demand for home computers.

4. Use a demand and supply diagram to show the effect of the following events on the shoe market: (L.O.8)

    (a) a decision by a provincial government to eliminate the sales tax on shoes;

    (b) an announcement that the price of shoes will increase by at least 25% within the next month;

    (c) the immigration into Canada of a large number of refugees;

    (d) the invention of a machine that greatly reduces the cost of manufacturing shoes.

5. College students have a choice of living in residence at college or living in private accommodation. The demand for college residence accommodation (rooms) is shown in Table 4.9. The college has 1100 places available at $20 per place per week and cannot build more accommodation. (L.O.8)

TABLE 4.9	Price per week ($)	Number of students per week
Demand for college accommodation.	30	300
	28	420
	26	500
	24	580
	22	650
	21	800
	20	1 200
	19	1 600
	18	2 000

    (a) What problem results from the college's current pricing policy?

    (b) How might the college solve this problem?

    (c) Give a rough estimate of a price that would clear the market.

(d) Suppose that prices for private accommodation and transportation fares increase, while the price of college rooms remains unchanged. How will these price increases affect the demand for college accommodation?

6. In an attempt to deal with the problem of high residential rents, many cities have introduced rent controls. What is the effect of rent controls? (L.O.8)

7. The government imposes a tax of $10 on each pair of shoes sold, regardless of price. What effect will this tax have on the sales of more expensive shoes relative to the sales of cheaper shoes? Does this effect violate the law of demand? (L.O.8)

8. It is sometimes argued that minimum wage legislation creates unemployment. Use demand and supply analysis to show how this might be possible. (L.O.8)

9. The demand for and supply of video cassette tapes are given in Table 4.10. (L.O.7,8)

    (a) On a graph, plot the demand and supply curves for video cassette tapes.

    (b) What are the equilibrium price and quantity?

    (c) Suppose that the government imposes a tax of $1 on each video cassette produced and sold in Canada. Fill in the column showing quantity supplied after the tax. (Hint: At a price of $8, the quantity supplied before the tax was 36 000. With the tax, this quantity will be supplied only at a price of $9).

    (d) On your graph, plot the new supply curve after the imposition of the tax.

    (e) What are the new equilibrium price and quantity?

TABLE 4.10	Price ($)	Quantity demanded (000)	Quantity supplied (000)	Quantity supplied after tax (000)
Demand and supply for video cassette tapes.	9.00	20	44	36
	8.50	24	40	
	8.00	28	36	
	7.50	32	32	
	7.00	36	28	
	6.50	40	24	
	6.00	44	20	

(f) How much of the $1 tax is passed on to the consumers in the form of an increase in price, and how much is paid by the producers?

(g) How much revenue does the tax produce for the government?

10. Assume that a technological breakthrough allows the production of three times as much electricity from given resources. Use the demand-supply model to predict how this will affect the equilibrium price and quantity in the market for electricity and the market for oil for heating purposes. Use diagrams to illustrate your answer. (L.O.8)

 11. The tuition at Private College (a fictitious college) in 1985 was $5000 per year and in that year, the college enrolled 6000 students. Ten years later, in 1995, when the tuition had risen to $8000 per year, the college enrolled 7000 students. This information was brought to the attention of students in an introductory economics class. Clearly, when the price (tuition fee) rose, the quantity of students increased. The students therefore immediately concluded that this was an excellent example of an upward sloping demand curve for places at Private College. Were the students correct? Explain.

MATHEMATICAL APPENDIX

INTRODUCTION

The main purpose of this mathematical appendix is to provide you with another type of tool that can be used to analyze demand, supply, and market price determination. No mathematics beyond elementary algebra is used. The actual mathematics used in economic analysis is much more complex and sophisticated than the elementary algebra used here, but even this rudimentary presentation will give you a bit of the flavour of a mathematical approach to economic analysis.

THE DEMAND FUNCTION

The demand function for a commodity can be expressed as

$$Q_d = Q(P, Y, Pr, T, Ex, Po) \tag{1}$$

where Q_d = quantity demanded
       P = price of the commodity
       Y = income
     Pr = prices of related goods
       T = taste
    Ex = expectations
    Po = population

The effect of each of the independent variables on quantity demanded has been discussed earlier in this chapter.

Let us assume that income, the prices of related goods, tastes, expectations, and population are constant. The demand function now becomes a relation between price and quantity demanded and may be expressed as the demand function:

$$Q_d = Q(P) \tag{2}$$

The independent variables in equation (1) that have been assumed constant are called *shift parameters*; if they change, they cause the demand curve to shift. According to the law of demand, the relation between price and quantity demanded is an inverse one. If we assume a linear relationship between price and quantity demanded, then we can express the demand function as

$$Q_d = a - bP, \ a > 0, \ b > 0 \tag{3}$$

The value of *a* represents the quantity demanded at a price of zero, and −*b* represents the slope of the demand function, which is appropriately negative since the demand curve is downward sloping. A demand function, for example, could take the form of an equation such as

$$Q_d = 100 - 50P \tag{4}$$

THE SUPPLY FUNCTION
The supply function for a commodity can be expressed as:

$$Q_s = Q(P,N,Pr,Te,Ex,Pi) \tag{5}$$

where Q_s = quantity supplied
  P = the price of the commodity
  N = number of sellers
  Pr = prices of related goods
  Te = technology
  Ex = expectations
  Pi = input prices

If we assume that the number of sellers, the prices of related goods, technology, expectations, and the prices of inputs are constant, then the supply function can be expressed as

$$Q_s = Q(P) \tag{6}$$

There is a direct relation between price and quantity supplied. As in the case of the demand function, let us assume a linear relationship between price and quantity supplied. We can express the supply function as

$$Q_s = c + dP, \; d > 0 \tag{7}$$

where c is a constant and d is the slope of the supply function. The positive slope means that the supply curve is upward sloping. A supply function could be of the form

$$Q_s = -60 + 20P \tag{8}$$

Assuming that the price is expressed in dollars, the negative sign here means that unless the price is above \$3, sellers will not offer the product for sale.

MARKET EQUILIBRIUM
To determine equilibrium price and quantity, we must bring the demand and supply functions together in a model of price determination. The demand and supply equations give us two equations in three unknowns (Q_d, Q_s, and P). We know that equilibrium occurs when the price is such that there is neither a shortage nor a surplus in the market, hence

$$Q_d = Q_s \tag{9}$$

This equation completes the model and allows us to obtain a unique solution. The complete model is

$$Q_d = a - bP \tag{10}$$

$$Q_s = c + dP \tag{11}$$

$$Q_d = Q_s \tag{12}$$

By solving this system of equations for P and Q, we will obtain the market equilibrium price and quantity.

EXAMPLE 4-1

Consider the following demand and supply equations:

$$Q_d = 50 - 4P$$

$$Q_s = -10 + 8P$$

Since in equilibrium $Q_d = Q_s$, we know that

$$50 - 4P = -10 + 8P$$

Therefore $12P = 60$, so $P = 5$

By substituting this value of P in either the demand or the supply equation, we obtain $Q = 30$. Hence, the equilibrium price is 5 and the equilibrium quantity is 30.

EXERCISES

1. Solve each of the following equations to determine the equilibrium price and the equilibrium quantity:

    (a) $Q_d = 32 - 3P$
    $Q_s = -12 + 8P$

    (b) $Q_d = 60 - 3P$
    $Q_s = -40 + 7P$

    (c) $Q_d = 900 - 20P$
    $Q_s = -100 + 30P$

2. You are given the following demand and supply equations:

$$Q_d = 130 - 3P$$
$$Q_s = -20 + 12P$$

   (a) Complete the following demand and supply schedules.

Price	Quantity demanded	Quantity supplied
5		
10		
15		
20		

   (b) What are the equilibrium price and quantity?

   (c) Solve the demand and supply equations for P and Q and compare your answer with the answer obtained in part (b).

3. The demand and supply equations are

$$Q_d = 28 - 2P$$
$$Q_s = 5P$$

   (a) What are the equilibrium price and quantity?

(b) Set up demand and supply schedules based on these equations for prices: $7, $6, $5, $4, $3, $2, $1.

(c) Use your demand and supply schedules to plot the demand and supply curves.

4. The market demand and supply curves are given by the following equations:

$$Q_d = 18 - 2P$$
$$Q_s = 3 + 5P$$

(a) By selecting prices ranging from $1 to $6, plot the demand and supply curves.

(b) Solve the equations for the equilibrium price and the equilibrium quantity.

VIDEO CASE

Ice Storm Effects

Background

In early January 1998, a massive ice storm struck eastern Ontario and southern Quebec. The freezing rain persisted for several days causing what has been titled *The Ice Storm of the Century.* Electrical power lines were broken by the sheer weight of the ice, or by falling ice-entombed trees. Candles, flashlights, and (for those who could get them) generators were people's best friends. Millions of people were without light and heat for hours, days and weeks. Without electricity, farmers were unable to milk their cows. It is safe to assume that eastern Ontario and Quebec will not soon forget the ice storm of 1998.

Many sectors of the economy were affected, and supplies of numerous products were drastically reduced. With much of economic activity at a virtual halt, shortages emerged in many markets. The market response to shortages is higher prices. Some suppliers seemed to have "helped the market along" by engaging in a practice that has been labelled "price extortion" — jacking up prices far beyond what may be considered to be reasonable under the circumstances.

While many products were in short supply, merchants in the areas affected by the ice storm suffered a big slump in sales — the direct result of a lull in economic activity. In Quebec, retailers suffered a 5% drop in sales in January 1998. The direct cost of the damage caused by the ice storm is estimated at $2 billion (some analysts offer significantly higher estimates).

Farmers Took A Big Hit

The results of the ice storm were also felt in the labour market. Thousands of people suffered temporary unemployment as the pulse of economic activity slowed down. In Quebec alone, the number of unemployed people increased by 30 000. Much of this could be attributed to the ice storm.

Ontario and Quebec farmers were hit hard by the ice storm. With no electricity to cool the milk, dairy farmers had to dump as much as 30 000 L of milk over a one-week period. That loss was onerous. Fortunately, financial assistance was available from the federal government to help defray "eligible" costs. The following costs were among those eligible for reimbursement:

- milk that had to be dumped during the ice storm;
- rental of electrical generators;
- animals that died as a result of the storm;
- repair of assets damaged by the ice storm, and loss of inventories because of power outages.

A great deal of farm equipment was damaged by the ice storm. This had an adverse effect on farm output, at least in the short term. Animal feed also was in short supply, and there was the expected increase in demand for imported animal feed and farm equipment. Clearly, the effects of the ice storm were widespread.

QUESTIONS

1. What are the main points of this case?
2. Identify demand and supply elements in this case and indicate what changes could be expected from the interplay of these market forces.
3. What are some of the costs of the 1998 ice storm? (Consider both direct and indirect costs).
4. Most economists expected an increase in economic activity *after* the ice storm. Explain why this might be a reasonable expectation.

Video Resource: "Farmers," *National Magazine* (January 1998)

CHAPTER 5

ELASTICITY

Learning Objectives

After studying this chapter, you should be able to:

1 understand the concept of elasticity

2 interpret the elasticity coefficient

3 explain the relationship between elasticity of demand and total revenue

4 identify the factors that affect price elasticity of demand

5 discuss cross elasticity and income elasticity

6 understand elasticity of supply

7 identify the determinants of price elasticity of supply

8 understand the uses of the elasticity concept

The elasticity (or responsiveness) of demand in a market is great or small as the amount demanded increases much or little for a given fall in price, and diminishes for a given rise in price.

Alfred Marshall, *Principles of Economics*

INTRODUCTION

Elasticity: a measure of
responsiveness.

The concept of **elasticity** is an important aspect of the demand-supply analysis presented in Chapter 4. We know that, other things being equal, a fall in the price of a product causes the quantity demanded to increase. But does quantity increase by just a little or by much? What effect does an increase or decrease in price have on a seller's total revenue? The answers to these questions depend on the price elasticity of demand for the product. This chapter will introduce you to the very important economic concept of elasticity. You will study various types of elasticity, how to measure them, and how to interpret the measurements. We will also consider some applications of the elasticity concept.

THE MEANING OF ELASTICITY OF DEMAND

Learning Objective 1:
understand the concept
of elasticity

Price elasticity of demand
measures the change in
quantity demanded result-
ing from a change in price.

Elasticity of demand is a measure of the degree to which quantity demanded responds to changes in one of the variables that can affect quantity demanded. For some goods and services, a small change in price greatly affects quantity demanded. For others, a small change in price has no appreciable effect on quantity demanded. **Price elasticity of demand** measures the percentage change in quantity demanded as a result of a small change in price. We often refer to this concept as *own price elasticity of demand* to distinguish it from cases where changes in the prices of other goods (substitutes and complements) affect the demand for a good.

THE POINT ELASTICITY FORMULA

Own price elasticity is often expressed by the formula

$$E_d = \frac{\% \text{ change in quantity demanded}}{\% \text{ change in price}}$$

or, alternatively, as

$$E_d = \frac{\text{change in quantity demanded}}{\text{original quantity}} \div \frac{\text{change in price}}{\text{original price}}$$

where E_d denotes own price elasticity of demand.

The symbol Δ (delta) is commonly used in economics. The sign means *a change in.* We can write the above expression for own price elasticity of demand as

$$E_d = \frac{\Delta Q}{Q} \div \frac{\Delta P}{P}$$

where E_d represents elasticity, Q represents quantity, and P represents price. This formula is sometimes called the *point elasticity of demand* formula because it measures elasticity at a point on the demand curve. The value obtained for E_d is just a number like 2 or 5 or $\frac{1}{2}$ and is referred to as the **coefficient of elasticity**.

The coefficient of elasticity is
used to measure the
degree of elasticity or
inelasticity.

Recall that an increase in price causes quantity demanded to decrease, and that a decrease in price causes quantity demanded to increase. Since price and quantity demanded move in opposite directions, E_d always has a negative value. It is common practice in economics to discard the negative sign and express elasticity of demand as a positive number. In other words, we take the absolute value of E_d. The following example illustrates how the formula may be used to calculate own price elasticity of demand.

EXAMPLE 5-1

If a reduction in the price of a product from $10 to $8 causes quantity demanded to increase from 1200 units to 1800 units, what is the coefficient of elasticity of demand?

Solution: The formula for E_d is given by

$$E_d = \frac{\Delta Q}{Q} \div \frac{\Delta P}{P}$$

The change in quantity $(\Delta Q) = (1800 - 1200) = 600$. The original quantity was 1200, i.e., $Q = 1200$. The change in price $(\Delta P) = (\$8 - \$10) = -\$2$. The original price was $10. By substituting, we obtain

$$E_d = \frac{600}{1200} \div \frac{-2}{10}$$

$$= \frac{600}{1200} \times \frac{10}{-2} = \frac{-5}{2} = -2.5$$

Discarding the negative sign, we obtain

$$E_d = 2.5$$

The use of this formula may lead to confusion since different values can be obtained for the coefficient of elasticity depending on whether the price increases or decreases. In the above example, we considered a price decrease. Now consider a price increase in the following example. Note that in both examples, the prices and quantities used are identical.

EXAMPLE 5-2

If an increase in the price of a product from $8 to $10 causes quantity demanded to decrease from 1800 units to 1200 units, what is the coefficient of elasticity of demand?

Solution:

$$E_d = \frac{\Delta Q}{Q} \div \frac{\Delta P}{P}$$
$$\Delta Q = (1200 - 1800) = -600$$
$$Q = 1800$$
$$\Delta P = (10 - 8) = 2$$
$$P = 8$$

By substituting, we obtain

$$E_d = \frac{-600}{1800} \div \frac{2}{8}$$

$$= \frac{-600}{1800} \times \frac{8}{2} = -1.3$$

Again, discarding the negative sign, we obtain

$$E_d = 1.3$$

For a price decrease, we obtain an elasticity measure of 2.5. For a price increase, we obtain an elasticity measure of 1.3. This is because we are measuring elasticity at different points on the demand curve. To remedy this situation, economists refined the above formula so that the same value is obtained regardless of the direction of the price change. Let us now turn to that refined formula.

THE ARC ELASTICITY FORMULA

By taking the average of the two prices and the average of the two quantities, we obtain the following formula for the price elasticity of demand:

$$E_d = \frac{\dfrac{Q_0 - Q_1}{Q_0 + Q_1}}{2} \div \frac{\dfrac{P_0 - P_1}{P_0 + P_1}}{2}$$

$$= \frac{Q_0 - Q_1}{Q_0 + Q_1} \div \frac{P_0 - P_1}{P_0 + P_1}$$

The average formula measures elasticity between two points on the demand curve.

where Q_0 = original quantity demanded, P_0 = original price, Q_1 = new quantity demanded, P_1 = new price. This new formula is called the *average elasticity of demand* formula, or the *arc elasticity of demand* formula because it measures E_d between two points on the demand curve. We would like to obtain a measure of elasticity of demand that is the same regardless of the direction in which we move. The arc elasticity formula provides us with that measure. By using this formula, we obtain the same value whether there is a price increase or a price decrease. Let us confirm this assertion by calculating the price elasticity of demand for the price and quantity changes in Example 5-2.

$$E_d = \frac{Q_0 - Q_1}{Q_0 + Q_1} \div \frac{P_0 - P_1}{P_0 + P_1}$$

$$Q_0 - Q_1 = 1800 - 1200 = 600$$

$$Q_0 + Q_1 = 1800 + 1200 = 3000$$

$$P_0 - P_1 = 8 - 10 = -2$$

$$P_0 + P_1 = 8 + 10 = 18$$

$$E_d = \frac{600}{3000} \div \frac{-2}{18} = -1.8$$

The price elasticity of demand is therefore 1.8. Now, see if you can verify that the value for the coefficient of elasticity will remain the same for a price fall from \$10 to \$8. Note that the value (1.8) obtained for the elasticity coefficient when we use the average formula is about the average of the values obtained for the elasticity coefficients (2.5 and 1.3) in Examples 5-1 and 5-2 above. This is to be expected, since the average formula takes the average of the quantities and the average of the prices.

Arc elasticity of demand treats the price and quantity as if they were midway between the initial and new prices and quantities, and then uses the point elasticity at this midpoint.

DEGREES OF ELASTICITY OF DEMAND

A change in the price of a product may have no effect whatever on the quantity demanded. In other words, the same quantity will be bought whatever the price may be.

We can say in this case that demand is **perfectly inelastic**. The demand for a drug prescribed by a physician is probably close to perfectly inelastic.

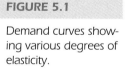

Demand may be perfectly inelastic, inelastic, unitary elastic, or perfectly elastic.

On the other hand, a small change in price may lead to an infinitely large change in quantity demanded. In this case, we can say that demand is **perfectly elastic**. If there are 100 sellers in a fruit market all selling the same type of grapes at the same price, and one of those sellers raises his or her price, the quantity demanded from that particular seller would probably fall to almost zero. In that case, the demand for grapes from that seller is probably close to perfectly elastic. You will encounter this situation in a later chapter.

Between the two extremes of perfectly elastic and perfectly inelastic demand, there are three important cases of elasticity of demand. If a certain percentage change in price leads to a greater percentage change in quantity demanded, then demand is said to be elastic with respect to price. If a certain percentage change in price leads to an equal percentage change in quantity demanded, then demand is said to have **unit elasticity**. Finally, if a certain percentage change in price leads to a smaller percentage change in quantity demanded, then demand is said to be **inelastic**.

Applying the elasticity formula will help us to determine the degree of price elasticity of demand. The five cases are as follows:

1. If E_d is infinitely large, then demand is perfectly elastic;

2. If E_d is greater than 1 but less than infinity (that is, $1 < E_d < \infty$), then demand is elastic;

3. If E_d is equal to 1, then demand is unitary elastic;

4. If E_d is less than 1 but greater than 0 (that is, $0 < E_d < 1$), then demand is inelastic;

5. If E_d is equal to 0, then demand is perfectly inelastic.

FIGURE 5.1

Demand curves showing various degrees of elasticity.

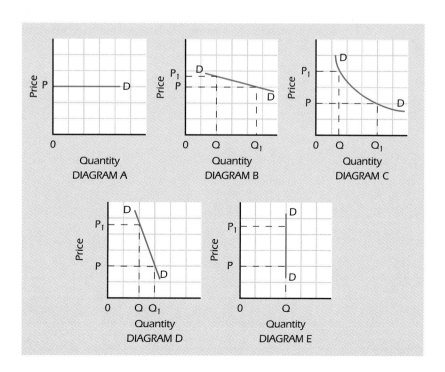

These different degrees of elasticity of demand can be illustrated geometrically as shown in Figure 5.1. The diagrams in Figure 5.1 are intended to serve for comparative purposes only. The units in which the axes are measured will have some effect on the slopes of the demand curves. Diagram A illustrates the case of perfectly elastic demand, which is depicted by a horizontal straight line. In this case, an infinitely large amount can be sold at the going price. Diagram B illustrates the case of elastic demand. An increase in price from P to P_1 causes a more-than-proportional decrease in quantity demanded as shown by the change in quantity from Q_1 to Q. The case of unit elasticity is illustrated by Diagram C. A change in price from P to P_1 causes a proportional change in quantity demanded. Diagram D shows the case of inelastic demand. A change in price causes a less-than-proportional change in quantity demanded. Finally, Diagram E illustrates the case of perfectly inelastic demand. A change in price leaves quantity demanded unchanged at Q units.

INTERPRETING THE ELASTICITY COEFFICIENT

Learning Objective 2: interpret the elasticity coefficient

Previously, we meticulously computed the price elasticity of demand using the average formula and obtained a value of 1.8 for the elasticity coefficient. But what does this number really mean? On the basis of what you learned in the previous section, you will quickly say that an elasticity coefficient of 1.8 means that the demand for the product is elastic; $E_d > 1$. But it tells us more than that. Let us investigate. We know that

$$E_d = \frac{\% \, \Delta Q}{\% \, \Delta P} = 1.8$$
$$\% \, \Delta Q = 1.8 \times \% \, \Delta P$$

Thus, if there is a 10% fall in price, the resulting increase in quantity demanded is

$$\% \, \Delta Q = (1.8 \times 10) = 18\%$$

If the coefficient of elasticity of demand is 1.8, then a 10% change in price causes quantity demanded to change (in the opposite direction) by 18%.

PROBLEM SOLVING 5-1

The manager of the Kyushu Uniform Boutique knows that the price elasticity of demand for uniforms at current prices is 2.8. What effect will a price increase of 15% have on the quantity of uniforms sold by the boutique?

PRICE ELASTICITY ALONG A LINEAR DEMAND CURVE

The price elasticity of demand varies along a linear demand curve.

Let us compute the price elasticity of demand at each price change shown in Table 5.1. The calculation for the first coefficient only is shown below. The other coefficients are entered in column three of Table 5.1, and plotted in Figure 5.2. Note that in Table 5.1, because price elasticity deals with changes in quantity and changes in price, the elasticity coefficients are placed in between the lines rather than on the same lines as price and quantity.

$$E_d = \frac{Q_0 - Q_1}{Q_0 + Q_1} \div \frac{P_0 - P_1}{P_0 - P_1}$$

$$= \frac{2}{10} \div \frac{1}{17} = 3.40$$

	Price ($) (1)	Quantity demanded (2)	Elasticity (3)
TABLE 5.1	9	4	3.40
Demand schedule.	8	6	2.14
	7	8	1.44
	6	10	1.00
	5	12	

This exercise clearly demonstrates two things: first, elasticity and slope are not identical — the slope of this demand curve is 1/2 at every point on the curve (you should verify this); and second, the price elasticity of demand varies along a linear demand curve. The price elasticity of demand decreases as price falls, i.e., as we move down the demand curve.

FIGURE 5.2

Demand and elasticity.

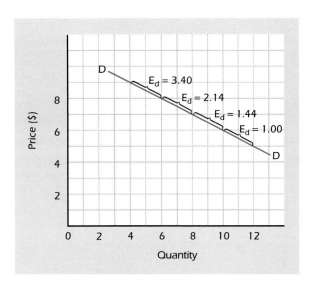

ELASTICITY OF DEMAND AND TOTAL REVENUE

If demand is elastic, price reductions result in increases in total revenue.

Learning Objective 3: explain the relationship between elasticity of demand and total revenue

Another way of looking at price elasticity of demand for a good or service is to see what happens to total revenue as the price of the good or service changes. Total revenue (TR) derived from the sale of any product is the price of the product (P) multiplied by the quantity sold (Q). That is,

$$TR = P \times Q$$

If the demand for a good or service is elastic, a fall in its price causes a more-than-proportional increase in quantity demanded. Hence, total revenue increases. Table 5.2 illustrates a case in which the demand for the product is elastic for all price ranges considered. As price falls, quantity demanded increases by a greater proportion than the fall in price, so total revenue increases.

	Price ($)	Quantity demanded	Total revenue ($)
TABLE 5.2	2.00	70 000	140 000
	1.90	90 000	171 000
Hypothetical demand	1.80	110 000	198 000
schedule for a	1.70	130 000	221 000
product with an	1.60	150 000	240 000
elastic demand.	1.50	170 000	255 000
	1.40	190 000	266 000
	1.30	210 000	273 000
	1.20	230 000	276 000

If demand is unitary elastic, a fall in price leaves total revenue unchanged.

    In the case of unitary elastic demand, a fall in the price of the product causes a proportional increase in quantity demanded, leaving total revenue unchanged. Table 5.3 illustrates the case of unit elasticity of demand.

	Price ($)	Quantity demanded	Total revenue ($)
TABLE 5.3	0.80	60 000	48 000
	0.60	80 000	48 000
Hypothetical demand	0.48	100 000	48 000
schedule for a	0.40	120 000	48 000
product with unit	0.30	160 000	48 000
elasticity of demand.	0.24	200 000	48 000
	0.20	240 000	48 000
	0.16	300 000	48 000
	0.12	400 000	48 000
	0.10	480 000	48 000

If demand is inelastic, price reductions result in decreases in total revenue.

    If the data in Table 5.3 were plotted on a graph, the result would be a demand curve with a constant elasticity of 1.0. Such a demand curve would be a rectangular hyperbola conforming to the equation $P \times Q = 48\ 000$, as shown in Figure 5.3. Constant elasticity demand curves are used extensively in econometric (statistical) studies of elasticity of demand.

FIGURE 5.3

Demand curve with constant elasticity.

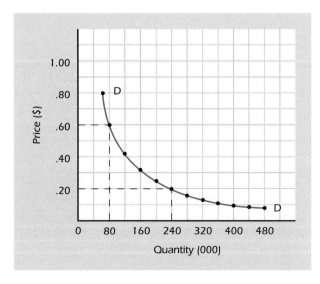

If the demand for a product is inelastic, a fall in the price of the product causes a less-than-proportional increase in quantity demanded; hence, total revenue falls as price falls. The demand schedule for a product with inelastic demand is given in Table 5.4.

	Price ($)	Quantity demanded	Total revenue ($)
TABLE 5.4	0.50	48 000	24 000
	0.46	50 000	23 000
Hypothetical demand	0.42	52 000	21 840
schedule for a product	0.38	54 000	20 520
with inelastic demand.	0.34	56 000	19 040
	0.30	58 000	17 400
	0.26	60 000	15 600
	0.22	62 000	13 640
	0.18	64 000	11 520
	0.14	66 000	9 240

However, the demand for a product may be elastic in one price range and inelastic in another price range. Consider the demand schedule in Table 5.5.

	Price ($)	Quantity demanded	Total revenue ($)
TABLE 5.5	12	10	120
	10	20	200
Demand and total	8	30	240
revenue.	6	40	240
	4	50	200
	2	60	120

Total revenue rises from $120 to $240 as the price falls from $12 to $8; thus demand is elastic within the price range from $12 to $8. Total revenue remains constant at $240 when price falls from $8 to $6; thus demand is unitary elastic between $8 and $6. As the price falls from $6 to $2, total revenue falls from $240 to $120; thus demand is inelastic within the price range from $6 to $2.

Figure 5.4, which is based on Table 5.5, is helpful in consolidating your understanding of the relation between elasticity of demand and total revenue. We have seen that if demand is elastic, a fall in price results in an increase in total revenue. Thus, for price decreases within the price range above $8, where the demand is elastic, total revenue rises. This is shown in Diagram B by the rising section of the total revenue curve. If demand is unitary elastic (between $8 and $6 in Diagram A), an increase or decrease in price leaves total revenue unchanged at $240. This is shown in Diagram B where $E_d = 1$. Finally, if demand is inelastic, a fall in price results in a fall in total revenue. Price reductions within the under $6 range cause total revenue to fall as shown in Diagram B by the downward-sloping section of the total revenue curve.

The relation between price elasticity of demand and total revenue is conveniently summarized in Table 5.6 for quick reference.

The demand for most products is either elastic, unitary elastic, or inelastic. The extremes of perfectly elastic and perfectly inelastic demand are rare. You will see in a later chapter, however, that, under certain conditions, the demand for the product of a seller may be perfectly elastic.

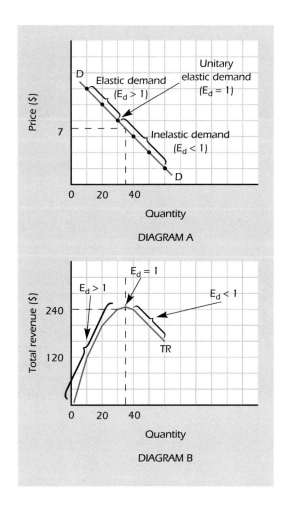

FIGURE 5.4

Relation between total
revenue and elasticity
of demand.

DIAGRAM A

DIAGRAM B

	Elasticity of demand	Direction of price change	Effect on total revenue
	inelastic	increase	increase
	inelastic	decrease	decrease
	elastic	increase	decrease
	elastic	decrease	increase
	unitary	any change	unchanged

TABLE 5.6

Elasticity and total
revenue.

FACTORS AFFECTING PRICE ELASTICITY OF DEMAND

Learning Objective 4:
identify the factors that
affect price elasticity of
demand

We have seen that the demand for a commodity (good or service) may be elastic in
one price range and inelastic in some other price range, as shown in Table 5.5 and
Figure 5.4. It is important to note also that the demand for a commodity may be found
to be elastic at a certain time and inelastic at some other time. In this section, we discuss
the major factors that are likely to affect the price elasticity of demand for a product.

SUBSTITUTES

*Availability of substitutes
affects elasticity.*

One of the most important factors likely to influence the price elasticity of demand for
a good or service is whether or not substitutes are available. If a commodity has many

close substitutes, its demand is likely to be elastic. This is so because, if the price of that commodity rises, buyers will switch to some of the many close substitutes available. Hence, the quantity demanded of that commodity will tend to fall significantly. Consider the case of a certain brand of coffee. If the price of that particular brand increases, consumers will buy other available brands instead. Thus, we find that the demand for products with many brands tends to be elastic. On the other hand, if there *are not* many close substitutes, quantity demanded will still tend to fall as a result of the higher price, but not by much. Consider the effect of a two-cent-per-litre increase in the price of gasoline at the pumps. There will probably be a large increase in the quantity demanded just before the increase comes into effect, but after that, we will probably observe no significant reduction in the quantity demanded as a result of the price increase.

NUMBER OF USES

The number of uses affects elasticity.

In general, the greater the number of uses a commodity has, the more elastic the demand for that commodity is likely to be. Consider a fall in the price of a commodity (eggs, for example) that has a large number of uses. As the price falls, more of it will be bought to be allocated to those different uses. On the other hand, if the commodity has only one or two uses (for example, tarragon — a plant whose leaves are used for flavouring salads), it is unlikely that a fall in its price will cause a significant increase in quantity demanded.

PERCENTAGE OF INCOME SPENT ON THE COMMODITY

The importance of the product in the budget affects elasticity.

Another factor that is likely to affect elasticity of demand is the proportion of income spent on the commodity. If only a negligible percentage of consumers' income is spent on the commodity, the demand for that commodity is likely to be inelastic. An increase in the price of such a commodity has no appreciable effect on the consumer's budget. Hence, expenditure patterns will hardly be affected. As an example of this point, consider the fraction of total income spent on matches. If the price of matches were to increase from three cents to five cents (an increase of 67%), the fall in quantity demanded is unlikely to be anywhere near 67%. As a matter of fact, the reduction in quantity demanded is likely to be minuscule. On the other hand, consider the fraction of total income spent on a television set — a relatively costly item. An increase in the price of television sets will probably result in a significant reduction in the quantity demanded. Similarly, a reduction in the price of television sets will probably result in a significant increase in the quantity demanded; many people might then consider buying a second or third set.

THE NATURE OF THE PRODUCT

The demand for necessities is likely to be inelastic.

The demand for luxuries is likely to be elastic.

Whether the product is a luxury or a necessity has some effect on its price elasticity of demand. Most people consider milk a basic necessity in the diets of children. If the price of milk increases by, say, 10%, the quantity demanded will probably not fall by that proportion. Consumers will probably sacrifice some other commodity rather than allow their children to go without milk. The demand for an item that is a basic necessity is likely to be inelastic. On the other hand, an increase in the price of a vacation package to Antigua (a small Caribbean island) is likely to cause a more-than-proportional decrease in the number bought — other things being equal, of course. In general, the demand for a luxury item is elastic. Luxury items that are also extremely expensive, however, may not quite fit into this general pattern. The demand for luxurious yachts is likely to be inelastic; the people in the market for them are so wealthy that a small increase in price is unlikely to cause any significant reduction in the quantity demanded.

TIME

The time period being considered will also have some effect on the elasticity of demand for a product. In general, the longer the time period being considered, the more elastic the demand is likely to be. This is due largely to the fact that it takes time for people to adjust to new situations. If the price of gasoline rises, people will respond by buying less gasoline, but within a short time span, they are unlikely to buy a great deal less. As time goes by, however, they are likely to use public transportation more, make more use of car pools, and ultimately purchase smaller and more fuel-efficient cars.

PROBLEM SOLVING 5-2

Based on the determinants of price elasticity of demand discussed in this section, state whether you expect demand for each of the following to be elastic or inelastic.

1. **The services of medical doctors**
2. **Toilet paper**
3. **Diamond necklaces**
4. **Telephone services**

OTHER ELASTICITY CONCEPTS

We should look at two other important demand elasticity concepts at this point: the concepts of cross elasticity of demand and income elasticity of demand.

CROSS ELASTICITY OF DEMAND

The cross elasticity of demand for a product is the relative change in the quantity demanded of that product divided by the relative change in the price of a related product.

Learning Objective 5: discuss cross elasticity and income elasticity

In Chapter 4, we noted that changes in the prices of other commodities may have some effect on the quantity of a commodity demanded. A change in the price of limes affects the quantity of lemons demanded, and a change in the price of battery-operated toys affects the quantity of batteries demanded. (Remember substitutes and complements?) **Cross elasticity of demand** measures the effect of a change in the price of a related good on the quantity demanded of the good under consideration. The cross elasticity of demand for a product A is the relative change in the quantity demanded of product A divided by the relative change in the price of product B.

Using the point formula and the notation introduced earlier in this chapter, we can express cross elasticity of demand as

$$(E_A P_B) = \frac{\Delta Q_A}{Q_A} \div \frac{\Delta P_B}{P_B}$$

Or, we may use the average formula and express cross elasticity as

$$(E_A P_B) = \frac{\Delta Q_A}{Q_{A0} + Q_{A1}} \div \frac{\Delta P_B}{P_{B0} + P_{B1}}$$

Substitutes have positive cross elasticity of demand.

Complements have negative cross elasticity of demand.

Independent goods have zero cross elasticity of demand.

where $E_A P_B$ equals cross elasticity between A and B, Q_A equals quantity of product A demanded, P_B equals price of product B, Q_{A0} and Q_{A1} are the two quantities, and P_{B0} and P_{B1} are the two prices. If A and B are substitutes, then an increase in the price of B causes an increase in the quantity of A demanded. **Substitutes** therefore show a positive cross elasticity of demand. If A and B are complementary goods, then an increase in the price of B causes a decrease in the quantity of A demanded. **Complements** therefore show a negative cross elasticity of demand. If A and B are not at all related, then a change in the price of B will have no effect on the quantity of A demanded. Therefore, independent goods show a zero cross elasticity of demand. The foregoing discussion may be summarized as follows:

1. If A and B are substitutes, then $E_AP_B > 0$;

2. If A and B are complements, then $E_AP_B < 0$;

3. If A and B are independent, then $E_AP_B = 0$.

INCOME ELASTICITY OF DEMAND

Income elasticity of demand: a measure of buyers' response to changes in income.

Other things being equal, an increase in income leads to an increase in quantity demanded if the good is normal. If the good is an inferior good, then an increase in income leads to a decrease in quantity demanded. But by how much will quantity increase or decrease? This depends on the income elasticity of demand. We may define **income elasticity of demand** as the relative change in quantity demanded divided by the relative change in income. If E_y denotes income elasticity of demand, then

$$E_y = \frac{\text{change in quantity demanded}}{\text{original quantity demanded}} \div \frac{\text{change in income}}{\text{original income}}$$

Demand for normal goods increases with an increase in income, while demand for inferior goods decreases as income increases.

You will recall that in Chapter 4, we discussed normal goods and inferior goods. For most goods, as income rises, the quantity demanded also rises. These are normal goods. The income elasticity of demand for **normal goods** will be positive. There are instances, however, when smaller quantities of certain goods are demanded as income rises. These are inferior goods. The income elasticity of demand for **inferior goods** will be negative. We may summarize the foregoing discussion as follows:

1. For normal goods (and this includes most goods), $E_y > 0$.

2. For inferior goods, $E_y < 0$.

As in the case of price elasticity of demand, either of the two formulas may be used to compute income elasticity of demand. You simply substitute income for price. It is obviously of great importance for producers to have some idea of the effect of income changes on the sale of their products. In other words, they need to know something about income elasticity of demand for their products.

PROBLEM SOLVING 5-3

1. **Farmers have been informed that the income elasticity of demand for beef is 2.2. If the price of beef is fixed, and on average, people's incomes are expected to increase by 10%, what change should beef farmers make in their production of beef?**

2. **You operate a small store that specializes in the sale of coffee. The cross elasticity of demand between coffee and tea is estimated to be 2.5. If the price of tea rises by 6%, what change should you expect in the demand for coffee?**

ELASTICITY OF SUPPLY

Price elasticity of supply measures sellers' response to changes in price.

The concept of elasticity of supply closely parallels that of elasticity of demand. For that reason, we need not devote a great deal of time to the elasticity of supply. This, of course, in no way detracts from the importance of elasticity of supply. The degree to which quantity offered for sale responds to changes in price is known as the price elasticity of supply. **Price elasticity of supply** is the percentage change in quantity supplied divided by the percentage change in price. Using the point formula, we may express price elasticity of supply as

Learning Objective 6:
understand elasticity of
supply

$$E_s = \frac{\Delta Q}{Q} \div \frac{\Delta P}{P}$$

where E_s equals price elasticity of supply, Q equals quantity supplied, and P equals price. Using the average formula, we can compute the coefficient of elasticity of supply as

$$E_s = \frac{Q_0 - Q_1}{Q_0 + Q_1} \div \frac{P_0 - P_1}{P_0 + P_1}$$

The value obtained for E_s is the *coefficient of elasticity of supply.* We say that supply is elastic if a change in price leads to a more-than-proportional change in quantity supplied. If a change in price leads to a less-than-proportional change in quantity supplied, then we say that supply is inelastic. Notice how closely the analysis parallels that of price elasticity of demand.

We can illustrate various degrees of price elasticity of supply graphically. A linear supply curve indicates an elastic supply if it cuts the vertical (price) axis. If a linear supply curve passes through the origin, supply is unitary elastic regardless of its slope. If a linear supply curve cuts the horizontal (quantity) axis, supply is inelastic. Perfectly elastic supply is depicted by a horizontal supply curve; perfectly inelastic supply by a vertical supply curve. Figure 5.5 shows supply curves with different elasticities.

FIGURE 5.5

Supply curves
showing various
degrees of elasticity.

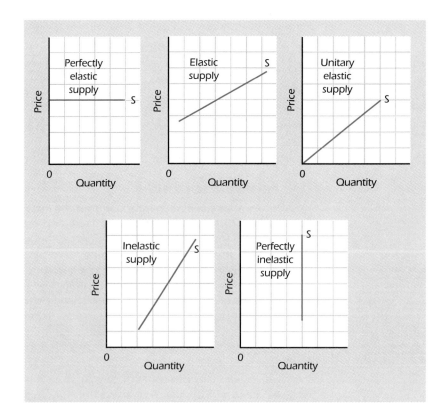

FACTORS AFFECTING PRICE ELASTICITY OF SUPPLY

TIME

The amount of time producers have to respond to changes in price is a major determinant of elasticity of supply.

Learning Objective 7: identify the determinants of price elasticity of supply

During the very short period (market period) an increase in price does not significantly affect the quantity offered for sale.

Reservation price: the lowest price a seller is willing to accept for a product.

The time period under consideration has a significant effect on the price elasticity of supply. If the time period is very short, then an increase in price does not significantly affect the quantity offered for sale. If a certain quantity of a commodity has already been produced and brought to market, then an increase in price does not cause a larger quantity to be offered for sale, because the quantity is fixed. We sometimes refer to this situation as the **very short period** or the **market period**. As the period under consideration becomes longer, supply tends to become more elastic. Sellers will be able to respond more easily to changes in the prices of their products. It is of interest to note that even in the very short period, sellers may withdraw their products from the market rather than sell them below certain prices. This is likely to happen in the case of goods that are not perishable and that do not have high storage costs. The price below which producers refuse to sell is referred to as a **reservation price**.

STORAGE COST

Storage cost affects elasticity of supply.

The elasticity of supply for goods that are not perishable and that can be stored at a relatively low cost tends to be greater than the elasticity of supply for perishables and goods with high storage cost. If the price of an item that can be stored cheaply falls, sellers may respond by withdrawing the item from the market and storing it. If the price of such an item rises, suppliers may be in a position to release some extra quantities from storage onto the market. These options may not be feasible in the face of high cost of storage.

PRODUCTION SUBSTITUTES AND COMPLEMENTS

Production substitutes and complements affect elasticity of supply.

If a product has a large number of substitutes in production, its supply is likely to be elastic. If the price of such a product falls, producers can shift resources into the production of any of the many substitutes. If the price of cabbage falls, producers can easily switch to lettuce or cucumbers. Because of the ease with which producers can respond to a change in the price of cabbage, its supply is elastic.

Production complements, you will recall, are goods that are produced together. When one is produced, the other is produced as a direct result. These are joint products. The supply of a relatively minor joint product is likely to be inelastic. Consider the case of beef and hides. A small increase in the price of hides is unlikely to induce farmers to butcher their cattle. Moreover, once cattle are slaughtered for beef, the hides will be sold at whatever the price may be. Therefore the supply of hides is likely to be inelastic.

PROBLEM SOLVING 5-4

The cost of producing Hollywood sunglasses is $10. Andrei Turgenev has a fixed supply of these sunglasses, which he will not sell unless he can make a profit of at least 10%. There are no storage costs and the product is durable. What will Andrei do (sell or not sell) if the market price is (a) $20, (b) $15, (c) $12, or (d) $10?

APPLICATIONS

Learning Objective 8:
understand the uses of
the elasticity concept

The concept of elasticity of demand has important applications in business decisions and in government policies. It will be helpful to refer to Table 5.6 on page 92. Suppose that farmers are contemplating an increase in the price of tomatoes in order to increase their revenues from the sale of tomatoes. The success of such a move depends on the price elasticity of demand for tomatoes. As can be seen from Table 5.6, if the demand for tomatoes is price inelastic, then a small increase in price causes total revenue to increase. If the demand for tomatoes is elastic, an increase in price causes total revenue to fall. The farmers will then fail to achieve their objective.

The following example illustrates the importance of price elasticity of demand in government tax policy. Suppose the government of Prince Edward Island wants to increase its revenue from taxation. What commodities can it tax in order to achieve this objective? Does a tax on gasoline, for example, increase tax revenues? Yes, a tax of two cents per litre produces an increase in the government's tax revenues, since the demand for gasoline seems to be inelastic at current prices. If the government increases the tax on a commodity whose demand is elastic, the resulting fall in quantity demanded will be relatively greater than the increase in the tax. This implies a fall in tax revenues.

In this section so far, we have concentrated on the price elasticity of demand. Is the price elasticity of supply also important? Certainly, we can learn a great deal about certain prices through elasticity of supply. Why, for example, are rare paintings so expensive? One answer, of course, is that there is a great demand for them. But that is only a part of the explanation. The other important aspect is that the supply of such paintings is, for all practical purposes, perfectly inelastic. A higher price will not cause another one to be produced. In such a case, the supply curve will be vertical as shown in Figure 5.6. Any increase in demand is reflected fully in an increase in price, since there can be no increase in quantity supplied to absorb or dampen the effect of the increase in demand.

FIGURE 5.6

Perfectly inelastic
supply.

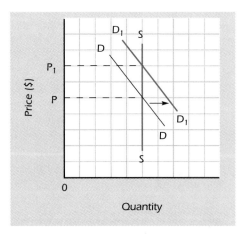

CHAPTER SUMMARY

1. Price elasticity of demand is measured by the relative change in quantity demanded divided by the relative change in price. The resulting value is the coefficient of elasticity.

2. The demand for a product may be perfectly elastic, elastic, unitary elastic, inelastic, or perfectly inelastic. Perfectly elastic demand and perfectly inelastic demand are extreme cases. The demand for most goods and services is elastic, unitary elastic, or inelastic.

Income Elasticity of Food Around the World

In developing countries where it is often a struggle to get enough food to eat, even a small increase in income is spent on food. In other words, the income elasticity of demand for food is relatively high. On the other hand, in advanced countries where it is hardly a problem to obtain food, and where people are usually consuming just about as much food as they wish, increases in income are usually spent on things other than food. In other words, the income elasticity of demand for food in advanced countries is relatively low.

India, Nigeria, and Indonesia have relatively low per capita incomes, averaging 5.6%, 6.7%, and 7.2% respectively of the U.S. per capita income, and, as can be seen from the following graph, their income elasticities of demand for food are high relative to those in Germany, Canada, and the United States.

Note: For graphical display, the income elasticity figures have been multiplied by 100. Thus, a value of 76 on the graph must be read as 0.76.

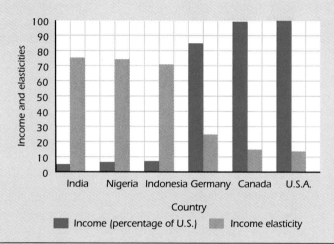

Source: Ching-Fun Cling and James Peale, Jr., "Income and Price Elasticities," in Henri Theil, ed., *Advances in Econometrics Supplement* (Greenwich, CT: JAI Press, 1989).

3. If the demand for a product is elastic, then a fall in price causes total revenue to increase. If the demand is unitary elastic, then a change in price leaves total revenue unchanged. If demand is inelastic, then a fall in price causes total revenue to fall.

4. Among the factors that affect price elasticity of demand are the availability of substitutes, the number of uses to which the commodity can be put, the proportion of income spent on the commodity, whether the commodity is a luxury or a necessity, and the time period under consideration.

5. Other important elasticity concepts are cross elasticity of demand and income elasticity of demand. Cross elasticity of demand measures the effect of a change in the price of good B on the quantity demanded of another good, A. If A and B are substitutes, their cross elasticity of demand will be positive. If they are complements, their cross elasticity of demand will be negative. If A and B are independent goods, then their cross elasticity will be zero.

6. Income elasticity of demand measures the effect of a change in income on quantity demanded. Normal goods have positive income elasticity of demand. Inferior goods have negative income elasticity of demand.

7. Price elasticity of supply measures the degree to which quantity offered for sale responds to changes in price. We measure price elasticity of supply by dividing the relative change in quantity supplied by the relative change in price.

8. Important determinants of elasticity of supply are the time being considered, storage cost, and the existence of production substitutes and production complements.

9. The elasticity concept has important applications to decisions concerning pricing and output in business and in government policy. It also helps us to understand the behaviour of certain prices.

TERMS FOR REVIEW

elasticity (84)
price elasticity of demand (84)
coefficient of elasticity (84)
perfectly inelastic (87)
perfectly elastic (87)
unit elasticity (87)
inelastic (87)
cross elasticity of demand (94)

substitutes (94)
complements (94)
income elasticity of demand (95)
normal goods (95)
inferior goods (95)
price elasticity of supply (95)
very short period (market period) (97)
reservation price (97)

QUESTIONS FOR REVIEW AND DISCUSSION

1. Under what circumstances will the own price elasticity of demand for a product be (L.O.1)

   (a) elastic

   (b) inelastic

   (c) perfectly inelastic

2. Make up a list of six products. Indicate, giving reasons, whether the demand for each product in your list is elastic or inelastic in relation to the price. (L.O.1,4)

3. Indicate the nature of the price elasticity of demand (elastic, inelastic, etc.) for each of the following commodities: (L.O.1,4)

   (a) bubble gum

   (b) beef

   (c) yachts

   (d) tea

   (e) Lloyd's electronic hand calculators

   (f) public transportation in Toronto

4. How would you interpret a value of –3.6 for the coefficient of price elasticity of demand for a product? (L.O.2)

5. Is the price elasticity of demand for a product the same as the slope of the demand curve for that product? Explain. (L.O.1)

6. What are the main determinants of price elasticity of demand? (L.O.4)

7. The government of British Columbia wants to increase its tax revenues. If lumber has a coefficient of price elasticity of demand of 2.5, while salmon has a coefficient of price elasticity of demand of 0.86, on which of these products will an increase in tax yield the larger tax revenue? (L.O.3)

8. Explain why an increase in the price of farm products may lead to larger incomes for farmers. (L.O.3)

9. Explain why a fall in the supply of farm products may lead to larger incomes for farmers. (L.O.6)

10. What are the main determinants of price elasticity of supply? (L.O.7)

11. You run a fish boat in Burgeo, Newfoundland. You have caught a certain amount of fish, which you must sell within a certain time because you have no cold-storage facilities and you do not want the fish to go bad. What is the price elasticity of supply in this situation? Would it be different if you had cold-storage facilities? (L.O.7)

12. Explain how price elasticity of supply may help us to understand the high prices of antiques. (L.O.8)

PROBLEMS AND EXERCISES

1. When the price of stopwatches falls from $15 to $12, the quantity demanded increases from 200 to 270. Compute the coefficient of price elasticity of demand for stopwatches using (L.O.1)

   (a) the point elasticity formula

   (b) the arc elasticity formula

2. Repeat Exercise 1 but with a price change from $12 to $15 and a quantity change from 270 to 200. (L.O.1)

3. Table 5.7 shows a demand schedule for good Y. (L.O.1,4)

   (a) Use the data in the first two columns to draw the demand curve for Y.

TABLE 5.7

Demand schedule for Y.

Price ($)	Quantity	Elasticity (E_d)
10	50	
8	60	
6	70	
4	80	
2	90	

   (b) Use the arc elasticity formula to compute the price elasticity coefficient at each price change, and complete the third column. (Remember that elasticity values go between the lines).

   (c) From this exercise, what have you observed about the price elasticity of demand at higher prices compared to the price elasticity of demand at lower prices?

4. (a) Construct a demand schedule for a product whose demand is perfectly inelastic within the price range $8, $7, $6, $5, $4, $3. Select your own quantities.

   (b) Graph the demand curve.

   (c) Name a good or service for which this demand is likely. (L.O.1,4)

5. Table 5.8 gives data for Fez Imports.

   (a) Complete the total revenue column. (L.O.1,3)

TABLE 5.8

Data for Fez Imports.

Price ($)	Quantity demanded	Total revenue	Elasticity coefficient
10	100		
9	120		
8	140		
7	160		
6	180		
5	200		

(b) Compute the price elasticity of demand for each price change and complete the elasticity column.

(c) Explain the relation that you observe between total revenue and price elasticity of demand.

6. When the price of X increases from $50 to $55, the quantity of Y demanded rises from 400 to 450. Use the arc elasticity formula to calculate the cross elasticity of demand between X and Y. (L.O.5)

7. When average income increases from $5000 to $8000, the quantity of automobiles demanded increases from 100 000 to 120 000. (L.O.2,5)

(a) Calculate the income elasticity of demand.

(b) What information does this elasticity coefficient give?

8. Assume that Canadian farmers face a price elasticity of demand for wheat of 0.65. How will a bad harvest that sends wheat prices up by 15% affect wheat growers? (L.O.8)

9. Show that if the demand for a product is perfectly price inelastic, then the burden (incidence) of a specific tax imposed on each unit produced (sold) will be shifted fully onto consumers. (L.O.8)

10. Show that if the supply of a product is perfectly price inelastic, then the burden (incidence) of a specific tax imposed on each unit produced (sold) will be borne entirely by the producers (sellers). (L.O.8)

11. On the basis of what you have learned in this chapter about price elasticity of demand, state whether you would expect the demand for gasoline to be elastic or inelastic. Gasoline prices have been fluctuating over a long period of time, which gives us a good opportunity to study the nature of the price elasticity of demand for gasoline in Canada. Interview local suppliers of gasoline (retail outlets) and ask them how customers respond to changes in gasoline price. Use the information that you receive to determine the nature of the price elasticity of demand for gasoline. Compare your result of this study with your expectation based on the material studied in this chapter.

CHAPTER 6

THE THEORY OF CONSUMER BEHAVIOUR

Learning Objectives

After studying this chapter, you should understand:

1 the concept of utility

2 the principle of utility maximization

3 the water-diamond paradox

4 the relationship between utility and demand

5 the derivation of the market demand curve

6 the concept and significance of consumer surplus

7 the idea of life-cycle saving

8 the motives for saving

The utility of articles valued for their beauty depends closely upon the expensiveness of the articles.

Thorstein Veblen, *The Theory of the Leisure Class*

INTRODUCTION

Households make three basic economic decisions. They decide how to spend their income on goods and services in the product market in order to maximize their satisfaction. They also decide how much of their income they will consume and how much they will save. Finally, they decide how to sell their resources, especially labour services, in the factor market. In this chapter, we will study the household's decision regarding how to allocate a given amount of money between various quantities of goods and services. We will also discuss the household's saving decision. A discussion of the household's behaviour in the labour market is deferred to a later chapter.

In Chapter 4, we analyzed the demand for a particular product. The total demand (or market demand) studied there is simply the sum of the demands of all the consumers in the market for that particular product. Let us now turn our attention to individual households, whose demands are added to obtain the total demand for a product.

In a very real sense, the satisfaction of wants is at the heart of economic activity. Production, consumption, and exchange are all carried out with the ultimate objective of satisfying wants. Wants are satisfied largely by the consumption of goods and services. It follows that an understanding of consumer behaviour is essential for an understanding of economic activity. This chapter will equip you with a theoretical apparatus for analyzing how a household will spend a given amount of money so that the satisfaction of the household will be maximized.

THE CONCEPT OF UTILITY

Learning Objective 1:
the concept of utility

Utility is a measure of satisfaction derived from consuming goods and services.

Util: a measure for a unit of satisfaction or utility.

Total utility is total satisfaction.

Marginal utility is extra satisfaction.

Economists use the term **utility** to refer to the satisfaction derived from the consumption of goods and services. Suppose that we could actually measure satisfaction in the same way that we can measure distances or weights. Then, after a very enjoyable meal, a consumer would be able to tell us exactly how many units of satisfaction he or she obtained from that particular meal. Well, if you have not already noticed, economists are very ingenious people. They have invented a measure for a unit of satisfaction or utility, and have labelled it a **util**. The utility derived from the consumption of a good or service varies from individual to individual, and from time to time for the same individual. Although utility cannot actually be measured (you might be the one to invent a meter that can somehow be hooked up to the brain to measure the amount of satisfaction experienced), and is not subject to interpersonal comparison, the concept is nevertheless important in enabling us to understand how consumers exercise choice over the various commodities that they can buy. The concept of making decisions at the margin, which we shall develop here, will help us in other areas of economics.

It is extremely important for us to know the difference between total utility and marginal utility. **Total utility** is the total satisfaction derived from the consumption of a good or service. For example, if you are really fond of ice cream, the more you consume per week (within reason, of course), the greater will be your total utility. **Marginal utility** is the extra or additional satisfaction derived from the consumption of additional units of a good or service. We can express marginal utility as

$$MU = \frac{\Delta TU}{\Delta Q}$$

where MU is marginal utility, TU is total utility, and Q is quantity. Table 6.1 shows hypothetical schedules of total and marginal utility for ice cream for a particular consumer for one week.

	Quantity of ice cream consumed (cones per week)	Total utility	Marginal utility
TABLE 6.1	0	0	
Hypothetical utility schedules for ice cream.			40
	1	40	
			30
	2	70	
			25
	3	95	
			20
	4	115	
			10
	5	125	
			5
	6	130	
			3
	7	133	
			1
	8	134	

The sum of all of the marginal utilities equals the total utility.

Note that the marginal utility values are placed between the lines of the total utility values. Note also that by adding all of the marginal utilities in the third column of Table 6.1, we obtain the total utility derived from all eight cones of ice cream.

FIGURE 6.1

Total utility and marginal utility.

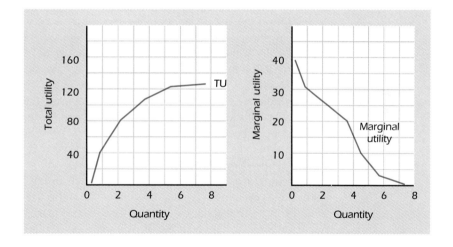

We can also illustrate total and marginal utility diagrammatically, as shown in Figure 6.1. The total utility column in Table 6.1 and the total utility graph in Figure 6.1 show that, although total utility increases as additional cones of ice cream are consumed, it does so at a decreasing rate. This phenomenon is called **the law of diminishing marginal utility** and can be stated as follows:

Marginal utility diminishes as quantity consumed increases.

> **As a consumer consumes more of a commodity, the utility or satisfaction derived from each additional unit diminishes.**

The following example will help to clarify the hypothesis. On a hot summer afternoon, you would probably really appreciate an ice cream cone. You might appreciate a second cone, though to a lesser extent than the first. You would likely enjoy a third cone even less than you enjoyed the second, and a fourth less than you enjoyed the third, and so on. Even though your total enjoyment increased, each cone of ice cream would give you less and less extra satisfaction. In other words, the marginal utility would diminish.

PROBLEM SOLVING 6-1

Assume that you have been given a case of Cherry Coke, and you must decide how much of it to consume within a given time. If, according to your subjective evaluation, the total utility derived after you have consumed the third bottle of Cherry Coke is 16 utils, and the marginal utility is positive but decreasing, should you consume more Cherry Coke?

THE CONSUMER'S PROBLEM: UTILITY MAXIMIZATION

Consumers achieve equilibrium when they maximize their satisfaction.

Learning Objective 2:
the principle of utility maximization

Let us assume that the objective of consumers is to maximize their total utility. Consumers act in such a way as to ensure that they obtain maximum satisfaction from their purchases of goods and services. When this happens, consumers have achieved their objectives, and we say that they are in equilibrium. Consumers in equilibrium have no desire to rearrange their purchases of goods and services, since any rearrangement will only result in a lower level of satisfaction.

Consider now the case of Erich Alda, a consumer who has a given amount of money to spend (budget) on two commodities, asparagus and bacon. Let us assume that Erich has spent his budget in such a way that the last dollar spent on asparagus gives more satisfaction than the last dollar spent on bacon. Let us assume, specifically, that the utility derived from the last dollar spent on asparagus is 15, while the utility derived from the last dollar spent on bacon is 10. Obviously, since an extra dollar spent on asparagus yields greater satisfaction than an extra dollar spent on bacon, Erich can increase his total satisfaction by buying more asparagus and less bacon. If the utility of the last dollar spent on bacon were greater than the utility of the last dollar spent on asparagus, then Erich could increase his satisfaction by buying more bacon and less asparagus. As long as the utility of the last dollar spent on asparagus is different from the utility of the last dollar spent on bacon, Erich can increase his total satisfaction by rearranging his purchases. It is only when the utility of the last dollar spent on each commodity is equal that the consumer will be maximizing his satisfaction.

Utility is maximized when the utility of the last dollar spent on each good is equal.

Let us return to the specific case in which the utility derived from the last dollar spent on asparagus is 15 and that derived from the last dollar spent on bacon is 10. As Erich buys more asparagus and less bacon, the marginal utility of asparagus will fall, while the marginal utility of bacon will increase (remember the hypothesis of diminishing marginal utility). If the utility of the last dollar spent on asparagus falls to 12 while the utility of the last dollar spent on bacon increases to 12, Erich will maximize his satisfaction and therefore have no desire to rearrange his purchases. When such a situation is attained, Erich will be in equilibrium. Any change from this position will result in a reduction in Erich's level of satisfaction.

So far, we have not introduced the prices of asparagus and bacon explicitly into the analysis. Erich's equilibrium position can be restated in terms of marginal utility and price. The marginal utility per dollar of asparagus is the marginal utility of asparagus divided by the price of asparagus. Similarly, the marginal utility per dollar of bacon is the marginal utility of bacon divided by the price of bacon. Thus, the condition to be met for Erich (or any other consumer) to be in equilibrium can be formulated as follows:

Learning Objective 2:
the principle of utility maximization

For a consumer purchasing two goods, A and B, to maximize satisfaction, the marginal utility of A divided by the price of A must equal the marginal utility of B divided by the price of B.

The utility maximization rule is often expressed in the following compact form:

$$\frac{MU_A}{P_A} = \frac{MU_B}{P_B}$$

Equimarginal principle: equating marginal values to maximize or minimize a variable.

where MU_A is the marginal utility of A, MU_B is the marginal utility of B, P_A is the price of A, and P_B is the price of B. This rule, known as the **equimarginal principle**, may also be expressed as

$$\frac{MU_A}{MU_B} = \frac{P_A}{P_B}$$

Expressed verbally, this formula says that the consumer will be in equilibrium (maximizing his or her satisfaction) when the ratio of the marginal utilities equals the ratio of the prices.

Of course, the consumer is usually confronted with more than just two commodities. The equilibrium condition can be extended to cover the situation of many commodities. In such a case, the equilibrium condition becomes

$$\frac{MU_A}{P_A} = \frac{MU_B}{P_B} = \frac{MU_C}{P_C} = \cdots = \frac{MU_Z}{P_Z}$$

for many goods from A to Z. The following example provides an opportunity to look at the consumer's allocation problem.

EXAMPLE 6-1

Consider the utility schedules of a consumer of two commodities, A and B, presented in Table 6.2. If the consumer, Yuki Hino, has a budget of $11 to spend on A and B, how should she allocate her funds between A and B in order to maximize her satisfaction?

TABLE 6.2

Schedule of marginal utility.

$ worth of A	MU_A	$ worth of B	MU_B
1	80	1	58
2	70	2	56
3	60	3	52
4	50	4	48
5	40	5	44
6	30	6	40
7	20	7	35
8	10	8	30
9	5	9	25
10	1	10	20

If Yuki spends the first dollar on A, she obtains 80 units of satisfaction (80 utils) but if she spends it on B, she obtains only 58 units of satisfaction. The first dollar should therefore be spent on A. The second dollar spent on A will yield 70 units of satisfaction, but if that dollar is spent on B, it will yield only 58 units of satisfaction. It should therefore be spent on A. For the same reason, the third dollar should be spent on A. Now, if the fourth dollar is spent on A, it will yield 50 units of satisfaction as compared with 58 if it is spent on B. The fourth dollar should therefore be spent on B. By similar reasoning, the fifth and sixth should be spent on B, the seventh on A, the eighth, ninth, and tenth on B, and the eleventh on A. We find that in the end, Yuki will have bought $5 worth of A and $6 worth of B. Note that this allocation accords with the principle stated earlier: that consumers will maximize their satisfaction when they allocate their incomes in such a manner that the utility of the last dollar spent on commodity A equals the utility of the last dollar spent on commodity B.

PROBLEM SOLVING 6-2
Referring to the data in Table 6.2, suppose that Yuki's spending money (budget) increases to $14. How will she rearrange her purchases in order to maximize her satisfaction?

THE WATER-DIAMOND PARADOX: THE PARADOX OF VALUE

Learning Objective 3:
the water-diamond paradox

Diamonds are more expensive than water not because they are more useful but because the marginal utility of diamonds is high relative to the marginal utility of water.

The **water-diamond paradox** or the **paradox of value** plagued numerous classical economists including Adam Smith (1723–1790), the man considered to be the father of economics as a discipline. The paradox lies in the question, "Why is water so much cheaper than diamonds when water is so much more useful than diamonds?" One solution is that diamonds are relatively scarce while water is relatively abundant. In price determination, marginal utility — not total utility — is the relevant concept. Water is useful but its marginal utility is low, while the marginal utility of diamonds is high. And since price is proportional to marginal utility, the price of diamonds is higher than the price of water.

THE CONSUMER'S DEMAND CURVE

The analysis presented above can be used to determine how a change in the price of a commodity affects the quantity demanded. Let us assume again that there are two goods, A and B, that the consumer can buy. If the price of A falls, then the marginal utility per dollar of A

$$\frac{MU_A}{P_A}$$

Learning Objective 4:
the relationship between utility and demand

increases. This being the case, the consumer will buy more of A. The following example helps us to illustrate the point. Let us assume that the price of A is $10 and that the marginal utility of A is 40 when the consumer is in equilibrium. The marginal utility per dollar of A is

$$\frac{40}{10} = 4$$

Since the consumer is in equilibrium, we know that the marginal utility per dollar of A equals the marginal utility per dollar of B — that is,

$$\frac{MU_A}{P_A} = \frac{40}{10} = \frac{MU_B}{P_B} = 4$$

Now, if the price of A falls to $8, then

$$\frac{MU_A}{P_A} = \frac{40}{8} = 5$$

which is now greater than

$$\frac{MU_B}{P_B}$$

To restore equilibrium, the consumer purchases more of A and less of B so that the MU_A falls while the MU_B rises until

$$\frac{MU_A}{P_A}$$

again equals

$$\frac{MU_B}{P_B}$$

A fall in the price of A, therefore, causes the quantity of A that the consumer will buy to increase. In other words, the consumer's demand curve slopes downward from left to right.

We can use an alternative approach to demonstrate the relation between marginal utility and the consumer's demand curve. Consider the demand curve in Figure 6.2 for your favourite consumer, you, for oranges per month. We can interpret this demand curve as follows: For a quantity of three bags of oranges, the maximum price you are willing to pay is $18. If the price were higher than $6 per bag, you would not buy the third bag of oranges.

FIGURE 6.2

Demand curve for oranges.

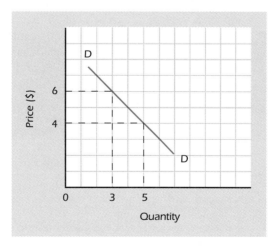

Why are you not willing to pay more than $6 for the third bag of oranges? The answer is that according to your subjective evaluation of the extra satisfaction derived from the third bag (i.e., its marginal utility), it is worth just $6 but no more. Likewise, you will not buy the fifth bag for a price exceeding $4 because that is your subjective evaluation of the marginal utility derived from the fifth bag. As we noted earlier in this chapter, the more oranges that you consume per month, the less satisfaction that you derive from each additional orange, and hence, the less you are willing to pay for extra bags of oranges. This approach clearly brings out the relation between marginal utility and demand.

Consumer demand reflects marginal utility.

MARKET DEMAND

Once we obtain a demand curve for each consumer of a particular product, we simply add these individual demand curves to obtain the market demand curve discussed in Chapter 4. Let us assume, for the sake of simplicity, that there are only three consumers, Maria Gabor, Emil Torecky, and Joan Day, in the market for a particular product. The individual demand schedules for these three consumers are given in Table 6.3, along with the market demand.

	Maria's demand		Emil's demand		Joan's demand		Market demand	
TABLE 6.3	**P**	**Q**	**P**	**Q**	**P**	**Q**	**P**	**Q**
Individual demand schedules.	8	2	8	0	8	3	8	5
	6	3	6	2	6	5	6	10
	4	4	4	4	4	7	4	15

At a price of $8, Maria will buy two units a week, Emil will buy none, and Joan will buy three units a week. Notice that at a price of $8, Emil is effectively out of the market. The total quantity demanded at $8 is therefore five units. This is shown in the market demand schedule. At a price of $6, Maria will buy three units a week, Emil will now enter the market and buy two units, while Joan will buy five units. The total quantity demanded at a price of $6 is thus 10 units, as shown in the market demand schedule. At a price of $4, Maria will buy four units, Emil will buy four, and Joan will buy seven; so together, they will buy a total of 15 units at a price of $4. You have seen, then, that the market demand is the sum of the demands of the individual consumers in the market.

Learning Objective 5:
the derivation of the market demand curve

The market demand curve is the horizontal summation of the individual demand curve.

Can we derive the market demand curve from the individual demand curves? Let us investigate. Figure 6.3 shows the demand curves for Maria, Emil, and Joan. At a price of $8, the total quantity demanded by all three consumers is five units. This combination of price and quantity gives one point on the market demand curve. At a price of $6, the total quantity demanded by all three consumers is 10 units a week. This combination of price and quantity gives another point on the market demand curve. The third point on the demand curve is obtained in a similar manner. Thus, we can conclude that the market demand curve is the horizontal summation of the individual demand curves.

CONSUMER SURPLUS

Learning Objective 6:
the concept and significance of consumer surplus

Consumer surplus is the difference between what consumers are willing to pay and what they actually pay.

We can now look at a useful economic concept called **consumer surplus**. Suppose apples are sold at $0.50 per kilogram. Quite possibly, consumers might be willing to pay $3 for the first kilogram, but they pay only $0.50 because this is the market price. They might possibly be willing to pay $2 for the second kilogram, but they still pay only $0.50. For the third kilogram, they might be willing to pay $1.20, but again, they pay only $0.50. They might be willing to pay $0.60 for the fourth kilogram, but once more they pay only $0.50. Table 6.4 shows the relevant data.

The consumer surplus is the difference between the amount that a consumer would have paid for a product and the amount that he or she actually paid.

Consumer surplus can also be shown on a graph. Consider Figure 6.4. The equilibrium price and the equilibrium quantity established by the market for this good or service are $0.50 and 5 kg respectively. Many buyers would have been willing to pay a higher price than $0.50 to obtain this commodity. But because they have to pay only $0.50, they actually receive a surplus or gain, which is referred to as consumer surplus.

FIGURE 6.3

Derivation of the market demand curve.

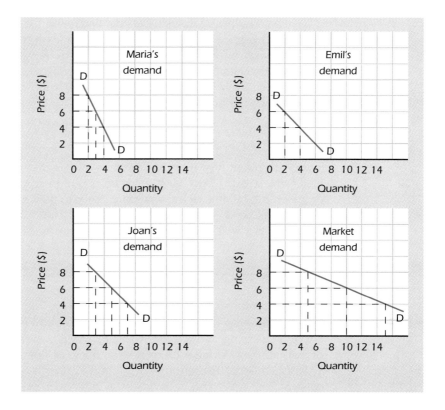

TABLE 6.4

Illustration of consumer surplus.

Apples (kg)	Total amount the consumer would have paid	Total amount actually paid	Consumer surplus
1	$3.00	$0.50	$2.50
2	5.00	1.00	4.00
3	6.20	1.50	4.70
4	6.80	2.00	4.80

FIGURE 6.4

Consumer surplus.

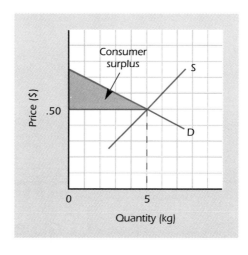

Consumers often derive a greater amount of satisfaction from a good than is suggested by the price of the good.

Each consumer's surplus differs depending on the price that he or she is willing to pay. And this price, as you have seen, depends on the consumer's evaluation of the utility derived from the product. The shaded area in Figure 6.4 measures total consumer surplus. The economic significance of the concept of consumer surplus is that consumers often derive a greater amount of satisfaction or utility from a good or service than is suggested by the price of the good.

THE SAVING DECISION

The total amount of savings in Canada is the result of the savings of individual households who decide to put aside a certain part of their income. People save for a variety of reasons: to be able to leave an inheritance to their children or grandchildren, to pay for their children's education, to purchase a car or a house, to take a cruise on a luxury ship, or to live well in retirement. These motives for saving will be discussed in greater detail.

MOTIVES FOR SAVING

The life-cycle motive for saving

Learning Objective 7:
the idea of life-cycle saving

Life-cycle saving is long-term saving, often for retirement.

Life-cycle saving refers to the idea that people will organize their consumption, and hence their saving, in such a way that they will be able to maintain an adequate level of consumption during retirement. The name of Franco Modigliani, a Nobel laureate at Massachusetts Institute of Technology (MIT), is most often associated with this concept.

Figure 6.5 illustrates the idea of life-cycle saving. We assume that this individual, Sally, obtains her first job at age 20, retires at age 65, and expects to live until she is 90. (Secretly, she thinks that she will live to be 100). As the graph shows, Sally's savings are zero before age 20. Thereafter, her savings increase until she reaches the age of 65. After age 65 she is in retirement so she has no income, except perhaps for interest earned on her savings. She then begins to use her savings to finance her consumption. At age 90, she has little or no savings left.

FIGURE 6.5

Life-cycle savings.

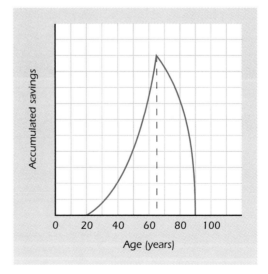

The precautionary motive for saving

Life is filled with uncertainties, risks, and unexpected events, many of which require funds. People are able to buy insurance against some of these events — car insurance, fire insurance, etc. But there are other risks against which they may not be able to purchase insurance. For example, a writer may not be able to buy insurance against the risk of a significant decline in demand for her book. Thus, people save for unexpected events. Such savings are referred to as **precautionary savings**. The amount of precautionary savings that people undertake depends on the ease of contracting loans, and the availability of insurance against risks.

Precautionary saving is for unexpected events.

The inheritance motive

To many people, the prospect of leaving an inheritance or bequest to their children and/or grandchildren is a matter of some importance. Such people are quite willing to sacrifice current consumption so that their children and grandchildren can enjoy higher levels of consumption. This motive for saving is called the **bequest** or **inheritance motive**. Experience seems to support the existence of a bequest motive for saving since many people are known to leave considerable amounts of money for their children and grandchildren. The fact that many people do not leave substantial amounts for their children and grandchildren may be due to lack of ability rather than to the absence of a bequest motive.

Inheritance saving is for one's heirs.

Target saving

Saving for specific purposes is often referred to as **target saving**. A student who has a part-time job may save toward the purchase of a stereo system or a computer. A couple may save toward the downpayment on a car or a house. Many people believe that it is important for their children to get a college or university education, so they save for that specific purpose. In Canada, students can obtain Canada or Quebec student loans and grants. This has reduced the burden of saving for parents to educate their children.

Target saving is for a specific purpose, such as the purchase of a car or house.

SAVING AND INCOME

The amount that people are able to save depends on the level of their disposable income. (Disposable income is income left after income taxes are deducted). People with high disposable incomes will tend to spend more on consumption, and they are likely also to save more than people with low disposable incomes. Because saving varies directly with the level of disposable income, an increase in income taxes will reduce disposable income and hence saving. Conversely, a reduction in income taxes will tend to increase household saving.

SAVING AND THE RATE OF INTEREST

The rate of interest exerts considerable influence on a household's decision to save. Higher interest rates encourage saving, while lower interest rates discourage saving. When interest rates are high, households will find it attractive to postpone consumption. But high interest rates also mean bigger interest earnings on savings, so people with savings feel better off when interest rates are high. This may lead to greater current consumption. Therefore, higher interest rates are likely to cause households to consume more both now and in the future.

GLOBAL PERSPECTIVE

Trade and Global Maximization of Satisfaction

In our discussion of consumer behaviour, we have shown how, given their income and the prices of goods and services, consumers within a given economy seek to maximize their satisfaction by purchasing goods and services freely. In the same way, nations could maximize their economic well-being if they could freely exchange goods and services among themselves.

International trade is one means whereby consumers all over the globe can attempt to maximize their satisfaction. Canadians need coffee, tea, cane sugar, British-made cars, oranges, pineapple and countless other items that either we do not have or that we could produce only by diverting scarce resources from more efficient to less efficient uses. We also benefit from trade because competition from other countries forces us to use cost-saving technology in our domestic industries. Through international trade, people of all nations are able to enjoy a greater variety of goods.

In this chapter, we also discussed households' savings decisions. The greater the return on your saving, other things being equal, the better off you will be. The ability to move funds across international borders also helps global consumers to maximize their satisfaction. Consider two countries: Canada and the United States. Let's assume that a shortage of capital in Canada results in a rate of interest of 12%, while the United States has plenty of capital, reflected in a U.S. rate of interest of 4%. If American citizens can invest their savings in Canada, they will earn a return of 12% compared to 4% if they invest in the United States. This transfer of funds benefits the citizens of both countries. Americans earn considerably more on their savings, whereas Canadians acquire more capital, enabling them to save less and increase their current consumption.

Among the major objectives of free trade agreements among countries and trade agreements under the General Agreement on Tariffs and Trade (GATT) and its new replacement, the World Trade Organization (WTO), are the mutual benefits to be derived from international trade and freer access to international capital. International trade and the free flow of capital between countries allow the global economy to use its scarce resources efficiently and thus maximize satisfaction globally.

CHAPTER SUMMARY

1. Utility refers to the amount of satisfaction derived from the consumption of goods and services. Utility is not measurable, and one person's utility cannot be meaningfully compared with that of another.

2. Total utility is the total amount of satisfaction derived from consuming goods and services. Marginal utility is the additional satisfaction derived from consuming additional units of goods and services. We can obtain total utility by adding all of the marginal utilities derived from each additional unit.

3. The law of diminishing marginal utility states that, as a consumer consumes more of a commodity, the utility or satisfaction derived from each additional unit diminishes.

4. We assume that the objective of consumers is to maximize their satisfaction. They do this by equating the marginal utilities of a dollar's worth of each of the commodities on which they spend their incomes. In this position, consumers are said to be in equilibrium.

5. We can derive the consumer's demand curve from utility analysis. The consumer's demand curve reflects marginal utility.

6. The market demand curve for a particular commodity is the sum of the demand curves of the consumers in the market for that commodity.

7. The consumer's surplus is the difference between what the consumers are willing to pay and what they actually pay. The existence of consumer's surplus suggests that consumers derive more satisfaction from a good than is suggested by the price.

8. The idea of life-cycle saving is that people will save in order to be able to maintain a certain level of consumption during retirement.

9. People also save in order to provide for unforeseen contingencies, to leave an inheritance to their children or grandchildren, or to finance some specific consumption.

10. The level of disposable income and the rate of interest are likely to affect households' saving decisions.

TERMS FOR REVIEW

utility (104)	water-diamond paradox (paradox of value) (108)
util (104)	
total utility (104)	consumer surplus (110)
marginal utility (104)	life-cycle saving (112)
law of diminishing marginal utility (105)	precautionary saving (113)
equimarginal principle (107)	inheritance (bequest) saving (113)
	target saving (113)

QUESTIONS FOR REVIEW AND DISCUSSION

1. Give an example to show that you understand the difference between total utility and marginal utility. (L.O.1)

2. Do you think that the utility analysis of consumer behaviour is important even though utility cannot be measured? Why or why not? (General)

3. State the law of diminishing marginal utility. Do you think that this law applies to all goods and services? (L.O.1)

4. Demonstrate your understanding of the conditions that must exist for a consumer to be in equilibrium. (L.O.2)

5. Explain the relation between marginal utility and consumer demand. (L.O.4)

6. What is the relation between the individual demand curve and the market demand curve? (L.O.5)

7. Outline briefly the procedure for deriving the market demand curve from the individual consumers' demand curves. (L.O.4)

8. Explain the water-diamond paradox. (L.O.3)

9. In a few sentences, explain consumer surplus. (L.O.6)

10. What is the economic implication of consumer surplus? (L.O.6)

11. Discuss some reasons why households might save. (L.O.7,8)

PROBLEMS AND EXERCISES

1. Given the information in Table 6.2, how should Yuki Hino allocate a budget of $17 between commodities A and B in order to maximize her satisfaction? (L.O.2)

2. Given the data shown in Table 6.5 on the utilities of A and B, and given that the price of A is $2 and the price of B is $3: (L.O.2)

	Quantity of A	MU$_A$	$\dfrac{MU_A}{P_A}$	Quantity of B	MU$_B$	$\dfrac{MU_B}{P_B}$
TABLE 6.5						
Utilities of A and B.	1	16		1	21	
	2	18		2	24	
	3	16		3	18	
	4	14		4	15	
	5	10		5	12	
	6	6		6	6	
	7	2		7	3	

(a) Fill in the MU$_A$/P$_A$ and the MU$_B$/P$_B$ columns.

(b) How should a customer allocate a budget of $12 between A and B?

(c) What change should be made in the consumer's purchases if his or her budget increases to $22?

3. The market for salmon consists of three consumers: Sol, Luci, and Clare. Their demand schedules for salmon are given in Table 6.6.

	Sol's demand		Luci's demand		Clare's demand	
TABLE 6.6	**P**	**Q**	**P**	**Q**	**P**	**Q**
Demand schedules for salmon.	10	8	10	6	10	5
	8	10	8	8	8	7
	6	12	6	10	6	9

(a) Construct the market demand schedule for salmon.

(b) Draw the demand curve for each consumer and then draw the market demand curve. (L.O.5)

4. Table 6.7 shows the demand schedule for beef for Annie Lamb. Plot Annie's demand curve. If the market price of beef is $4 per kilogram, show Annie's total consumer surplus on your graph and calculate its value. (L.O.6)

	Price ($)	Quantity demanded per week (kg)
TABLE 6.7		
Annie's demand for beef.	7	0
	6	1
	5	2
	4	3
	3	4

5. How would you expect households to react to each of the following in terms of their motivation to save? (L.O.7,8)

(a) the elimination of an inheritance tax

(b) the introduction of easily available insurance for a wide range of risks

(c) more liberal loans and grants for students

(d) a marked decline in the birth rate

Internet Site

http://www.wto.org

This is the Web site for the World Trade Organization. Information about the WTO and its activities can be found here.

INTERNET EXERCISE

1. Go to the home page for the WTO.
2. Click on *About the WTO.*
3. List the four guiding elements which make up the General Agreement on Trade in Services (GATS).
4. List four services, other than banking, that fall under the jurisdiction of the GATS.

CHAPTER 7

BUSINESS ORGANIZATION, SPECIALIZATION, AND INDUSTRIAL LOCATION

Learning Objectives

After studying this chapter, you should be able to:

1 discuss various forms of business organization

2 state the advantages and disadvantages of each form of business organization

3 discuss business financing

4 discuss advantages and disadvantages of specialization

5 account for the location of certain industries

The nature of our industrial organization does not lend itself to neat classification.

George J. Stigler, *Five Lectures on Economic Problems*

INTRODUCTION

The production of goods and services in Canada is undertaken by numerous firms operating under different forms of business organization. These firms may be classified in several ways. For example, we could classify them as small, medium or large, either on the basis of their annual sales, their share of the market, or on their number of employees. We could also classify them as domestic or foreign owned firms. Each classification would, of course, depend on the purpose for which the classification was made. In this chapter, we shall discuss the various forms of organization that a firm may take, the concept of specialization, and the location of production. Forms of business organization include the single proprietorship, the partnership, the corporation, and the cooperative. Numerous examples of each form of organization can be found all over the country. These various forms of business organization do not merely represent the financial arrangement under which the firm operates. They dictate the extent to which the owners are liable for the debts of the business, which laws will apply to its operation, the owner's role in running the business, and the type of taxes to be paid.

In this book, we will focus our attention on firms that operate for profit. You must realize, however, that there are many organizations that use resources to produce goods and services, but whose objectives do not include profit-making. Such organizations are often referred to as not-for-profit organizations and include charitable, social, religious, philanthropic, scientific, and educational institutions. These non-profit-seeking organizations also exist in the same four forms mentioned above.

THE SINGLE PROPRIETORSHIP

Single (or sole) proprietorship: a firm with a single private owner who is solely responsible for all decision-making.

Learning Objective 1: discuss various forms of business organization

Let us imagine a person, Cyril Khan, who believes that he can earn a handsome income by selling worms as fishing bait. He gets his supply of worms, and serves his customers from his garage. Cyril has established a single proprietorship. Or imagine a lawyer, Andrea Malozzi, who has left the firm of Briggs, Cahill, and Morin to start her own practice. She too has established a single proprietorship. **Single** (or **sole**) **proprietors** own their own businesses, finance them themselves (perhaps with the help of family), and make all of the decisions regarding the operation of their businesses. If their businesses prosper, the proprietors enjoy the profits; if their businesses fail, the proprietors suffer the losses. The single proprietorship is found mainly in small businesses such as confectioneries and farms and in certain professions such as accounting and business and economic consulting.

Advantages of the single proprietorship

The single proprietorship has certain advantages:

Learning Objective 2: state the advantages and disadvantages of each form of business organization

1. Single proprietors derive a certain amount of satisfaction, pride, and independence from owning their own businesses. You can sense the feeling of accomplishment when someone proudly states, "I own my own business."

2. Knowing that they can lose all of their possessions if their businesses fail, single proprietors are likely to make special efforts to run their businesses efficiently.

3. In situations demanding swift action, single proprietorships enjoy a considerable advantage over other forms of business organization, since owners do not need to consult with or seek the agreement of anyone other than themselves.

4. Single proprietors are likely to be more concerned about developing good working relations with the few employees that they may have, and with securing the

goodwill of their customers. If single proprietors are successful, the quality of their services will be high, and the effect on their revenues favourable.

5. Single proprietors may enjoy tax benefits. The earnings of single proprietors are subject to tax once only. We will see later that corporations do not enjoy this advantage.

Disadvantages of the single proprietorship

The single proprietorship has the following disadvantages:

Learning Objective 2:
state the advantages and disadvantages of each form of business organization

1. Single proprietors are at a distinct disadvantage in situations requiring huge capital outlays. Not many single proprietors are in a position to raise the large sums of money required in many of today's modern businesses. Hence, we do not find many single proprietors owning large industrial plants.

2. The single proprietorship form of business organization suffers from the uncertainty about the continuation of the business in the event of the death or retirement of the owner. It must be observed, however, that some single proprietorships have been known to survive through several generations in the hands of the same family.

3. The biggest disadvantage of the single proprietorship, however, is the fact that the owners are legally responsible for all debts incurred by their businesses. Single proprietors are not protected by limited liability. This means that if their businesses fail, single proprietors are fully liable and can lose personal assets such as cars, furniture, or even homes since, in this form of business organization, there is no legal distinction between personal assets and business assets.

THE PARTNERSHIP

Learning Objective 1:
discuss various forms of business organization

A partnership: an agreement between two or more people to own and operate a business together. The partners are jointly and personally liable for all debts of the business.

Suppose our hypothetical worm-seller, Cyril, is doing so well that he believes that he can rent a small building two blocks away and move the business out of his garage. Since the business has grown, it requires more money to run it. He now needs someone to share the rental cost and perhaps manage the store when he is out gathering worms. He discusses the idea (a business proposition?) with two of his friends who attended high school with him. They agree to go into business with him — thus forming a partnership. A **partnership** is a form of business organization in which two or more individuals agree to own and operate a business. The partners usually draw up an agreement (contract) outlining the amount of capital that each has invested in the business, the responsibilities of each partner, and the manner in which the profits will be divided among them. Partnerships are quite common among lawyers, doctors, business and management consultants, and small retail stores. Why do people form partnerships? The answer is that there are certain advantages in forming a partnership.

Advantages of the partnership

The following are the major advantages of the partnership:

Learning Objective 2:
state the advantages and disadvantages of each form of business organization

1. The partnership has the ability to raise more capital than the single proprietorship is able to raise.

2. The partnership, like the single proprietorship, is not subject to tax. Individual partners, of course, pay taxes on their incomes, but the business itself pays no tax on its earnings.

3. Discussion is likely to take place among the partners before any important action is taken. These discussions are likely to lead to more sober decisions than those reached by single proprietors who do not need to engage in such discussions. According to the old adage, two heads are better than one.

4. The partnership may benefit from the variety of special talents and skills possessed by the partners. One may have expertise in marketing, another in management, another in accounting, etc., and all contribute to the successful operation of the business.

Disadvantages of the partnership

The partnership suffers from the following disadvantages:

1. The partnership lacks continuity. If one partner dies or if agreement cannot be reached among the partners, the partnership may have to be dissolved.

2. Although the partnership may be able to raise more capital than the single proprietorship, it is still severely limited in the amount of funds it can raise.

3. The partnership does not have limited liability. This is probably its most serious drawback. Each partner is fully liable to the extent of his or her personal possessions for any debts incurred by the business. It is possible for one partner to make a bad business decision in the name of the partnership, thus jeopardizing the financial security of the other partners, since they are severally and jointly liable.

THE LIMITED PARTNERSHIP

Learning Objective 1:
discuss various forms of business organization

In a limited partnership, some partners are protected by limited liability, but at least one partner must have unlimited liability.

Learning Objective 2:
state the advantages and disadvantages of each form of business organization

A modified version of the ordinary partnership, called the limited partnership, has emerged. The limited partnership reduces, to a certain extent, the problems of unlimited liability associated with the ordinary partnership. In a **limited partnership**, certain partners have limited liability. Such partners are liable only to the extent of the amount of money they have invested in the partnership, but they may legally take part neither in managing it nor in conducting any business in its name. A limited partnership requires at least one partner to assume unlimited liability. The limited partnership arrangement increases the ability of the partnership to raise funds, because some partners have limited liability. Knowing that they can lose, at worst, only their investment in the business, limited partners may be attracted to the partnership.

> **PROBLEM SOLVING 7-1**
> **Why is a partnership the ideal form of business organization for a law firm, from the viewpoint of the client?**

THE CORPORATION

Learning Objective 1:
discuss various forms of business organization

Corporation: a form of business organization in which shareholders have limited liability.

Let us return to our hypothetical worm-seller, Cyril. Cyril's partnership is extremely successful. Customers from 30 km away have begun asking about fishing equipment. The partners of the business decide, therefore, to expand their operation. They want to open stores all over the city. And, in addition to selling worms and other types of bait, they want to stock all types of fishing equipment and books about fishing. They also plan to expand their business into neighbouring provinces, and ultimately, to have a chain of stores stretching from coast to coast.

For the moment, however, their focus is on expanding city-wide and offering fishing equipment as well as bait. This expansion requires a great deal of capital and, instead of gathering worms, as they do now, the partners plan to breed worms scientifically. To do so, they need to obtain very expensive equipment. If they could lure a few wealthy persons into the partnership, they would probably be able to afford the new equipment and larger facilities required. But it is extremely difficult to find people who are willing both to invest huge sums of money and to be fully liable for the debts of the business. Cyril and his partners can overcome this problem, however, by forming a **corporation**.

A corporation is a form of business organization in which a group of persons agree to engage in business in which they have limited liability. They obtain permission from either the federal government or from one of the provincial governments to incorporate. The corporation can raise vast amounts of money by selling shares to the public. The purchasers of these shares (the shareholders, or stockholders, as they are often called) are the owners of the business. A board of directors is elected by the shareholders, and this board hires senior executive officers. Legally, the corporation is an entity that exists apart from the shareholders. It can sue or be sued, enter into contracts, and be taxed just like an individual. Naturally, we would expect the corporation to be the dominant form of organization in large businesses. A corporation is identified by the word *Corporation*, *Incorporated* (or its abbreviation *Inc.*), or *Limited* (or its abbreviation *Ltd.*) at the end of the name of the firm. The following firms would be corporations: The ABC Corporation; Advicecon, Inc.; and Econoserve, Ltd.

In the modern corporation, the decision-making process is divorced from the risk-taking process, since the risk is borne by the shareholders, who are the owners of the business. A hired manager may not even own shares in the company. The profits of the corporation accrue to (are distributed to) the shareholders as dividends. Portions of the profits of the corporation may be retained to be reinvested in the business. These are known as **retained earnings** or *undistributed profits*.

Retained earnings are not paid to shareholders, they are retained for reinvestment.

Advantages of the corporation

Learning Objective 2: state the advantages and disadvantages of each form of business organization

The corporation has a number of important advantages:

1. It has a tremendous ability to raise huge amounts of money. The shares of the corporation can easily be transferred from one owner to another. If you hold shares in a corporation, you can sell your shares to any person who is willing to buy them. Investment in corporate stock is thus considered to be very attractive.

2. This form of business organization has the continuity that is lacking in the single proprietorship and the partnership. If a shareholder dies, the corporation continues as usual.

3. The corporation can usually afford to hire the services of experts. It can hire a staff of researchers, economists, top management personnel, accountants, lawyers, and experts in other fields. Policy decisions are, therefore, likely to be sound.

Shareholders have limited liability – liability only for the total of their investment.

4. In a corporation, each owner (shareholder) is liable only to the extent of his or her investment in the business. That is, the owners have **limited liability**. If the company fails, each shareholder's liability is limited to the amount of money spent in buying shares in the business. This is undoubtedly the greatest advantage of the corporation.

Disadvantages of the corporation

Despite the significant advantages of the corporation, it still suffers from the following disadvantages:

1. The earnings of the corporation are taxed twice. The corporation pays a tax before its profits are distributed, and the shareholders also pay a tax on their dividends.

2. The owners of the corporation may have little or no control over its operation, and those who make the day-to-day decisions of the corporation may not have the same incentives as the owners.

3. The size of the corporation often forces a wedge between labour and management, and also destroys the close personal relationship between owner and customer that is typical of the single proprietorship.

PROBLEM SOLVING 7-2

1. **The profitable partnership Hitchcock, James, and Chill Filmmakers finds that it could earn even larger profits if it expanded its operation. Potential partners are unwilling to join the partnership because of unlimited liability. What course of action might the firm take to overcome this difficulty?**

2. **If a government is primarily interested in increasing its tax revenue, should it favour the formation of corporations?**

THE COOPERATIVE

Learning Objective 1: discuss various forms of business organization

A **cooperative** is a form of business organization that is owned, financed, and controlled by its member-patrons, who share the risks and benefits in proportion to their patronage. A cooperative is established to reap the benefits of large-scale selling and buying. It is similar to a corporation in many respects. In fact, it is a modified version of the corporation. A cooperative raises funds by selling shares, and its shareholders enjoy the advantage of limited liability.

Unlike the corporation though, in which a shareholder is entitled to one vote for each share he or she owns, each member of the cooperative has only one vote no matter how many shares he or she controls. Hence, a true cooperative exhibits democratic control. Also, dividends are distributed not in proportion to the number of shares held, as in the case of a corporation, but in proportion to the amount of business that each member conducts with the cooperative.

Cooperative: a form of business organization in which members provide the capital, and in which dividends are distributed according to patronage.

TYPES OF COOPERATIVES

Cooperatives may be classified in a variety of ways depending on the main objectives of the cooperatives. Thus there are consumer cooperatives, producer cooperatives, purchasing cooperatives, and marketing cooperatives. Each of these types will be briefly discussed.

A *consumer cooperative* is formed by a group of consumers who join together to operate a business that provides consumer goods and services. Since dividends are distributed among the members in proportion to the volume of business that each member does with the cooperative (i.e., according to patronage), the members find it advantageous to do as much business as possible with the cooperative.

A *producer cooperative* is formed by a group of producers who believe that by banding together they can better serve their interests. A group of dairy farmers or fruit growers, for example, may form a cooperative for the purpose of increasing efficiency through joint action.

Purchasing cooperatives and *marketing cooperatives* are formed to take advantage of large-scale purchasing and marketing. The main objective of a purchasing cooperative is to buy on a large scale and obtain the benefits of lower costs. Similarly, marketing cooperatives can sell on a large scale and thus increase their profits.

Advantages of the cooperative

Learning Objective 2: state the advantages and disadvantages of each form of business organization

1. The cooperative can take advantage of the benefits of large-scale operation. For example, a consumer cooperative can obtain its supplies more cheaply by buying in large quantities, and thus take advantage of quantity discounts. A producer cooperative can establish and operate a distribution system for its products more cheaply than if each producer did his or her own marketing.

2. The managers and customers of a cooperative are likely to work together towards the success of the business.

Disadvantages of the cooperative

1. The cooperative may fail to look beyond its own membership for expert management.

2. The cooperative may be limited by its inability to raise huge amounts of capital. This may be the case for two main reasons. First, only those individuals who intend to conduct a large volume of business with the cooperative are likely to purchase its shares. Second, its members are unlikely to contribute additional funds since dividends are distributed not in proportion to funds invested but by patronage.

3. The democratic control that is a feature of cooperatives may limit decision-making severely. The membership may not be sufficiently informed to vote intelligently on certain major policy issues.

PROBLEM SOLVING 7-3

You have come up with an idea for a good or service that you believe will be successful on the market, and you would like to experiment with this idea. It does not require a great deal of money to get it started. What form of business organization would you choose to establish your business?

BUSINESS FINANCING

Learning Objective 3:
discuss business financing

It would be helpful for you, as a student of economics, to have at least a general idea of business financing. This section provides that general knowledge. The method of financing available to a business enterprise depends on the specific form of business organization of the enterprise.

You have already learned that a single proprietorship is financed by the resources of its owner. The owner may raise the capital by borrowing from a financial institution, such as a bank, or from family members. In any case, the financial burden rests squarely on the shoulders of the owner. The partnership is financed in a similar fashion, except that the burden is shared among all of the partners. Once the firm becomes a going concern and begins to earn profits, funds for expansion and new investment may come from those profits.

A corporation may finance its operations internally from retained earnings, or externally by debt financing or equity financing.

Unlike the single proprietorship and the partnership, the corporation has a number of options that it may use to raise capital. First, it may rely on internal financing; that is, the firm may decide not to distribute all profits after taxes to its shareholders, but to retain a certain amount for investment. Retained earnings provide the main source of funds for total investment.

Financing through bond issue

A bond is a certificate stating that a corporation or the government owes you a certain amount of money at a specific time.

Second, the corporation may raise capital by issuing bonds. A **bond** is a certificate printed on fancy paper that is issued by a government or a corporation, promising to pay a certain amount of money as interest payment periodically (annually or semi-annually, for example) until the bond matures. The issuer of the bond (the borrower) promises to pay whoever owns it (the lender) the full amount of its face value when the bond becomes due, that is, when it matures. If you buy a $1000 bond from a corporation that promises to pay $100 every year for a period of five years, the corporation is actually borrowing $1000 from you. You will earn $100 every year for five years; and you will receive the principal of $1000 at the end of the five-year period on the maturity date of the bond.

What happens, you may well ask, if the corporation expected to earn an annual return averaging 15% but actually earns only 8%? Is it still obliged to pay you the amounts promised by the bond? The answer is yes. Your payments are not conditional upon the corporation's earnings. Failure on the part of the corporation to meet the terms specified by the bond constitutes a default of obligations and exposes the corporation to legal proceedings and the consequences prescribed by law.

Financing through bank credit

Third, a corporation may negotiate a loan with a bank or other financial institution. The corporation and the lending institution negotiate the terms of the loan. Whereas a bond is usually for a long period of time, bank credit is usually short-term — up to three years, and frequently maturing within a year. The rate of interest that the corporation pays depends largely on the lending institution's evaluation of the degree of risk associated with the corporation. The rate of interest that banks charge their most credit-worthy corporate borrowers is called the **prime rate**.

> The prime rate is the interest rate charged to a financial institution's best customers.

Financing through shares

Fourth, a corporation may issue shares. When you buy shares in a company, you are actually buying part ownership in the corporation. As a part owner, you are entitled to a share of the profits, but you must also suffer any losses that may occur.

The capital raised by issuing bonds and by using bank credit is referred to as **debt capital**. The capital obtained from selling shares is called **equity capital**.

> Debt capital is acquired by issuing bonds or obtaining bank loans; equity capital is acquired from selling shares in the corporation.

SPECIALIZATION

The corporation makes large-scale production possible, and one of the reasons for efficiency in large-scale operations is the ability to take advantage of specialization. There are two main forms of specialization: specialization by occupation and specialization by task.

> Specialization may involve concentration on a particular occupation or task.

Specialization by occupation occurs when an individual specializes in a particular trade, occupation, or profession, instead of engaging in a number of separate occupations (generalizing). Occupational specialization is visible in the fact that some individuals are plumbers, some are farmers, some are college professors, some are sculptors, and some are doctors.

Specialization by task occurs when the production of a certain good is divided into a number of different tasks, and each worker performs one of these tasks. Adam Smith's description of the process of pin-making is such a vivid account of the process of specialization by task that we should look at the entire passage:

> One man draws out the wire, another straightens it, a third cuts it, a fourth grinds it at the top for receiving the head; to make the head requires two or three distinct operations; to put it on, is a peculiar business, to whiten the pins is another; it is even a trade by itself to put them into the paper; and the important business of making a pin is, in this manner, divided into about eighteen distinct operations, which, in some manufactories, are performed by distinct hands, though in others the same man will sometimes perform two or three of them.*

The assembly-line production method of the automobile industry is another classic example of specialization by task.

---

*Adam Smith, *The Wealth of Nations* (New York: The Modern Library, 1937), pp. 4–5

Advantages of specialization

The advantages of specialization are numerous. Consider two people, Simon Peter and Diana Nimrod. Simon fishes well, but hunts poorly. Diana hunts well, but fishes poorly.

1. Obviously, the combined output of both people will be larger if Simon concentrates (i.e., specializes) on fishing and Diana on hunting than if both fish and hunt individually. In general, specialization allows people to choose the jobs for which they are best suited.

2. Specialization saves time. It takes a great amount of time for a worker to acquire the skills for a new job even if that worker is exceptionally clever. It also takes a certain amount of time to change from one set of tools to another. Changeover time is eliminated by specialization.

3. Specialization maximizes the use of machines. Without specialization, tools and equipment would lie idle for considerable lengths of time. For example, if Diana Nimrod and Simon Peter do not specialize, then we would find that when Diana is hunting, her fishing tools would be idle, and when she is fishing, her hunting tools would be idle. The same would be true of Simon. It does not make good economic sense for each farmer, for example, to have his or her own flour mill, which would be idle for long periods, when milling can be concentrated in the hands of millers.

4. The repeated performance of a certain task causes performers to develop skills to increase their efficiency. Also, their general knowledge of their jobs is likely to increase with the length of time spent at the job.

Disadvantages of specialization

There can be little doubt that specialization has contributed significantly to increases in productivity. There are, however, some disadvantages associated with it:

1. Specialization restricts the sphere of competence of workers. Workers develop the skills necessary for the performance of their particular tasks or jobs, but have no competence in other areas.

2. Workers who are performing the same tasks day after day become bored. There is little scope for creativity, since after a while, jobs lose their challenge. Complaints from assembly-line workers that they are hardly more than machines are common.

3. Specialization implies a certain degree of interdependence. In the case of Diana Nimrod and Simon Peter, once they specialize, Diana must depend on Simon for fish while Simon must depend on Diana for venison. Thus, each will lose a certain amount of independence.

These disadvantages notwithstanding, we expect specialization to remain a permanent feature of industrial production.

INDUSTRIAL LOCATION

Up to this point, you have studied the various forms of business organization, the advantages and disadvantages of each type, the methods of financing available, and specialization in production. What we haven't yet considered, though, is that a businessperson might choose an appropriate form of business organization for a business enterprise, and the enterprise might be adequately financed, yet it still might fail to prosper if the location is inappropriate. The location of a business enterprise is of the utmost importance to the success of the operation. You should consider the understanding of industrial location an important aspect of your study of economics.

In the final analysis, the decision regarding industrial location will be guided primarily by cost considerations. In the production process, three distinct cost elements can be identified: the cost of obtaining raw material, the cost of manufacturing the product, and the cost of distributing the product to its users. These cost elements play an important part in determining where particular industries will be located. In the following sections, we will look at some of the factors that affect the location of particular industries.

DETERMINATION OF INDUSTRIAL LOCATION

The source of raw materials; availability of water, fuel, power, etc.; transportation; labour supply; population; and the political setting affect industrial location.

Many industries tend to be located near the source of raw materials used in the production process. This is particularly true in cases where the manufacturing process results in a substantial loss of weight between the raw materials and the finished products. Thus, we find sawmills in close proximity to timber, and fish canneries near the ocean.

Some industries require large supplies of water, fuel, or power. Such industries tend to be located where these supplies can be obtained at low cost. It is unlikely that a paper mill that requires a large supply of water for its operation will be located at a site where the water supply is inadequate. It is equally unlikely that a site with poor water supply will be chosen as the location for a brewery. The availability of fuel and electric power is also a crucial determinant of the location of many manufacturing industries.

Raw materials needed for production often have to be transported to the manufacturing site, and the outputs of the various industries certainly have to be transported to their users. It follows then that transportation plays an important role in determining the location of many industries. The existence of good roads, railways, water routes, and air service all feature prominently in the choice of the location for a plant.

The availability of labour is another important determinant of the location of some industries. Industries that require large amounts of labour tend to be located where labour is cheap and plentiful. In some cases, special skills may be required by the industry. If these skills are readily available in a certain area, the industry will tend to move into that area.

Certain industries tend to be located near the major markets for their products. Banks, bakeries, barber shops, and beauty salons are usually located close to their customers. Also of importance in determining the location of industries is the government's attitude toward industries. A heavy tax burden, for example, may discourage the establishment of some industries in certain areas, whereas a lenient tax structure may encourage their establishment.

A favourable political climate will tend to attract industries provided that other favourable factors exist. On the other hand, political uncertainty, fear of government takeover of certain businesses, and unwieldly tax burdens are likely to discourage the establishment of industries, and to encourage existing industries to relocate to areas where political conditions are more favourable.

PROBLEM SOLVING 7-4

In an attempt to reduce poverty, the Province of Esperanza sets its minimum wage well above that of any other province. Will this have any effect on industrial location?

CHAPTER SUMMARY

1. The single proprietorship, the partnership, and the corporation are the major forms of business organization. Single proprietors own and manage their businesses, enjoy the profits, and bear the losses. Single proprietors are fully liable for all debts incurred by their businesses and may lose all of their personal possessions if their businesses fail.

2. A partnership is a form of business organization in which two or more people own and operate a business. The partnership, like the sole proprietorship, has unlimited liability. In a limited partnership, however, some partners enjoy limited liability.

3. A corporation is a form of business organization in which a group of people (shareholders) agree to engage in business. The shareholders enjoy limited liability and the corporation is considered in law to be an entity apart from its owners.

4. A cooperative is a business owned by its members, who have only one vote each. The dividends of a cooperative are paid out to members in proportion to the amount of business that each one does with the cooperative. Cooperatives are classified as consumer cooperatives and producer cooperatives. They are also classified as purchasing cooperatives and marketing cooperatives.

5. Single proprietorships and partnerships are financed by funds that their owners are able to raise, or out of any profits that the business may make.

6. A corporation may be financed out of retained earnings, through bond issue, through bank credit, or through issuing shares. Financing through bonds or bank credit is called debt financing, while financing through issuing shares is called equity financing.

7. Specialization takes two main forms: specialization by occupation and specialization by task. Specialization has advantages and disadvantages, but the advantages generally far outweigh the disadvantages.

8. Some of the factors likely to affect the location of industries are: the proximity to raw materials; the availability of water, fuel, and power; transportation; labour availability; the market; and political factors.

GLOBAL PERSPECTIVE

Beer Brewing —On the Move Globally

Labatt and Molson are Canadian beers, Heineken is Dutch, and Coors, Budweiser, and Miller are American. Of course, through international trade, Canadians have been able to obtain beers brewed in other countries. If there is a very limited demand for Coors in Canada, it would not be cost efficient to establish a plant in Canada to brew Coors beer for a small market. Instead, it would make more sense for Canadians to simply import Coors from the United States.

Over the past thirty years or so, however, the beer brewing industry has become increasingly globalized, mainly because of increases in world demand for different types of beer. The main component of beer is water. The theory of industrial location suggests that if an industry uses large amounts of water, it makes good economic sense to set up the industry close to a good source of water supply. In the case of beer, this will significantly reduce shipping cost. Consequently, beer producers have entered into licencing agreements to brew each other's beer. For example, Molson produces Coors in Canada and Labatt produces Budweiser in Canada. Carlsberg, a Danish beer, is brewed in Canada by Labatt. Asahi, a Japanese company, brews Molson in Japan. Beer brewing is certainly on the move — globally.

TERMS FOR REVIEW

single (or sole) proprietorship (119)   bond (124)
partnership (120)   prime rate (125)
limited partnership (121)   debt capital (125)
corporation (121)   equity capital (125)
retained earnings (122)   specialization (by occupation,
limited liability (122)   by task) (125)
cooperative (123)

QUESTIONS FOR REVIEW AND DISCUSSION

1. Small, single-owner firms enjoy certain economic advantages. What are these advantages? Mention some industries in which you would expect small, single-owner firms to flourish. (L.O.1,2)

2. What are the major advantages and disadvantages of the single proprietorship? (L.O.2)

3. What are the advantages and disadvantages of the partnership? (L.O.2)

4. What considerations might cause a group of people to form a partnership? (L.O.1,2)

5. What is a limited partnership? What are its advantages? (L.O.1,2)

6. Discuss the advantages and disadvantages of the corporation. (L.O.2)

7. What methods are available to a corporation for raising capital? Briefly discuss each method. (L.O.3)

8. What is the difference between: debt capital and equity capital? (L.O.3)

9. What are the advantages and disadvantages of the cooperative? (L.O.2)

10. What is the difference between: (L.O.1)

    (a) a consumer cooperative and a producer cooperative?

    (b) a purchasing cooperative and a marketing cooperative?

11. What is the difference between specialization by occupation and specialization by task? (General)

12. Name some advantages and disadvantages of specialization. (General)

13. "The political climate is an important determinant of industrial location." Discuss this statement. (L.O.5)

14. What are the major determinants of industrial location? (L.O.5)

PROBLEMS AND EXERCISES

1. What type of business organization would you consider most suitable for each of the following types of businesses? Give reasons for your choice. (L.O.1)

    (a) a corner newspaper stand

    (b) a small confectionery shop

    (c) a firm producing men's clothes on a large scale

    (d) a small accounting firm

    (e) a hotel chain

    (f) a firm producing computers for the world market

2. You currently earn $75 000 per year. You own shares in Bell Canada. Would you prefer to receive annual dividends from Bell or would you prefer those earnings to be reinvested by Bell? (General)

3. What form of business organization is implied by each of the following situations? (L.O.1)

   (a) You invest $50 000 of your money to start a business and hire three people to work for you.

   (b) You and your old college buddy invest $50 000 each to start a business, with an agreement that you will divide the profits equally among you. You and your buddy manage the business and hire ten people to work for you.

   (c) You invest $50 000 of your money and borrow $20 000 from your friend to start a business. You manage the business and hire your friend and five other people as your employees.

   (d) You discuss a business idea with four of your friends. They like your idea, so you and your four friends apply for and obtain a charter from the federal government for your business. To raise the capital, you sell 500 shares at $200 per share. You manage the business and hire ten people to work for you.

   (e) You believe that prices at the college bookstore are too high so you call a meeting of the student body. At the meeting, you agree to form an association consisting of members of the student body who pay $50 each to join the association. With the proceeds, you establish The Student Bookstore to sell books to the student members. You employ members of the association to run the bookstore. (L.O.1)

4. A business enterprise can raise capital by equity financing or by debt financing. For each of the following, use D to indicate debt financing and E to indicate equity financing. (L.O.3)

   (a) The firm issues 1000 shares at $50 a share.

   (b) The firm sells $2 000 000 worth of bonds with a ten-year maturity date.

   (c) The firm borrows $50 000 from a bank and uses its building as collateral.

   (d) The owner of the firm borrows $10 000 from a friend and agrees to pay 10% interest on the loan.

5. Outline how you would go about establishing a department store on the principle of a cooperative. How would you convince people to join the cooperative? (L.O.1,2)

6. Choose four industries in your area or province and suggest explanations for the location of each. (L.O.5)

 7. Talk with two or three members of your class about a business venture. The discussion should lead to a determination of a business enterprise that your group could establish. Write down the details of the venture:

   (a) name of business;

   (b) product or service to be offered;

   (c) your main customers;

   (d) location;

   (e) capital required;

   (f) who will manage it;

   Draw up a partnership agreement for the business venture.

Internet Site

http://www.strategis.ic.gc.ca
This is the Web site for Industry Canada. It contains all kinds of valuable information on and for businesses in Canada.

INTERNET EXERCISE

1. Go to the Industry Canada Web site.
2. List four ways a small-business owner could use this site.
3. List four types of information that a consumer could get from this site.

CHAPTER 8

THEORY OF PRODUCTION

That roundabout methods lead to greater results than direct methods is one of the most important and fundamental propositions in the whole theory of production.

Eugen von Bohm-Bawerk, *Positive Theory of Capital*

INTRODUCTION

It is via the production process that resources are converted into consumer and producer goods and services. It is worth noting that production is not limited to manufacturing. It includes other activities such as providing consulting services, transportation, and banking services. A warehouse operator who stores goods so that they can be available for distribution when needed is involved in production, just as is the car manufacturer who uses labour, machines, and materials to produce automobiles.

A firm is the unit that trans-forms inputs into outputs.

The **firm** may be defined as the business enterprise involved in producing goods and services. The goods and services produced may be consumer goods and services such as microwave ovens and banking services, or they may be inputs such as steel and bricks to be used by other firms. The firm may be organized as a sole proprietorship, a partnership, a corporation, or a cooperative. Although some firms produce more than one product, we assume here that the firm produces only one type of product such as computer software or photo albums. In this chapter, you will study the principles of production. The firm buys factors of production (inputs) and through the production process, transforms these inputs into outputs for sale to other firms and to consumers. In Chapter 6, we noted that the entity that makes decisions about consumption is the consumer or household. In the case of the firm, the decision-maker may be the **entrepreneur** (sole owner) or a hired manager. Technically, it is the owner who has final responsibility for actions taken by the firm, for the owners are the risk-takers.

An entrepreneur organizes factors of production to produce a good or service.

THE OBJECTIVES OF THE FIRM

Learning Objective 1:
the objectives of the firm

In economic theory, it is assumed that the firm seeks to maximize its profits.

In order to analyze the firm's behaviour and to predict what course of action it will take under various circumstances, we must pinpoint its goal. In economic theory, we assume that the firm seeks to maximize its profits. The firm's profits may be defined as the difference between its revenues (that is, its receipts from the sale of its products) and its costs. Symbolically,

$$\pi = TR - TC$$

where π is profit, TR is total revenue, and TC is total cost.

Other objectives that a firm may pursue are sales maximization, public image, and the welfare of consumers.

The assumption of profit maximization has come under attack from economists and non-economists alike. Critics of the profit maximizing assumption claim that firms pursue objectives other than profit maximization. These critics do agree that a certain profit level must be achieved to provide earnings for the firm's owners. Once this level is reached, however, they feel that the firm pursues other objectives including maximizing sales, public image, and the satisfaction and general welfare of consumers. It has also been suggested that these other objectives are merely avenues through which the firm may maximize profits in the long run. Despite the criticisms of the profit maximizing assumption, we will take this assumption to be correct. The profit maximizing assumption has enabled economists to analyze and predict the behaviour of firms with a great degree of success.

PROBLEM SOLVING 8-1

If the only objective of a firm is to maximize its profits, will it discriminate against workers on the basis of sex or race in its hiring practices?

ECONOMIC EFFICIENCY VERSUS TECHNOLOGICAL EFFICIENCY

Learning Objective 2:
economic efficiency and technological efficiency

The method that is technically most efficient is the one that uses the fewest inputs.

One of the basic decisions that the firm has to make pertains to the method of production. Usually, there are several ways of combining the factors of production in order to produce a given output. The method that uses the least inputs is said to be the most technically efficient. The concept of **technical** or **technological efficiency** is illustrated by Table 8.1. Suppose A, B, and C are three methods by which 10 000 shirts per week can be produced. Method B uses more labour and more capital than method A and method C do. Method B is therefore technically least efficient.

TABLE 8.1	Method	Capital	Labour	Output per week (shirts)
Technological efficiency.	A	100	500	10 000
	B	180	900	10 000
	C	50	800	10 000

The method that is economically most efficient is the one with the lowest cost.

But what of methods A and C? Method A uses more capital than method C does but, at the same time, uses less labour than method C does. Both methods are technically efficient. How does the firm choose between methods A and C? The firm could choose the method that has the lower cost — that is, the method that is **economically more efficient**. In order to determine whether A or C has the lower cost, we must know the prices of the factors of production — in this case, the prices of capital and labour.

Suppose the prices of capital and labour are $40 and $5 respectively. We can compute the cost associated with each method as follows:

$$C_a = (100 \times \$40) + (500 \times \$5) = \$6500$$

$$C_c = (50 \times \$40) + (800 \times \$5) = \$6000$$

where C_a is the cost associated with method A, and C_c is the cost associated with method C. Given the above prices, method C is economically more efficient than method A.

Now suppose the prices were $20 for capital and $10 for labour. The cost associated with each method would be as follows:

$$C_a = (100 \times \$20) + (500 \times \$10) = \$7000$$

$$C_c = (50 \times \$20) + (800 \times \$10) = \$9000$$

In this case, method A would be economically more efficient than method C. Note also that a method that is technically inefficient is also economically inefficient. To choose the economically most efficient method is to choose from among technically efficient methods the one with the lowest cost.

ECONOMIC EFFICIENCY RATIOS

We can easily determine the most economically efficient method when the output produced by all methods is the same, as in the previous example. In that case, we need only compare costs. If, however, we are confronted with different costs for different output levels, then the problem of deciding on the most economically efficient method becomes a bit more difficult. In what follows, we assume that the demand for the product is given.

Economic efficiency ratio: the ratio of the value of the output to the cost of the inputs.

To choose the most economically efficient method in situations involving different costs and different output levels, we can use the concept of the **economic efficiency ratio**, which is defined as follows:

$$EER = \frac{\text{value of output}}{\text{cost of input}}$$

where EER represents the economic efficiency ratio. The higher the economic efficiency ratio, the more efficient the method.

Now, consider Table 8.2. Let us assume that the prices of capital and labour are given as $20 and $10 respectively. The values of the inputs, using methods A and C, have already been calculated as $7000 and $9000 respectively.

TABLE 8.2

Production methods with varying output levels.

Method	Capital	Labour	Output per week (shirts)
A	100	500	10 000
C	50	800	11 000

If we assume that the price of a shirt is $5, then the value of the output from method A is $50 000 (10 000 × $5). The value of the output from method C is $55 000 (11 000 × $5).

$$EER \text{ (method A)} = \frac{50\ 000}{7000} = 7.1$$

$$EER \text{ (method C)} = \frac{55\ 000}{9000} = 6.1$$

Since method A has a higher economic efficiency ratio, it is economically more efficient than method C. In method A, for every $1 of input, the firm receives $7.10 in output. In method C, for every $1 of input, the firm receives $6.10 in output.

PROBLEM SOLVING 8-2

You are contemplating going into business to produce pen-holders. You are faced with the methods of producing pen-holders shown in Table 8.3. The prices of capital and labour are $5 and $6 respectively, and the market price of pen-holders is $10. Which method should you choose?

TABLE 8.3

Production methods for pen-holders.

Method	Capital	Labour	Output
1	10	6	24
2	15	2	25

PRODUCTION RUNS OR PERIODS

Learning Objective 3: production runs or periods

Quantities of fixed production factors cannot be varied quickly, quantities of variable factors are more easily adjusted.

In the short run, the firm has at least one fixed factor.

The firm's decisions about the efficient use of existing equipment and the expansion or contraction of its scale of operation can be grouped into short-run and long-run decisions respectively. In order to define the short run and the long run, it is necessary to examine the nature of the firm's inputs. These inputs or productive factors are classified into fixed and variable factors. **Fixed factors** are those whose quantities cannot be varied within the period under consideration. Those productive factors whose quantities can be varied are called **variable factors**. A firm's fixed factors may be its land and its capital equipment. Its variable factors may be labour and raw materials.

The **short run** is defined as a situation in which the firm has at least one fixed factor of production. The short run is such that the firm does not have sufficient time to vary

In the long run, the firm has only variable factors.

all of its inputs. The **long run** is a situation in which the firm is able to vary all of its factor inputs. There are no fixed productive factors in the long run. As an example, consider the following case. You are operating a small photocopy business with two photocopy machines in a rented space near your college or university. After three years, you decide to get out of the photocopy business and move on to some more lucrative pursuit. Your lease on the space has just expired but you have two photocopy machines, which you cannot get rid of for three weeks. Since it will take you three weeks to get out of the business, then the short run for you would be any time within three weeks. After three weeks, you are able to vary all your inputs — in this case getting rid of your machines — so your long-run situation would be any time after three weeks. The definitions of the short run and the long run and the example just given make it quite clear that these time horizons (the short run and the long run) do not correspond to any definite periods of calendar time. In some industries, the short run may be quite long, while in others, the long run may be quite short. For example, the long run may be only a few hours for a shoe shine business, but it may be several years for a business such as a public utility.

THE PRODUCTION FUNCTION

The production function is a technically determined relationship between inputs and output.

Learning Objective 4: the production function

Economists use the term **production function** to refer to the relation between the firm's inputs and its output of goods and services. To simplify the analysis, we shall discuss a production scenario in which there are only two factors of production: labour and land. Furthermore, we shall assume that land is a fixed factor while labour is a variable factor, and that all workers are equally efficient. This technical or engineering relation between the firm's inputs and its output may be expressed as follows:

$$Q = Q(L, \bar{T})$$

where Q represents output, L represents the quantity of labour, and T represents the fixed quantity of land. The bar over the T indicates that T is fixed. Since there is a fixed factor, this production function is a short-run production function. Table 8.4 shows how output varies as units of labour are added to a fixed quantity of land.

TOTAL, MARGINAL, AND AVERAGE PRODUCT

TOTAL PRODUCT

Total product: total output per period of time.

Learning Objective 5: total, marginal, and average product

Total product (TP) refers to the total output of the firm per period of time. Column two of Table 8.4 shows how output changes with variations in the quantity of the variable factor (labour in this case). Note that as the number of units of the variable factor increases, total product increases, reaches a maximum of 144 units when eight or nine units of labour (workers) are hired, and then declines as more workers are hired.

If all workers are assumed to be equally efficient, you would expect that each additional worker would contribute equally to total output. In the example in Table 8.4, the first worker hired added 15 units of output per week. You would probably expect the second worker to add another 15 units per week, but instead, that worker added 19 units. Why? One worker alone cannot take advantage of specialization and the division of labour. But when the second worker is hired, there can be some specialization and division of labour that result in increased productivity.

	Units of variable factor (per week)	Total product (units per wk.)	Marginal product (units per wk.)	Average product (units per wk.)
TABLE 8.4	0	0		
			15	
Relation between inputs and output (hypothetical data).	1	15		15
			19	
	2	34		17
			23	
	3	57		19
			31	
	4	88		22
			22	
	5	110		22
			16	
	6	126		21
			14	
	7	140		20
			4	
	8	144		18
			0	
	9	144		16
			−4	
	10	140		14
			−19	
	11	121		11
			−25	
	12	96		8

MARGINAL PRODUCT

Marginal product of a variable factor is the extra output obtained by using one more unit of the variable factor.

Marginal product (MP) is the change in total product resulting from using an additional unit of the variable factor. We can express marginal product as follows:

$$MP = \frac{\Delta Q}{\Delta L}$$

where L is the quantity of labour, and Q is the total product or output. Table 8.4 shows that the first unit of labour causes output to increase by 15 units. Thus the marginal product is 15. Another unit of labour increases total output from 15 units to 34 units, thus the marginal product at that point is 19. Values of the marginal product are given in column three of Table 8.4. Note that the values of the marginal product are placed in between the lines on which the total product values are placed. Special attention will be paid to the behaviour of marginal product as the quantity of the variable input is increased.

AVERAGE PRODUCT

Average product is the output per unit of the variable factor.

Average product (AP) is total product divided by the number of units of the variable factor. That is, average product is simply the total output per unit of the variable factor. We can express average product symbolically as

$$AP = \frac{Q}{L}$$

Values of the average product are calculated and recorded in column four of Table 8.4. Note that the average product rises, reaches a maximum at 22 units of output when four or five workers are hired, and then diminishes as more workers are hired.

The relation between total, average, and marginal products can also be illustrated graphically, as shown in Figure 8.1. Part A shows the total product curve while part B shows the average and marginal product curves. The two diagrams are lined up in order to emphasize the relation between the three curves. The relation between marginal product and total product, and that between marginal product and average product are set out below.

FIGURE 8.1

Total, average, and marginal products.

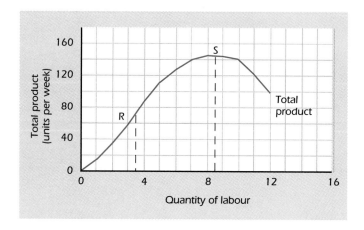

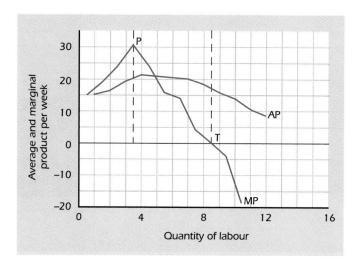

RELATIONS BETWEEN MARGINAL PRODUCT AND TOTAL PRODUCT

1. When the marginal product is rising, the total product increases at an increasing rate. In Part B of Figure 8.1, the marginal product rises to point P, and the total product shown in Part A increases at an increasing rate to point R.

2. When the marginal product is positive, the total product is increasing. This is necessarily so since the marginal product is the change in total product as an additional unit of the variable factor is employed. If this number is positive, then the total product must increase. In Table 8.4 and Figure 8.1, the marginal product is positive up to the point when the eighth worker is hired; hence, total product increases up to that point. Note, however, that when the marginal product is positive but declining

(between points P and T in Part B), total product increases at a diminishing rate (between points R and S in Part A).

3. When the marginal product is negative, the total product falls. This is necessarily so since a negative number is being added to the total product; that is, some quantity is being taken away from the total product. In Table 8.4 and Figure 8.1, total product begins to decline after the employment of the ninth unit of labour. At that point, the marginal product is negative.

4. When the marginal product is zero, the total product ceases to rise, but does not fall either. It has reached its maximum. In Table 8.4 and Figure 8.1, this occurs at an output of 144 units when nine units of labour are used.

RELATIONS BETWEEN MARGINAL PRODUCT AND AVERAGE PRODUCT

To help you to understand and remember the relationship between marginal product and average product, think of the marginal product as a magnet that pulls the average product to it.

1. When marginal product is greater than average product, average product will rise. In Table 8.4 and Figure 8.1, this is the case until the addition (employment) of four workers. Note that when the marginal product curve is above the average product curve, it pulls the average product curve up. To illustrate this relation further, let us consider a case to which you can easily relate. If, in a class of 30 economics students, the average mark on an economics examination is 69%, and a new student enters the class and gets a mark of 77%, the new mark (the marginal mark), being higher than the class average, will pull up the class average. As another example, suppose your final grade is based on four examinations written during the term. You have written three examinations and your average is 70%. Your mark on the fourth examination will be the marginal mark of the fourth examination. If your mark on the fourth examination is better than 70%, your average will increase. In the same way, a marginal product curve that is higher than the average product curve pulls up the average product curve.

2. When marginal product is less than average product, average product will fall. This can be seen in Table 8.4 and Figure 8.1 after the employment of the fifth worker. Note that in Figure 8.1, when the marginal product curve is below the average product curve, the average product curve falls. Can you explain why? Consider what would happen to your average grade if the mark of your fourth examination was under 70%.

3. When marginal product is equal to average product, average product is at its maximum. The marginal product curve shown in Figure 8.1 cuts the average product at the maximum point on the average product curve. In Table 8.4, this occurs when the average product is 22 units and between four and five units of labour are employed.

THE LAW OF DIMINISHING RETURNS

As increasing amounts of a variable factor are added to a fixed factor, a point will be reached where the marginal product diminishes.

Learning Objective 6: the law of diminishing returns

Our observation of the short-run behaviour of total product as units of a variable factor are added to a fixed factor has given rise to a famous hypothesis in economics that has been called the **law of diminishing returns**. This law may be stated as follows:

> **As additional quantities of a variable factor are added to a given quantity of fixed factors, after a point the marginal product will diminish.**

The point of diminishing marginal productivity occurs at the level of output at which the marginal product is at a maximum. In Figure 8.1, it occurs at point P. This means that after that point, the increase in output will diminish. The point of diminishing average productivity occurs at the level of output at which the average product is maximal. Maximum average product occurs when average product is 22 units in Table 8.4, and at point Q in Figure 8.1.

Observe that the law of diminishing returns states what will happen to physical returns rather than what will happen to monetary returns. In other words, the law deals with a physical rather than a monetary phenomenon. The existence of the law of diminishing returns presents a constant challenge to humankind to find more efficient ways of production.

A P P L I C A T I O N

The Effectiveness of Advertising

The principle of diminishing marginal returns has numerous applications, one of which will be considered in this section. Let us consider an advertising message — a commercial — prepared for radio. If the same message is heard repeatedly, it may be effective, but after a while, its impact may diminish, i.e., diminishing returns may set in. To counteract this, advertisers and sponsors tend to use different versions of the script and vary the voice or voices used to convey the message. By so doing, they may actually increase the effectiveness of the advertising message.

EFFICIENCY IN THE USE OF INPUTS

Earlier in this chapter, we used cost to define economic efficiency. The most economically efficient method is the one with the lowest cost for a given output level. In this section, we will discuss the firm's choice of inputs. The problem faced by the firm is similar in many ways to the problem faced by the consumer in deciding how to allocate a given amount of money among various commodities.

Learning Objective 7: efficiency in the use of inputs

To simplify our analysis, let us assume that the firm purchases only two factors of production: labour and capital. The firm's objective is to maximize its profits. It will therefore seek to produce any given level of output at the lowest possible cost. To minimize cost, the following condition must be satisfied:

$$\frac{MP_K}{P_K} = \frac{MP_L}{P_L}$$

where MP_K is the marginal product of capital, that is, the extra output obtained by using an additional unit of capital; MP_L is the marginal product of labour, that is, the extra output obtained by using an additional unit of labour; P_K is the price of capital; and P_L is the price of labour.

Compare the above condition with the condition for utility maximization discussed in Chapter 6. Obviously, if the last dollar spent on capital, that is

$$\frac{MP_K}{P_K}$$

causes output to increase by 15 units, and the last dollar spent on labour, that is

$$\frac{MP_L}{P_L}$$

causes output to increase by only six units, then it would benefit the firm to purchase more capital and less labour, provided that labour and capital are substitutable. On the other hand, if the last dollar spent on capital causes output to increase by a lesser amount than the increase in output resulting from an extra dollar spent on labour, that is, if

$$\frac{MP_K}{P_K} < \frac{MP_L}{P_L}$$

then the firm would benefit by purchasing more labour and less capital. It follows that the firm will be in the best position (minimizing its costs) when

$$\frac{MP_K}{P_K} = \frac{MP_L}{P_L}$$

We can also express this cost-minimizing condition as

$$\frac{MP_K}{MP_L} = \frac{P_K}{P_L}$$

The least-cost combination of inputs is achieved when the ratio of the marginal products equals the ratio of input prices.

In other words, the optimum input mix for the firm occurs when the ratio of the marginal product of capital to the marginal product of labour equals the ratio of the price of capital to the price of labour. This is another example of the equimarginal principle introduced earlier in this text.

THE PRINCIPLE OF SUBSTITUTION

Learning Objective 8: the principle of substitution

To minimize cost the firm will tend to use more of the cheaper factor and less of the more expensive factor.

If capital is cheap relative to labour, and the two are substitutable, the firm will tend to use more capital and less labour. But if labour is cheap relative to capital, then the firm will tend to use more labour and less capital. This tendency for the firm to substitute the cheap factor for the more expensive factor is known as the **principle of substitution** and may be stated as follows:

If two factors of production are substitutable and the price of one rises relative to the price of the other, the firm will tend to use less of the more expensive factor, substituting the less expensive factor for it.

The principle of substitution relates to the cost-minimizing condition of the firm:

$$\frac{MP_K}{P_K} = \frac{MP_L}{P_L}$$

If the price of capital (P_K) falls, then

$$\frac{MP_K}{P_K} > \frac{MP_L}{P_L}$$

In order to maintain the cost-minimizing condition, the firm will use more capital. This then causes MP_K to fall and MP_L to rise, thus restoring equality between the two ratios. It should be noted that in the short run, the firm may not be able to substitute one factor for another, or may be able to do so only to a limited extent. In the long run, substitution of factor inputs is less difficult.

GLOBAL PERSPECTIVE

Productivity Among the Major Industrial Countries

A common and useful method of measuring productivity is output per worker. It is informative to know how labour productivity has changed in Canada over time, and how the Canadian experience compares with those of other countries. This capsule and the following table give us a global perspective of labour productivity.

Labour productivity among the major industrial countries, 1980-89 and 1990-99

1980-89		1990-99	
Country	Annual percent change	Country	Annual percent change
France	4.1	Germany	4.6
Italy	4.0	France	4.0
United Kingdom	3.9	U.S.A.	3.0
Japan	3.0	Italy	2.7
U.S.A.	2.8	United Kingdom	2.4
Germany	2.6	Canada	1.7
Canada	1.7	Japan	1.5

Source: International Monetary Fund, *World Economic Outlook*, May 1998: 158.

Between 1980 and 1989, the average annual change in labour productivity in Canada was 1.7%. Of all the major industrial countries (the so-called G-7 countries), Canada had the unenviable position of last place in terms of changes in labour productivity. It is important to understand that here we are talking about *changes* in productivity rather than *levels* of productivity. France had the highest annual average change (4.1%) during that period.

For the period 1990-99, Germany took sole possession of first place with an average annual change in labour productivity of 4.6%, while Canada, still with 1.7%, was second to last. Germany was second to last in the 1980-89 period with 2.6%. Japan fell from fourth place in the 1980-89 period (3.0%) to last place with 1.5% in the 1990-99 period. The United States jumped from fifth place in the 1980-89 period with 2.8% to third place in the 1990-99 period with 3.0%.

CHAPTER SUMMARY

1. The firm buys factor inputs and transforms them into output. The decision-maker for the firm is the entrepreneur, and the objective of the firm is to maximize its profits.

2. Technological efficiency refers to the use of inputs in physical terms, while economic efficiency refers to the use of inputs in terms of cost.

3. The method that is technologically most efficient is the one that uses the fewest inputs. The method that is economically most efficient is the one with the lowest cost.

4. The short run defines a situation in which the firm is unable to vary all its factor inputs. The long run is a situation in which the firm can vary all its inputs. These terms do not equate with any particular periods of calendar time.

5. The relation between a firm's inputs and its output of goods and services is called the production function.

6. The average product of a variable factor is total product divided by the quantity of the variable factor.

7. The marginal product of a variable factor is the change in total output or product resulting from using one more unit of the variable factor.

8. The law of diminishing returns states that, as additional quantities of a variable factor are added to a given quantity of fixed factors, the marginal product will diminish after a point. This law is a short-run phenomenon. It deals with the behaviour of physical output rather than monetary returns.

9. We can obtain the least-cost combination of inputs by equating the ratio of the marginal product of the factors to the ratio of their prices.

10. The principle of substitution states that if the price of a factor of production rises relative to the price of another factor, the firm will tend to substitute the less expensive factor for the more expensive factor.

TERMS FOR REVIEW

firm (133)
entrepreneur (133)
technical (technological)
  efficiency (134)
economic efficiency (134)
economic efficiency ratio (134)
fixed factors (135)
variable factors (135)

short run (135)
long run (136)
production function (136)
total product (136)
marginal product (137)
average product (137)
law of diminishing returns (139)
principle of substitution (141)

QUESTIONS FOR REVIEW AND DISCUSSION

1. Which of the following would you consider to be a firm and why? (General)
   (a) a Manitoba farmer
   (b) the Tizoc Driving School
   (c) a small private radio station
   (d) a college teachers' union

2. Economic theory assumes that the objective of the firm is to maximize its profits. How are profits calculated? What criticisms have been made about the profit-maximizing assumption? (L.O.1)

3. What other objectives besides profit maximization might firms pursue? (L.O.1)

4. What is the difference between technological efficiency and economic efficiency? (L.O.2)

5. What is the difference between:
   (a) the long run and the short run?
   (b) fixed factors and variable factors?
   Give examples of fixed factors and variable factors. (L.O.3)

6. What is meant by a short-run production function? (L.O.4)

7. Describe the behaviour of total product when marginal product is: (L.O.5)
   (a) positive;
   (b) negative;
   (c) positive but falling.

8. Describe the behaviour of average product when marginal product is: (L.O.5)

    (a) greater than average product;

    (b) equal to average product;

    (c) less than average product;

    (d) falling.

9. "Diminishing returns may be in operation even when total product is rising." Explain. (L.O.6)

10. Explain the law of diminishing returns. How does this law pertain to rapid population growth? (L.O.6)

11. Explain how a firm decides on its use of inputs in order to minimize cost. (L.O.7)

12. What is the principle of substitution? What is the relation between the cost-minimizing condition and the principle of substitution? (L.O.7,8)

PROBLEMS AND EXERCISES

1. Table 8.5 shows units of labour and capital required to produce 100 units of output. (L.O.2)

TABLE 8.5	Combination	Labour	Capital	Output
Combinations of labour and capital required for 100 units of output.	A	8	15	100
	B	9	20	100
	C	6	20	100

   (a) Which of these methods is technically inefficient and why?

   (b) If labour costs $3 per unit and capital $5 per unit, which method is economically most efficient?

   (c) If the price of labour doubles while the price of capital remains the same, which method will be economically most efficient?

2. Referring to the problem on page 135, if the price of capital changes to $6 and the price of labour changes to $5, which method would you choose? (L.O.2)

3. (a) Given the production schedule in Table 8.6, compute the marginal products of the variable factor.

   (b) Does this production schedule depict diminishing returns? (L.O.5,6)

TABLE 8.6	Units of fixed factor	Units of variable factor	Total product
Production data.	20	0	0
	20	1	25
	20	2	45
	20	3	60
	20	4	70
	20	5	75

4. The Zodiac Production Company has the production schedule shown in Table 8.7. (L.O.5,6)

TABLE 8.7	Capital	Labour	Output
Production data for Zodiac Production Company.	30	0	0
	30	1	10
	30	2	30
	30	3	45
	30	4	55
	30	5	63
	30	6	68
	30	7	68
	30	8	63
	30	9	58

(a) Does the production schedule for Zodiac depict diminishing returns?

(b) Compute average and marginal product schedules for labour.

(c) On a graph, plot the total product curve.

(d) On another graph, just below the total product curve (as in Figure 8.1), plot the marginal and average product curves.

5. A firm uses two variable inputs, labour and capital, to produce its output. The price of labour is $2 per hour and the price of capital is $5 per hour. The production schedules for the firm are set out in Table 8.8. (L.O.5,7)

	Labour			Capital		
	Quantity per hr.	TP per hr.	MP_L per hr.	Quantity per hr.	TP per hr.	MP_K per hr.
TABLE 8.8						
Production data.	0	0		0	0	
	1	20		1	25	
	2	30		2	40	
	3	38		3	50	
	4	43		4	55	
	5	45		5	55	
	6	45		6	50	

(a) Complete the table by filling in the marginal product of labour and the marginal product of capital columns.

(b) If the firm wants to spend $9 per hour on labour and capital, how much of each should it purchase?

(c) How should the firm allocate a total cost of $30 between labour and capital in order to minimize production cost?

6. Table 8.9 shows variations in output as units of a variable factor are added to a fixed factor. (L.O.5)

TABLE 8.9	Units of variable factor	Total product	Marginal product	Average product
	0	0		
	1	12		
	2	30		
	3	51		
	4	68		
	5	80		
	6	84		
	7	84		
	8	80		
	9	72		

Production data.

(a) Complete the table by filling in the marginal and average product columns.

(b) Use graph paper and plot the marginal and average product curves on the same diagram.

(c) Locate the maximum point on the average product curve and label it M. Compare the values of the average product and the marginal product at that point.

7. Visit a local manufacturing plant and observe the production process in the plant. Describe the product or service that is produced (the output) and then write an account of the production process, including a statement of the inputs (factors of production) used in the process. Identify both fixed and variable factors. State whether the technology used is labour intensive or capital intensive, and try to find out whether the production technology has changed over the past ten years.

Internet Site

http://www.statcan.ca
The Statistics Canada site contains useful data on virtually all aspects of the Canadian economy and society.

INTERNET EXERCISE

1. Go to the Statistics Canada Web site.
2. Click on *Canadian Statistics*.
3. Click on the *Economy in Detail*.
4. Click on *Manufacturing and Construction, Employment*.
5. List three industries that had fewer employees in 1997 than in 1993.
6. List three industries that had more employees in 1997 than in 1993.
7. What year saw the biggest increase in the number of employees in all industries?

CHAPTER 9

THE COSTS OF PRODUCTION

Learning Objectives

After studying this chapter, you should be able to:

1 analyze costs in the short run

2 describe the relations between marginal cost and marginal product, and between average variable cost and average product

3 analyze costs in the long run

4 understand returns to scale

5 understand economies of scope

In calculating the expenses of production of a commodity, we must take account of the fact that changes in the amounts produced are likely, even when there is no new invention, to be accompanied by changes in the relative quantities of its several factors of production.

Alfred Marshall, *Principles of Economics*

INTRODUCTION

The cost function is a relation between cost and output.

In Chapter 8, you studied how a firm decides on the various quantities of inputs to purchase in order to produce a certain volume of output. The relationship between the firm's inputs and its output is one aspect of the information that the firm needs in order to decide on the optimum level of output. The other aspect needed is information on the relationship between costs and output. When a firm increases its output, it uses more resources (labour, space, material, etc.), and it thus incurs greater costs. It follows that the benefits from increases in production must outweigh the additional costs of greater production in order for firms to have an incentive to increase output. This chapter examines the relation between a firm's costs of production and its volume of output. This relation is often referred to as the firm's **cost function**, which may be expressed as

$$C = C(Q)$$

where C represents cost and Q represents output. The firm incurs costs by engaging in production. There is therefore a close relationship between production and cost. This chapter highlights that close relationship.

THE FIRM'S COSTS

An explicit cost is a direct outlay. An implicit cost is an opportunity cost where no direct payment is made to anyone outside the firm.

Cost may be defined as payments for the factors of production that the firm uses to produce goods and services. These payments include wages and salaries, rent for land and buildings, expenditures for raw materials, fuel and electricity, and taxes. Costs of this nature are called **explicit costs**. In addition to these direct business outlays, the firm may use its own resources. In this case, a cost is incurred although no direct payment is made to anyone outside the firm. Such costs are known as **implicit costs** or *imputed costs*, and must be taken into account when calculating the firm's costs.

An example of an implicit cost is provided by the case of Cyril, the worm-seller who served his customers from his garage. Cyril incurred a cost by using his garage as a store. This cost can be estimated by invoking the concept of opportunity cost. In this case, the opportunity cost would be the best possible alternative use to which Cyril could put his garage. Suppose a man chooses to work on his farm instead of accepting paid employment elsewhere at a salary of $15 000 per year. The implicit cost of working on his farm is $15 000.

To further illustrate the concept of implicit cost, suppose that Peter Bright invests $100 000 of his own money to start the Bright Look Company. The money is used to purchase machines. Suppose Peter could have earned 8% interest annually by leaving his money in the bank. Then at the end of the year, Peter should include $8 000 (i.e., 8% of $100 000) as a part of his costs (implicit cost of capital). Moreover, during the year, Peter's machines would have suffered a certain amount of wear and tear through use. This **depreciation** or loss of value of the machines also represents an implicit cost and should be considered as a part of the cost of capital.

Depreciation is the loss in value of capital stock over time.

Business managers and accountants tend to focus on explicit costs. Economists believe, however, that decisions should be based on considerations of total cost, both explicit and implicit.

PROBLEM SOLVING 9-1

You decide to go into house painting for the summer months. You spend $50 to place an advertisement in the local newspaper. You use your own car to transport your tools. You spend $550 for paint, brushes, rollers, etc. At the end of the summer, your total receipts from your painting business amount to $2000. Did you make a profit?

COSTS IN THE SHORT RUN

In the short run, the firm has both fixed costs and variable costs.

Learning Objective 1: analyze costs in the short run

Some costs incurred by the firm affect its decisions in the short run while others do not. For example, the decision to increase output by a few extra units may require only that the firm hires more workers and uses more raw materials without adding to its existing stock of machines. For this reason, a distinction is made between these two types of costs. The firm's total cost (TC) consists of total fixed costs (TFC) and total variable costs (TVC):

$$TC = TFC + TVC$$

Fixed (overhead) costs do not vary with output.

Fixed costs are those costs that do not change as output changes. These costs remain the same whether the firm produces a little or a lot. They are incurred even if the firm temporarily suspends its operation. Examples of fixed costs are insurance costs, interest payments on borrowed money, certain taxes (property taxes, for example), rental payment on factory building, and management salaries. In common business language, fixed costs are referred to as **overhead costs**. Fixed costs apply only to the short run because fixed factors of production exist only in the short run.

Variable costs depend on the volume of output.

Variable costs are those costs that change with the volume of output. Examples of variable costs are payments for raw materials, labour costs, fuel, and depreciation associated with production. In other words, variable costs are the operating costs of production. Variable costs are incurred both in the short run and in the long run.

AVERAGE COST

Average cost or average total cost (ATC) is the sum of average fixed cost and average variable cost.

For many purposes, it is important to know the firm's average cost; that is, cost per unit of output. **Average cost** (AC) or **average total cost** (ATC) is total cost divided by the number of units produced. Thus, if Q represents the quantity of output produced, we can define average total cost as follows:

$$ATC = \frac{TC}{Q}$$

Average total cost (also called unit cost) consists of average fixed cost (AFC) and average variable cost (AVC):

$$ATC = AFC + AVC$$

Average fixed cost (AFC) is total fixed cost divided by the number of units produced.

Average fixed cost (AFC) is total fixed cost divided by the number of units produced. Symbolically,

$$AFC = \frac{TFC}{Q}$$

Average variable cost (AVC) is total variable cost divided by the number of units produced.

Average variable cost (AVC) is total variable cost divided by the number of units produced. That is,

$$AVC = \frac{TVC}{Q}$$

Note that we can obtain average total cost by dividing each component of total cost by quantity, as follows:

$$TC = TFC + TVC$$

$$ATC = \frac{TC}{Q} = \frac{TFC}{Q} + \frac{TVC}{Q}$$

$$ATC = AFC + AVC$$

MARGINAL COST

Another cost concept that we shall use quite frequently is marginal cost (MC). **Marginal cost** is the extra or additional cost incurred by producing an additional unit of output. Accountants and business executives often use the term **incremental cost** when referring to marginal cost. Symbolically,

$$MC = \frac{\Delta TC}{\Delta Q}$$

The marginal cost concept is similar to the marginal utility concept discussed in Chapter 6 and the marginal product concept discussed in Chapter 8. For example, if the total cost of producing nine units of output is $200, and the total cost of producing 10 units is $220, then the marginal cost of increasing output by 10 units (that is, the extra cost of producing one more unit) is $20. The various cost concepts are summarized below, and the relation between them is illustrated in Table 9.1.

SUMMARY OF COST CONCEPTS

TC = total cost

ATC = average total cost

TFC = total fixed cost

TVC = total variable cost

AFC = average fixed cost

AVC = average variable cost

MC = marginal cost

$$TC = TFC + TVC$$

$$ATC = \frac{TC}{Q} = \frac{TFC}{Q} + \frac{TVC}{Q}$$

$$ATC = AFC + AVC$$

$$MC = \frac{\Delta TC}{\Delta Q}$$

The various levels of output produced per period of time are given in column one of Table 9.1. Column two shows the firm's total fixed cost. This amount ($200 in the example) remains unchanged for any level of output. Note that even when the firm produces no output at all (Q = 0), it still has to pay for its fixed factor inputs. Total variable cost is given in column three. Total variable cost rises continuously as output expands: from $400 for the first unit to $15 000 for 12 units of output. In order to produce a greater quantity of output, the firm must use more of its variable inputs (more labour, more raw materials, etc.) so its total variable cost increases. Column four shows total cost, which is obtained by adding total fixed cost and total variable cost. Total cost rises continuously because total variable cost rises continuously with increasing output.

Figure 9.1 shows total cost, total fixed cost, and total variable cost curves. The total fixed cost curve (TFC) is a horizontal straight line, indicating that total fixed cost is constant at $200 for any level of output. The total variable cost (TVC) curve rises continuously with increasing output. The total cost (TC) curve is obtained by adding the total fixed cost curve to the total variable cost curve. Since the total fixed cost curve is a horizontal straight line, the total cost curve will have the same shape as the total variable cost curve but will lie above the total variable cost curve. The vertical distance between the TC curve and the TVC curve at any level of output is the TFC.

Column five of Table 9.1 shows the average fixed cost of the firm, which is obtained by dividing column two by column one. Average variable cost is given in column six and is obtained by dividing column three by column one. Column seven, the average total cost column, is obtained by adding average fixed cost to average variable cost. Alternatively, column seven may be obtained by dividing column four by column one. Column eight gives marginal cost, which can be obtained from column three or from column four. Can you see why?

TABLE 9.1

Hypothetical cost data for a firm.

Quantity of output (units) (1)	TFC ($) (2)	TVC ($) (3)	TC ($) (4)	AFC ($ per unit) (5)	AVC ($ per unit) (6)	ATC ($ per unit) (7)	MC ($ per unit) (8)
0	200	0	200	—	—	—	
							400
1	200	400	600	200.00	400.00	600.00	
							200
2	200	600	800	100.00	300.00	400.00	
							100
3	200	700	900	66.67	233.33	300.00	
							100
4	200	800	1 000	50.00	200.00	250.00	
							300
5	200	1 100	1 300	40.00	220.00	260.00	
							400
6	200	1 500	1 700	33.33	250.00	283.33	
							700
7	200	2 200	2 400	28.57	314.28	342.85	
							800
8	200	3 000	3 200	25.00	375.00	400.00	
							1 000
9	200	4 000	4 200	22.22	444.44	466.66	
							2 000
10	200	6 000	6 200	20.00	600.00	620.00	
							4 000
11	200	10 000	10 200	18.18	909.09	927.27	
							5 000
12	200	15 000	15 200	16.67	1 250.00	1 266.67	

FIGURE 9.1

Total cost curves.

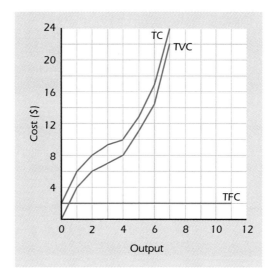

Figure 9.2 shows the relation between average fixed cost (AFC), average variable cost (AVC), average total cost (ATC), and marginal cost. The average fixed cost curve declines continuously as output expands. This is so because as output expands, the fixed cost is spread over more and more units of output. The average variable cost curve first declines, reaches a minimum at point K, and then rises. The average total cost curve also declines

FIGURE 9.2

Average and marginal
cost curves.

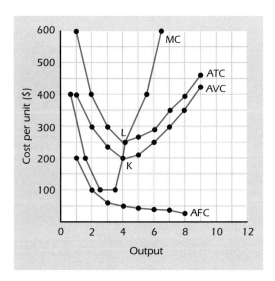

The marginal cost curve
cuts the average variable
cost curve and the average
total cost curve at their
minimum points.

at first, reaches a minimum at point L, and then rises thereafter. The marginal cost curve falls and then rises as output increases.

Note that the rising marginal cost curve cuts the average variable cost curve and the average total cost curve at their minimum points. It is easy to see why this is so: If the marginal cost is less than the average cost, the average cost will fall. If the marginal cost is greater than the average, the average cost will rise. When the marginal cost equals the average cost (at the point of intersection), the average cost ceases to fall and is about to rise. The average cost must therefore have reached its lowest point at its intersection with the marginal cost. Note also that the average variable cost reaches its minimum point at a lower level of output than the average total cost does. This is so because of the effect of the falling AFC, which is added to AVC to obtain ATC.

The relations between marginal cost and average cost are conveniently summarized below. Remember the magnetic effect of the marginal on the average — the marginal pulls the average to it like a magnet.

RELATIONS BETWEEN MC AND AVC

1. When MC < AVC, AVC will fall (the marginal pulls the average down). This occurs over the range of output from zero to four units in the example in Figure 9.2.

2. When MC > AVC, AVC will rise (the marginal pulls the average up). This occurs over the range of output from five units and above.

3. When MC = AVC, AVC will neither rise nor fall; it will be at its minimum. This occurs somewhere between the fourth and fifth units of output.

RELATIONS BETWEEN MC AND ATC

1. When MC < ATC, ATC will fall.

2. When MC > ATC, ATC will rise.

3. When MC = ATC, ATC will be at its minimum.

RELATIONS BETWEEN MC AND MP, AND BETWEEN AVC AND AP

Learning Objective 2:
describe the relations between marginal cost and marginal product, and between average variable cost and average product

By this time, you might have concluded intuitively that a relation exists between marginal product and marginal cost. Let us explore this relation. In Table 9.2, we present hypothetical cost and product data. Let us assume that each additional unit of the variable factor (for example, each worker, if the variable factor is labour) is hired at a constant price of $5 per unit of time. The marginal cost per unit of extra output is simply the extra cost ($5) divided by the extra output (marginal product) contributed by the worker. Thus, provided that the marginal product of each additional worker is rising, the marginal cost of each additional unit will fall.

TABLE 9.2

Hypothetical cost and product data.

Quantity of varia-ble factor (workers)	Total product (units per week)	Marginal product (units)	Average product (units)	Marginal cost per unit of ex-tra output	AVC per unit of extra output
0	0		—		—
		5		1.00	
1	5		5		1.0
		7		0.71	
2	12		6		0.83
		9		0.56	
3	21		7		0.71
		7		0.71	
4	28		7		0.71
		6		0.83	
5	34		6.8		0.74
		4		1.25	
6	38		6.3		0.79
		2		2.50	
7	40		5.7		0.88

In Table 9.2, the marginal product of the first worker is five, but the extra cost of hiring this worker is $5, so the marginal cost per unit of extra output is $5/5 = $1. The marginal product of the second worker is seven, but the extra cost of hiring that worker is again $5, so the marginal cost per unit of extra output is $5/7 = $0.71. The other marginal cost values are obtained in a similar manner.

Note, however, that after the third worker is hired, diminishing returns set in. Since the marginal product is now falling, the marginal cost rises.

Given the price of a variable factor, increasing marginal product (increasing returns) implies decreasing marginal cost; and diminishing marginal product (diminishing returns) implies increasing marginal cost.

These relations are illustrated graphically in Figure 9.3. Similar relations that exist between the average product and the average variable cost are also shown in Figure 9.3.

SUMMARY OF RELATIONS

The marginal cost and average variable cost curves are mirror reflections of the marginal product and average product curves.

The following six points provide a convenient summary of the relations discussed in this section.

1. When marginal product rises, marginal cost falls.

2. When marginal product falls, marginal cost rises.

FIGURE 9.3

Relations between marginal product and marginal cost, and average product and average variable cost.

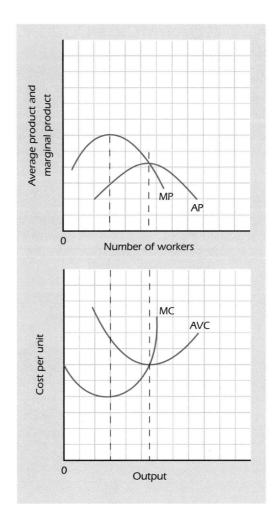

3. When marginal product is at its maximum, marginal cost is at its minimum.

4. When average product rises, average variable cost falls.

5. When average product falls, average variable cost rises.

6. When average product is at its maximum, average variable cost is at its minimum.

COSTS IN THE LONG RUN

Learning Objective 3:
analyze costs in the long run

In the long run, all the firm's inputs are variable, therefore all its costs are variable.

Up to this point in our analysis, we have concentrated on the situation in which the firm had at least one fixed factor of production; our analysis dealt with a firm in the short run. We now turn our attention to the situation where the firm is able to vary all of its factor inputs; our analysis now turns to the firm in the long run.

In the long run, all of the firm's factors of production can be varied. In this situation, the firm has no fixed factors of production, and hence no fixed costs. The firm is in a position to be able to make any adjustment to the size of its plant and to its scale of operation that it deems necessary. The profit-maximizing firm will, of course, choose the minimum cost for each level of output.

FIGURE 9.4

Short-run cost curves of three plants.

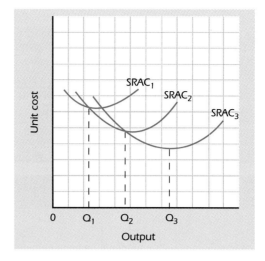

To illustrate how the firm chooses in the long run, let us assume that the firm has three plants of different sizes. Figure 9.4 shows the short-run average cost curves of the three plants, and allows us to compare the average cost of producing any given level of output in each of the three plants. $SRAC_1$ is the short-run average cost curve for plant 1, $SRAC_2$ is the short-run average cost curve for plant 2, and $SRAC_3$ is the short-run average cost curve for plant 3. If the firm contemplates an output of less than Q_1 units, it will choose plant 1. This is so because plant 1 has the lowest average cost at that output level. If the firm contemplates an output between Q_1 and Q_2, it will choose plant 2. For an output level greater than Q_2, the firm will choose plant 3, which evidently has the lowest average cost at that level of output.

The firm will choose the plant size that minimizes cost for any desired output level.

For any desired level of output then, the firm will choose the plant size for which the average cost is lowest. In Figure 9.4, we have assumed that the firm has only three plant sizes from which to choose. Let us assume instead, that the firm has an infinite number of plants of different sizes from which to choose. Figure 9.5 illustrates this situation.

FIGURE 9.5

Derivation of the long-run average cost curve.

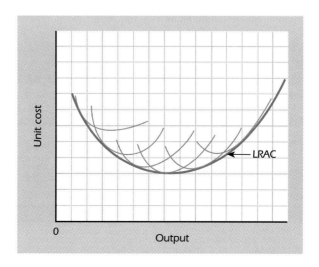

Here, several short-run cost curves appear. The firm's long-run average cost (LRAC) curve is tangent to the infinite number of short-run average cost curves. For this reason, the LRAC curve is sometimes called the **envelope curve** — geometrically, the LRAC curve envelops the SRAC curves.

Note that when the LRAC curve is falling, the points of tangency lie to the left of the minimum points of the SRAC curves. When the LRAC curve is rising, the points of tangency lie to the right of the minimum points of the SRAC curves. A firm's long-run average cost is the lowest cost per unit at which the firm can produce a given level of output in a situation where the firm can vary all its factors. Figure 9.6 shows a long-run average cost curve without the associated short-run average cost curves.

An envelope curve is a firm's long-range average cost curve.

Long-run average cost: the lowest cost per unit at which a firm can produce a given level of output when it can vary all its inputs.

FIGURE 9.6

Long-run average cost curve.

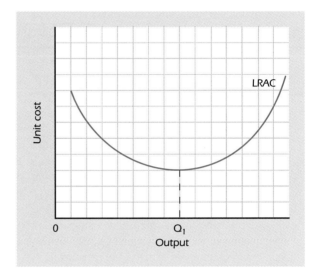

RETURNS TO SCALE

You will recall that in Chapter 8 you studied how a firm's total output will respond when increasing quantities of a variable input are added to a fixed input. There, we discussed the law or principle of diminishing returns. In this section, we shall discuss how a firm's total output responds to changes in all its inputs. You will now study the following cases: increasing returns to scale, constant returns to scale, and decreasing returns to scale.

INCREASING RETURNS TO SCALE

Learning Objective 4: understand returns to scale

Increasing returns to scale: a more-than-proportional increase in output resulting from an increase in all inputs.

If a firm increases all of its factors of production by some proportion (that is, its entire scale of operation) and as a result, increases its output proportionately more than it increases its factors of production, we say that the firm operates under conditions of **increasing returns to scale**. If we assume that factor (input) prices remain unchanged, increasing returns to scale imply that unit cost is falling.

The relation between increasing returns to scale and unit long-run cost can be illustrated as follows. For simplicity, let us assume that the firm uses only two factors of production: labour (L) and capital (K). Let us assume further that the price of labour is $2 per unit of time, the price of capital is $1 per unit of time, and the firm uses three units of labour and two units of capital to produce one unit of output. In this case, when the firm doubles all its inputs, its output more than doubles. In fact, its output triples. This is precisely the meaning of increasing returns to scale. Production and cost information are shown in Table 9.3. Note that long-run average cost falls from $8 to $5.33.

	Inputs		Output (units)	Total Cost ($)	Long-run average cost ($)
L		**K**			
3		2	1	8	8/1 = 8
6		4	3	16	16/3 = 5.33

TABLE 9.3

Production, cost, and increasing returns to scale.

Economies of scale: the decline of average cost as the firm's scale of operation expands.

As a consequence of this relation, the terms *increasing returns to scale* and *decreasing costs* are often used synonymously. Figure 9.7 shows decreasing costs or increasing returns to scale as the downward-sloping section of the long-run average cost curve. The firm enjoys increasing returns to scale over the range of output from 0 to Q_1. We say that a firm operating under conditions of decreasing cost enjoys **economies of scale**.

FIGURE 9.7

Long-run average cost curve showing returns to scale.

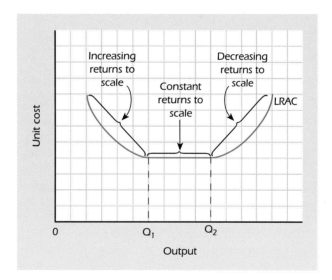

CONSTANT RETURNS TO SCALE

Constant returns to scale: a proportional increase in output resulting from an increase in all inputs.

A firm operates under **constant returns to scale** if an increase in all of its inputs results in a proportional increase in output. Constant returns to scale imply that unit long-run cost remains unchanged as output increases. Consider the information given in Table 9.4. In this case, as the firm doubles its inputs, its output also doubles. Note that long-run average cost remains unchanged at $8. Figure 9.7 illustrates the case of constant returns to scale. The firm operates under constant returns to scale over the range of output from Q_1 to Q_2.

The level of output at Q_1 has some significance. At this level of output, increasing returns to scale are exhausted and constant returns to scale begin. At a level of output less than Q_1, the firm is not taking full advantage of economies of scale, and there are no economies of scale to be gained at any level of output beyond Q_1. The level of output at which economies of scale end and constant returns to scale begin (Q_1 in Figure 9.7) is referred to as the firm's **minimum efficient scale**.

Minimum efficient scale: the level of output at which economies of scale end.

| TABLE 9.4 | Inputs | | Output | Total Cost | Long-run average |
	L	K	(units)	($)	cost ($)
Production, cost, and constant returns to scale.	3	2	1	8	8/1 = 8
	6	4	2	16	16/2 = 8

DECREASING RETURNS TO SCALE

Decreasing returns to scale: a less-than-proportional increase in output resulting from an increase in all inputs.

If an increase in all of the firm's inputs results in a less-than-proportional increase in the firm's output, then the firm is experiencing **decreasing returns to scale**. Decreasing returns to scale imply increasing long-run average cost. This situation is illustrated in Table 9.5.

| TABLE 9.5 | Inputs | | Output | Total Cost | Long-run average |
	L	K	(units)	($)	cost ($)
Production, cost, and decreasing returns to scale.	3	2	1	8	8/1 = 8
	6	4	1.5	16	16/1.5 = 10.67

Diseconomies of scale: a situation in which long-run costs rise as output increases.

In this case, when the firm doubles its inputs, the resulting output is less than double. Note also that long-run average cost is illustrated graphically in Figure 9.7 by the rising portion of the long-run average cost (LRAC) curve. The firm faces increasing costs over the range of output beyond Q_2. At any point beyond Q_2, **diseconomies of scale** are said to be in effect.

REASONS FOR INCREASING AND DECREASING RETURNS TO SCALE

Increasing returns to scale may result from specialization, large volume purchasing, and the greater efficiency of larger plants.

Constant returns to scale would seem to be the normal condition to expect. If one plant can produce 500 units of output per day, then two plants of the same type should produce 1000 units per day. In fact, many firms do experience constant returns to scale over certain ranges of output.

But why do increasing returns to scale and decreasing returns to scale occur? Increasing returns to scale may result from specialization, which may not be practical in a small-scale operation. Also, decreasing cost may result from the firm's ability to purchase inputs in large quantities and thus take advantage of quantity discounts for which smaller orders may not qualify. For these reasons, larger plants tend to be more efficient than smaller ones (at least up to a point), so the firm may enjoy decreasing costs as it expands its operation. The reason generally given for increasing costs is inefficiency in management. As the size of the operation grows, management becomes more complex and the decision-making process becomes ensnared in red tape.

Decreasing returns to scale are due largely to management inefficiency.

ECONOMIES OF SCOPE

In our discussion of the costs of production up to this point, we have assumed that the firm produces only one product or service. In fact, many firms produce more than one product. One firm may produce radios, televisions, VCRs, and other electronic goods. The

Learning Objective 5:
understand economies
of scope

Economies of scope exist
when the costs of produc-
tion are less for producing
different goods together
than they would be if produced separately.

production of audio tapes might affect the cost of producing videotapes since there might be some common elements in the production of both.

When the costs of production fall by producing a set of different goods together rather than separately, **economies of scope** are said to exist. This explains why we find certain firms producing several different but closely related products at the same time. We should not at all be surprised to find the same firm producing refrigerators, washers, dryers, air-conditioning units, dishwashers, ovens, and even vacuum cleaners.

A P P L I C A T I O N

Two Ways to Reduce Unit Cost

Knowledge of the behaviour of cost can help a firm to reduce unit cost. If increasing returns to scale exist, then the firm may reduce unit cost by increasing output. That is, it may take advantage of economies of scale. But it may also be able to lower its long-run average cost curve. For example, as the workers gain experience and learn to perform their respective functions with greater proficiency, the average cost curve will shift downward. This is one of the great benefits of training, and it explains why firms are willing to spend hundreds of thousands of dollars in providing training for their employees.

G L O B A L   P E R S P E C T I V E

Unit Labour Cost: An International Comparison

In this chapter, emphasis was placed on the costs of production. For most industries, the cost of labour con-stitutes the biggest cost. Rapidly rising labour cost has been known to present severe problems for many firms, and many companies have been influenced by labour costs when making decisions about the location of their plants.

This capsule compares unit labour costs in manu-facturing in seven industrial countries. The average annual change between 1990 and 1999 is used as the index for comparison. Over the period under consider-ation, unit labour costs grew fastest in the U.K., among the seven countries selected (see the accompanying table). The values for Germany and France were nega-tive. The average annual growth rate of unit labour cost in Canada over the 1990-99 period was 0.8%. In Italy it was relatively high at 2.6%.

Unit labour cost

Country	Unit Labour Cost (%)
Canada	0.8
United States	0.7
Japan	1.4
Germany	–0.7
France	–0.3
Italy	2.6
United Kingdom	3.1

Source: International Monetary Fund, *World Economic Outlook,* May 1998. Washington, D.C., 1998: 158.

CHAPTER SUMMARY

1. The firm incurs costs by purchasing and using factors of production to produce its output of goods and services.

2. The cost function is the relation between cost and the quantity of output produced.

3. Explicit costs are those costs for which direct payment is made for factor inputs. Implicit costs or imputed costs are those costs for which no direct payment is made since the resources are already owned by the firm.

4. The firm's total cost in the short run consists of fixed costs and variable costs. Fixed costs are those costs incurred even if the firm suspends its operation temporarily. Variable costs are the costs that change with the level of output.

5. Average total cost is total cost divided by the number of units produced. Average fixed cost is total fixed cost divided by the number of units produced. Average variable cost is total variable cost divided by the number of units produced. Average total cost is the sum of average fixed cost and average variable cost.

6. Marginal cost or incremental cost is the extra cost incurred by producing an extra unit of output.

7. Total fixed cost does not vary with the volume of output produced. Total cost and total variable cost rise as the volume of output increases.

8. Average fixed cost declines continuously; average variable cost and average total cost first decline, reach a minimum, and then rise. Marginal cost cuts average variable cost and average total cost at their minimum points.

9. Increasing marginal product implies decreasing marginal cost, and diminishing marginal product implies increasing marginal cost. Similar relations exist between average product and average variable cost.

10. In the long run, the firm has only variable costs since it has no fixed inputs.

11. The long-run average cost is the lowest unit cost at which the firm can produce a given level of output in a situation where the firm is able to vary all its inputs.

12. Increasing returns to scale (also known as decreasing costs) exist when an increase in all the inputs leads to a more-than-proportional increase in output. Increasing returns to scale are illustrated by the downward sloping portion of the long-run average cost curve.

13. Constant returns to scale exist when an increase in all the inputs results in a proportional increase in output. Constant returns to scale are illustrated by the flat (horizontal) portion of the long-run average cost curve.

14. The minimum efficient scale for a firm occurs at the level of output at which economies of scale are exhausted and constant returns to scale begin.

15. Decreasing returns to scale (also referred to as increasing costs) exist when an increase in all the inputs leads to a less-than-proportional increase in output. Decreasing returns to scale are illustrated by the upward-sloping portion of the long-run average cost curve.

16. Economies of scope refer to the gain in economic efficiency that results from producing different products together rather than separately.

TERMS FOR REVIEW

cost function (148)
explicit costs (148)
implicit costs (148)
depreciation (148)
fixed (overhead) costs (149)
variable costs (149)
average cost (149)
average total cost (ATC) (149)
average fixed cost (AFC) (149)
average variable cost (AVC) (149)

marginal (incremental) cost (150)
envelope curve (156)
increasing returns to scale (156)
economies of scale (157)
constant returns to scale (157)
minimum efficient scale (157)
decreasing returns to scale (158)
diseconomies of scale (158)
economies of scope (159)

QUESTIONS FOR REVIEW AND DISCUSSION

1. What do economists mean by the term *cost function*? (General)

2. Distinguish between explicit costs and implicit costs. (General)

3. What is the difference between fixed costs and variable costs? Give an example of a cost that is likely to be fixed and one that is variable. (L.O.1)

4. Your family plans to open a gas station along the Trans-Canada Highway. Make a list of possible cost items for the operation of this business, then state which ones are fixed and which ones are variable. (L.O.1)

5. What is the relation between (L.O.1)

   (a) marginal cost and average cost?

   (b) marginal cost and total cost?

6. Explain why the average fixed cost curve declines continuously. (L.O.2)

7. State the relation between (L.O.2)

   (a) marginal product and marginal cost.

   (b) average product and average variable cost.

8. Explain each of the following terms: (L.O.3)

   (a) increasing returns to scale;

   (b) constant returns to scale;

   (c) minimum efficient scale;

   (d) decreasing returns to scale.

9. What is the difference between diminishing returns and decreasing returns to scale? (L.O.3)

10. What reasons can you give for the existence of decreasing costs? (L.O.3)

11. Distinguish between economies of scale and economies of scope. (L.O.4,5)

PROBLEMS AND EXERCISES

1. Table 9.6 shows cost data for a firm. (L.O.1)

TABLE 9.6		Q	TFC	TVC	TC	AFC	AVC	ATC	MC
Cost data for a firm.		1	100	25					
		2	100	40					
		3	100	48					
		4	100	60					
		5	100	80					
		6	100	108					
		7	100	140					
		8	100	192					
		9	100	270					
		10	100	380					
		11	100	550					
		12	100	780					

(a) Complete the table by filling in the remaining five columns.

(b) On graph paper, plot curves for the average fixed cost, the average variable cost, the average total cost, and the marginal cost.

(c) At what levels of output does the marginal cost curve cut the average variable cost curve and the average total cost curve? Compare these levels with the output levels at which the average variable cost curve and the average total cost curve reach a minimum.

2. You are given the data contained in Table 9.7 for Providex Ltd. (L.O.1)

TABLE 9.7	Output	AFC ($)	AVC ($)
Cost data for Providex, Ltd.	0	—	—
	1	20.00	30.00
	2	10.00	28.00
	3	6.67	27.00
	4	5.00	26.00
	5	4.00	24.00
	6	3.33	23.00
	7	2.86	24.00
	8	2.50	26.00
	9	2.22	29.00
	10	2.00	32.00

Calculate each of the following at each level of output.

(a) TFC

(b) TVC

(c) MC

3. Use your answer from Question 2 above to graph the TFC, TVC, and TC curves for Providex. (L.O.1)

4. A firm has total fixed costs amounting to $400. Draw the firm's average fixed cost curve for output ranging from one unit to eight units. (L.O.1)

5. The cost data in Table 9.8 are for the Excelcom Corporation. (L.O.1)

	Output	TC	MC	TVC	ATC	AVC
TABLE 9.8	0	60				
	1	65				
Cost data for Excelcom	2	70				
Corporation.	3	75				
	4	80				
	5	85				
	6	96				
	7	112				
	8	136				
	9	162				
	10	190				

(a) Compute MC, TVC, ATC, and AVC and fill in the appropriate columns.

(b) Compute AFC values for Excelcom.

(c) Graph Excelcom's AFC, AVC, ATC, and MC curves all on the same diagram.

6. A textbook publisher finds that at an output of 10 000 books, its average fixed cost (per book) is $5. What will the firm's average fixed cost be if it increases its output to 15 000 books? (L.O.1)

7. The Unipro Company uses labour as its only variable input. Table 9.9 shows production data for Unipro. The wage rate is $5 per hour. (L.O.1)

	Number of workers	Total product units
TABLE 9.9	0	0
	1	15
Production data for	2	25
Unipro.	3	33
	4	38
	5	42
	6	44

(a) Compute total variable cost for the range of output indicated.

(b) Compute Unipro's AVC for each level of output indicated.

(c) Plot Unipro's AVC curve.

8. Table 9.10 shows short-run cost schedules for the production of T-shirts, using three different plant sizes. (L.O.1,3)

	Plant 1		Plant 2		Plant 3	
TABLE 9.10	Q	AC	Q	AC	Q	AC
	10	20	10	30	10	35
Short-run cost	20	18	20	25	20	32
schedules for the	30	17	30	16	30	23
production of T-shirts.	40	19	40	13	40	16
	50	25	50	12	50	13
	60	40	60	18	60	10
	70	65	70	27	70	15
	80	102	80	46	80	25
	90	150	90	78	90	45

(a) For what output range should the firm use plant 1?

(b) For what output range should the firm use plant 2?

(c) For what output range should the firm use plant 3?

(d) On the basis of the information given in Table 9.10, complete a table of the firm's long-run cost schedule for Q from 10 to 90 in increments of 10.

9. How would economic efficiency be affected if General Electric (a company that produces a wide variety of products) were broken up into a number of companies, each producing only one product? Explain your answer. (L.O.4,5)

10. A hypothetical small firm manufactures plastic clips used largely in the furniture industry. The firm employs 10 workers and pays rent of $12 000 annually for its facilities. The owner-manager is concerned about the rising costs of production. Make up a list of possible causes of the increase in cost and recommend steps that may be taken to reduce cost in this firm.

CHAPTER

THE PURELY COMPETITIVE FIRM

Learning Objectives

After studying this chapter, you will be familar with:

1 market structures

2 short-run output decisions in a purely competitive firm

3 the purely competitive firm's short-run supply curve

4 the short-run industry supply curve

5 long-run equilibrium and adjustment

6 the importance of the purely competitive model

Monopoly, besides, is a great enemy to good management, which can never be universally established but in consequence of that free and universal competition which forces everybody to have recourse to it for the sake of self-defence.

Adam Smith, *Wealth of Nations*

INTRODUCTION

In Chapter 8, you studied the aspects of the firm's behaviour that deal with its choice of inputs, and in Chapter 9, you studied how the firm's production costs are related to its volume of output. These are all aspects of supply. In this chapter, you will study yet another aspect of supply — supply under perfect competition. The aspect of supply that we will now study deals with the firm's pricing and output decisions under specific market conditions. The firm's pricing and output decisions depend, to a great extent, on the characteristics of the market within which the firm operates. This chapter focuses mainly on the behaviour of a firm in a purely competitive industry.

MARKET STRUCTURES

Learning Objective 1:
market structures

Market structures, such as pure competition and monopoly, affect pricing and output decisions.

An industry is a group of firms producing similar products.

The term **market structures** refers to certain market characteristics that influence the firm's pricing and output behaviour. These market characteristics define, in part, the environment within which the firm operates. In discussing market structures, you will find the concept of the industry quite useful. An **industry** is defined as a group of firms producing similar products. A firm that is the only one in an industry will most likely behave quite differently from a firm that is just one among many in the industry.

Different markets have different characteristics, but economists have managed to group these characteristics into four broad categories of market structures. These market structures are:

1. pure or perfect competition

2. monopoly

3. monopolistic competition

4. oligopoly

Imperfect competition includes monopolistic competition and oligopoly.

As you will see shortly, pure competition and monopoly are at opposite ends on a continuum of market structures (see Table 10.1). Between these polar opposites are monopolistic competition and oligopoly, which, together with monopoly, are frequently referred to by economists as **imperfect competition**. We shall deal with each of these market structures in turn.

PURE COMPETITION

Pure (perfect, atomistic) competition is a market structure characterized by a large number of firms, homogeneous products and freedom of entry and exit.

A price taker is a firm that, by itself, cannot affect the market price of its product.

The market structure termed **pure competition** or **perfect competition** is defined by the following characteristics:

1. The market consists of a large number of firms — so many of them that no single firm has any control over the price of its product. The purely competitive firm is therefore a **price-taker**. Each firm produces such a small fraction of the total output of the product that output will not be noticeably affected by one firm producing and selling as much as it can or by ceasing production. Because each firm represents such a tiny fraction of the industry, the term **atomistic competition** is sometimes used to define pure competition.

   Farming, the stock market, and international money markets are usually cited as good examples of perfect competition. It is not easy to find many other good examples of purely competitive markets in the real world. Even in the case of agriculture, government programs influence the price at which the farmers sell their products. Pure competition, therefore, does not really exist in these markets.

2. The products of the firms are homogeneous or standardized. Because the products are identical, buyers have no preference for purchasing from one firm rather than from another.

3. There is freedom of entry into and exit from the industry. There are no entry or exit barriers, so resources are perfectly mobile in and out of the market.

4. Buyers know the price charged by each firm. If one firm attempts to charge a price higher than the market price, it will lose all of its customers.

Note: When a distinction is made between pure competition and perfect competition, the distinguishing feature is that in perfect competition, consumers have perfect knowledge regarding the prices charged by the firms in the market. In our analysis, we will make no distinction between pure competition and perfect competition; the two terms may be used interchangeably.

It is important to note that in order for competition to exist in a market, only two features are essential. These are: numerous sellers (firms), and freedom of entry and exit. The conditions for the existence of pure competition are therefore more restrictive in scope than the conditions for competition.

MONOPOLY

A monopolized market or monopoly is an industry with a single firm producing a product that has no close substitutes.

In contrast to a purely competitive market, a **monopolized market** is one that is dominated by a single firm. A **monopoly** exists when there is one firm in an industry producing a good or service that has no close substitutes. The firm in monopoly has significant control over the price that it charges for its product. The entry of other firms into the industry is precluded by a variety of barriers. Ontario Hydro, Hydro-Québec, and Bell Canada (to some degree) are examples of monopolies.

MONOPOLISTIC COMPETITION

Monopolistic competition exists when there is a large number of firms selling differentiated products.

Monopolistic competition is a market structure consisting of a large number of firms, each selling a differentiated product and exerting some slight influence on the market price. Price differences are likely to be small among products sold by firms in monopolistic competition because, although consumers acknowledge differences among the products, they perceive these differences as minor. For example, many different stores sell clothing, and we do observe differences in price as we move from one store to the next. Not very often, however, do we observe startling differences in the prices of suits of similar quality.

OLIGOPOLY

Oligopoly exists when there are few interdependent firms in the industry.

Oligopoly is a market structure in which there are only a few sellers. Since each firm in this situation usually produces a substantial portion of the total output of the industry to which it belongs, it will take account of the policies and strategies adopted by its rivals. A firm in an oligopoly situation has considerable influence on the price of its product. If the firms happen to agree to act as a group to control price and output, their influence increases substantially. Examples of oligopolistic firms are those in the automobile industry, the brewing industry, and the tobacco industry. The four largest firms in each of these industries produce over 90% of the total output of these industries. Table 10.1 illustrates the spectrum of market structures with their major characteristics.

We shall analyze the behaviour of the purely competitive firm in the remaining sections of this chapter. Pure competition is one of the best known and most widely used models in economics. It is also one of the most widely criticized. The following two chapters will discuss the behaviour of firms in the other market structures. In Chapter 4, we saw how the price of a product is determined in a purely competitive market. We shall now study in some detail the behaviour of a purely competitive firm seeking to maximize its profits.

TABLE 10.1	Pure competition	Monopolistic competition	Oligopoly	Monopoly
Market structures and their characteristics.	Large number of firms	Large number of firms	Few firms	Only one firm
	Identical products	Differentiated products	Similar or differentiated products	Product has no close substitutes
	No barriers to entry and exit	Freedom of entry and exit	Some barriers to entry	Effective barriers to entry
	No control over market price	Small control over market price	Substantial control over price	Significant control over price

PROBLEM SOLVING 10-1

Can you expect a single firm in a purely competitive industry to advertise its product?

THE SHORT-RUN OUTPUT DECISION IN A PURELY COMPETITIVE FIRM

A purely competitive firm must decide on the level of output that will maximize its profits.

Recall that a purely competitive firm has no control over the price at which it sells its output. Since the firm in pure competition must accept the market price as a given, such a firm must determine only what level of output to produce in order to maximize its profits. Actually, there are two ways in which a firm can determine the level of output that will earn maximum profits: the total cost/total revenue method and the marginal method. These two methods will be discussed in turn.

THE TOTAL COST/TOTAL REVENUE APPROACH TO PROFIT MAXIMIZATION

Learning Objective 2: short-run output decisions in a purely competitive firm

Profit is the difference between total revenue and total cost. If TR > TC, then $\pi > 0$; if TR = TC, then $\pi = 0$; and if TR < TC, then $\pi < 0$. To maximize its profits, the firm can choose that level of output at which the difference between total revenue and total cost is greatest. The procedure for calculating maximum profit is outlined in Table 10.2.

Column one of Table 10.2 shows various levels of output. The price of the product is $10, as shown in column two. Total revenue in column three is obtained by multiplying price by quantity of output. Column four gives total cost, and column five, the total profit column, is obtained by subtracting column four from column three. As we can see from the table, total profit is at a maximum when the firm produces an output level of seven or eight units.

We can also illustrate the total cost/total revenue approach to profit maximization diagrammatically. Figure 10.1 plots the cost and revenue data shown in Table 10.2. The firm's total revenue (TR) is represented by a straight line through the origin. If there is no output, there will be no revenue. As output expands, total revenue rises in proportion to the increase in output — given a fixed price. Total cost rises as output expands. The profit-maximizing output appears where the difference between total revenue and total cost (TC) is greatest.

	Output (units) (1)	Price ($) (2)	Total revenue ($) (3)	Total cost ($) (4)	Profit ($) (5)
TABLE 10.2	1	10	10	30	−20
	2	10	20	35	−15
Hypothetical revenue,	3	10	30	39	−9
cost, and profit	4	10	40	41	−1
data for a purely	5	10	50	44	6
competitive firm.	6	10	60	49	11
	7	10	70	56	14
	8	10	80	66	14
	9	10	90	80	10
	10	10	100	95	5

FIGURE 10.1

Total revenue and total cost.

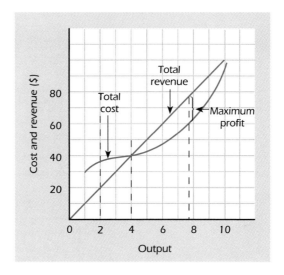

THE MARGINAL APPROACH TO PROFIT MAXIMIZATION

Learning Objective 2: short-run output decisions in a purely competitive firm

Marginal revenue is the additional revenue received from selling one more unit of output.

The firm maximizes profits when it produces a level of output that equates its marginal revenue and its marginal cost.

Remember that marginal cost is the extra or additional cost incurred in producing one more unit of output. **Marginal revenue** is the extra revenue obtained from selling an additional unit of output. Marginal revenue and marginal cost are calculated in columns six and seven of Table 10.3.

If the cost of producing an additional unit of output is less than the revenue obtained from that unit, then it will pay the firm to produce that additional unit. In other words, as long as the marginal cost is less than the marginal revenue, the firm will expand its output. If, however, the cost of producing an additional unit of output is greater than the revenue obtained from that unit, then the firm will not produce the additional unit. To do so would reduce the firm's profits. In other words, as long as marginal cost exceeds marginal revenue, the firm will reduce its output. It follows that, when its marginal revenue equals its marginal cost, the firm will be in the best profit position.

This profit-maximizing condition is illustrated in Figure 10.2. At a level of output of nine units, the marginal cost exceeds the marginal revenue. Hence, the firm will reduce its output. At a level of output of three units, marginal revenue exceeds marginal cost. Hence, the firm will increase its output. At an output level between seven and eight units, the firm cannot increase its profits by changing its output. Hence, an output between

	Quantity (units) (1)	Price ($) (2)	Total revenue ($) (3)	Total cost ($) (4)	Profit ($) (5)	Marginal revenue ($) (6)	Marginal cost ($) (7)
TABLE 10.3 Hypothetical revenue, cost, and profit data for a purely competitive firm.	1	10	10	30	−20		
						10	5
	2	10	20	35	−15		
						10	4
	3	10	30	39	−9		
						10	2
	4	10	40	41	−1		
						10	3
	5	10	50	44	6		
						10	5
	6	10	60	49	11		
						10	7
	7	10	70	56	14		
						10	10
	8	10	80	66	14		
						10	14
	9	10	90	80	10		
						10	15
	10	10	100	95	5		

FIGURE 10.2

Marginal revenue and marginal cost.

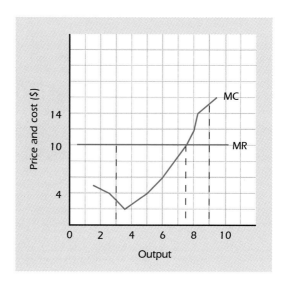

seven and eight units is the output level that maximizes the firm's profits. Note that the profit-maximizing level of output occurs where the rising marginal cost curve cuts the marginal revenue curve.

You may ask, "Why increase output to the point where MR = MC? Why not stop at some level of output just before seven units where MR > MC?" The reason for trying to operate where MR = MC may become much clearer if you think of the difference between MR and MC as extra profits. As long as MR > MC, the firm will earn extra profits by increasing its output. When there are no more extra profits to be made (i.e., when MR = MC), the firm will be in a profit-maximizing position.

PROBLEM SOLVING 10-2

Many people who manage firms know nothing about marginal revenue and marginal cost. Does this mean that they can never maximize their profits?

PRICE, AR, AND MR IN PURE COMPETITION

The relation between price, average revenue, and marginal revenue in a purely competitive market structure is something we should understand. Recall that a purely competitive firm is a price-taker. The price at which it sells its output is given. Since variations in the output of a purely competitive firm will have no appreciable effect on the market price of the product, the purely competitive firm faces a perfectly elastic demand curve. This kind of curve appears on a graph as a horizontal straight line (see Figure 10.3).

The demand curve for a purely competitive firm is perfectly elastic.

FIGURE 10.3

Average revenue and marginal revenue in pure competition.

The demand curve for a purely competitive firm coincides with its average and marginal revenue curves.

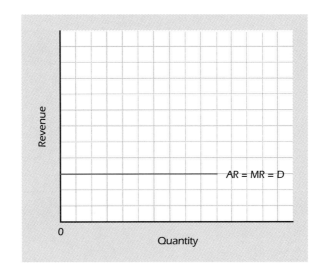

Average revenue is total revenue divided by number of units sold.

Average revenue and price are identical.

Average revenue (AR) is simply total revenue divided by the number of units sold. But this is exactly the same as price. The following simple algebraic exercise demonstrates that average revenue and price are identical.

$$TR = P \times Q$$

$$AR = \frac{TR}{Q} = \frac{P \times Q}{Q} = P$$

Therefore AR = P.

Note that in Table 10.3, marginal revenue remains constant and equals price or average revenue. This relation holds only in a situation of pure competition, where the price is given. The profit-maximizing condition for a purely competitive firm is often stated as:

$$MR = MC = P$$

We shall see later that pure competition is the only market structure in which profits are maximized when marginal cost equals price.

THE COMPETITIVE FIRM'S PROFIT LEVEL: THE SHORT RUN

The firm earns a profit provided that the price is above its ATC. It incurs a loss if the price is below its ATC.

The purely competitive firm maximizes its profits and will therefore be in equilibrium when it produces at an output level at which marginal cost equals price. But how large or how small are these profits? A quick look at Figure 10.4 will reveal whether or not the firm is earning a profit. For this purpose, you must remember that a firm's total profit is the difference between TR and TC. We can therefore determine the firm's profit per unit of output by dividing its total profit by the number of units produced and sold.

$$\text{Profit per unit} = \frac{\text{TR} - \text{TC}}{\text{Q}}$$

$$= \text{AR} - \text{ATC}$$

$$= \text{P} - \text{ATC}$$

FIGURE 10.4

The competitive firm's profit level.

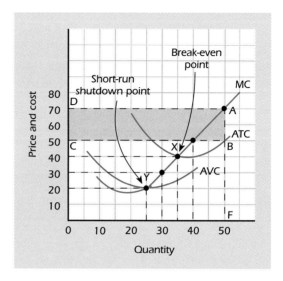

By comparing price and average total cost, we can easily determine whether or not the firm is earning a profit.

$$\text{If P} > \text{ATC, then } \pi > 0;$$

$$\text{If P} = \text{ATC, then } \pi = 0;$$

$$\text{If P} < \text{ATC, then } \pi < 0.$$

In Figure 10.4, if the price of the product is $70, the profit-maximizing firm will produce an output of 50 units where MR = P = MC. At this level of output, ATC = $50, so the firm makes a profit of $70 − $50 = $20 on each unit of output. At a price lower than $70, the firm's profit is reduced. In fact, it is possible for the price to be so low that the firm earns no profit at all and may even incur a loss. At a price of $30, for example, the firm does not cover its ATC (the price is below ATC); hence, the firm incurs losses.

We can also use Figure 10.4 to determine the firm's total revenue, total cost, and total profit at various price-output combinations. Let us assume that the price of the product is $70. The firm seeking to maximize its profits will produce 50 units of output. The firm will receive a total revenue of $70 × 50 = $3500. This total revenue is illustrated by the rectangle 0DAF. The total cost (ATC × Q) of producing an output of 50 units is $50 × 50 = $2500, and is illustrated by the rectangle 0CBF. The firm's total profit is the difference between its total revenue (0DAF) and its total cost (0CBF). This is shown by the area of the shaded rectangle ABCD, which is 20 × 50 = $1000.

THE SHORT-RUN SUPPLY CURVE OF THE PURELY COMPETITIVE FIRM

Learning Objective 3:
the purely competitive firm's short-run supply curve

At the break-even point, total revenue equals total cost, and profits are zero.

The break-even level of output is that output level at which the firm's total cost is just equal to its total revenue.

If price falls below AVC in the short run, the short-run shutdown point has been reached and the firm should close its plant.

The foregoing analysis provides a method of determining the short-run supply curve of the purely competitive firm. The firm is doing the best it can in the short run provided that it produces an output at which MR = MC. Figure 10.4 shows that at a price of $70, the firm earns a profit. In fact, the firm earns a profit if the price is anywhere above $40. At a price of $40, the firm makes neither a profit nor a loss; it just breaks even. The price equals its average total cost (or its total revenue equals its total cost). This point is sometimes called the **break-even point**. In Figure 10.4, point X is the break-even point and the output of 35 units is the **break-even level of output**. If the price falls below $40, the firm incurs losses. At a price of $30, for example, the firm is doing its best in the short run when it produces an output of 30 units (MR = MC), yet it is incurring losses. Any different level of output will merely increase the firm's losses. A firm in such a situation is said to be *minimizing its losses*.

Since the firm incurs losses when the price falls below $40, is it not better for the firm to cease operation? The answer is no. As long as the firm covers its average variable cost in the short run, it should continue to operate. If it suspends its operation, it still has its fixed costs; whereas if it continues to operate, its losses will be less than its total fixed costs. When the price falls below $20, the firm does not cover its variable costs and should therefore shut down. This point is called the **short-run shutdown point**. In Figure 10.4, point Y is the short-run shutdown point. Points along the marginal cost curve show the various quantities that the firm will supply at various prices. Note, however, that no output will be supplied at prices below $20. The various quantities supplied at various prices are shown in Table 10.4.

TABLE 10.4	Price ($)	Quantity supplied
The short-run supply schedule for a competitive firm.	70	50
	60	45
	50	40
	40	35
	30	30
	20	25
	Less than 20	0

The short-run supply curve is that portion of the MC curve that lies above the AVC curve.

This, of course, is the short-run supply schedule for a purely competitive firm. It corresponds with the marginal cost (MC) curve above the average variable cost (AVC) curve in Figure 10.4. Thus, the **short-run supply curve** of the purely competitive firm seeking to maximize its profits is the section of its marginal cost curve that lies above its average variable cost curve.

Let us return for a moment to Figure 10.4. We said that in the short run, if the price of the product is between $20 and $40, the firm should continue to operate even though it is incurring losses. When does a firm operating in that position go out of business? A firm will not continue to incur losses forever. In the long run, the firm has no fixed factors. In the long run therefore, a firm that is incurring losses will leave the industry. We will study the firm's adjustment to the long run later in this chapter.

PROBLEM SOLVING 10-3

"Any firm operating at a loss would be better off closing down." **Do you agree?**

THE SHORT-RUN INDUSTRY SUPPLY CURVE

You know that a purely competitive industry consists of a large number of firms. However, in order to illustrate geometrically the derivation of the short-run industry supply curve, we will assume that there are only three firms, A, B, and C, in an industry, D. Table 10.5 shows the various quantities supplied by each firm at each possible price.

TABLE 10.5

Derivation of short-run industry supply.

Price ($)	Output firm A	Output firm B	Output firm C	Output industry D
3	2 000	3 000	2 000	7 000
6	3 000	5 000	4 000	12 000
9	4 000	7 000	6 000	17 000
12	5 000	9 000	8 000	22 000
15	6 000	11 000	10 000	27 000
18	7 000	13 000	12 000	32 000
21	8 000	15 000	14 000	37 000
24	9 000	17 000	16 000	42 000

Learning Objective 4:
the short-run industry supply curve

The industry supply curve is derived from the horizontal summation of the supply curves of the individual firms. This is shown in Figure 10.5. At a price of $3, firms A and C supply 2000 units each and firm B supplies 3000 units.

The total quantity supplied by the industry at a price of $3 is:

$$2000 + 3000 + 2000 = 7000$$

This gives us point E on the industry supply curve. At a price of $6, firm A supplies 3000 units, firm B supplies 5000 units, and firm C supplies 4000 units. The total quantity supplied by the industry at a price of $6 is:

The short-run industry supply curve is derived by adding horizontally the supply curves of all the firms in the industry.

$$3000 + 5000 + 4000 = 12\ 000$$

This gives point E_1 on the industry supply curve. In a similar manner, we can plot the other points on the industry supply curve as shown in Figure 10.5.

FIGURE 10.5

Derivation of the industry supply curve.

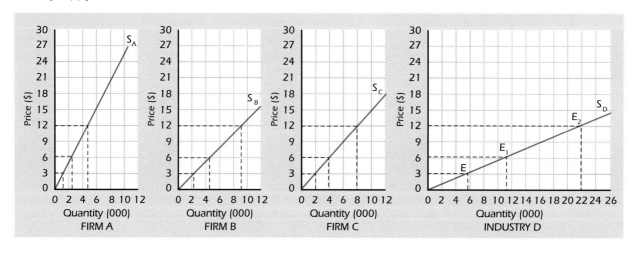

LONG-RUN EQUILIBRIUM

Learning Objective 5:
long-run equilibrium and adjustment

In a purely competitive market structure, firms are free to enter or to leave the industry: there are no barriers to entry or exit. If the firms in the industry earn profits in the short run, other firms will enter the industry. The entry of these new firms will increase total industry supply and, assuming no change in demand occurs, the price will tend to fall. New firms will tend to enter the industry provided that there are positive profits to be made. If firms in the industry are suffering losses, they will not remain in the industry in the long run. The exit of firms from the industry will cause total supply to fall and the price of the product will tend to rise.

A purely competitive firm in long-run equilibrium earns zero economic profits, called normal profits.

Movement of firms into and out of the industry will cease when each firm in the industry is earning zero profits — sometimes referred to as **normal profits**. You may wonder why a firm would stay in an industry if it were making zero profits, but the matter is easily clarified if we remind ourselves that profits are defined as total revenue minus total cost, and that total cost includes opportunity cost (that is, what the resources could earn in their best alternative uses). When a firm earns zero profits, it earns a return just equal to what the inputs could have earned if they were employed in their best alternative use.

The firm's long-run equilibrium position can be illustrated diagrammatically. If the price of the product is \$15, as determined by the demand and supply curves for the industry shown in Figure 10.6, the firm will earn positive economic profits. New firms will enter the industry. As this happens, the industry supply curve shifts to the right, say, to S_1. This causes the price to fall to \$6. At this price, firms will incur losses and therefore leave the industry. This exit of firms from the industry causes the industry supply curve to shift to the left (from S_1S_1 to S_0S_0 in Figure 10.6) resulting in an increase in price from \$6 to \$10. At this price, each firm earns zero profits. Note that this price equals average cost, and that the firm is in equilibrium, since marginal revenue equals marginal cost.

FIGURE 10.6

Long-run equilibrium of the purely competitive firm.

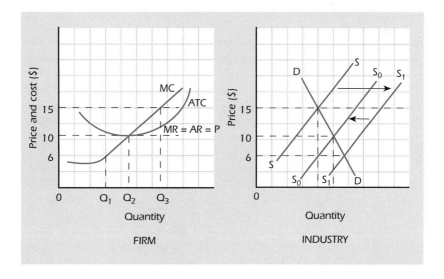

FIRM

INDUSTRY

In long-run equilibrium in pure competition, price equals minimum average cost.

Note further that in equilibrium, price equals marginal cost; but marginal cost passes through the minimum point of the average cost curve, so the price equals minimum average cost. This is important. The firm is in long-run equilibrium when

$$MR = MC = AC = P$$

MR equals MC and AR equals AC when an industry is at long-run industry equilibrium.

When each firm in the industry is in long-run equilibrium, and when there is no incentive for firms to enter or leave the industry, the output of the industry will remain steady — the industry supply curve will not shift. In this case, we say that the industry is in long-run equilibrium. Long-run **industry equilibrium** exists when both marginal revenue equals marginal cost and average cost equals average revenue.

LONG-RUN INDUSTRY ADJUSTMENT

Learning Objective 5:
long-run equilibrium and adjustment

The long-run supply curve shows all of the goods that an industry will supply in long-run equilibrium.

In a constant-cost industry, costs remain unchanged as the industry expands.

In the previous section, we assumed implicitly that the industry operates under constant cost. In this section, we explicitly analyze constant-cost and increasing-cost industries. There is some controversy as to whether an industry can have decreasing cost. However, we will not pursue this issue. Regardless, the long-run industry supply curve is extremely important in our analysis. The **long-run supply curve** of a purely competitive industry shows the various quantities of a good that all the firms in the industry will be willing to supply at various prices when the industry is in long-run equilibrium.

CONSTANT-COST INDUSTRIES

A **constant-cost industry** is one in which the prices of the factors of production, and hence the costs of production, remain constant as the industry's output expands by the entry of new firms into the industry. When the industry is in long-run equilibrium, the price equals minimum long-run average cost. In a constant-cost industry, the expansion of industry output by the entry of new firms has no effect on cost. The entry and exit of firms cause total output to change, but the price of the product always returns to the point where it is equal to the minimum average total cost. Thus, in the long run, the industry supplies various quantities at a constant price. This means that:

> the long-run supply curve of a constant-cost industry is horizontal (perfectly elastic) at the minimum average total cost.

FIGURE 10.7

Constant-cost industry adjustment.

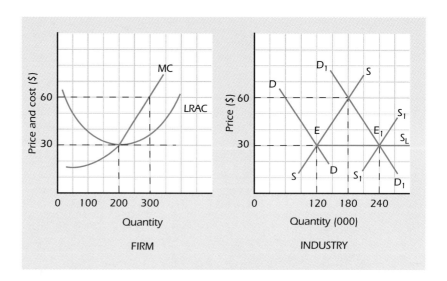

FIRM   INDUSTRY

Let us continue our analysis with the help of Figure 10.7, which shows a firm and an industry, both in equilibrium. The firm shown in the diagram is typical of all of the firms in the industry. It produces 200 units of output, and the price of the product is $30.

The industry demand curve is DD, the supply curve is SS, and the quantity produced by the industry is 120 000 units.

Let us assume now that the demand for the product increases from DD to D_1D_1 as shown in Figure 10.7. This causes the price to rise from $30 to $60. This price is now above average cost, so the firms now earn positive economic profits. At a price of $60, the typical or representative firm increases its output to 300 units. The output of the industry increases along SS from 120 000 units to 180 000 units. Because profits are being earned in this industry, it attracts new firms. The entry of these new firms shifts the supply curve from SS to S_1S_1, and forces the price back to $30. With the price now back at $30, the initial firms reduce their output along their marginal cost curves. Each firm in the industry now produces 200 units, but because there are now more firms, the industry output increases to 240 000 units. Profits are again zero; and there is no movement of firms into or out of the industry. We started with an initial price of $30 and a total quantity of 120 000 units. We end up with a price of $30 and a total quantity supplied of 240 000 units. By joining points E and E_1, we obtain the long-run supply curve (S_L) of the industry.

INCREASING-COST INDUSTRIES

An **increasing-cost industry** is one in which the prices of the factors of production, and hence production costs, increase as the industry's output expands by the entry of new firms into the industry. Although many industries seem to have constant cost in the long run, it is reasonable to expect that as an industry expands, the increase in demand for scarce factors of production will raise the prices of inputs, and thus increase production costs.

Figure 10.8 will be helpful in our analysis. The firm and the industry are in equilibrium at a price of $30. The typical firm produces 100 units of output. DD and SS are the initial demand and supply curves of the industry, and the total output of the industry is 50 000 units.

FIGURE 10.8

Increasing-cost industry adjustment.

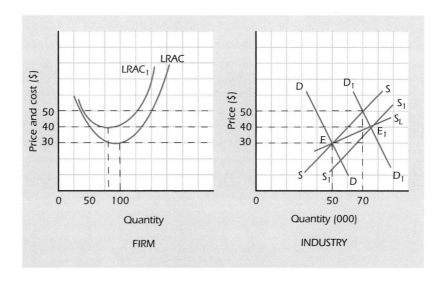

FIRM

INDUSTRY

Suppose that the demand for the output of the industry increases from DD to D_1D_1. This causes the price to rise from $30 to $50. The existing firms increase their output, moving along their marginal cost curves (not shown), and the industry output increases along SS from 50 000 to 70 000 units. New firms enter the industry, thus causing the supply curve to shift from SS to S_1S_1, but the cost rises, as shown by the shift of the long-run average cost curve from LRAC to $LRAC_1$. Therefore, the increase in supply resulting from the entry of new firms does not force the price back to its initial level of $30, but only to $40. We obtain the long-run supply curve (S_L) of the industry by joining points E and E_1. This analysis shows that:

the long-run supply curve of an increasing-cost industry has a positive slope.

THE IMPORTANCE OF THE PURELY COMPETITIVE MODEL

Learning Objective 6:
the importance of the purely competitive model

The marginal cost pricing strategy sets price equal to marginal cost.

The purely competitive model serves as an ideal by which other market structures may be judged.

We saw earlier in this chapter that real-world examples of pure competition are not easy to find. Why then do economists spend so much time analyzing behaviour in this type of market structure? It is easier to understand the issue if you view pure competition as a model. Let us remind ourselves first that the competitive solution occurs where price equals marginal cost. This **marginal cost pricing** (a characteristic feature of pure competition) implies that the firm sells its product at a price just equal to the opportunity cost. Let us also remind ourselves that long-run competitive equilibrium occurs where price equals minimum average cost. Hence, resources are efficiently employed in the purely competitive model.

The purely competitive model serves as an ideal situation by which we can measure other market structures. We can, in fact, consider it a kind of measuring rod. Moreover, many of the predictions of the purely competitive model hold true even in situations where pure competition does not prevail.

PARETO EFFICIENCY

Pareto optimality (efficiency) exists when it is impossible to make someone better off without at the same time making someone else worse off.

If all markets are purely competitive, Pareto optimality will be realized.

One of the objectives of economic science is to allocate resources efficiently. How do we know if resources are allocated efficiently? One way is to test for **Pareto optimality** or **efficiency**. Pareto optimality (named after the Italian-born economist Vilfredo Pareto) states that efficiency exists if it is impossible to rearrange inputs and outputs so as to make someone better off without making anyone else worse off. Stated slightly differently, if it is possible to make someone better off without making someone else worse off, the economy is not operating at maximum efficiency.

The following conditions are necessary to the existence of Pareto optimality:

1. Each consumer must have the opportunity to maximize his or her own satisfaction.
2. For each consumer, the ratio of the marginal utilities of any two goods must be the same. This means essentially that all consumers must pay the same price for each good.
3. Each firm must produce an output level at which marginal cost equals price.
4. The production of each good must be at the lowest possible cost.
5. Each factor of production must be employed in its most efficient use.
6. Each household must have the opportunity to supply as many factor services as it chooses.
7. People must be free to enter whatever occupation they choose.

It can be shown that if pure competition exists in all markets, all of the above conditions will prevail and Pareto efficiency will be attained. We can conclude then, that there is some basis for the popular notion that competition is good.

GLOBAL PERSPECTIVE

Global Competition

Competition among firms in an industry in one country may have nothing to do with competition among the firms in the same industry in another country. For example, competition among small retail stores in Canada is virtually independent of competition among similar retail stores in Britain. In many cases, however, a firm's competitive position is truly global rather than national or domestic. In this capsule, we will take a quick glance at global competition.

Global competition refers to competition among firms in many different countries. Manufacturers of tires, television sets, and automobiles, for example, sell their products internationally. Such firms face global competition. A Canadian firm that might have great monopoly power at home might find itself with little or no market strength as a global competitor. Telecommunications equipment

is one of the areas in which Canadian firms are believed to have acquired some competitive advantage on the global market. The behaviour of such firms in the domestic market will be different from their behaviour in the global market. The pricing and output decisions of such firms will tend to reflect the competitive environment in which they operate.

In an effort to increase their strengths in the global market, many firms have adopted a strategy of global alliance. Examples of such alliances are: GM and Toyota; Boeing, Kawasaki, and Fuji; and alliances among firms in the aerospace industry in Britain, France, Germany, and Spain. An alliance between American Airlines and Canadian Airlines has been approved by the National Transportation Agency, and other alliances between Canadian and American airline companies are quite possible.

CHAPTER SUMMARY

1. Economists have grouped different market structures into four categories. These categories are: pure competition, monopoly, monopolistic competition, and oligopoly.

2. Pure or perfect competition and monopoly are at opposites ends of a continuum of market structures. Monopoly, monopolistic competition, and oligopoly are usually referred to collectively as market structures of imperfect competition.

3. In a purely competitive market, there are many firms selling a homogeneous product. The sellers are so numerous that no single firm has any noticeable effect on the price of the product. Each seller (firm) is a price-taker. In this type of market structure, firms are free to enter or to leave the industry. Pure competition is also called atomistic competition.

4. A market is said to be monopolized when it is dominated by a single firm. In a pure monopoly, there is only one firm in the industry. This firm (the monopolistic firm) produces a product that has no close substitutes. The monopolist has a great deal of control over the price of its product.

5. In a market characterized by monopolistic competition there are many firms, each selling a differentiated product. Each firm has a small amount of influence on the price of the product.

6. An oligopoly is a market structure in which there are only a few sellers. In this market situation, each firm has substantial influence over the price of the product, and each firm is likely to be affected by the behaviour of the other firms in the industry.

7. A firm's profit is the difference between its total revenue and its total cost. The firm maximizes its profits by producing that output at which the difference between total revenue and total cost is greatest, or by producing an output level at which marginal revenue equals marginal cost.

8. The purely competitive firm faces a perfectly elastic (horizontal) demand curve. Its average revenue curve is the same as its marginal revenue curve.

9. A firm in pure competition earns positive short-run profits provided that the price at which it sells its product is above its average total cost. When the price just equals average total cost, the firm is in a break-even position.

10. If the firm is covering its variable costs but not its total costs, and if it produces an output level at which marginal revenue equals marginal cost, we say that it is minimizing its losses. The firm is better off doing this in the short run than closing down. The short-run shutdown point is the point at which the firm is just barely covering its variable cost with nothing left over.

11. The competitive firm's short-run supply curve is the portion of its marginal cost curve that lies above its average variable cost curve. We can obtain the short-run industry supply curve by adding horizontally the supply curves of the firms in that industry.

12. At long-run equilibrium, the purely competitive firm earns zero profits. The long-run equilibrium position may be stated as "marginal revenue equals marginal cost equals average cost equals price." The industry is in equilibrium when each firm is in equilibrium and when there is no entry or exit of firms into or out of the industry.

13. The long-run supply curve of a purely competitive industry shows the various quantities of the product that the firms in the industry will supply at various prices in long-run equilibrium.

14. A constant-cost industry is one in which the cost of production remains unchanged as the industry expands by the addition of new firms. Constant-cost industries have horizontal long-run supply curves.

15. An increasing-cost industry is one in which production costs rise as the industry expands by the addition of new firms. Increasing-cost industries have upward sloping long-run supply curves.

16. Although examples of pure competition may be hard to find in the real world, the purely competitive model is useful as an ideal situation by which we may evaluate other types of market structures.

17. Pareto optimality exists when one person cannot be made better off without making someone else worse off.

18. If all markets are purely competitive, Pareto optimality will be realized.

TERMS FOR REVIEW

market structures (166)
industry (166)
imperfect competition (166)
pure (perfect, atomistic)
 competition (166)
price-taker (166)
monopolized market (167)
monopoly (167)
monopolistic competition (167)
oligopoly (167)
marginal revenue (169)
average revenue (171)

break-even point (173)
break-even level of output (173)
short-run shutdown point (173)
short-run supply curve (173)
normal profits (175)
industry equilibrium (176)
long-run supply curve (176)
constant-cost industry (176)
increasing-cost industry (177)
marginal cost pricing (178)
Pareto optimality (efficiency) (178)

QUESTIONS FOR REVIEW AND DISCUSSION

1. What are the characteristics of each of the following market structures? (L.O.1)

    (a) pure competition

    (b) monopoly

    (c) monopolistic competition

    (d) oligopoly

2. Why would you expect a single price to prevail in a purely competitive market? (L.O.1)

3. "The purely competitive firm is a price-taker and a quantity-adjuster." Explain. (L.O.1)

4. Distinguish between competition and perfect competition. (L.O.1)

5. Why are marginal revenue and price identical for a firm in pure competition? (L.O.1,2)

6. Show that a firm will maximize its profits when it produces a level of output at which marginal revenue equals marginal cost. (L.O.2)

7. Explain how to derive the short-run supply curve for a firm trying to maximize its profits in pure competition. (L.O.3)

8. Explain the process of deriving the industry's short-run supply curve. (L.O.4)

9. Explain how a firm could be in equilibrium in the short run when it is incurring losses. (L.O.2)

10. "The objective of the firm is to maximize its profits. If this objective is achieved, the firm is in equilibrium. The firm cannot therefore be in equilibrium if it is not making a profit." Discuss this statement. (L.O.2)

11. Describe the process by which a purely competitive industry reaches long-run equilibrium. (L.O.5)

12. "The purely competitive model is completely useless in a world where pure competition rarely exists." Discuss. (General)

13. How useful is the economic model of perfect competition? (General)

14. What is Pareto optimality? Mention at least four conditions that are necessary for the existence of Pareto optimality. (General)

15. Is there any relation between pure competition and Pareto optimality? Explain. (General)

PROBLEMS AND EXERCISES

1. The demand schedule facing a firm is shown below in columns 1 and 2 of Table 10.6. (General)

TABLE 10.6

Demand and revenue data.

Price (1)	Quantity (2)	TR (3)	AR (4)	MR (5)
$5	1			
5	2			
5	3			
5	4			
5	5			
5	6			

(a) Compute total revenue, average revenue, and marginal revenue, and complete the table.

(b) Plot average revenue and marginal revenue on a graph.

(c) On the same graph, plot the demand curve.

(d) What do you notice about the demand curve and the average revenue curve?

2. The Wisepro Manufacturing Company has the cost data shown in Table 10.7. The market price of the product is $5. (L.O.2)

TABLE 10.7

Cost data for Wisepro.

Quantity (units)	Total cost ($)
0	10
1	14
2	17
3	19
4	20
5	21
6	23
7	26
8	30
9	35
10	44

(a) What is Wisepro's total revenue at each level of output?

(b) Calculate Wisepro's total profit or loss at each level of output.

(c) At what level of output does Wisepro earn maximum profits?

(d) Graph the total revenue and the total cost curves for Wisepro and indicate the maximum total profit.

3. Referring to Table 10.7, and given that the price of the product is $5: (L.O.3)

(a) compute the firm's marginal cost and marginal revenue at each level of output;

(b) graph the firm's marginal cost and marginal revenue curves;

(c) from your graph, determine the firm's optimal (best) output level.

4. Table 10.8 refers to a purely competitive firm whose objective is to maximize its profits. (L.O.2,3)

TABLE 10.8

Cost and revenue data for a firm.

Q	TFC	TVC	TC	AFC	AVC	ATC	MC	MR	TR
0	100	0	100						0
1	100	25							100
2	100	35							200
3	100	50							300
4	100	100							400
5	100	180							500
6	100	340							600
7	100	560							700

(a) Determine the price of the product.

(b) Complete the table.

(c) If the price were $80, should the firm continue to operate? Why or why not?

(d) If the price were to fall to $40, should the firm continue to operate? Why or why not?

(e) What is the minimum price this firm must receive in order for it to continue to operate in the short run?

5. Referring to Table 10.8, draw the firm's short-run supply curve. (L.O.3)

6. You find that you are operating your small grocery store at a loss but are covering your variable costs. Should you continue to operate in the short run? Explain. (L.O.2)

7. The information in Table 10.9 is provided for the Best Hits Recording Company, which is a purely competitive firm. The price of its product is $20. (L.O.2)

TABLE 10.9

Cost data for Best Hits Recording Company.

Q (units)	TR ($)	MR ($)	TC ($)	MC ($)	Profits ($)
1			30		
2			40		
3			48		
4			58		
5			70		
6			90		
7			120		
8			160		

(a) Complete the table and determine what level of output the firm should produce in order to maximize its profits.

(b) On graph paper, draw the total revenue and total cost curves. At what level of output is the difference between total revenue and total cost greatest?

(c) On graph paper, draw the marginal revenue and marginal cost curves. At what level of output do these curves intersect?

8. Referring to Figure 10.9, describe the firm's position in terms of profitability for each marginal revenue curve shown. (L.O.2)

FIGURE 10.9

ATC, AVC, MC, and MR curves.

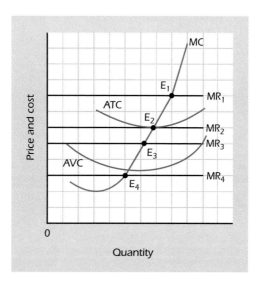

9. Figure 10.10 is for a purely competitive firm that is a profit-maximizer. The price of the product is $50. (L.O.2)

FIGURE 10.10

Price and cost for a purely competitive firm.

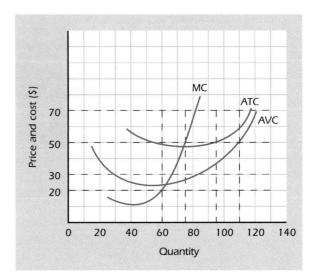

(a) What is the maximum profit this firm can make on all units produced?

(b) At this profit level, what is the firm's total revenue?

(c) What is the firm's total cost at the profit-maximizing level of output?

 10. "Introductory economics textbooks are very much alike." Go to the library and pick out a few modern textbooks on introductory economics. Look through the textbooks and see if your research supports the above assertion. Using your knowledge of a competitive industry, explain why introductory economics textbooks are so much alike.

11

THE THEORY OF MONOPOLY

Learning Objectives

After studying this chapter, you should be able to:

1 discuss barriers to entry

2 describe the demand curve for a firm in monopoly

3 describe the marginal revenue of a monopolist

4 discuss the profit level of the monopolist

5 understand the relation between elasticity and marginal revenue

6 compare monopoly with pure competition

7 understand monopoly regulation

8 discuss price discrimination

The price of monopoly is upon every occasion the highest which can be got.

Adam Smith, *Wealth of Nations*

INTRODUCTION

In the previous chapter, we examined the determination of price and output under pure competition. In this chapter, we shall look at the opposite extreme and examine price and output determination under monopoly. The pure monopolist is the sole producer of a product that has no close substitutes. The firm and the industry are identical. Although this definition seems simple and straightforward enough, it raises some important issues. First, the notion of close substitutes is subjective and arbitrary. While most people may agree that coffee and tea are close substitutes, they may not agree so readily on electricity and oil. Electricity and oil may be considered close substitutes for heating purposes, but very poor substitutes, or not substitutes at all, for lighting purposes. Second (and this is related to the first), the definition of monopoly and the product that is monopolized are inseparable.

A definition of monopoly should indicate the market that is monopolized.

Just as it is difficult to find examples of pure competition in the real world, so too is it difficult to find examples of pure monopoly. The term **monopoly** often conjures up an image of a large firm that mercilessly takes advantage of consumers, controls price and output, and earns unconscionably large profits. But not all monopolies deserve this "bad guy" image. Public utilities are often monopolies. You may be able to think of some local monopolies in your area: the local public transit system or the water supply system, for example.

BARRIERS TO ENTRY

Monopolies exist because of certain barriers that block the entry of potential competitors.

For a monopoly to exist, there must be circumstances that restrict the entry of other firms into the particular monopolized industry. These prohibitive factors or circumstances are called **barriers to entry**. Let us look at some of these barriers.

Learning Objective 1:
discuss barriers to entry

BARRIERS CREATED BY THE GOVERNMENT

You are a very enterprising economics student and you have come up with an idea that you believe will earn you a great deal of money. You and your friends are going to pick up letters, mainly from businesses, and deliver them to their destination anywhere within a radius of 30 km from the downtown core. You know you can do this at a cost significantly below what the post office charges and still make a very good profit.

Patents and franchises are barriers to entry.

Hold it! You can't do it. The government won't let you. It's illegal, so you will have to dream up some other scheme for making your million dollars. The government prevents other firms from entering certain industries and competing with the existing firms. This type of legal barrier is quite common and quite effective in maintaining monopolies. A patent is one of the legal devices used to maintain monopolies. A **patent** is an exclusive right that the government grants to a producer to produce a product. During the term of the patent (a period of 17 years), the producer is protected against potential competitors. Patents can often be circumvented, however, for although other firms are not allowed to produce an identical product, they can produce a product that is quite similar. The government grants approximately 21 000 new patents each year.

Ownership or control of an essential input can be an effective barrier to entry into a monopolized market.

A government may also grant an exclusive **franchise** to a producer to operate a business or provide a service in a certain area. The granting of a franchise means that no other producer may legally operate an identical business or provide an identical service in the same area. You should not interpret the foregoing to mean that only governments can grant franchises. Private concerns may also grant franchises. If you obtain a franchise from McDonald's, you are protected against competition from any other McDonald's restaurant, since another one will not be established within the boundaries of your business area.

You will enjoy a monopoly on McDonald's hamburgers, but you will face competition from Harvey's, Wendy's, Burger King, and other restaurants.

BARRIERS CREATED BY OWNERSHIP OR CONTROL OF ESSENTIAL RAW MATERIALS

If a particular firm owns a certain raw material essential to the production of a certain product, and if the firm does not allow any other firm to use that essential material, then obviously a monopoly situation will develop. For example, bauxite is a necessary ingredient in the production of aluminum. If one company owns or controls all sources of bauxite in the country, and if the import of bauxite or aluminum is strictly forbidden by law, then that company will have a monopoly in the domestic market for aluminum. One South African company has a virtual monopoly on the world's diamond market since it owns or controls most of the world's diamond mines.

BARRIERS CREATED BY ECONOMIES OF SCALE

Substantial economies of scale may effectively block the entry of new firms into an industry.

Because of substantial economies of scale, one firm may be able to supply the entire market more cheaply than two or more firms. Often, the cost of establishing an efficient plant in this case is enormous, and the minimum average cost will be covered only at a level of output large enough to supply the entire market. If there are two or more firms in this type of industry, the average cost will be quite high. This is so because these firms divide among them the total market supply. Consider how much it would cost to start up a telephone company to provide telephone service to people in a certain area. Now compare that cost with the cost to an existing telephone company of providing the same service to those people. The market situation in which a single firm is likely to be more efficient than two or more firms is often referred to as **natural monopoly**.

In a natural monopoly, a single firm is more efficient than two or more firms.

Examples of natural monopolies are telephone companies, gas companies, and electrical power companies like Hydro-Québec and Ontario Hydro.

THE DEMAND CURVE FOR A FIRM IN MONOPOLY

The monopolistic firm's demand curve is identical to the total demand curve for its product.

In Chapter 4, we noted that the market demand curve slopes downward from left to right. Since the monopolistic firm is the only firm in the industry, the demand curve of the monopolistic firm is exactly the same as the industry or market demand curve. If the monopolistic firm wishes to sell a larger quantity, it can do so by lowering the price of its product. If it increases the price of its product, the quantity that it can sell will decrease.

Learning Objective 2: describe the demand curve for a firm in monopoly

The monopolist cannot control both price and output at the same time.

Figure 11.1 shows a hypothetical demand curve for a monopolistic firm. At a price of $8, the monopolistic firm can sell 120 units. When the price is $4, it can sell 240 units. Note that the monopolistic firm is not a price-taker: it does have significant control over the price it charges for its product. However, it cannot completely control both price and quantity. If the monopolist has the demand curve shown in Figure 11.1, it cannot, for example, charge a price of $8 and sell more than 120 units. Once it sets the price, the quantity that it can sell at that price is determined by the demand curve. The monopolistic firm must operate within the constraint imposed on it by its demand curve. The fact that the demand curve facing the monopolistic firm slopes downward tells us that the demand for its product is not perfectly inelastic.

PROBLEM SOLVING 11-1

A monopolistic firm is in an enviable position because it can charge any price it wishes and sell as much as it pleases at that price. Is this a true statement?

FIGURE 11.1

A monopolistic firm's demand curve.

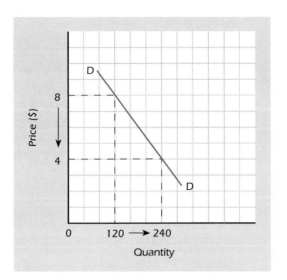

The monopolist faces a downward-sloping demand curve.

THE MARGINAL REVENUE OF THE MONOPOLIST

Learning Objective 3: describe the marginal revenue of a monopolist

Recall that, under pure competition, demand (or average revenue) and marginal revenue are identical. Under monopoly however, this is not the case. It becomes necessary then, to distinguish between demand or average revenue and marginal revenue. Marginal revenue is crucial in deciding whether or not the firm should produce a little more or a little less in order to maximize its profits. A declining average revenue implies a declining marginal revenue. (Remember the magnetic effect of the marginal on the average). Moreover, the marginal revenue will fall at a faster rate than the average revenue. This must be the case since, in order to sell a larger volume of output, the monopolistic firm receives a lower price on those units it could have sold at a higher price had it not chosen to increase its output. Table 11.1 helps to illustrate this idea.

Table 11.1 shows that the monopolistic firm can sell one unit of output if the price is $10. The firm can sell two units only if it charges a price of $9. Total revenue is now $18 — an increase of $8 due to the sale of the additional unit. In other words, marginal revenue is now $8. The firm could have sold the first unit for $9, thus losing $1 of the selling price on that unit. Similarly, the firm can sell three units only if the price is $8. Total

TABLE 11.1

Hypothetical demand and marginal revenue for a monopolist.

P ($)	Q (units)	TR ($)	MR ($)
10	1	10	
9	2	18	8
8	3	24	6
7	4	28	4
6	5	30	2
5	6	30	0
4	7	28	-2
3	8	24	-4

The marginal revenue of the monopolistic firm is less than its average revenue.

revenue is now $24 and marginal revenue $6. The firm could also have sold the first two units for $9 each, thus losing $1 of the selling price on each of the first two units. This exercise shows that:

for a monopoly, marginal revenue is less than average revenue, and falls at a faster rate than average revenue.

Notice that price and average revenue are identical — a relation you learned in the previous chapter. Figure 11.2 shows the relation between average revenue and marginal revenue.

FIGURE 11.2

Average revenue and marginal revenue of a monopolist.

When the average revenue curve slopes downward, the marginal revenue curve slopes downward also, but more steeply than the average revenue curve.

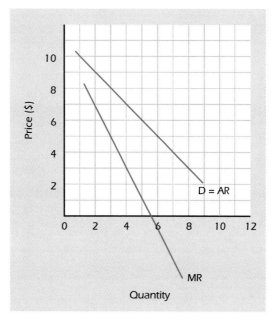

Note that if both the demand and marginal revenue curves are linear and downward sloping, then the marginal revenue curve will bisect any horizontal line between the vertical axis and the demand curve. In Figure 11.3, the marginal revenue curve bisects 0Q and HK.

FIGURE 11.3

Relation between linear demand and marginal revenue curves.

The marginal revenue curve lies halfway between the demand curve and the vertical axis at all points.

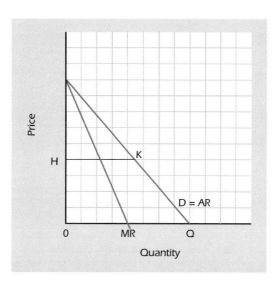

We have seen that the concept of marginal revenue is important in determining the output level at which the firm maximizes its profits. (Recall the MR = MC condition discussed in the previous chapter). Let us now determine the equilibrium position of a monopolistic firm.

EQUILIBRIUM UNDER MONOPOLY

The monopolist must decide how much to produce and what price to charge in order to maximize profits.

The firm in pure competition is a price-taker and a quantity adjuster. That is, the purely competitive firm accepts the price determined by the market for the product, and then decides on the level of output that will maximize its profits. For a monopolistic firm, the price of the product is not given. The monopolistic firm, therefore, faces two problems in terms of its profit maximization objective: the problem of deciding what price to charge for its product and the problem of deciding what level of output to produce. Once it sets the price, the maximum amount that it can sell at that price is determined by its demand curve.

The monopolistic firm maximizes its profits when its marginal cost equals its marginal revenue.

We can reasonably assume that the monopolistic firm faces a cost situation similar to that faced by a firm in any other type of market structure. Table 11.2 contains hypothetical cost and revenue figures for a firm in a monopoly situation. Profits are maximized at a level of output of four units, where the difference between total revenue ($28) and total cost ($21) is greatest at $7, and the price $7. Alternatively, using the marginal-revenue-equals-marginal-cost condition, we arrive at the same conclusion that the monopolistic firm maximizes its profits by producing four units and selling at a price of $7.

Figure 11.4 illustrates graphically the relations between the data shown in Table 11.2. In this figure, MR = MC at a level of output of four units. If the monopolistic firm charges a price of $7, it will maximize its profits. The maximum profit is shown on Diagram A as the greatest distance between TR and TC, and as the shaded area in Diagram B.

A monopolist may deliberately earn less than maximum profits.

We have determined the price-output combination that maximizes the profits of the monopolistic firm. Given the conditions of demand and cost, any other price-output combination results in lower profits for the monopolist. But whether or not the monopolist will choose to charge that particular price at which profit is greatest is another

	Price ($)	Quantity (units)	Total cost ($)	Marginal cost ($)	Total revenue ($)	Marginal revenue ($)	Profits ($)
TABLE 11.2 Hypothetical cost and revenue data for a monopolist.	11	0	10		0		−10
				2		10	
	10	1	12		10		−2
				3		8	
	9	2	15		18		3
				2		6	
	8	3	17		24		7
				4		4	
	7	4	21		28		7
				5		2	
	6	5	26		30		4
				7		0	
	5	6	33		30		−3
				10		−2	
	4	7	43		28		−15
				17		−4	
	3	8	60		24		−36

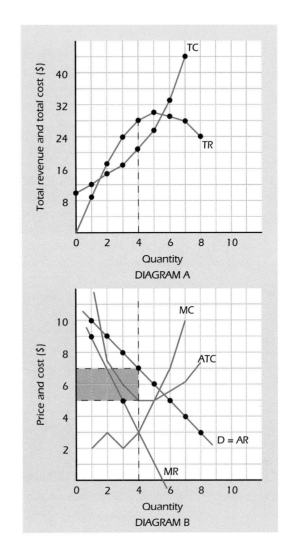

FIGURE 11.4

Profit maximization for a monopolist.

question. For several reasons, the monopolist may decide against earning maximum profits. First, extremely high profits provide incentive for other firms to attempt to break through the barriers and end the monopoly. Second, social conscience may prevent those who make the decisions in the monopolistic firm from undertaking measures necessary to maximize profits. Public opinion may enter into such a decision. In this case, the firm may decide to earn a satisfactory profit instead of trying to earn maximum profits. Third, the monopolist may want to avoid provoking the government to regulate its price and other profit factors.

The firm shown in Figure 11.4 is earning positive economic profits (its price is above its average total cost). This situation could continue even in the long run since there are barriers that effectively block the entry of new firms into this industry. If potential firms are able to surmount the entry barriers and compete with the monopoly, the monopoly will be destroyed and the positive economic profits will dwindle away in the long run.

PROBLEM SOLVING 11-2

Can a monopolistic firm always succeed in increasing its profits by raising its price?

THE MONOPOLIST'S PROFIT LEVEL

Even a monopolist may suffer losses.

Learning Objective 4: discuss the profit level of the monopolist

A commonly held misconception is that monopolistic firms always make huge profits. In fact, while some monopolies make large profits, others incur losses. In some cases, excessively high production costs result in losses to the firm. Such a situation is illustrated in Figure 11.5. At an output level of Q_1, this monopolistic firm is doing the best it can under the existing circumstances. Nevertheless, the firm is suffering losses because the price, P, is below average total cost. The price is, however, above the firm's average variable cost. The firm, then, will likely continue to operate in the short run in order to minimize its losses. These losses are shown as the shaded area in Figure 11.5. In the long run, however, the firm will likely shift its resources into more profitable uses.

The firm may try to improve its profit position by increasing its total revenue. It would be possible to increase total revenue if the firm could raise its price without reducing quantity demanded. Quite often, this is easier said than done. The firm's demand curve would have to shift to the right. Advertising is one means of trying to shift the firm's demand curve to the right.

FIGURE 11.5

A monopolist incurring losses.

Marginal revenue and marginal cost may be equal at a price below average cost.

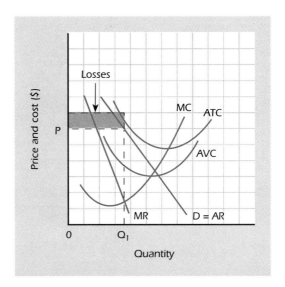

APPLICATION

Research and Development

We have seen that not all monopolies make huge profits. However, if firms in an industry perceive that it is profitable to become a monopolist, they will vie for monopoly position. One way of winning the race to become a monopoly is through research and development (R&D) that will enable a firm to be the first to introduce a product on the market. Pharmaceutical companies spend hundreds of thousands of dollars on R&D. A question well worth asking is, why do firms spend so much money on R&D?

Let's assume that a pharmaceutical company estimates that there is a very high demand for a drug that increases intelligence. The first company that produces such a drug and obtains government approval to market it will enjoy monopoly power. The winning firm will be able to sell the product at a monopoly price and earn enormous profits for the duration of the time that it has the sole right to market that drug. Although the firm that wins the race earns impressive profits, we must note that the losers also spend a great deal on R&D even though they do not produce and market the drug.

THE INEFFICIENT MONOPOLIST

Inefficiency will reduce the monopolist's profits.

X-inefficiency is the failure to use resources in their most economically efficient way.

A monopolistic firm that adopts the attitude that customers have no alternative but to buy the product from that firm may not feel the need to control cost adequately. Such inefficiency can destroy the profit potential of the monopoly. The term **X-inefficiency** is used to describe the situation in which the firm does not produce its output at the lowest possible cost. X-inefficiency may result from keeping on unproductive workers out of loyalty, putting unproductive relatives and friends on the payroll, or padding executives' expense accounts.

Figure 11.6 illustrates the effect of X-inefficiency on the profit level of the monopolistic firm. Diagram A shows an efficient monopolist, while Diagram B shows an inefficiently run monopolistic firm. The demand and marginal revenue curves of both firms are identical. The efficient monopolist produces its output at an average total cost of C_1. Note that the average total cost (ATC_1) of the inefficient monopolist is higher than that (ATC) of the efficient monopolist. This illustrates X-inefficiency. The smaller profit earned by the inefficient monopolist is due to X-inefficiency.

FIGURE 11.6

The effect of X-inefficiency.

X-inefficiency raises the costs of the monopolistic firm and reduces its profits.

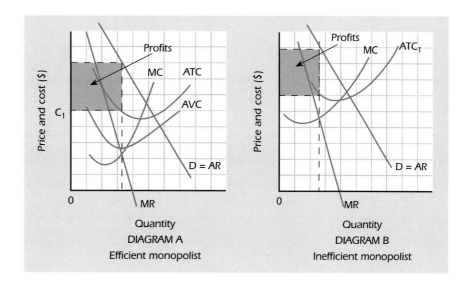

DIAGRAM A — Efficient monopolist; DIAGRAM B — Inefficient monopolist

ELASTICITY, TOTAL REVENUE, AND MARGINAL REVENUE

Remember that if the demand for a product is elastic, a reduction in price will cause total revenue to increase. But total revenue can increase only if marginal revenue is positive. It follows, therefore, that if marginal revenue is positive, the demand for the product in that range must be elastic.

When the price elasticity of demand is unitary, a reduction in the price of the product will not change total revenue. If total revenue is stable, then marginal revenue must be zero. Therefore, it follows that when marginal revenue is zero, the elasticity of demand for the product at that price must be one.

Learning Objective 5: *understand the relation between elasticity and marginal revenue*

An inelastic demand implies that a reduction in price will cause total revenue to fall. But total revenue can fall only if marginal revenue is negative. Hence, when marginal revenue is negative, the demand for the product must be inelastic. Table 11.3 shows the relation between demand, total revenue, and marginal revenue for a monopolist.

TABLE 11.3	Q (units)	P ($)	TR ($)	MR ($)
Demand, total revenue, and marginal revenue for a monopolist.	0	10.50	0	
				10
	1	10.00	10	
				9
	2	9.50	19	
				8
	3	9.00	27	
				7
	4	8.50	34	
				6
	5	8.00	40	
				5
	6	7.50	45	
				4
	7	7.00	49	
				3
	8	6.50	52	
				2
	9	6.00	54	
				1
	10	5.50	55	
				0
	11	5.00	55	
				−1
	12	4.50	54	
				−2
	13	4.00	52	
				−3
	14	3.50	49	
				−4
	15	3.00	45	
				−5
	16	2.50	40	
				−6
	17	2.00	34	
				−7
	18	1.50	27	
				−8
	19	1.00	19	
				−9
	20	0.50	10	

The relationship is illustrated graphically in Figure 11.7. At an output level less than Q_1, the marginal revenue is positive, the total revenue is rising, and the demand for the product is elastic in that range. At an output level of Q_1, marginal revenue equals 0, total revenue is at its maximum, and demand is unitary elastic at a price of P. At an output level greater than Q_1, marginal revenue is negative, total revenue is falling, and the demand is inelastic at any price below P.

The monopolistic firm incurs additional costs as it increases its output — that is, its marginal cost is positive. This implies that marginal revenue and marginal cost will intersect at some positive value. But if marginal revenue is positive, the demand is elastic. This leads to the following proposition:

A profit-maximizing monopolistic firm will operate only within that range where the demand for its product is elastic.

FIGURE 11.7

Relation between demand, total revenue, marginal revenue, and elasticity.

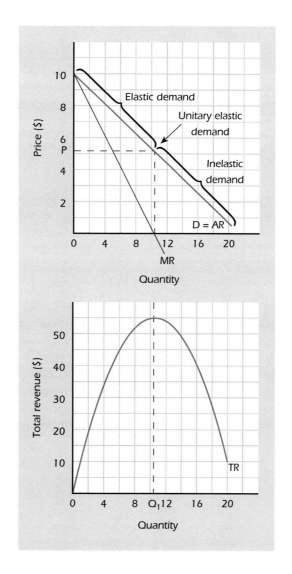

PROBLEM SOLVING 11-3

Demonstrate that if marginal cost is zero, the monopolistic firm will maximize its profits by producing at that point where the price elasticity of demand is one.

MONOPOLY VERSUS PURE COMPETITION

Learning Objective 6: compare monopoly with pure competition

Allocative efficiency exists when resources are optimally allocated. This occurs when price equals marginal cost.

In the previous chapter, we noted that the model of pure competition served as a convenient reference for the evaluation of other market structures. It is a useful exercise to compare the price and output behaviours of a purely competitive industry with those of a monopoly.

First, in a purely competitive market, each firm charges a price that just equals its marginal cost. Economists refer to this situation as **allocative efficiency**. In pure competition, resources are allocated efficiently. In a monopoly, on the other hand, the price is above marginal cost. Therefore, resources are not allocated efficiently. This situation is illustrated graphically in Figure 11.8. We assume that the cost curves are the same in both market structures. AR represents the demand or average revenue of the monopolist, which is the same as the industry demand curve. For convenience, we show the position of one of the firms in the competitive industry. The subscript F indicates that the reference is to the firm. To maximize profits, the monopolist produces an output of Q_m and charges a price of P_m, thus equating marginal revenue and marginal cost. The purely competitive price will be P_c, which equals marginal cost. Note that P_m is greater than marginal cost.

FIGURE 11.8

Monopoly vs. competition.

The monopolist charges a price that is higher than MC.

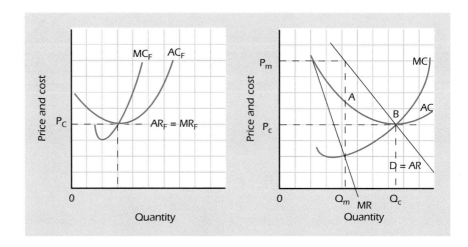

Compared with pure competition, the monopoly output is less, and unit cost is higher.

Second, the purely competitive output is produced at a minimum unit cost. This is not the case under monopoly. The monopolist produces its output at a higher unit cost. Figure 11.8 shows that the profit-maximizing monopolist produces at point A on the average cost curve. In the long run, however, production in a purely competitive industry takes place at point B, the minimum point on the average cost curve.

Third, other things being equal, the monopolist produces less output than the competitive industry does. As illustrated in Figure 11.8, the monopolist produces an output of Q_m while the competitive industry produces an output of Q_c. This suggests that employment will be greater in the competitive industry than in the monopolistic firm. The monopolist charges a higher price and supplies a smaller quantity than the purely competitive industry does.

A monopolist may earn positive profits even in the long run.

Finally, if the monopolistic firm's price is greater than its average cost, it will earn positive profits. If the firms in a purely competitive industry earn positive profits in the short run, other firms will enter the industry and compete until profits settle down at zero in the long run. In the case of the monopolist, however, positive profits may remain because of barriers preventing other firms from entering the industry.

PROBLEM SOLVING 11-4

How does the existence of economies of scale affect the general conclusion that pure competition results in a lower price for the consumer and a larger quantity of output than monopoly does?

THE REGULATED MONOPOLY

Learning Objective 7:
understand monopoly
regulation

A firm exhibiting monopoly
power (market power) can
control either output or
price, but not both.

Regulated monopolies are
controlled by government
legislation.

The analysis presented in the previous section suggests that monopolies have certain social consequences that are less desirable than those associated with pure competition. Compared with pure competition, for example, the monopolist produces a smaller output at a higher unit cost and sells at a higher price, other things being equal. This ability to exert control over price and output is called **monopoly power** or **market power**. The misallocation of resources associated with monopolies has no parallel in the purely competitive market structure. The prices charged by many natural monopolies are determined by government regulatory agencies. Let us now turn our attention to the ways in which a government or its regulatory agencies may **regulate monopolies**, and the consequences of such regulation.

MARGINAL-COST PRICING

One of the things we noted about a firm in a monopoly situation is that it will operate at a point where price is greater than marginal cost. From a social point of view, resources are optimally allocated when price equals marginal cost. Let us examine the consequences of a regulatory body setting the monopolist's price at a level equal to its marginal cost. Figure 11.9 will help to clarify the effects of monopoly regulation.

FIGURE 11.9

Monopoly regulation.

Regulation may force a
monopolist to equate price
and marginal cost, or to
equate price and average
cost, or to produce that
output at which average
cost is at its minimum.

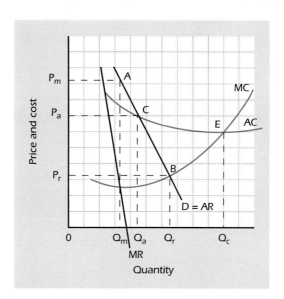

The diagram illustrates a natural monopoly. Note that because of huge fixed costs, the average revenue curve cuts the average cost curve while the latter is still falling. The unregulated monopolist, who is a profit-maximizer, produces an output of Q_m and sells at a price of P_m since, at this point, marginal revenue equals marginal cost (position A in Figure 11.9). A regulation that sets price equal to marginal cost will cause the monopolist to produce an output of Q_r at a price of P_r (position B). By setting a price of P_r, the regulatory agency prevents the monopolist from restricting output in order to exact a higher price. *Marginal-cost pricing regulation* does not necessarily result in losses for the monopolist, but it sometimes does. The firm depicted in Figure 11.9 incurs a loss by operating where price equals marginal cost. Since no firm wants to continue to incur losses indefinitely, this firm will have to take measures to survive, or leave the industry. If the monopoly is considered to be essential, the government may decide to take over its operation and endure the losses resulting from marginal-cost pricing, or it could subsidize the monopoly. But the notion of a government subsidizing a private monopoly is likely to incite public indignation.

AVERAGE-COST PRICING

If the regulatory agency considers marginal-cost pricing to be inappropriate, it may consider average-cost pricing as an alternative. *Average-cost pricing regulation* sets the price of the product equal to the average cost (position C in Figure 11.9). The monopolist will produce an output of Q_a at a price of P_a. This alternative eliminates any monopoly profits that the monopolist may otherwise have made. Average-cost pricing accords with the idea of a fair return on the owners' resources. Note that average-cost pricing results in a level of output that, though greater than the unregulated monopoly output, is still less than the socially optimum output of Q_r, where price equals marginal cost.

MINIMUM AVERAGE-COST PRICING

Finally, the regulatory agency may choose to have the monopolist operate at the lowest point on the average cost curve (point E in Figure 11.9). If the average cost curve declines over a large range of output as in Figure 11.9, this minimum point could occur at a level of output too large for the market served by the monopolist.

In order to operate at the minimum point on the average cost curve, this monopolist would have to produce a level of output of Q_c — clearly more than the firm would be able to sell at any price. The alternative chosen by the regulatory body ultimately depends on its objective. In any case, the regulated monopoly produces a larger output and sells at a lower price than if the monopoly were not regulated.

THE DISCRIMINATING MONOPOLIST

Learning Objective 8:
discuss price discrimination

Up to this point in our analysis, we have assumed implicitly that the monopolist charges all of its customers the same price. In certain circumstances, the monopolist may find it profitable to charge different prices to different buyers for the same good or service. This practice is called **price discrimination**, defined as the practice of selling a product to different buyers or groups of buyers at different prices for reasons unrelated to cost differences.

Bell Canada, for example, charges commercial users of its telephone service one price and residential users a different price. Many suppliers of electricity also have different rates for commercial and residential users. Similarly, lawyers may charge a wealthy client more than they charge a poor one for a similar case; or a company may sell goods in a foreign market at a lower price than it charges in the domestic market.

To practice price discrimination, the monopolist must be able to group buyers into different classes on some basis, and prevent arbitrage dealings.

Arbitrage transactions occur when product is bought in a low-price market for resale in a high-price market.

For price discrimination to be possible, two conditions must be satisfied. First, the monopolistic firm must be able to group the buyers of its product into different classes such as rich and poor, adults and children, or residential and commercial. Second, the monopolist must be able to maintain a separation between the markets in which the product is sold so that buyers will not be able to engage in **arbitrage transactions** (buying in one market and selling in another, thereby making a profit by the price differential in the two markets). Those who buy in the market with the lower price must not be able to sell in the market with the higher price. If the monopolist cannot separate the markets in this way, the price will tend to rise in the cheaper market and fall in the more expensive market until the price differential is eliminated. The two conditions stated above are necessary for price discrimination to exist. They do not, however, ensure the profitability of price discrimination. Price discrimination will be profitable only if the price elasticity of demand is different in each market in which the monopolist sells its product.

The following example illustrates why price discrimination is profitable. Suppose there are only two groups of people — students and professors — buying a certain product. Suppose also that students are willing to pay $10 per unit while the professors are willing to pay only $6. Obviously, the monopolistic firm can increase its profits by charging a price of $10 to the students and a price of $6 to the professors. By not charging a single price of $6, the monopolist has succeeded in preventing the students from paying only $6 when they would be willing to pay $10. If, on the other hand, the monopolist charges a single price of $10, the professors will not purchase any of the product. We can use the concept of consumer's surplus discussed in Chapter 6 to illustrate why the monopolist benefits from price discrimination. By charging each consumer the maximum amount that he or she is willing to pay, the monopolist captures the entire amount of the consumers' surplus.

> Price discrimination will be profitable only if the price elasticity of demand in each market is different.

THE DISTRIBUTION OF OUTPUT BETWEEN THE MARKETS

We now turn our attention to the decision faced by the discriminating monopoly. The discriminating monopoly must decide how much to sell in each market and at what price. We can analyze the behaviour of the discriminating monopoly with the help of Figure 11.10. Diagrams A and B show the demand and marginal revenue curves in two markets, A and B. Here we assume, for simplicity, that the marginal cost is constant in each market at 0C. In order to maximize profits, the monopolistic firm will sell, in each market, an amount such that marginal revenue equals marginal cost. The firm will therefore sell Q_a units in market A and Q_b units in market B. The price in market A will be P_a, while the price in market B will be P_b. Note that the higher price occurs in the market with the less elastic demand.

FIGURE 11.10

The distribution of output by a discriminating monopolist.

To maximize profits, the discriminating monopolist will allocate output in the various markets in such a way that marginal revenue equals marginal cost in each of the markets.

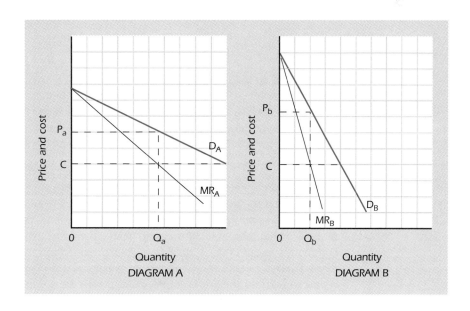

DIAGRAM A

DIAGRAM B

THE EFFECTS OF PRICE DISCRIMINATION

We have seen that by engaging in price discrimination, the monopolistic firm can increase its profits. Let us now compare the output of a discriminating monopoly with that of a non-discriminating monopoly. Figure 11.11 illustrates that a non-discriminating monopoly will produce an output of Q_1, where marginal revenue equals marginal cost. If it engages in complete price discrimination, selling each unit at the maximum price that a consumer is willing to pay, its demand curve will, in effect, become its marginal revenue curve. The discriminating monopoly will equate marginal revenue and marginal cost and thus produce an output of Q_2 units. It is unlikely that the monopolist will be able to practise complete price discrimination, because this would require the firm to know exactly the maximum price that each buyer is willing to pay. However, we can conclude that a discriminating monopoly will produce a greater output than a non-discriminating monopoly.

FIGURE 11.11

Discriminating and non-discriminating monopolists.

Price discrimination allows the monopolist to produce a greater output than would be the case without price discrimination.

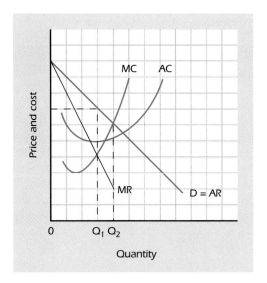

IS PRICE DISCRIMINATION BAD?

There can be little doubt that many of those who pay the higher prices under price discrimination consider the practice to be unfair. It is also clear that price discrimination is beneficial to the monopolists who practise it. Let us now proceed beyond these obvious facts and delve more deeply into the pros and cons of price discrimination.

The pros

Many goods and services might not be produced if the monopolist were not able to practise price discrimination.

On the positive side, we may note that many goods and services might not be produced at all if the monopolist were not to engage in price discrimination. For example, physicians in small remote communities may find it worthwhile to keep their practices in those communities only if they can charge their wealthy clients a higher price than they can their poorer clients. Similarly, price discrimination in airfares makes it possible for many parents to take their children on vacation. Price discrimination along these lines seems to be desirable and therefore should not be condemned.

The cons

Price discrimination may lead to misallocation of resources.

On the negative side, the practice of price discrimination may be carried to the point where the price falls below marginal cost. For example, price discrimination in electricity rates could result in such low rates to residential users that they end up wasting electricity. When price is allowed to fall below marginal cost, a misallocation of resources results. The amount of resources that would flow into the industry is above the social optimum. As another example, consider the case of a public transit system. Price discrimination is usually practised in favour of children and the elderly. If price discrimination is carried too far in this case, taxpayers may have to subsidize the transit system. Resources that could be better allocated elsewhere would be diverted into this industry.

APPLICATIONS

The analytical tools that we have introduced in this chapter can help us to organize our thoughts properly on certain issues relating to decisions in a monopolistic situation. In this section, we shall study the effects of taxes on monopolistic behaviour. First, we shall study the effect of an excise tax. (You will recall that an excise tax is a tax imposed on a particular commodity that is domestically produced.) We shall then study the effect of a tax on the profits of the monopolist.

THE EFFECT OF AN EXCISE TAX

Let us assume that a monopolist has to pay an excise tax on each unit of a product that it sells. Will the monopolist raise the price by the amount of the tax? Many people would answer yes to this question, but let us analyze the situation with the help of Figure 11.12. We assume, for simplicity, that the demand and marginal revenue curves are linear, and that the monopolist has constant marginal cost. AR and MR are, as usual, average revenue and marginal revenue and MC is marginal cost before the imposition of the tax. According to Figure 11.12, the monopolist produces a quantity of Q and charges a price of P in order to maximize profits. After the tax is imposed, the marginal cost curve shifts up by the amount of the tax, to MC_t. The firm now produces an output of

FIGURE 11.12

The effect of an excise tax.

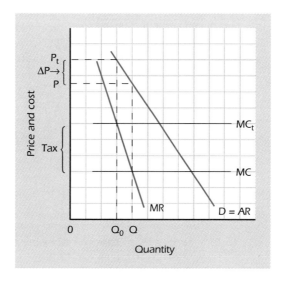

Q_0 and charges a price of P_t. The increase in price from P to P_t is less than the tax (the distance between MC and MC_t). We can therefore draw the following conclusion:

If an excise tax is imposed on each unit of a commodity sold by a monopolist, the price will rise, but by an amount less than the tax.

THE EFFECT OF A TAX ON PROFITS

In Canada, as in many other countries, firms are required to pay taxes on their profits. Let us assume that a monopolist has to pay 30% of its profits in taxes. Should it raise its price by 30% in order to shift the burden of the tax on to its customers? Let us investigate. Let us assume that the monopolist is maximizing its profits by equating its marginal revenue and its marginal cost. If it raises its price, its profits will fall. It makes more sense to pay the tax out of the maximum profits than out of reduced profits that would result from an increase in price.

The data in Table 11.4 illustrate this point. Clearly, the price that maximizes profits before taxes is $5. After taxes, the price that maximizes profits is still $5.

	Price	Profits before tax	30% tax	Profits after tax
TABLE 11.4				
Profits before and after tax.	$6	$10 000	$3 000	$ 7 000
	5	15 000	4 500	10 500
	4	9 500	2 850	6 650

GLOBAL PERSPECTIVE

De Beers and Diamonds

The De Beers Company of South Africa provides a famous example of a monopoly over a commodity — diamonds. De Beers has exercised control over the world production of diamonds for many years, either through ownership of diamond mines or by entering into marketing agreements with other mine owners. De Beers Consolidated Mines has interests in 19 diamond mines in Africa, and through its cartel, the Central Selling Organization (CSO), it wields tremendous control over much of the world's diamond production.

But the power of the cartel has been challenged by diamond producers in Angola, Australia, Canada, and Russia. Moreover, monopoly pricing practices by De Beers have made the production of diamond substitutes attractive. In the past, it was relatively easy even for a nonprofessional in the field to distinguish a real diamond from a synthetic diamond, so the synthetic product was not really considered a close substitute for the real product. However, technological advances in the production of synthetic diamonds have made them so close in appearance to real diamonds that it is now extremely difficult for most purchasers of diamonds to distinguish between real and synthetic. The production of close substitutes for diamonds has weakened the monopoly position of De Beers in the world market for diamonds.

CHAPTER SUMMARY

1. In a monopoly situation, only one firm sells a product that has no close substitutes. Since substitutes can be found for most products, examples of pure monopoly are hard to find in the real world.

2. Monopolies exist because of barriers to entry into a market. Such barriers include legal barriers such as patent rights, ownership of essential raw materials, and economies of scale.

3. Since the monopolistic firm is the only firm in the industry, its demand curve is identical to the industry demand curve and slopes downward from left to right.

4. Because the demand curve of the monopolistic firm slopes downward, the marginal revenue curve must also slope downward. Also marginal revenue will be less than demand or average revenue in the case of a monopoly.

5. The monopolist maximizes profits at a level of output at which marginal revenue equals marginal cost. However, the monopolist's price will exceed marginal cost. Fear of government regulation, fear of the entry of other firms into the market, and a desire not to incite public outcry are some of the factors that may prevent a monopolist from seeking maximum profits.

6. When marginal revenue is positive, demand is elastic. When marginal revenue is zero, demand is unitary elastic; and when marginal revenue is negative, demand is inelastic. The profit-maximizing monopolist will never operate at an output level at which demand is inelastic.

7. Compared with purely competitive firms, the monopolist produces a smaller output and sells at a higher price. Also, the monopolist may earn positive economic profits in the long run. Any positive profits that a competitive firm may earn in the short run will disappear in the long run due to competition.

8. Because of certain socially undesirable consequences of monopolization, the government may regulate certain monopolies. The regulated monopoly usually produces a greater output and sells at a lower price than would be the case if the monopoly were unregulated.

9. Price discrimination is the practice of charging different prices among different buyers for the same product or service. Price discrimination is possible only if the buyers can be grouped into different classes and if the monopolist can prevent purchases in one market for resale in another.

10. Price discrimination is possible only if the price elasticity of demand in each market is different. The discriminating monopolist tries to capture the consumers' surplus.

11. The discriminating monopolist will produce an output at which marginal revenue equals marginal cost, and will distribute this output among the markets in such a way that marginal revenue equals marginal cost in each market.

12. The discriminating monopolist produces a greater output and sells at a lower price than a non-discriminating monopolist.

13. Price discrimination may result in the wasteful use of the product, but, on the other hand, it may make certain goods and services available to consumers, which might not be possible in the absence of price discrimination.

TERMS FOR REVIEW

monopoly (186)	allocative efficiency (195)
barriers to entry (186)	monopoly power (market power) (197)
patent (186)	regulated monopoly (197)
franchise (186)	price discrimination (198)
natural monopoly (187)	arbitrage transactions (198)
X-inefficiency (193)	

QUESTIONS FOR REVIEW AND DISCUSSION

1. What difficulty is involved in defining a monopoly? (General)
2. Name and discuss factors that give rise to monopolies. (L.O.1)
3. Explain why a monopolist faces a downward-sloping demand curve. (L.O.2)
4. Give examples of monopolies in your area and explain why they are monopolies. (L.O.2)
5. Do monopolies always earn large positive economic profits? Explain. (L.O.4)
6. Explain why a monopolistic firm seeking to maximize its profits will not operate at a level of output and price range at which the demand for its product is inelastic. (L.O.5)
7. What considerations may lead a monopolist to seek less than maximum profits? (General)
8. "A profit-maximizing monopolist will always charge the highest possible price for its product." Discuss. (General)
9. By examining pricing and output decisions under monopoly, explain how monopolies affect the allocation of resources. (L.O.6)
10. Explain the term monopoly power. What actions might a government take to prevent the abuse of monopoly power? (L.O.7)
11. What problem may result from marginal-cost pricing regulation of a monopoly? (L.O.7)
12. From a social point of view, what advantages does pure competition have over monopoly? (L.O.6)
13. What is price discrimination? What circumstances encourage a monopolist to practise price discrimination? (L.O.8)
14. When is price discrimination possible? When is it profitable? (L.O.8)
15. Explain how a discriminating monopolist allocates output between two markets with different price elasticities of demand in order to maximize profits. (L.O.8)
16. What are the economic effects of price discrimination? (L.O.8)
17. Do you think that we should always condemn price discrimination? (L.O.8)
18. What are the pros and cons of price discrimination? (L.O.8)

PROBLEMS AND EXERCISES

1. Table 11. 5 shows the demand schedule for Clockwise Ltd., a monopolistic firm. (L.O.2,3)

   (a) Compute the marginal revenue for Clockwise at each level of output.

   (b) On a graph, plot the average revenue and the marginal revenue curves for Clockwise.

TABLE 11.5	Quantity	Price
Demand schedule for Clockwise.	1	$20.00
	2	17.50
	3	15.00
	4	12.50
	5	10.00
	6	7.50

2. Figure 11.13 represents Power Plus, a monopolistic firm. (L.O.4)

FIGURE 11.13

Revenue and cost curves for Power Plus.

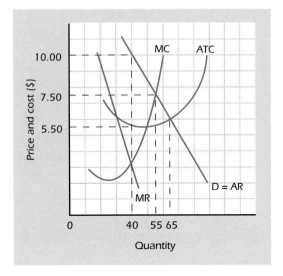

(a) What output should Power Plus produce in order to maximize its profits?
(b) What price should it charge?
(c) What is the maximum total profit that this firm can earn?
(d) What is the firm's total revenue at the profit-maximizing output?
(e) What is the firm's total cost when it is maximizing its profits?

3. The data presented in Table 11.6 are for the Isotemp Corporation, which is a monopoly. (L.O.3,4)

(a) Construct a table showing Isotemp's marginal cost and marginal revenue.

(b) Plot Isotemp's marginal revenue and marginal cost curves.

(c) What level of output should Isotemp produce so as to maximize profits?

(d) At what price will this output sell?

TABLE 11.6

Isotemp's cost and revenue.

Quantity	Total cost ($)	Total revenue ($)
0	10	0
5	15	15.00
10	21	27.50
15	28	37.50
20	36	45.00
25	45	50.00
30	55	52.50
35	66	52.50

4. Figure 11.14 shows the revenue curves for the Safe-T Transport Company (a monopoly). The cost of transporting an additional passenger from point A to point B is practically zero. (L.O.4)
(a) What price should this firm charge in order to maximize its profits?
(b) What level of output should it produce?

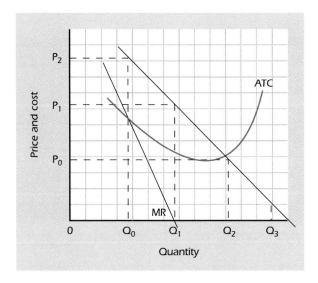

FIGURE 11.14

Cost and revenue for Safe-T Transport.

5. Show that if marginal cost is zero, the monopolistic firm maximizes its profits by producing at the point where the price elasticity of demand is 1. (L.O.5)

6. Table 11.7 contains data for a monopolistic firm called Monopole. (L.O.3,4)

TABLE 11.7

Price and cost data for Monopole.

P	Q	TR	MR	TC	MC	Total profit
$900	0			$ 400		
800	1			500		
700	2			550		
600	3			650		
500	4			850		
400	5			1 150		
300	6			1 430		
200	7			1 800		

(a) Complete the table.

(b) What output should Monopole produce in order to maximize its profits?

(c) What price will Monopole charge?

(d) What will Monopole's total profit be at this price?

7. Use the data in Table 11.7 to draw the demand and marginal revenue curves for Monopole. What do you notice about the relation between demand and marginal revenue? (L.O.2,3)

8. Figure 11.15 shows the average revenue and marginal cost curves for a monopolist called Unifirm. (L.O.3,4)

(a) Draw in the marginal revenue curve.

(b) What price will maximize Unifirm's profit?

(c) What output should the firm produce?

FIGURE 11.15

Unifirm's MC and AR curves.

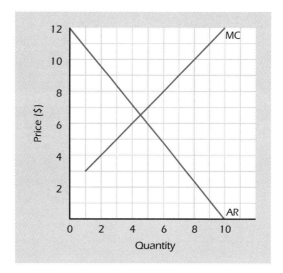

9. A monopolistic firm, Coverall Ltd., produces a particular type of garment. Coverall has to pay a tax of 40% of its profits. Should Coverall raise its price and thus try to pass the tax on to its customers? (L.O.4)

10. To a large extent, Bell Canada enjoys a monopoly in the sale of telephone service. If the federal government imposes a tax of $2 on each unit of telephone line installed by Bell, will Bell increase the price of each unit by $2? (L.O.4)

 11. Municipal governments have a monopoly on garbage collection and disposal, and people pay for this service through their taxes. Discuss the pros and cons of breaking up the government's monopoly and permitting private contractors to enter the garbage collection business, selling their services privately to households and firms.

Internet Site

http://www.bayer.ca
This site is the home page for Bayer Inc.-Canada. This company is heavily involved in the research and development of pharmaceutical and other products worldwide.

INTERNET EXERCISE

1. Go to the Bayer site listed above.
2. Click on *Bayer Facts.*
3. Click on *Bayer and Innovations.*
4. List five breakthrough products developed by Bayer.
5. In one short paragraph, outline Bayer's attitude to R&D.
6. Click on *Bayer and Its Products.*
7. Click on one room of the house, and list all of the Bayer products found there.

12

C H A P T E R

IMPERFECT COMPETITION: MONOPOLISTIC COMPETITION AND OLIGOPOLY

Learning Objectives

After studying this chapter, you should:

1 understand the concept of monopolistic competition

2 be familiar with demand and marginal revenue of the firm in monopolistic competition

3 understand short-run equilibrium in monopolistic competition

4 know the conditions for long-run equilibrium in monopolistic competition

5 know the differences and similarities between monopolistic competition and pure competition

6 understand the effects of advertising

7 understand the behaviour of firms in oligopoly

8 understand oligopolistic pricing and output

9 be familiar with the kinked demand curve model

10 understand alternative pricing strategies

11 understand cartels and other forms of collusion

12 know the theory of contestable markets

Each firm in any sector of the system in which monopolistic competition prevails offers products that differ in some way from the products of every other firm in the sector, and thus supplies a special market of its own.

Joseph A. Schumpeter, *Business Cycles*

INTRODUCTION

Imperfect competition is neither monopolistic nor pure competition.

In this chapter, we shall concern ourselves mainly with the pricing and output decisions of firms in monopolistic competition and oligopoly markets. Economists often use the term **imperfect competition** to refer to a market structure that is neither purely competitive nor purely monopolistic. Hence, the term encompasses both monopolistic competition and oligopoly. In Canada, most firms operate in market structures that are neither purely competitive nor purely monopolistic, but lie somewhere between these two opposites. Most firms in Canada operate in monopolistically competitive or oligopolistic market structures.

MONOPOLISTIC COMPETITION

Learning Objective 1: understand the concept of monopolistic competition

As the name implies, monopolistic competition contains elements of both pure competition and monopoly. In this type of market structure, there are many firms selling similar but differentiated products. The characteristics of monopolistic competition are set out below. As these characteristics are outlined, you will recognize the similarity between this market structure and pure competition. You may find it helpful to refer to Table 10.1 on page 168 to review market structure characteristics.

1. RELATIVELY LARGE NUMBER OF FIRMS

Monopolistic competition involves a relatively large number of firms.

A monopolistically competitive market structure (monopolistic competition) consists of a relatively large number of firms. The number need not be as large as in pure competition. Although a specific number will only be arbitrary, most students still like to have an idea of what is relatively large when referring to monopolistic competition. For this purpose, a number between 30 and 100 will suffice. Because the number of firms is relatively large, each one's share of the total market, though not negligible, is relatively small — just enough to cause each firm to have a slight influence on price. Also, the number of firms is sufficiently large to make it impractical for the firms to get together to act jointly to control price and output in the market. Each firm acts independently of the others because the action of any one will have a very small (almost unnoticeable) effect on the others.

2. DIFFERENTIATED PRODUCTS

Product differentiation is characteristic of firms in monopolistic competition.

You will recall that in pure competition, the firms produce identical products. In monopolistic competition, the firms produce differentiated products. Indeed, product differentiation is a key feature of monopolistic competition. **Product differentiation** is a situation in which firms use a number of devices to distinguish their products from those of other firms in the same industry.

An important point to grasp here is that it does not matter much whether the products *are* different. What matters is whether buyers *perceive* them to be different. The true test of the existence of product differentiation is whether or not buyers prefer to purchase the item from one seller rather than from another.

Product differentiation may be achieved in many ways. First, it may be achieved through product characteristics such as distinctive designs, packaging, trademarks, colour, durability, and brand names. Some trademarks and brand names have become so popular that the product is identified by the brand name or trademark. Examples that may come to mind are Kleenex (for tissues), Band-Aid (for plastic bandage strips), Xerox (for photocopy), Scotch tape (for transparent adhesive tape), Q-tips (for cotton swabs), Vaseline (for white petroleum jelly), and Walkman (for mini stereo cassette players).

Second, product differentiation may be achieved through product image. The idea is to create a certain image of the product with the hope that it will appeal to certain buyers. For example, a product that has a conservative image will likely appeal to people who behave conservatively. A certain type of car, for example, may portray this conservative image.

Finally, product differentiation may be achieved through emphasizing certain features of the firm. These features may include convenient location, attention given to customers by the firm's employees, and the services provided along with the product. A beauty salon may provide reading material or free coffee while its clients are waiting to be served. A furniture store may offer free delivery anywhere in the city and surrounding areas. These services differentiate these firms from those that offer no such services. A car dealer may build a reputation on the basis of the service offered to its customers after they purchase a car. Product differentiation on the basis of services rendered is an attempt to compel consumers to view the product and the service offered with it as a single item. This type of product differentiation is particularly prevalent in retail outlets where it is difficult or impossible to differentiate the physical characteristics of the product. The video cassettes rented from one video outlet are identical to those of other outlets. The service, however, may vary from one outlet to another.

Monopolistic competition is prevalent in service industries. The many different beauty salons, barber shops, and restaurants operating in any large city are good examples of monopolistic competition. Other examples include bakeries, gasoline stations, shoe stores, men's and women's clothing stores, automotive garages, stationery stores, and florists.

3.   FREEDOM OF ENTRY AND EXIT

In the case of pure competition, there is freedom of entry into, and exit from, the industry. In the case of monopolistic competition, entry and exit are relatively easy. Entry may not be as easy as in pure competition because of the need to differentiate one's product in a monopolistically competitive market. Also, to break into the monopolistically competitive industry may require significant advertising, the financial burden of which may be a factor limiting entry into the market.

There is relative freedom of entry and exit in monopolistic competition.

PROBLEM SOLVING 12-1

You operate a pharmacy in your neighbourhood. Will you set your prices significantly above the prices in other pharmacies?

DEMAND AND MARGINAL REVENUE OF THE FIRM IN MONOPOLISTIC COMPETITION

Learning Objective 2: be familiar with demand and marginal revenue of the firm in monopolistic competition

The firm in monopolistic competition is one among many. However, because its product is perceived to be different from those of its competitors, the monopolistic competitor is able to exercise some control over price. If the monopolistic competitor raises its price, it will lose some of its customers. But those who strongly prefer the product in question may remain; brand loyalty will cause them to stay with their preferred brand. If the firm lowers its price, it will attract some customers from its competitors. But all buyers will not be attracted by the small reduction in price. This implies that the demand curve for the monopolistic competitor slopes downward. Because there are so many close substitutes for the product of any one firm in monopolistic competition, the demand for the product of any one firm is likely to be relatively elastic. The degree of elasticity will depend on the degree of product differentiation that the firm is able to achieve.

A downward-sloping demand curve implies a downward-sloping marginal revenue curve. The firm in monopolistic competition can sell a greater quantity only by lowering the price. Hence, each additional unit adds a smaller amount to total revenue. Demand and marginal revenue curves for a firm in monopolistic competition are shown in Figure 12.1.

FIGURE 12.1

Demand and marginal revenue curves for a firm in monopolistic competition.

The average and marginal revenue curves of a firm in monopolistic competition slope downwards.

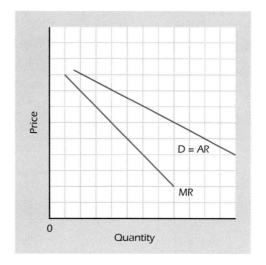

SHORT-RUN EQUILIBRIUM IN MONOPOLISTIC COMPETITION

Learning Objective 3: understand short-run equilibrium in monopolistic competition

The individual firm in a monopolistically competitive industry must decide on the price and output combination that will maximize its profits. Profits will be maximized when marginal revenue equals marginal cost. The short-run equilibrium (profit-maximizing) position of a monopolistically competitive firm is shown in Figure 12.2. The firm shown in the diagram will earn maximum profits by producing an output of 0Q and selling at a price of 0P. The firm is earning positive economic profits since its price of 0P is greater than its unit cost of 0C. The profit is shown by the shaded rectangle in Figure 12.2.

A firm in monopolistic competition may incur losses in the short run. Figure 12.3 illustrates this situation. We assume that this firm is covering its variable costs. The firm is doing

FIGURE 12.2

Short-run equilibrium of a firm in monopolistic competition.

The monopolistically competitive firm will be in equilibrium when its marginal revenue equals its marginal cost.

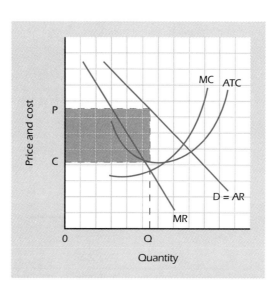

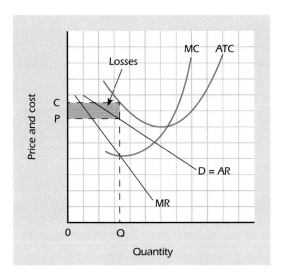

A monopolistically competitive firm incurring losses.

A firm in monopolistic competition may incur losses in the short run when its marginal revenue equals its marginal cost.

the best it can in the short run by producing an output of 0Q and charging a price of 0P. It is, however, incurring losses because its price, 0P, is below its average total cost, 0C. The losses are illustrated by the shaded area in Figure 12.3.

LONG-RUN EQUILIBRIUM IN MONOPOLISTIC COMPETITION

In monopolistic competition, as in pure competition, entry into and exit from the industry are easy. If the firms in the industry are earning positive economic profits, new firms will be attracted into the industry. As this happens, the demand curve for each firm will shift to the left, as shown in diagram A of Figure 12.4, as each firm's share of the total industry demand falls. D is the original demand curve, representing the firm's share of the market demand, and D_0 is the new demand curve after the adjustment to the entry of new firms into the industry. The firm is still earning profits since its demand curve is still above its average total cost curve.

Effects of the entry of new firms.

Entry and exit in monopolistic competition change the firm's share of the market.

Learning Objective 4: know the conditions for long-run equilibrium in monopolistic competition

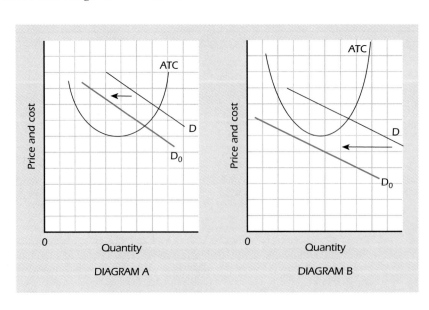

If too many firms enter the industry, the demand curve will shift below the average cost curve. The firm will then incur losses. This occurrence is shown in diagram B of Figure 12.4. Here, the demand curve has shifted from D to D_0, which is now below the average total cost curve. This drop will cause some firms to leave the industry, and as a result, the demand curve will shift back to the right.

When each firm in the industry is earning only normal profits (that is, when P = ATC), the entry and exit of firms will cease, and long-run equilibrium will be achieved. This situation is illustrated in Figure 12.5. The firm will produce an output of 0Q units at a price of 0P. Note that in long-run equilibrium, marginal revenue equals marginal cost, and price equals average cost.

FIGURE 12.5

Long-run equilibrium of a firm in monopolistic competition.

In long-run equilibrium, a firm in monopolistic competition earns only normal profits.

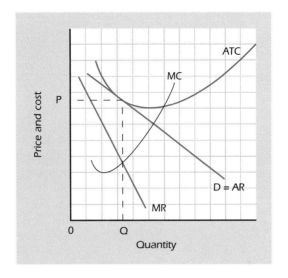

MONOPOLISTIC COMPETITION COMPARED WITH PURE COMPETITION

Learning Objective 5: know the differences and similarities between monopolistic competition and pure competition

A monopolistically competitive firm in long-run equilibrium will operate with excess capacity.

We can evaluate the efficiency of monopolistic competition relative to pure competition with the help of Figure 12.6. This diagram shows that, in pure competition, price equals marginal cost. In monopolistic competition, price exceeds marginal cost. This means that resources are not optimally allocated in monopolistic competition. An increase in output by the monopolistically competitive firm would benefit the society. The firm in monopolistic competition is wasteful in the sense that it does not produce at the lowest point of its average cost curve as the purely competitive firm does. The fact that the monopolistic competitor does not produce at minimum average cost implies that the firm has excess or under-utilized capacity. This concept has been termed the **excess capacity theorem**, and may be stated as follows:

> **In long-run equilibrium, a firm in monopolistic competition will operate with excess capacity. That is, it will operate at a point to the left of the minimum point on its long-run average cost curve.**

Figure 12.6 also shows that the purely competitive firm produces a greater output (Q_{pc}) than the monopolistically competitive firm does (Q_{mc}), and that the price charged by the monopolistically competitive firm (P_{mc}) is higher than the purely competitive price (P_{pc}).

FIGURE 12.6

A comparison of pure
competition and
monopolistic
competition.

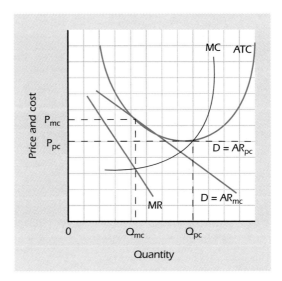

A question that is quite often asked is whether the consumer is better off under pure competition than under monopolistic competition. Under pure competition, the consumer pays a lower price, but his choice of product is limited. In a purely competitive industry, all of the firms in that industry produce identical products. In a monopolistically competitive industry, the consumer can choose from a wide variety of differentiated products. We can argue that the higher price under monopolistic competition is offset by the greater choice that the consumer enjoys. Whether or not the greater variety of products sufficiently compensates for the higher price is a normative matter and cannot be answered by economic analysis. The decision rests with the individual consumer.

ADVERTISING

A firm advertises in order to maintain or increase its share of the market.

Learning Objective 6: *understand the effects of advertising*

Advertising is, in itself, a form of non-price competition. A purely competitive firm need not spend money trying to increase the amount that it can sell. It can sell as much as it can produce at the going price. But for a monopolistic competitor, advertising may result in an increase in profits. It is obvious that for advertising to be profitable, it must add more to the firm's total revenue than it does to its total cost. If advertising is successful, it will increase the demand for the firm's product and will also make it less elastic. This will increase the market power of the monopolistically competitive firm. If advertising outlay is a fixed cost, then it will not affect marginal cost. And if advertising does not significantly affect demand for the firm's product, then the price and quantity at which MR = MC will not change appreciably. In that case, advertising will simply push up the firm's total cost and hence reduce the firm's profits.

PROBLEM SOLVING 12-2

You manage a café in Port Alberni. Another café across the street has just installed an air-conditioner. What will you do?

A P P L I C A T I O N

A Competitive Strategy

Firms in monopolistic competition can adopt a variety of competitive strategies. They can employ price competition, **quality competition**, or competitive advertising, in which product differentiation may be emphasized. A company that has built up a reputation for the high quality of its products may be able to keep its prices above those of its competitors. Whereas its competitors may compete on the basis of price, it may compete on the basis of quality. Historically, IBM typewriters and computers and Fisher Price toys have long been considered products of "superior value," and consequently these firms were able to charge a higher price for their products.

A competitive strategy based on superior-quality goods is likely to succeed when the market consists of buyers who are more quality-conscious than price-conscious. The model of monopolistic competition, with its product-differentiation feature, helps to explain the coexistence of higher-priced and lower-priced firms, and high-quality and lower-quality products, in the same industry.

THE PROS AND CONS OF ADVERTISING

Quality competition: competition by a firm attempting to make its products superior to the competitors'.

The issue of advertising has received a great deal of attention in economics and marketing literature. Does advertising increase or reduce prices? Is advertising wasteful? Does advertising hinder or promote competition? These issues are debatable. In this section, we shall take a quick look at the main arguments in favour of and against advertising.

The pros

Those who argue in favour of advertising make the following claims:

Advertising may create employment and income.

1. Advertising creates employment and income for people in the advertising business, and for people who work in the media. In addition, advertising increases the demand for goods and services, and since the production of goods and services requires the use of resources, including labour, it increases employment in general.

Advertising may lead to economies of scale.

2. Advertising enables firms to take advantage of economies of scale. This argument can be illustrated with the help of Figure 12.7. AC represents the firm's average cost without advertising. Suppose the quantity of the firm's product demanded without advertising is 0Q. This output will be produced at an average cost of 0C. Now, because of advertising, the firm's average cost curve shifts upward from AC to AC_a, and the quantity demanded now grows from 0Q to $0Q_1$. But the average cost of producing this greater output has fallen from 0C to $0C_0$. Here, the benefits from economies of scale outweigh the increase in average cost resulting from advertising. Consumers benefit by obtaining the product at a lower price with advertising than without it.

Advertising gives valuable information.

3. Advertising provides consumers with valuable information that enables them to make better decisions in the market. By informing consumers about new products, new locations and new firms, advertising greatly reduces search costs to consumers.

Advertising results in product improvement and development.

4. Advertising leads to product improvement and development. When a firm advertises its product, it emphasizes some advantage of its product over the products of its competitors. A firm must therefore improve its product in order to justify its advertising claims. Moreover, the fact that its competitors are also advertising puts pressure on the firm to improve its product and its service.

FIGURE 12.7

The effect of advertising.

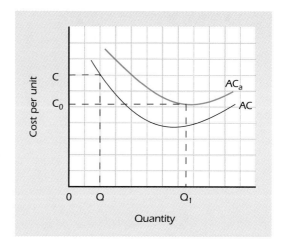

5. Advertising increases competition. Advertising makes it easier to successfully launch new products that are close substitutes for existing products. Thus, advertising increases the number of firms in the industry and makes it more competitive.

Advertising may make markets more competitive.

The cons

Those who argue against advertising raise the following points to support their case:

1. Advertising increases monopoly power. Firms in certain industries spend millions of dollars each year on advertising. In order to break into such industries, potential competitors must be willing to make those massive advertising outlays. This in itself may prove to be an effective barrier to new firms.

Advertising may increase monopoly power.

2. Advertising is wasteful. Resources that could be productively employed in other industries to produce goods and services to satisfy wants are wasted in advertising. Why, it is argued, use so much ink and paper in advertising, when those same resources could be used in producing educational books, which would improve the society's well-being?

Advertising may lead to a misallocation of society's resources.

3. Advertising may increase costs and prices. A good portion of advertising simply causes consumers to switch from brand to brand. The output of the industry does not increase as a result of advertising, but costs rise, the market share of each firm hardly changes at all, and consumers end up paying higher prices.

Advertising may result in higher costs and prices.

4. Advertising is mainly persuasive, not informational. Many of the advertisements on radio and television give very little useful information to consumers in terms of helping them to make rational choices. Some advertisements, it is claimed, may even give misleading or false information.

Most advertising is persuasive or competitive rather than informative.

5. Advertising imposes indirect costs on society. Unsightly billboards that mar the beauty of the landscape, tons of advertising circulars that must be disposed of, and advertisements that are in bad taste are some examples of the costs imposed on society by advertising.

Advertising forces society to incur indirect costs.

OLIGOPOLY

Learning Objective 7: understand the behaviour of firms in oligopoly

Duopoly: a market structure consisting of only two firms.

An oligopolistic industry consists of only a few firms.

Oligopolistic firms recognize their interdependence.

Entry barriers exist in oligopoly.

A differentiated oligopoly is a market with a few firms selling differentiated products.

Concentration ratios provide information about the competitive nature of an industry.

The term **oligopoly** has been applied to an industry that consists of a few firms, each producing a substantial share of the total output of that industry. This type of market structure is typical of the petroleum industry, the automobile industry, and the steel industry, to name only a few. If the industry consists of only two firms, the term **duopoly** is generally used. The main features of oligopoly are outlined below.

1. FEW FIRMS
The industry consists of only a few firms — so few that each produces a relatively large share of the total output of the industry. As in the case of monopolistic competition, any specific number given must be quite arbitrary, but one typically thinks of an oligopolistic industry as consisting of two to 15 firms.

2. INTERDEPENDENCE RECOGNIZED
As a consequence of the small number of firms in an oligopolistic industry, the actions taken by any one firm have a noticeable effect on the other firms. Acknowledging this interdependence is crucial in understanding the behaviour of firms in oligopolistic industries.

3. BARRIERS TO ENTRY
There are barriers to entry into an oligopolistic industry. These barriers often include the huge capital investment necessary to establish an oligopolistic firm, and the enormous advertising necessary to capture a worthwhile share of the market.

4. IDENTICAL OR DIFFERENTIATED PRODUCTS
Oligopolistic firms may produce identical products or they may produce differentiated products. For example, the cement produced by one firm is similar to that produced by the other firms. There is an obvious difference, however, between General Motors' compact cars and Ford's compact cars. The term **differentiated oligopoly** is used when the products of the firms in an oligopolistic market are differentiated.

CONCENTRATION RATIOS
The extent to which a market is dominated by a few firms can be determined by looking at **concentration ratios**. These ratios show the percentage of total market supply accounted for by a few of the largest firms in the industry, for example, a concentration ratio would tell you what percentage of the beer industry's business is done by only two of the largest breweries. The larger companies in highly concentrated industries usually have branches in several provinces and sell their output from coast to coast. Table 12.1 contains a list of manufacturing industries with relatively high concentration ratios.

TABLE 12.1

Industries with high concentration ratios.

Industry	
Tobacco products	Aircraft and aircraft parts
Breweries	Business and office machines
Motor vehicle manufacturing	Organic chemicals
Iron and steel mills	Publishing and printing
Electrical wire cables	Petroleum refining
Smelting and refining	Telecommunications material

Source: Statistics Canada, *Canada Yearbook, 1988.* (Latest data available).

OLIGOPOLISTIC PRICING AND OUTPUT

Learning Objective 8:
understand oligopolistic pricing and output

The oligopolistic firm produces a substantial portion of the total industry output and therefore has some control over the price of its product. Product differentiation by the oligopolistic firm may also increase its market power. The demand curve for the oligopolistic firm therefore slopes downward. Like firms in other market situations, the oligopolistic firm is assumed to be a profit-maximizer. The oligopolistic firm will therefore produce an output at which marginal revenue equals marginal cost. In Figure 12.8, the profit-maximizing output is 0Q, and the price charged is 0P.

FIGURE 12.8

Price and output in an oligopolistic firm.

The profit-maximizing oligopolist firm equates its marginal revenue and its marginal cost.

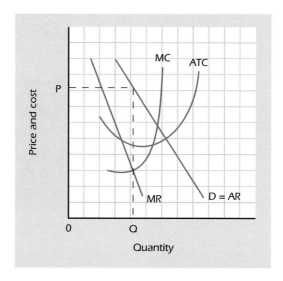

An increase in the cost of production will normally lead a firm to increase the price of its product. If an oligopolistic firm increases its price, however, some buyers will probably switch to substitutes offered by other firms. Such crossover may result in an increase in the prices of the substitutes.

PROBLEM SOLVING 12-3

Suppose that you are the manager of a grocery store, and there are only two other grocery stores in the area. Suppose also that you and your competitors are earning satisfactory profits but you know that you could increase your profits if you could increase your sales. Would you cut your prices in order to woo customers away from your competitors?

THE KINKED DEMAND CURVE

It has been observed that prices tend to remain relatively stable in oligopoly markets. One explanation for this relative price stability is that firms in oligopolistic industries realize that a price cut by one firm will cause other firms to retaliate by cutting their prices also. Instead of engaging in a price war, which will hurt every firm, each firm tacitly agrees to live and let live by sharing the market — and the profits. This, of course, is a result of the strong interdependence of firms in oligopoly markets, which is absent in other market structures.

The kinked demand curve explains price rigidity.

The model of the **kinked demand curve,** advanced independently but almost simultaneously in 1939 by Paul Sweezy in the United States and by R. Hall and C. Hitch in

Learning Objective 9: be familiar with the kinked demand curve model

Britain, explains price rigidity in oligopolistic industries. The theory is based on two basic assumptions about firms' reactions to price changes by their rivals. The assumptions are:

1. a price increase by one firm will not be matched by similar increases in other firms;

2. a reduction in price by one firm will be matched by similar reductions in other firms.

Oligopolistic firms are assumed to behave in this manner in order to keep their customers or to capture a larger share of the market. If, for example, Coke increases the price of its cola, we can assume that Pepsi, in order to attract customers from Coke, will leave its price unchanged. But if Coke reduces its price, it is assumed that Pepsi will follow suit in order not to lose customers to Coke.

This situation is illustrated in Figure 12.9. Consider an oligopolist selling a product at price P. If the firm raises its price above P, its rivals, by assumption, will not raise their prices. Thus, the quantity of the firm's product demanded can be expected to fall significantly as buyers switch to the firm's rivals. This implies that the demand curve is relatively elastic at prices above P.

If the oligopolist lowers its price from P, its rivals will, by assumption, follow its lead and lower their prices in order not to lose their customers. Thus, the quantity of the firm's product demand as a result of lowering its price will not increase significantly. There is no price incentive for buyers to switch from the firm's rivals. This implies that the demand curve is relatively inelastic at prices below P. The demand curve is relatively elastic at prices above P and relatively inelastic at prices below P.

Thus, the demand curve has a kink at point A in Figure 12.9. The marginal revenue curve associated with such a demand curve is also illustrated. Note that the marginal revenue curve has a discontinuous section.

Figure 12.9 shows that if the marginal revenue and the marginal cost curves intersect within the range of the vertical section of the marginal revenue curve, an appreciable shift in the marginal cost curve will have no effect on the profit-maximizing price and output for the firm. For example, an increase in the marginal cost from MC_1 to MC_2 leaves price and output unchanged at 0P and 0Q respectively. Changes in cost will affect price and output only when they are very substantial.

FIGURE 12.9

The kinked demand curve.

An appreciable increase in cost leaves the price unchanged.

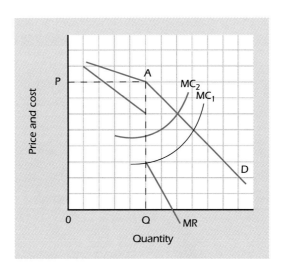

The model of the kinked demand curve explains how a kink occurs in the demand curve, but it does not explain where. Once the price is known, we can use the model to explain price rigidity, but it does not tell us anything about the determination or the establishment of the rigid price in the first place. To conclude, the model of the kinked demand curve is one explanation of relative price rigidity in oligopolistic markets, but it is not the only explanation, and it cannot be regarded as a general theory of price and output determination in oligopoly markets.

OTHER EXPLANATIONS OF STICKY PRICES

The kinked demand curve model does a good job of explaining "sticky" (inflexible) prices. In this section, we examine two other explanations of sticky prices that have been advanced. These are long-term contracts and small menu costs.

LONG-TERM CONTRACTS

Many firms enter into long-term agreements with their suppliers to provide inputs at pre-arranged prices. Many companies also enter into contracts to provide retail outlets with a certain amount of output at some pre-determined price. Such arrangements obviously contribute to price rigidity as they prevent prices from responding to short-run changes in demand and supply.

SMALL MENU COSTS

Menu costs are those costs incurred when changing prices.

There are costs involved in changing prices. The firm that is changing its prices has to pay employees to remove old price tags and replace them with new ones. New catalogues and price lists may have to be printed and distributed to customers. Such costs are referred to as **menu costs**. The existence of these menu costs may cause a firm to be hesitant to change its prices.

OTHER MODELS OF OLIGOPOLISTIC BEHAVIOUR

LIMIT OR PREDATORY PRICING

Predatory (limit) pricing serves as an effective barrier to the entry of new firms into a market.

Learning Objective 10: *understand alternative pricing*

In cases where significant economies of scale exist and initial capital outlays are high, the firms in an oligopoly situation may deliberately set the prices so low that it would be impossible for new firms to enter the industry and make a profit. This pricing strategy is known as **limit pricing** or **predatory pricing** and may be formally defined as the practice of setting the price of a product so low that it precludes the possibility of potential firms entering the industry and making a profit.

Figure 12.10 illustrates how predatory pricing works. The profit-maximizing price shown in diagram A is P_e. If the existing firms set a price of P_L, they still earn a profit at this low price because they control such a large share of the market. When the existing firms charge a price of P_L, the share of the market that can be captured by any potential competitor is represented by the demand curve D_N in diagram B of Figure 12.10. This price is too low for any new firm to make a profit. At any level of output, the new firm's demand curve lies below its average cost curve AC_N. The potential firm's share of the market, therefore, will be too small for profitable operation.

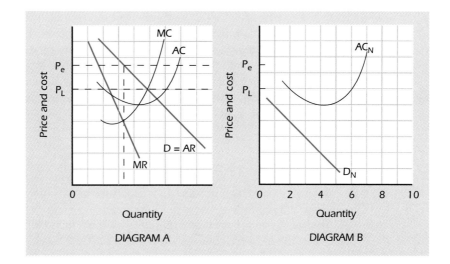

FIGURE 12.10

Predatory pricing.

Low industry price and small market share for potential entrants prevent entry.

PRICE LEADERSHIP

Price leadership means that one firm in an industry sets prices and the other firms adopt those prices.

The firms in an oligopolistic industry may refrain from engaging in price competition and, consequently, a situation of price leadership may emerge. **Price leadership** is a situation in which a single firm in an industry sets the price of its product, and the other firms follow the price set by the leader. Two types of price leadership exist: dominant price leadership and barometric price leadership. *Dominant price leadership* exists when the industry consists of a single large firm that dominates the industry, and a few smaller firms. Price changes are initiated by the dominant firm, and the smaller firms simply follow the leader.

In a situation of *barometric price leadership*, the industry may not be dominated by any single firm. Any firm may be the leader, or the leadership role may rotate in a rather orderly manner. Changes in demand and cost conditions in the industry may cause one firm to initiate a price change that is followed by the other firms in the industry.

Price leadership allows an orderly change from one price to another, but it may not benefit all firms equally.

Although price leadership may prevent the dangerous problem of a price war, in which all of the firms lose, the arrangement is unlikely to benefit all firms equally. As you know, a firm maximizes its profits by setting a price at which its marginal revenue equals its marginal cost. Since all of the firms in the industry are unlikely to have the same cost, it follows that if the leader sets a price that will maximize its profits, that single price will not benefit all firms equally. To reduce the risk of a price war, the price leader must take the situation of its followers into consideration when initiating price changes for the industry.

COST-PLUS PRICING

Many oligopolistic firms determine their prices by adding a mark-up to their average cost.

It is believed that many firms in oligopoly markets determine the prices of their products by adopting a method of pricing known as **cost-plus pricing** or **mark-up pricing**. The idea of cost-plus pricing is very simple. The firm simply adds a certain percentage mark-up to its average cost and thus determines its price. Thus, if the firm's average cost is $12, say, it may choose a mark-up of 25% and set its price at $15.

The advantage of this method of price determination is that it is easy to calculate and easy to understand. But it does have some problems. First, if the firm is trying to maximize its profits, how does it know that a mark-up of 25% rather than a mark up of 20% or 30% will equate its marginal revenue and its marginal cost? Second, the cost-plus method is practical only if the firm knows exactly how much it can sell at various prices. If it puts its mark-up at 25%, it may find that it can sell only 70% of its output at that price. It may then be forced to lower its mark-up.

CARTELS

Learning Objective 11: understand cartels and other forms of collusion

Collusion occurs when firms agree not to compete among each other.

A gentlemen's agreement is not put down on paper, and is usually concluded simply with a handshake.

Cartels engage in market sharing and price fixing.

It is certainly not uncommon for oligopolistic firms to act in unison to control the market for a particular product. Such **collusion** is often illegal in Canada. Nevertheless, firms still seem to get together informally and enter into so-called **gentlemen's agreements** to control price and output. Tacit agreement among firms is more likely to occur when the industry consists of only two or three firms.

The best-known form of collusion among firms in oligopoly is probably a **cartel**, defined as a group of independent producers who have entered into a formal agreement to control price and output in a particular industry.

In many international markets, agreements to control prices and output are legal. Therefore, many cartels operate in international markets. Cartels are quite common in markets for natural resources. The International Bauxite Association, the Organization of Petroleum Exporting Countries (OPEC), and the International Association of Airlines are examples of cartels.

Cartels may be *perfect* or *imperfect*. In a perfect cartel, all decisions regarding price and output are surrendered to a central decision-making body, and the profits distributed to each firm according to the terms of the cartel agreement. In an imperfect cartel, each firm reserves some decision-making powers, and may be allowed to keep whatever profits it may earn. This is the type of cartel likely to be found in practice.

Cartels face a variety of problems. However, we shall focus our attention on three common problems that plague cartels. First, individual independent firms are unlikely to be willing to surrender their decision-making powers to the central body. Second, there is a strong temptation for each firm in the cartel to cheat and produce more than its quota at the prospect of earning greater profits. Whether other cartel members cheat or not, there is a strong profit incentive for any individual firm to cheat. Here the firm's individual interest supersedes the interest of the cartel. The cartel may have to resort to industrial surveillance (spying) because of the enormous incentive to cheat. Third, there is the problem of the entry of new firms into the industry. If a new firm enters the cartel, and there is no increase in the total demand for the industry's product, the optimum output for the cartel remains unchanged, but the given profits of the group must now be shared among a greater number of members. If the new firm enters the industry but is not admitted into the cartel, then the survival of the cartel is threatened.

Cheating among cartel members is one of the most serious problems of a cartel.

PRICING AND OUTPUT POLICIES IN CARTELS

Joint profit maximization

If the cartel decides to maximize joint profits, it chooses a price-output combination that equates marginal revenue with marginal cost. In other words, the cartel behaves exactly like a monopolist producing its output in different plants.

Once the cartel decides on its price-output combination, it faces the further problem of allocating output and profits among cartel members. The allocation of output may be done in any of several ways, including the assignment of exclusive territories and the establishment of output quotas for members. The output quota approach is followed by OPEC — perhaps the best-known cartel.

EVALUATION OF OLIGOPOLY

Like monopoly, oligopoly has certain undesirable social consequences. Barriers to the entry of new firms into the industry may result in a price that exceeds average total cost in most oligopolistic firms. Thus, oligopolistic firms are likely to earn excess profits. Also, the price established in an oligopolistic market is likely to be above marginal cost. This imbalance between price and marginal cost implies a misallocation of resources. Furthermore, oligopolistic firms spend huge amounts of money on advertising in an attempt to maintain or increase their share of the market. Many people consider this enormous advertising outlay to be wasteful.

Under workable competition, an industry is competitive enough to maintain output and keep profits at reasonable levels.

Despite its disadvantages, oligopoly is not always socially undesirable. If there is **workable competition** — that is, if there is sufficient competition in the industry to ensure that output is not unduly restricted and that profits are not excessively high — oligopoly may not be totally undesirable. We can even argue that economies of scale under oligopoly may lead to lower cost and hence lower prices in oligopolistic firms.

Moreover, many firms in oligopoly do undertake a significant amount of research and development (R&D). New and important products are developed, new techniques are introduced — often with significant benefits to society.

A large percentage of the goods and services produced in the Canadian economy are produced by oligopolistic firms. It is obvious, therefore, that an understanding of the theories that attempt to explain the behaviour of firms in oligopolistic markets contributes to our understanding of the Canadian economy.

CONTESTABLE MARKETS

Learning Objective 12: know the theory of contestable markets

In discussing market structures, we have concentrated on the number of firms in the industry and the conditions for entry into the industry. In some cases, however, the number of sellers might not provide a proper indication of how the firms in the industry will behave.

Let us assume that Jane Justice is the only lawyer in town, and she also serves the neighbouring communities. There is not another lawyer in the area. Jane Justice is a monopoly. She will charge a price that equates marginal revenue and marginal cost. She may even be able to practice price discrimination and thus increase her profits.

Consider now the case of John Janitorial Services, a firm that specializes in cleaning services. Like Jane Justice, John Janitorial is a monopoly. However, the pricing behaviour of the two firms will likely be quite different. Whereas Jane Justice may set a price that results in positive economic profits, John Janitorial Services may behave like a pure competitor and deliberately earn only normal profit (zero economic profit).

Entry into a contestable market is easy and no firm can exercise monopoly power.

Why do these two firms adopt different pricing strategies? Entry into Jane Justice's market requires legal training and passing certain special examinations. Thus, her market is not easily contestable. On the other hand, it is relatively easy to enter John Janitorial's industry. His is a **contestable market**. A market with one or a few sellers is said to be contestable if entry into the industry is easy so that the threat of entry of potential competitors prevents the existing firms from exercising any monopoly power.

The concept of contestable markets suggests that looking at the number of firms in an industry is not enough to determine the extent of market power. The ease of entering the industry, and thus potential competitors, must also be considered.

GLOBAL PERSPECTIVE

Russian Caviar

Caviar is a seafood delicacy from a fish (the sturgeon) found primarily in the Caspian Sea. The supply of so-called *fine Soviet caviar* to Western countries was, for many years, controlled by a Soviet state cartel. This cartel limited the supply of caviar to the West to only about 7% of the annual production of approximately 2000 tonnes, and was thus able to command a relatively high export price.

With the collapse of the former Soviet Union, each independent state (Russia, Kazakhstan, Azerbaijan, and Turkmenistan) along with Iran that borders the Caspian Sea produces caviar for export. Concern with overfishing of sturgeon aside, the desire on the part of each independent state to earn foreign currency has resulted in an increase in the supply of caviar to the West and a significant reduction in price. In the absence of this cartel, the independent states mentioned above and individual fishermen have increased competition in the supply of caviar. The formation of a cartel can affect the world price of a commodity, but so too can the disbandment of a cartel.

CHAPTER SUMMARY

1. Monopolistic competition is a market structure characterized by a large number of firms selling a differentiated product.

2. Because of product differentiation, the monopolistically competitive firm has slight control over the price charged for the product. It can raise the price slightly without losing all of its customers and, thus, its demand curve slopes downward.

3. The firm in monopolistic competition maximizes profits when its marginal revenue equals its marginal cost. Its price exceeds marginal cost.

4. If the monopolistically competitive firm is earning positive economic profits in the short run, new firms will enter the industry and compete, and those profits will dwindle away. In long-run equilibrium, price equals average cost.

5. The excess capacity theorem states that a monopolistically competitive firm will have excess capacity in long-run equilibrium. The firm will not produce at the minimum point on the average cost curve.

6. Monopolistic competition gives consumers a relatively wide variety of products from which to choose.

7. Firms in monopolistic competition often engage in advertising in order to increase the demand for their products or to maintain their share of the market.

8. Oligopoly, a market structure involving few sellers, is typical in industries that require huge capital outlays. Duopoly refers to a situation in which there are only two firms in the industry. Because so few firms exist in this market structure, interdependence is crucial.

9. Concentration ratios show the percentage of total market supply accounted for by a few of the largest firms in the industry.

10. The oligopolistic firm exercises considerable market power. Like firms in other market structures, the oligopolistic firm maximizes profits when its marginal revenue equals its marginal cost.

11. The model of the kinked demand curve explains price rigidity in oligopolistic markets. Given the demand for the product, the price will change only when there is a substantial change in cost.

12. Predatory pricing or limit pricing may be used as a device to restrict the entry of firms into a particular market. When this happens, the price of the product is kept artificially low.

13. Price leadership, a situation in which a price charged by one firm is followed by the other firms, may develop in an oligopolistic industry. Various other forms of collusion may also result.

14. Cost-plus or mark-up pricing may be used by oligopolistic firms to establish the prices of their products.

15. A cartel is a group of firms that have formally agreed to unite for the purpose of controlling price and output in a particular industry. Cartels may be either perfect or imperfect. Perfect cartels, however, are not usually encountered in the real world.

16. Workable competition is the term applied to a situation in which there is sufficient competition in the industry to ensure that output is not unduly restricted and that the firms do not earn excessively high profits.

17. A contestable market exists when easy entry into an oligopolistic or monopolistic market forces the existing firms to deliberately earn only normal economic profits.

TERMS FOR REVIEW

imperfect competition (209)	menu costs (220)
product differentiation (209)	predatory (limit) pricing (220)
excess capacity theorem (213)	price leadership (221)
quality competition (215)	cost-plus (mark-up) pricing (221)
oligopoly (217)	collusion (222)
duopoly (217)	gentlemen's agreements (222)
differentiated oligopoly (217)	cartel (222)
concentration ratios (217)	workable competition (223)
kinked demand curve (218)	contestable market (223)

QUESTIONS FOR REVIEW AND DISCUSSION

1. What are the main features of a monopolistically competitive market? (L.O.1)

2. What do you understand by the term *product differentiation?* Name some devices used to achieve product differentiation. (L.O.1)

3. Name four industries, other than those listed in the text, that can be classified as monopolistically competitive. Give reasons for your choice. (L.O.1)

4. Explain why a firm in monopolistic competition faces a downward-sloping demand curve that is very elastic. (L.O.2)

5. With the help of an appropriate diagram, explain the profit-maximizing position of a firm in monopolistic competition. (L.O.3)

6. Explain why a monopolistically competitive firm earns only normal profits (zero economic profits) in the long run. (L.O.4)

7. How does the long-run equilibrium of a monopolistically competitive firm differ from that of a purely competitive firm? Illustrate with a diagram. Account for the difference. (L.O.4,5)

8. What arguments can you advance for and against advertising? (L.O.6)

9. Why might a firm in monopolistic competition advertise its product? (L.O.6)

10. What are the main characteristics of an oligopolistic industry? (L.O.7)

11. Why is it so difficult to develop any general theory of oligopolistic behaviour? (L.O.7,8)

12. What does the model of the kinked demand curve explain? (L.O.9)

13. Would you consider the kinked demand curve model to be an adequate model of price and output determination in oligopoly markets? Why or why not? (L.O.9)

14. The kinked demand curve model explains price rigidity in oligopoly markets. Discuss other explanations that have been offered for sticky prices.

15. What is the difference between each of the following pairs of concepts? (L.O.10,11)

    (a) dominant price leadership and barometric price leadership

    (b) cartel and gentleman's agreement

    (c) perfect cartel and imperfect cartel

    (d) collusion and workable competition

16. What is cost-plus pricing? Will it automatically lead to profit maximization? (L.O.10)

17. Explain how predatory pricing may be used as a technique to prevent potential competitors from entering an industry. (L.O.10)

18. What are some of the problems faced by cartels? (L.O.11)

19. "There is a great incentive to engage in product improvement and development when there is imperfect competition." Discuss. (General)

20. "Monopoly may be less undesirable from society's point of view than oligopoly." Discuss. (General)

PROBLEMS AND EXERCISES

1. Explain why people buy name brands of a product when in-house brands are available at lower prices. (L.O.1,2)

2. Is it possible for monopolistic competition to exist in an industry where many firms sell identical products? Explain. (L.O.1)

3. Table 12.2 shows data for Prodif, a firm in monopolistic competition. (L.O.2,3)

TABLE 12.2	P	Q	TR	MR	ATC	TC	MC	Profit
Price and cost data for Prodif.	200	1			210			
	190	2			175			
	180	3			160			
	170	4			155			
	160	5			155			
	150	6			165			
	140	7			170			
	130	8			180			

(a) Compute total revenue, marginal revenue, total cost, marginal cost, and profit for Prodif, and complete the table.

(b) How many units should Prodif sell in order to maximize profits?

(c) What should the price of each unit be?

(d) What will Prodif's total profit be?

4. Figure 12.11 represents a monopolistically competitive firm called Best-Brand Ltd. (L.O.3)

FIGURE 12.11

Cost and revenue curves for Best-Brand Ltd.

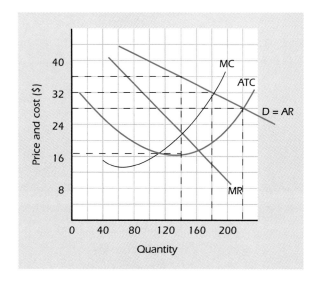

(a) What level of output should Best-Brand produce in order to maximize profits?

(b) What price should Best-Brand charge for this output?

(c) What is the maximum total profit that Best-Brand can earn?

5. Draw a demand curve for a firm in monopolistic competition, then draw another demand curve to show the effect of a successful advertising campaign on the firm's demand. Explain your diagram. (L.O.6)

6. You and your brother decide to enter a business that is monopolistically competitive. You have carefully calculated your costs, and you know the demand for your product. Your objective is to maximize your profits. Your brother, who has a degree in marketing, suggests that you take a sample of the prices being charged by your competitors, and then set your price as the average of your sample prices. Would you agree with your brother that this is the best pricing strategy? Explain. (L.O.3,10)

7. Figure 12.12 represents Oliotel, a firm in an oligopoly situation. Oliotel is a profit maximizer. (L.O.8)

(a) What output should Oliotel produce?

(b) What price should it charge?

(c) What price adjustment should Oliotel make following a $2.50 increase in marginal cost?

FIGURE 12.12

Oliotel's cost and revenue.

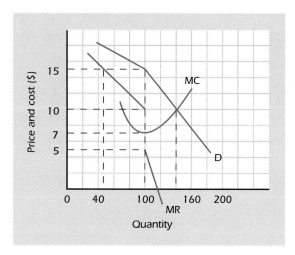

8. "Monopolists and oligopolists are both price-setters but their actions are guided by different considerations." Explain. (General)

9. Video rental stores are numerous in any Canadian city. There seems to be a good case for describing this industry as monopolistically competitive.

   a) What arguments can you advance for describing the video rental industry as monopolistically competitive?

   b) Telephone a few of these outlets to gather information on prices. Compare these prices.

   c) Visit three video rental outlets and see if you can detect any methods used to differentiate one outlet from another.

VIDEO CASE

The Newspaper Scene: A New Entrant

Background

For many years, the Globe and Mail, founded in 1844, has claimed to be Canada's only national daily newspaper. On October 27, 1998 a new Canadian publication, the National Post, billing itself as Canada's only truly national daily newspaper brought an end to the Globe and Mail's claim. Not surprisingly the Canadian newspaper market is highly concentrated. Not too many cities can support two or three daily papers. Toronto, Canada's largest city, is home to the Toronto Sun, the Toronto Star and now, the National Post, but some people doubt if even Toronto can support four daily newspapers.

The main player

The National Post will compete with existing newspapers, but its main competitor is the Globe and Mail. The man who dared to go head to head with the "Grand Old Man" (the Globe and Mail) is newspaper baron Conrad Black. Prior to October 1998, Mr. Black owned daily newspapers in all of Canada's major cities (Vancouver, Montreal, Winnipeg, Halifax) except Toronto. As of October 27, 1998, the exception no longer exists. Of 105 newspapers in Canada, Mr. Black controls 68 of them. That is power plus.

The market

Each of the newspapers mentioned above seems to appeal to a specific group of readers. For example, the Globe and Mail has traditionally been a rather conservative newspaper, appealing to the intellectuals, the business executives, the professionals, and the well-to-do, while the Toronto Star seems to cater to a more general readership. The Toronto Sun has a tabloid format and appears to cater to a younger generation of readers. By proclaiming itself to be a national newspaper, the National Post will probably compete more closely with the Globe and Mail than with the other newspapers. Clearly, the National Post will be in fierce competition for the advertising dollars of companies that advertise nationally (and locally too).

The theory

The theory of oligopoly should help us to understand the impact that the National Post will have on the behaviour of its competitors. The paper entered the market at a price below that of the Globe and Mail. Will that pricing strategy cause price-sensitive consumers to switch? Will the Globe and Mail match the lower price charged by the National Post? And what about product differentiation? Will the papers differentiate themselves by their content?

When the National Post arrived on the scene, its contents were similar in many ways to those of its major competitor. There was the colourful front page leading to the first section, followed by an *Arts and Life* section dealing with entertainment, fashion, and sports. And then there was the *Financial Post* section with business news, followed by *FP Investing* with reports on the financial markets.

The Globe and Mail is no longer that ultra conservative-looking newspaper. If its content has not changed much, its appearance certainly has. It is now a flashy paper. After the front section, there is the *Report On Business* (with colour) including the financial markets and a special *Careers* section. And how about sports coverage in the Globe and Mail? Well, it's right there in the A section — all five (more or less) pages.

As the theory predicts, the Globe and Mail has reacted — with colour, more excitement, and by apparently broadening its scope to attract women and younger readers. The possibility of a newspaper war exists, and whenever that happens in Canada, some casualty can be expected.

QUESTIONS

1. Isolate the main points in this case.

2. Do you see any danger in one man owning approximately 65% of the newspapers in Canada?

3. Do you think that an oligopoly model is appropriate for analyzing Canada's newspaper industry? Justify your answer.

4. How might the newspapers achieve product differentiation?

Video Resource: "2 × 1 Canadian," *National Magazine* (April 1998).

13

C H A P T E R

THE LABOUR MARKET

Learning Objectives

After studying this chapter, you will understand:

1 the demand for and supply of labour

2 competitive wage determination

3 predictions of the theory of wage determination

4 the effects of discrimination in the labour market

5 wage differentials

6 unions and collective bargaining

7 factors in wage negotiations

8 the effects of labour unions in the labour market

9 how unions affect resource allocation

When an attempt is made to apply to the labour market the ordinary principles of price determination — without making allowance for the type of market — the result appears at the first sight very odd.

J. R. Hicks, *The Theory of Wages*

INTRODUCTION

Up to this point, we have concentrated mainly on the product market, studying the demand for and supply of a product; households' decisions about how much of a product to buy in order to maximize satisfaction; and firms' decisions about how much to produce and what price to charge. In this chapter and the next, we concentrate on the factor market. Recall that households and firms operate in both markets. In the product market, the firms are the sellers while the households are the main buyers. In the factor market, however, the firms are the buyers while the sellers can be households or firms.

This chapter deals with labour — the most important resource used in the process of production. You will recall that the wage rate is the price of labour. We shall now study how the wage rate is determined in a competitive market structure, discuss wage differentials briefly, and take a quick look at labour unions and the collective bargaining process. In the process, you will see how the theory of wage determination applies to real-world situations.

In 1997, income from labour services in Canada amounted to $445 804 million or approximately 71% of total income earned from all sources. Table 13.1 shows the relative incomes from various sources, and Figure 13.1 compares the 1997 figures with the 1995 data. The distribution of income among the various factors of production is called the **functional distribution of income**.

Functional distribution of income is among the various factors of production.

TABLE 13.1	**Income Source**	**Value ($million)**	**% of total income**
Sources of income and relation to total income.	Labour income	445 804	70.7
	Corporate profits before taxes	78 988	12.5
	Government enterprise profits	6 707	1.1
	Interest and investment income	46 187	7.3
	Accrued net farm income	1 422	0.2
	Unincorporated business income	52 978	8.4
	Inventory valuation adjustment	–1 622	(0.2)
	Net domestic income	630 464	100.0*

*Note: Percentages may not add up to 100 because of rounding.

Source: Statistics Canada, Canadian Economic Observer, July 1998 (Cat. 11-010-XBP): 3.

FIGURE 13.1

Comparison of income shares.

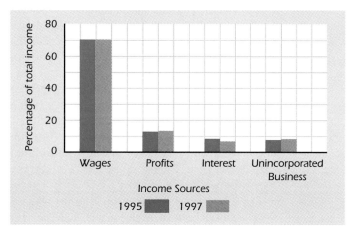

Source: Adapted from Table 13.1.

Figure 13.1 shows that the share of labour income remained constant at 70.7% from 1995 to 1997, while profits rose slightly from 13% in 1995 to 13.6% in 1997. The share of interest and investment income fell from 8.5% in 1995 to 7.3% in 1997, while unincorporated business income rose from 7.8% to 8.4%.

THE DEMAND FOR LABOUR

Learning Objective 1:
the demand for and supply of labour

A direct demand is a demand for goods and services.

The demand for labour is a derived demand.

The marginal physical product of labour is the extra output from adding one unit of labour.

The marginal revenue product is the additional revenue contributed by the last unit of a factor.

Consumers buy goods and services in the product market because they derive utility (satisfaction) directly from goods and services. The demand for goods and services is therefore a **direct demand**. In contrast, producers buy factors of production in the factor market to produce goods and services. Factor inputs do not give satisfaction directly as consumer goods and services do. The demand for factors of production (such as labour) depends on the demand for the goods and services that the factors of production are used to produce. If the demand for goods and services increases, then more factors of production are required to produce them. The demand for factors of production is therefore a **derived demand**.

In addition to firms that demand labour services to help with the production of goods and services, the various levels of government also demand labour services to offer the wide variety of services that governments provide. The government's use of labour services has some effect on the availability of workers for the private sector.

The principle of substitution (see Chapter 8) indicates that if the price of labour (the wage rate) falls, firms tend to use more labour. The following analysis helps to determine how a firm decides how many workers it will hire. We assume that the firm is in a purely competitive industry, and that it buys its inputs in a purely competitive market.

The marginal product of labour (MP_L) is the change in total output resulting from the use of one additional unit of labour. If this magnitude is expressed in physical terms, economists call it the **marginal physical product of labour** (MPP_L). The extra revenue resulting from the sale of the extra output produced by the additional unit of labour is called the **marginal revenue product** (MRP_L). The marginal revenue product, then, is simply the value of the marginal physical product (VMPP). We can calculate the value of the marginal physical product by multiplying the marginal physical product by the market price of the product. That is,

$$MRP_L = VMPP_L = MPP_L \times P$$

where P is the price of the product.

If an additional worker will contribute more to total revenue than to total cost, then it will pay the firm to hire the extra worker. Hence, if the marginal revenue product (MRP) is greater than the wage rate (W), the firm will likely employ additional units of labour. If the marginal revenue product is less than the wage rate, then the firm will likely reduce its employment of labour. It follows that the firm seeking to maximize its profits will employ labour up to the point where MRP = W. Figure 13.2 illustrates this fact.

Since marginal product declines as additional units of labour are employed (diminishing returns), the marginal revenue product curve slopes downward. The market wage rate is assumed to be 0W. If the firm were hiring $0Q_0$ units of labour at a wage rate of 0W, the marginal revenue product $0W_1$ would be greater than the wage rate, and the firm would benefit by hiring more labour. If it were hiring $0Q_1$ units of labour at a wage rate of 0W, the marginal revenue product $0W_0$ would be less than the wage rate, and the firm would benefit by hiring fewer units of labour. At a wage rate of 0W, the firm will hire 0Q units of labour since, with that amount of labour, the marginal revenue product

FIGURE 13.2

FIGURE 13.2

The firm's demand curve for labour.

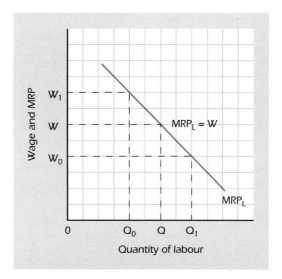

The firm employs labour up to the point where the marginal revenue product equals the wage rate.

of labour equals the wage rate. This concept, known as the **marginal productivity theory of wages**, may be stated as follows: under purely competitive conditions, a profit-maximizing firm will hire labour up to the point where the wage rate equals the value of the marginal product of labour.

The marginal productivity theory of wages states that labour should be employed to the point where the MRP equals the wage rate.

Note that if the wage rate were $0W_1$ instead of $0W$, then the firm would employ $0Q_0$ units of labour instead of $0Q$. If the wage rate were $0W_0$, then the firm would employ $0Q_1$ units of labour instead of $0Q$. As the wage rate falls, the firm employs more units of labour. The marginal revenue product curve shows the various quantities of labour that a firm will hire at various wage rates. The marginal revenue product curve, therefore, is the firm's demand curve for labour. Observe that a change in the wage rate causes a movement along, not a shift in, the firm's demand curve for labour. Factors such as changes in income, changes in tastes, and changes in market size, which affect the demand for the firm's product, will change the quantity of labour demanded by the firm at any given wage rate, and thus shift the firm's demand curve for labour. To obtain the market demand curve for labour, we add the demand curves of all the firms in the industry.

The marginal revenue product curve is the firm's demand curve for labour.

A complication arises, however, from this procedure. This is so because as the wage rate falls, the increased employment of labour by all firms in the industry is likely to increase the supply of the product. Such an increase in supply lowers the price of the product. For this reason, the market demand curve for labour will be less elastic than that derived by adding the demand curves of the individual firms. To overcome this complication, we can assume, just for analytical purposes, that the price of the product is not affected by the firm's employment of labour.

THE SUPPLY OF LABOUR

The supply curve of labour shows the number of units of labour offered at each possible wage rate. Of course, it is the households that supply labour services to the labour market. We assume that at low wage rates, only small amounts of labour are offered. Households regard both income and leisure as being desirable. As the wage rate increases, households will be more willing to sacrifice leisure and offer more labour services. We assume also that there is labour mobility between industries. One industry may attract

Learning Objective 1: the demand for and supply of labour workers by offering higher wage rates than those offered in other industries. The market supply curve of labour then slopes upward, as shown in Figure 13.3. At a wage rate of $0W_1$, the quantity of labour supplied is $0Q_1$. At the higher wage rate of $0W_2$, a larger quantity of labour ($0Q_2$) is offered for hire. You will observe here also that the change in the wage rate causes a movement along, not a shift in, the supply curve. Factors such as changes in taxes and changes in the size of the labour force will shift the supply curve of labour.

FIGURE 13.3

The supply curve of labour.

The higher the wage rate, the greater the quantity of labour offered by households.

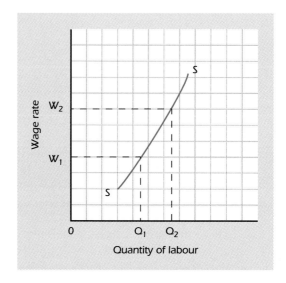

THE BACKWARD-BENDING LABOUR SUPPLY CURVE

A backward-bending labour supply curve shows the wage rates at which the number of hours worked decreases.

The labour supply curve discussed above is upward-sloping. There is, however, the possibility that the **supply curve of labour** could be negatively sloped (i.e., **backward-bending**) once the wage rate has reached a certain level. This situation is illustrated in Figure 13.4. At any wage rate up to W_1, a higher wage rate is an incentive to offer more hours of work. But at any wage rate above $0W_1$, the number of hours worked decreases

FIGURE 13.4

A backward-bending supply curve for labour.

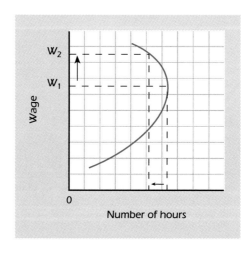

APPLICATION

A Question of Motivation

It is generally agreed that workers can be encouraged to work extra hours by offering them a higher wage. It is sometimes argued, however, that in many less-developed countries where workers have grown accustomed to a traditional lifestyle, their horizons are so limited that they are really not interested in earning extra income by working longer hours. This is the notion of the backward-bending supply curve of work effort in less-developed countries.

If such a supply curve of work effort does indeed exist, then higher wages will discourage rather than encourage greater effort. Thus, in order to motivate workers, incentives other than higher wages will be required. Such incentives may be provided by education aimed at changing attitudes and the way of life, and by providing opportunities for greater enjoyment of extra income. In other words, in such circumstances, it may be necessary to change the income-leisure choice.

as the wage rate increases. In this case, people prefer to choose leisure over additional income from labour services. It is suggested that some high-income-earning professionals, such as doctors and lawyers, who choose to work four days a week probably demonstrate the existence of a backward-bending supply curve for labour.

WAGE DETERMINATION IN A COMPETITIVE LABOUR MARKET

Learning Objective 2:
competitive wage determination

We can determine the equilibrium wage rate and the amount of labour employed in a competitive labour market by bringing together demand for labour and supply of labour. Figure 13.5 shows the demand curve for labour (D_L) and the supply curve for labour (S_L). At a wage rate of $0W_1$, the quantity of labour supplied exceeds the quantity demanded. This surplus of labour tends to force down the wage rate. At a wage rate of $0W_0$, the quantity of labour demanded exceeds the quantity supplied. At a wage rate of $0W$, the quantity demanded equals the quantity supplied. The labour market clears and the wage rate stabilizes. The equilibrium wage rate is $0W$, and $0Q$ units of labour are hired.

FIGURE 13.5

Equilibrium in the labour market.

The intersection of the demand and supply curves of labour determines the equilibrium wage rate.

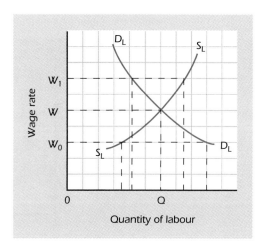

PREDICTIONS OF THE THEORY OF WAGE DETERMINATION

An increase in the demand for labour results in an increase in the wage rate.

Learning Objective 3:
predictions of the theory of wage determination

How does an increase in demand for labour in a particular industry affect wages in that industry? For help in answering this question, let us look at Figure 13.6. DD is the original demand curve, SS is the original supply curve, 0W is the initial equilibrium wage rate, and 0Q is the amount of labour hired. A shift in the demand curve upward and to the right (from DD to D_1D_1) shows an increase in the demand for labour. We can see that the wage rate increases from 0W to $0W_1$, and that the amount of labour employed increases from 0Q to $0Q_1$. Hence, we can conclude that:

an increase in the demand for labour, other things being equal, causes a rise in the wage rate and an increase in the quantity of labour hired.

FIGURE 13.6

Effect of an increase in the demand for labour.

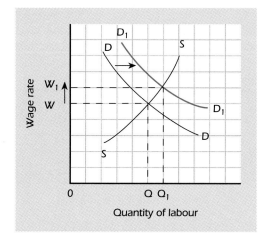

A reduction in the supply of labour results in an increase in the wage rate.

We can also easily determine the effects of a change in the supply of labour. Let us suppose that the supply of labour falls. Figure 13.7 shows such a fall as a shift in the supply curve from SS to S_0S_0. Assuming there is no change in demand for labour, the wage rate increases from 0W to $0W_1$, and the amount of labour falls from 0Q to $0Q_0$. In other words:

A reduction in the supply of labour, other things being equal, will cause an increase in the wage rate and a fall in the equilibrium quantity of labour.

FIGURE 13.7

Effect of a decrease in the supply of labour.

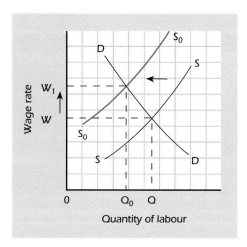

PROBLEM SOLVING 13-1

"The institution of minimum wage laws contributes to unemployment." Can this claim be valid?

DISCRIMINATION IN THE LABOUR MARKET

Learning Objective 4:
the effects of discrimination in the labour market

Discrimination affects the labour market and imposes a cost on society. To show the effect of discrimination in the labour market, let us refer to Figure 13.8. The demand and supply curves for labour in a particular profession (teaching, engineering, etc.) are shown as DD and SS respectively. The equilibrium wage rate is W and the quantity of labour employed is 0L. The effect of discrimination is reflected in its effect on the demand curve of labour for the group discriminated against. Because of discrimination, the demand curve for the group that is the victim of discrimination shifts from DD to D_0D_0. This demand shift results in a fall in wages from W to W_0 and a decrease in the quantity of labour employed from 0L to $0L_0$. Discrimination therefore causes members of the group discriminated against to earn less and to find less employment than would be the case in the absence of discrimination.

Discrimination results in a misallocation of labour resources.

This type of discrimination is costly to society in terms of the loss of goods and services that could have been provided by the group discriminated against. By shifting the demand curve and lowering wages, discrimination causes labour resources to be misallocated. In this case, labour is not paid the value of its marginal product.

FIGURE 13.8

Effect of discrimination in the labour market.

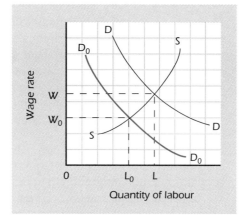

WAGE DIFFERENTIALS

Learning Objective 5:
wage differentials

There are significant differences in wage rates among occupations. In this section, we shall examine some of the reasons for these wage differentials. First, education, experience, and responsibility affect wage-earning potential. Material handlers require less training and skill than operators of complicated machines. Hence, we expect machine operators to be better paid than material handlers. A director of nursing at a large city hospital has greater responsibilities than a nursing assistant, so we expect the director to be better paid than the assistant. Quite often, responsibility is a function of experience and education; and wages are normally a function of responsibility. Of course, superior talent and ability cannot be overlooked. This accounts for the high salaries earned by superstars in sports and in entertainment. We shall return to this issue when we discuss the concept of economic rent in Chapter 14.

Second, the existence of unions in some occupations and professions may account for wage differentials. Unionized workers supposedly earn more than their non-union counterparts. It may be pointed out, however, that the evidence is not conclusive that unionized workers do in fact earn more than non-unionized workers in the same occupation.

Third, wage differentials may also be explained by the non-monetary benefits associated with certain occupations and professions. These benefits, referred to as **psychic income**, include such things as good working hours, pleasant working surroundings, long summer and winter vacations, and the enjoyment that some people derive from their jobs. Some employees may opt for psychic income in lieu of a higher money wage.

Finally, we should recognize that the degree of danger associated with various jobs affects wage differentials. The more hazardous the job, other things being equal, the greater the salary. For example, a nuclear medical technician will earn more than an audio-visual technician, not only because of a difference in training, but also because of a difference in the degree of danger associated with the job.

Of course, the reasons for these wage differentials are related largely to demand and supply. For example, there is enormous demand for athletes with superior ability and the supply is small; these people therefore earn high wages. Material handling, however, can be learned fairly easily by almost anyone. In this case, there is an enormous supply of material handlers and these people therefore earn low wages. Generally, then, wage differentials are a function of demand and supply.

Psychic income is the non-monetary rewards derived from a job.

Wage differentials are due basically to differences in the relative scarcities of different types of labour.

UNIONS AND COLLECTIVE BARGAINING

Learning Objective 6: unions and collective bargaining

Unions have played, and continue to play, an important role in the labour market. We have come to accept labour unions as quite normal in our society. But this was not always the case. The rights now enjoyed by labour unions were won only after bitter struggles. The union movement has contributed significantly to the pleasant working conditions that modern workers (unionized and non-unionized) now enjoy. For our purposes, let us define a union as an association of workers organized to promote the interests of its members in negotiations with their employers.

A craft or trade union's membership consists of workers in a single occupation.

There are different types of unions. In a **craft** or **trade union**, the membership comprises workers in a single occupation irrespective of where they work. In an **industrial union**, the membership comprises workers in a given industry. Unions have become an important institution in the modern economy.

All members of an industrial union work in a given industry.

Unions are organized at the local, national, and international levels.

Let us begin our examination of unions by looking at their structure and their organization. Unions are organized at four levels. First, there is the **local union**, to which the individual worker belongs directly. The local union holds meetings to discuss problems and to decide on courses of action. The local union also collects membership dues. Second, there is the **national union**, of which the local union is a member. The national union often does the bargaining and sets broad policy outlines. It receives a part of the dues paid to the locals. The Canadian Labour Congress (CLC), the Centrale des syndicats démocratiques (CSD), and the Confederation of Canadian Unions (CCU) are examples of national unions. Third, there is the **international union**, whose membership consists of local unions in different countries. The American Federation of Labour-Congress of Industrial Organizations (AFL-CIO) is an example of an international union. Finally, there is the **federation**, which is an association of national unions. The Confédération des Syndicats Nationaux (CSN), based in Quebec, is an example of a federation of unions. Table 13.2 shows union membership in Canada by type of union and affiliation.

A federation is an association of national unions.

	Type of affiliation	Number of unions	Membership Number	%
TABLE 13.2	International unions	51	1 216 725	29.9
	AFL-CIO/CLC	34	1 087 285	26.7
Union membership by type and affiliation, 1997.	AFL-CIO/CFL	8	99 400	2.4
	CLC only	2	6 830	0.2
	AFL-CIO only	4	17 980	0.4
	Unaffiliated unions	3	5 230	0.1
	National unions	233	2 662 550	65.4
	CLC	55	1 575 935	38.7
	CSN	10	251 420	6.2
	CEQ*	14	109 775	2.7
	CCU	9	17 275	0.4
	CSD	2	14 330	0.4
	CFL	2	1 780	0.0†
	Unaffiliated unions	141	692 035	17.0
	Directly chartered unions	401	60 600	1.5
	CSD	390	59 500	1.5
	CLC	11	1 100	0.0†
	Independent local organizations	326	134 025	3.3
	TOTAL	1 011	4 073 900	100.0

* Centrale de l'enseignement du Quebec
† Less than 0.1 per cent

Source: Human Resources Development Canada, *Directory of Labour Organizations in Canada*, 1998: XXIII

Many of the rights for which unions have fought over the years have now been incorporated into law. In many countries, there are labour codes that define the rights and privileges of workers, and governments have enacted legislation that protects workers. Yet unions continue to be popular. The number of unions in Canada increased from 911 in 1994 to 1011 in 1997, and union membership decreased slightly from 4 077 987 to 4 073 900 (a fall of about 0.10%) during the same period.

UNION SECURITY

A union tries to secure its position by a variety of methods. These methods include the closed shop and the union shop. The concept of an open shop helps to explain how a closed shop or a union shop arrangement helps the union. An **open shop** is an arrangement whereby an employee does not necessarily have to be a union member to obtain or keep a job. On the other hand, a **closed shop** arrangement is one in which membership in a union is a prerequisite for obtaining employment. Between these two practices is the **union shop**, in which the employee may be hired even if he or she is not a union member, but must join a union within a specified period of time. It should be obvious that unions are least likely to support open shops. A union is most powerful when all of the workers at an establishment are unionized.

Another technique that a union might use to increase the job security of its members and strengthen its own position is **featherbedding**. This is the practice of enforcing and insisting on work rules and methods that may be inefficient (at least in the view of the employer), but that may keep the employee in the position. Featherbedding represents an inefficient use of labour resources, but it also protects workers who might otherwise experience great difficulty in finding another job. The issue therefore involves a trade-off between economic efficiency on the one hand and humanitarianism on the other.

In an open shop, workers do not need to belong to a union.

Closed shop and union shop arrangements increase union security.

In featherbedding, workers are given unnecessary work to keep them on the payroll.

An important development in Canadian labour practice was the introduction in 1945 of the **Rand Formula**. Of enormous support to union security, the Rand Formula was named after Mr. Justice Ivan Rand, who passed an arbitration decision in a labour dispute at the Ford Motor Company of Canada. According to that decision, Ford workers were to pay union dues whether or not they were members of the union. These dues were to be deducted from the workers' pay by the company's administrators and then handed over to the union. Canadian industries now commonly use the Rand Formula or some version of it.

The Rand Formula makes it compulsory for a worker to pay union dues even if he or she is not a union member.

 PROBLEM SOLVING 13-2
Can an employer benefit from a closed shop?

THE COLLECTIVE BARGAINING PROCESS

A union is supposed to represent its members and protect their interests. It represents the collective voice of its members. Instead of individual employees negotiating directly with their employer, the union, representing all of its members, negotiates on their behalf. Sometimes, several different unions unite to form a common front when negotiating with an employer. This often happens with public-sector unions.

Employers and employees arrive at a contract (collective agreement) by collective bargaining.

Learning Objective 6:
unions and collective bargaining

Collective bargaining is the entire process by which unions and management arrive at an agreement through negotiations on the terms of employment. The contract arrived at (the **collective agreement**) specifies the responsibilities of employers and employees concerning wages, vacation, safety on the job, non-monetary benefits such as maternity leaves and training, job security, and other issues. The wage and other conditions of work determined by the collective bargaining process depend on the relative strengths of the bargaining parties and on the skills of the negotiators. In a period of heavy unemployment, the employer tends to have greater market power. In a period of general labour shortage and rising demand for labour, the unions enjoy greater market power.

Negotiations between the union and the employer usually begin well in advance of the expiry date of the existing contract. The union makes its demands, and the employer makes its proposals. Usually, each side finds something in the other's proposal that is unacceptable. Bargaining continues with each party making proposals and counterproposals until a settlement is reached and a contract is signed.

SETTLEMENT OF DISPUTES

It is reasonable to expect disputes between employers and employees. In cases in which a compromise cannot be reached by the two parties, there are several ways of attempting to settle such disputes. One procedure is to call in an outside neutral mediator to study the situation and suggest possible moves toward a settlement. This is the process of **conciliation** or **mediation**. There is no obligation on the part of either party to accept the conciliator's suggestions.

Labour disputes may be settled by conciliation (mediation) or by voluntary or compulsory arbitration.

Another procedure used in settling labour disputes is **voluntary arbitration**. Each party to the dispute agrees to submit its case to an impartial third party and to abide by the decision of the arbitrator. A third technique used to settle labour disputes is **compulsory arbitration**. The government compels the disputing parties to submit their disputes to an arbitrator, whose decision is binding upon both parties.

STRIKES AND LOCKOUTS

A strike is a temporary work stoppage by employees; a lockout is a temporary plant closing by the employer.

As a means of obtaining its demands, a union may resort to strike action. A **strike** is a temporary work stoppage by employees, designed to force an employer to grant their demands. From the employer's side, the equivalent of a strike is a **lockout**, which is a temporary closing of the plant by an employer, designed to win a dispute.

Most contract agreements are reached without resort to strikes or lockouts.

Contrary to popular belief, strikes and lockouts occur relatively infrequently in Canada. In most years, the working time lost because of strikes and lockouts amounts to only about 0.16% of overall working time. This means that the average unionized worker in Canada strikes for only about half a day per year. This suggests that the vast majority of collective agreements are reached without resort to strikes and lockouts.

THE COSTS OF STRIKES

Strikes impose costs on the parties directly involved, and on others not directly involved in the strike.

Strikes are costly. We are fortunate that they do not occur more frequently in this country. A proper analysis of the costs of strikes requires that these costs be grouped into at least two categories: direct costs and indirect costs.

Direct costs

It is relatively easy to pinpoint the direct costs of a strike. The cost to workers is lost wages. The cost to employers is lost production, lost sales, and lost profits.

Indirect costs

A strike in one industry affects other industries and the general public. For example, a strike by truck drivers affects grocery stores and other retail outlets, since they cannot obtain supplies during the strike. This is an indirect cost. If workers in the steel industry go on strike, the auto industry may have to shut down because of a shortage of steel, which is an important input in the auto industry. In many cases, strikes cause a great deal of inconvenience to the public — as, for example, when a public transportation company goes on strike. These indirect costs often outweigh the direct costs of the strike.

 PROBLEM SOLVING 13-3
Do strikes necessarily result in a reduction of total output in the economy?

FACTORS IN WAGE NEGOTIATIONS

Learning Objective 7: factors in wage negotiations

An escalator clause stipulates automatic wage increases to reflect price changes or cost of living changes.

Indexed wages rise with prices.

Cost of living, productivity, and profitability are important considerations in wage negotiations.

In the early stages of negotiation, both parties consider a variety of factors when drawing up their lists of proposals. In deciding on wage demands and wage offers, one factor that is likely to be particularly significant is the cost of living. Workers try to protect their purchasing power against a rising cost of living. The employer cannot easily ignore such a consideration. Unions try to protect their members' purchasing power by building escalator clauses into their contracts. An **escalator clause** is a provision in a contract specifying that wages will rise automatically to compensate for any increase in the cost of living. **Indexation** is the adjustment of wages to the rate at which prices rise. A **cost of living adjustment** (COLA) allows wages to be adjusted to the cost of living.

Another factor likely to carry some weight is productivity. Workers will naturally expect to share in any increase in their productivity. And employers are less likely to resist demands for wage increases in the face of productivity increases. By the same token, a fall in the productivity of workers is likely to result in the refusal of employers to grant anything but modest wage increases.

A third factor likely to feature significantly in wage demands and offers is the profitability of the business. If the firm has had a substantial increase in profits, the union will certainly use that fact as justification for higher wage demands. On the other hand, if the firm has undergone a period of declining profits, the employers will likely refuse to grant higher wages.

GLOBAL PERSPECTIVE

Labour Relations in Japan

You have probably heard a great deal about differences between Japanese and North American unions. This capsule takes a brief look at labour relations in Japan so that you can compare the Japanese and Canadian situations. Japanese unions operate on the concept of *enterprise unionism*, where a single union is organized within each enterprise rather than within a craft or an industry. The enterprise unions are then organized into industrial federations and central national labour organizations.

In the spring of each year, negotiations between labour and management take place in order to determine wages and other working conditions. These enterprise unions, also called company unions, work very closely with management. The attitude is one of cooperation rather than confrontation. In fact, union leadership in Japan is an extension of management since union leaders hold management positions in the companies. It is claimed that labour relations in Japan are better than they are in North America. The system seems to work well since there are very few strikes. Japanese workers know that they benefit from a profitable company.

EFFECTS OF LABOUR UNIONS IN THE LABOUR MARKET

Unions attempt to influence the wage rate by shifting the demand and supply curves for labour.

One of the objectives of a union is to secure higher wages for its members. Economic theory predicts that higher wages will result from an increase in the demand for labour. A union may therefore attempt to shift the equilibrium wage rate upward by shifting the labour demand curve to the right or by shifting the labour supply curve to the left.

INCREASING THE DEMAND FOR AND REDUCING THE SUPPLY OF LABOUR

Learning Objective 8: the effects of labour unions in the labour market

Recall that the demand for labour is a derived demand. That is, if the demand for a certain product increases, the demand for inputs (including labour) used to produce that product also increases. This relationship suggests that one way in which unions may increase the demand for labour is to increase the demand for the products of unionized producers. This increase in the demand for labour will likely increase the wage rate.

Many unions encourage their members to purchase union-made products. The effect of this practice is illustrated in Figure 13.9. DD and SS are the initial demand and

FIGURE 13.9

Effect of increasing the demand for labour.

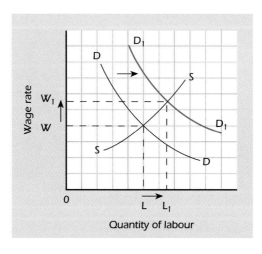

supply curves for labour. The equilibrium wage rate is W. A campaign to encourage people to buy union-made products, if successful, will increase the demand for labour. This increase in demand is shown by the new demand curve D_1D_1. Assuming that there is no change in supply, the wage rate increases to W_1, and the quantity of labour hired increases from L to L_1.

A union may shift the supply curve of labour upward and to the left by restricting the entry of newcomers into certain occupations and professions. The effect of this practice on the wage rate is illustrated in Figure 13.10. The initial demand curve in the particular occupation or profession is DD. The initial supply curve is SS. The initial wage rate is 0W. By limiting new entrants into the occupation or profession, the union shifts the supply curve from SS to S_0S_0. This has the effect of raising the wage rate from 0W to $0W_1$.

FIGURE 13.10

Effect of a decrease in the supply of labour.

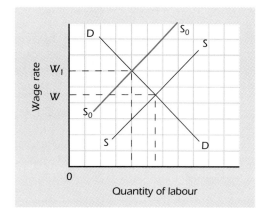

An increase in wage rates in one occupation or profession may spark demands for wage increases in other occupations and professions, leading to higher wages. This process by which wage increases in one occupation lead to wage increases in other occupations is referred to as the **wage transfer mechanism**. There is no doubt that wage rates have increased significantly in the various industries. Whether these higher wages result from union activities, however, is still a matter of considerable debate among economists. It is suspected that unions have played a role, but that other factors have also contributed.

A wage transfer mechanism adjusts wages in one occupation based on wage increases in another.

PROBLEM SOLVING 13-4

If all economists in Canada had to obtain a licence from an association called the Economics Association of Canada in order to work as economists, what would happen to the market for economists?

UNIONS AND RESOURCE ALLOCATION

Learning Objective 9: how unions affect resource allocation

Labour mobility is one requirement for market forces to allocate labour resources efficiently. Labour tends to move from low-wage occupations to high-wage occupations. The marginal productivity theory of wages discussed earlier in this chapter, moreover, asserts that high productivity is associated with high wages. It follows, then, that the movement of labour from low productivity jobs to high productivity jobs causes an increase in output.

Some critics have claimed, however, that unions restrict labour mobility and thus cause a misallocation of resources. Some have also argued that unions contribute to the

Union Objective Determines Strategy

Over four million Canadians are members of unions. Many of these union members have families and close relatives, therefore the agreements that are negotiated between unions and employers affect not only a few people. It has come to be generally accepted that unions have as their mandate to secure better working conditions for their members, to obtain higher wages, and to seek greater job security.

The analysis presented here shows that a union's objective will determine its negotiating strategy. The following diagram will facilitate the analysis.

Let us assume that there are L workers in the union. If the objective of the union is to have all of its members employed, it will negotiate for a wage rate of W. The quantity of workers demanded at a wage rate of W is L, as determined by the demand curve, so all members would be employed at a wage rate of W.

If, however, the objective of the union is to maximize total wages, it would adopt a different strategy and negotiate for the employment of L_o workers where the marginal revenue is zero. Recall that total revenue is at its maximum when marginal revenue is zero. The wage rate associated with the employment of L_o workers is W_1. This latter strategy leaves some workers ($L-L_o$) unemployed.

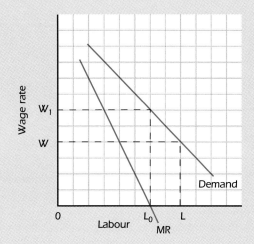

misallocation of labour resources by allowing promotions and job security on the basis of seniority rather than on the basis of competence. Often, a competent worker with low seniority loses his or her job, while a much less competent employee may be sheltered by seniority.

Supporters of labour unions, on the other hand, claim that the higher wages resulting from union activity actually serve as an incentive for greater productivity. Union supporters claim that discontented and disgruntled workers cannot be expected to have high productivity, but that good wages and working conditions contribute to good worker morale and productivity.

SOME UNSETTLED ISSUES

It goes without saying that unions occupy an important position in our economy and in our society. Their activities often touch our lives in significant ways. The economic, political, and social impact of unions has generated a number of debatable issues. We outline some of these issues in this closing section.

First, strikes in key industries can be crippling to the economy. This fact has led some critics to argue that strikes should be outlawed in key industries. Instead of strikes, would it not be better to settle disputes by compulsory arbitration? This is a debatable issue. Is a limitation on the right to strike an infringement on workers' rights? Should strike action by any group of workers be allowed to disrupt the lives of the majority of people?

Second, union wage demands have been blamed for inflation — rapidly rising prices. Currently, inflation is not a problem in the Canadian economy, but the Canadian economy has experienced bouts of inflation, and the effects have been costly. Should controls be imposed on wage increases? And if wages are controlled, should other prices be controlled as well?

Labour organized itself in order to achieve some monopoly power in the labour market. Organized labour has been able to win concessions from employers — concessions that would not have been possible if labour had not been organized into unions. Some people argue that unions now have too much power in the labour market while others argue just as emphatically that they do not have enough power. The debate rages on.

CHAPTER SUMMARY

1. Labour is a very important input into the production process. Income from labour accounts for approximately 71% of total income from all sources.

2. The demand for labour is a derived demand since it depends on the demand for goods and services, which labour is used to produce.

3. The marginal revenue product of labour (MRP_L) is the extra revenue obtained from selling an extra unit of output produced by an additional unit of labour. By multiplying the marginal physical product of labour (MPP_L) by the price of the product, we can obtain the marginal revenue product of labour.

4. The firm will employ labour up to the point where the marginal revenue product of labour equals the wage rate. The firm's demand curve for labour is the marginal revenue product of labour curve. We can approximate the industry demand curve for labour by adding the demand curves of all the firms in the industry.

5. The supply curve for labour slopes upward, generally. Higher wage rates serve as an incentive to increase the quantity of labour supplied. But in particular cases, the labour supply curve may be backward bending as extra income from labour causes people to work fewer hours.

6. The equilibrium wage rate is determined by the intersection of the demand and supply curves for labour. An increase in the demand for labour, other things being equal, results in an increase in the wage rate. An increase in the supply of labour results in a fall in the wage rate.

7. Differences in wages among occupations and professions are due to differences in education, skill and experience, responsibility, the existence of unions, and the degree of risk associated with the job. Psychic income also plays a role.

8. A union is an association of workers organized to promote the interests of its members in negotiations with their employers.

9. The membership of a craft or trade union consists of workers in a single occupation irrespective of where they work. The membership of an industrial union consists of workers in a particular industry.

10. Unions are organized at the local, national, international, and federation levels.

11. An open shop is an arrangement whereby an employee does not have to be a union member in order to obtain or keep a job. A closed shop requires membership in a union before employment can be obtained. A union shop allows for the hiring of workers who are not union members but who must become union members in a specified time.

12. The Rand Formula makes it compulsory for workers to pay union dues even if they are not members of the union.

13. Collective bargaining refers to the whole process whereby union and management arrive at an agreement about the terms of employment. The contract agreement deals with wages, vacation, safety, and other non-monetary matters such as job security.

14. Among the factors considered by the negotiating parties when deciding on wage demands and offers are productivity, profitability, and the cost of living.

15. An escalator clause is a provision in a contract specifying that wages will increase automatically to compensate for increases in the cost of living.

16. Unions can shift the wage rate up by increasing the demand for union-made products, and by restricting the entry of newcomers into certain occupations and professions.

17. Some critics claim that unions restrict labour mobility and thus contribute to misallocation of labour resources. Union supporters claim that union activity actually increases productivity.

TERMS FOR REVIEW

functional distribution
 of income (231)
direct demand (232)
derived demand (232)
marginal physical product
 of labour (232)
marginal revenue product (232)
marginal productivity theory
 of wages (233)
backward-bending labour
 supply curve (234)
psychic income (238)
craft or trade union (238)
industrial union (238)
local union (238)
national union (238)

international union (238)
federation (238)
closed shop, open shop, and
 union shop (239)
featherbedding (239)
Rand Formula (240)
collective bargaining (240)
collective agreement (240)
conciliation (mediation) (240)
voluntary arbitration (240)
compulsory arbitration (240)
strike (240)
lockout (241)
indexation, COLA, and escalator
 clause (241)
wage transfer mechanism (243)

QUESTIONS FOR REVIEW AND DISCUSSION

1. In what respect does the demand for an input such as labour differ from the demand for a product such as bread? (L.O.1)

2. Briefly explain the marginal productivity theory of wages. Do you think that the theory is relevant to present-day Canada? (L.O.1)

3. Explain how the wage rate is determined in a purely competitive labour market. (L.O.2)

4. Why might an increase in wages cause unemployment? (L.O.3)

5. If a provincial government sets the minimum wage in the province significantly above those in other provinces, what economic consequences (for labour) would you expect? (L.O.3)

6. You operate an apricot orchard in the Okanagan Valley. Your employees are not unionized. How would you decide on the number of employees to hire? (L.O.1,2)

7. Discuss the effect of discrimination in the labour market. (L.O.4)

8. Give some reasons for differences in wages among occupations in Canada. (L.O.5)

9. What is psychic income? How might psychic income influence a person's occupational choice? (L.O.5)

10. Give a brief account of union organization in Canada. (L.O.6)

11. How might a union secure higher wages for its members? (L.O.6,7)

12. Strikes are costly. What are some of the costs of strikes? (L.O.6,7)

13. Discuss some of the factors that union leaders and employers consider when deciding on wage demands and offers. (L.O.7)

14. "Unions cause resources to be misallocated." Do you agree with this assertion? (L.O.9)

PROBLEMS AND EXERCISES

1. Table 13.3 contains hypothetical data for a firm in pure competition. The labour market is also purely competitive, and the price of the firm's product is $2. (L.O.1)

TABLE 13.3

Wage and employment data.

Units of labour	Wage rate ($)	MPP$_L$	MRP$_L$
0	10		
		4	
1	10		
		6	
2			
		5	
3			
		4	
4			
		3	
5			
		2	
6			
		1	
7			

(a) Complete the table.

(b) On a graph, draw this firm's demand curve for labour.

(c) How many units of labour will this firm hire?

(d) Now, suppose that the wage rate falls to $6. How many units of labour will the firm hire?

2. The information in Table 13.4 is given for the Stanco Production Company, which operates in a purely competitive market. Stanco sells its product for $10, and pays its workers a wage of $50 per day. (L.O.1)

TABLE 13.4	Number of workers	Total product
Production schedule for Stanco.	0	0
	1	25
	2	35
	3	43
	4	48
	5	52
	6	52
	7	50

(a) How many workers will Stanco hire?

(b) How many workers would be hired if the wage rate were to rise to $80 per day?

3. The production schedule for the Minilite firm, which uses labour as its only variable input, is given in Table 13.5. Workers are paid $50 a day and Minilite's product sells for $5 in a purely competitive market. What is the optimum number of workers for Minilite to employ? (L.O.1,2)

TABLE 13.5	Number of workers	Total product
Minilite's production schedule.	0	0
	5	100
	10	175
	15	235
	20	285
	25	325
	30	350

4. Table 13.6 shows the demand and supply of labour. (L.O.1,2)

TABLE 13.6	Wage rate ($)	Quantity of labour demanded	Quantity of labour supplied
Demand and supply	4	11	1
	5	9	4
	6	7	7
	7	5	10
	8	3	13

(a) Draw the demand and supply curves on a graph.

(b) What is the equilibrium wage?

(c) How many workers will be hired at this wage rate?

5. Based on the information given in Question 4 above, suppose the government legislates a minimum wage rate of $7. How many units of labour will remain unemployed? (L.O.2,3)

6. With the help of diagrams, explain how each of the following will affect the labour market (ignore long-term effects): (L.O.3)

(a) an increase in the labour force due to immigration;

(b) a more optimistic economic outlook on the part of firms;

(c) an increase in the demand for Canadian goods because of the free-trade arrangement between Canada and the U.S.A;

(d) an increase in the tax rate, which reduces work incentive.

7. It is sometimes argued that labour unions, by demanding higher wages for their members, may end up hurting them. Discuss. (L.O.3)

8. Use a diagram to explain why, on average, lawyers earn more than service station attendants. (L.O.5)

 9. Many of the causes for which unions fought have now been incorporated into labour laws. Does this mean that unions have outlived their usefulness? Discuss.

Internet Site

http://labour-travail.hrdc-drhc.gc.ca/wip/othersites.html-ssi
This site takes you to several other sites dealing with labour.

INTERNET EXERCISE

1. Go to the Web site indicated above.

2. Click on *Unions* in *Canada* and then click on one of the sites that may be of interest to you.

You can learn about any of the unions listed on the site.

14 CHAPTER

RENT, INTEREST, AND PROFITS

Learning Objectives

After studying this chapter, you will know about:

1 the meaning of rent

2 rent determination

3 rent differentials

4 interest and interest rate determination

5 profit and its economic significance

Rent is that portion of the produce of the earth which is paid to the landlord for the use of the original and indestructible powers of the soil.

David Ricardo, *Principles of Political Economy and Taxation*

INTRODUCTION

In addition to labour services, firms use land (natural resources) and capital in the production process. Government also uses these factors of production in providing services for its citizens. These factors of production, like labour, are purchased in factor markets, and the sellers of these resources receive some form of factor income. Entrepreneurial services are also traded in factor markets, and the providers of such services receive another form of factor income. Recall that rent, interest, and profits are incomes derived from land, capital, and entrepreneurial services respectively.

According to Karl Marx, a nineteenth-century German philosopher and economist, rent, profits, and interest are surplus values obtained from oppressing workers whose labour services are, Marx felt, the source of all value. The demanding of rent, interest, and profits by landlords and capitalists was nothing but the exploitation of labour. In this chapter, we shall see whether Marxist views on rents, interest, and profits are valid. In doing so, we shall also determine what purposes are served by these types of income.

About 75% of total income goes to labour in the form of wages, salaries, and supplementary labour income. The remaining 25% is allocated between land, capital, and entrepreneurial services in the form of rent, interest, and profits. It is important for the student to be clear about the sense in which these terms are used; we will discuss their meanings in the next few sections.

THE MEANING OF RENT

Rent: the return to a factor whose supply is fixed.

Learning Objective 1: the meaning of rent

Pure economic rent: the income earned from a factor of production whose supply is completely price inelastic.

The monthly payment made by a tenant to a landlord for an apartment is commonly called rent. You can also rent a car for a weekend. Or you can rent tools from a tool rental company. These notions of rent, however, differ from the economic concept of rent. In economics, **rent** refers to the return on a productive factor the supply of which is fixed. **Pure economic rent** is the income earned by a factor of production whose supply is completely price inelastic. Land is often used as the best example of a factor of production that generates pure economic rent because, for practical purposes, the total quantity of land available is fixed.

Let us examine briefly this notion of a fixed quantity of land. Physically, the supply of land available to society is fixed. There is just so much land available to society, and offers of higher prices will not induce a greater quantity. The fertility of land, however, can be increased or reduced. Moreover, land can undergo a variety of improvements, such as drainage of swamps. But these improvements do not actually create new land. We can view these improvements to land as increasing capital rather than creating new land. It is important to note also that the quantity of land available for one use can be increased by reducing the quantity available for some other use. For example, farm land can be converted into land for residential purposes.

RENT DETERMINATION

Learning Objective 2: rent determination

Let us follow the classical tradition of using land to illustrate the determination of rent. Rent is determined in the market like any other price: by demand and supply. In Figure 14.1, the demand curve D_L slopes downward. This downward slope indicates that as the rent decreases, the quantity of land demanded increases. The vertical supply curve S_L shows that the supply of land is fixed at Q_L. The demand and supply curves intersect at R to give the market-determined rental value of r_e.

Demand and supply
curves for land.

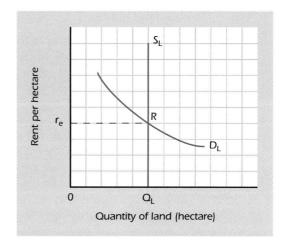

Rent is determined by the
intersection of the demand
and supply curves for land.

Because supply is fixed,
changes in rent are due to
changes in demand.

Note that changes in demand will change the rent per hectare of land. In Figure 14.2, if the demand for land is D_1, the rent per hectare will be r_1 and total economic rent will be the shaded area in the diagram ($Q_L \times r_1$). An increase in the demand for land from D_1 to D_2 will cause the rent per hectare to increase from r_1 to r_2, and the additional economic rent will be the unshaded area in Figure 14.2.

Effect of an increase in
demand for land.

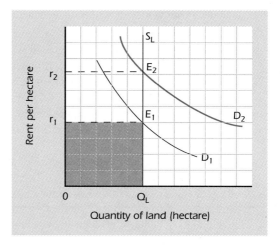

An increase in the demand
for land causes an increase
in rent.

RENT DIFFERENTIALS

Yield per hectare, resource
content, and location affect
the demand and hence the
rental value of land.

It is clear from the foregoing analysis that differences in rent are due to differences in demand for different parcels of land. In explaining rent differentials then, we must consider the factors that affect the demand for different parcels of land.

Let us consider a piece of land intended for wheat farming somewhere in Manitoba. Obviously, the demand by potential users depends on the expected yield per hectare. The higher the yield per hectare of this particular parcel of land, the greater the demand for it will be. And the greater the demand, the higher the rent.

Learning Objective 3:
rent differentials

Resource content also affects the demand for land — and thus rent. We can expect a parcel of land rich in mineral deposits to generate a higher rental value than a parcel with no mineral deposits. We base such an expectation on the assumption that the demand for the resource-rich parcel is likely to be higher than the demand for the barren parcel.

Finally, the location of land will have some effect on its demand and hence on its rental value. Compare the rent for land in the heart of a large city such as Montreal, Toronto, or Vancouver with the rent for land in a more remote area such as Petty Harbour, Newfoundland.

PROBLEM SOLVING 14-1

The downtown area of many cities is cluttered by high-rise buildings. In outlying areas, however, high rises are few. Explain this phenomenon.

ECONOMIC RENT AND TRANSFER EARNINGS

We defined rent earlier as the income earned by a factor of production whose supply is perfectly price inelastic. Another way of understanding rent is to view it as a return to a factor of production over and above its opportunity cost. Many superstars in music, sports, and entertainment earn exceptionally high incomes, and many people openly express dissatisfaction with the huge incomes earned by these individuals. Criticism of superstar salaries, however, is actually aimed at the rent portion of their incomes.

What is the rent portion of the income of a hockey player who earns $450 000 annually? To answer this question, we must determine the next best employment alternative for this hockey player. In other words, what is the opportunity cost? Or what is the minimum that this hockey player must earn playing hockey to decide not to quit hockey and take up some other job? This minimum is sometimes called **transfer earnings**, which is the amount of money that a factor of production can earn in the next best employment alternative.

Let us assume that the best employment this hockey player could get outside of hockey is a job that pays $30 000 a year. Then the excess ($420 000) is the rent portion of the hockey player's income. Superstars are paid very high salaries because their employers judge their marginal revenue products to be very high. Note that resources other than land are fixed in supply only in the short run. Incomes derived from such resources are usually called **quasi rent** to distinguish them from pure economic rent.

An issue often raised in connection with the rent portion of income is the economic effect of taxing away such income. Some people argue that taxing away the rent portion of income does not affect incentives or resource use. For example, if the rent portion of a hockey player's income is taxed, that person will likely continue to be a hockey player. Hockey players are unlikely to quit hockey for other careers because their incomes as hockey players are higher than the incomes that they could earn in other occupations.

However, if the rent portion of income is taxed away, will individuals still push themselves to achieve that rare quality that makes them superstars? Will they still take the time and trouble to develop and maintain those talents and skills that contribute to their exceptionally high incomes? How many would continue to strive for perfection? These questions are not easy to answer. One could conclude that rents are essential because they provide incentives for certain resources to be maintained.

A TAX ON LAND

The incomes of superstars can be explained, at least partly, by their practice and hard work in order to excel at what they do. But what about landowners? Consider the owner of a piece of land in some isolated area. Population growth or a population shift could increase the demand for the land, thus raising its price twentyfold within a relatively short time. This massive economic rent on the land would be a matter of luck rather than exerted effort or diligent work. For this reason, many argue that the economic rent from

Many salaries consist of rent and transfer earnings.

Transfer earnings is the minimum payment required to attract resources away from other uses.

Quasi rent is the return on a factor whose supply is fixed only in the short run.

Rent may be necessary to maintain certain resources.

land should be taxed. Such a tax, it is argued, is neutral in that it affects neither the incentives to produce nor the allocation of resources. The landowner simply pays the tax, and that's it. The incidence (burden) of the tax falls entirely on the landowner.

In practice, however, a land tax as suggested above may have some difficulties. Rarely is the payment for land limited to the land itself. It often includes payment for investment made to improve the land, and it may not be easy to separate the improvements made to the land from the land itself. Taxing the economic rent from land under such circumstances would adversely affect investment such as land clearing and drainage.

INTEREST

Interest is the payment for or the income derived from a loan.

Learning Objective 4:
interest and interest rate determination

Quite simply stated, interest is the payment for the use of money for a specified period of time. In order to purchase capital (machines, buildings, tools, etc.), many firms borrow funds and pay interest to those who lend these funds. Households also borrow money from financial institutions such as banks to purchase certain items such as cars, furniture, and appliances, and pay interest to these lenders. People lend money directly to corporations by purchasing corporate bonds, or indirectly by depositing funds in banks and other financial institutions that accept deposits. People lend money to the federal government by purchasing Canada Savings Bonds. To the lenders, interest represents income, while to the borrowers, it represents a cost. We can look at interest in a slightly different way. If I lend you $500, I am foregoing consumption that I could have had with my money. In order to induce me to forego that consumption, you must pay me something. This payment is interest.

It is important at this point to distinguish between interest and the rate of interest or interest rate. Clearly, from the discussion so far, interest is a sum of money. The amount lent or borrowed is called the principal. The rate of interest is the ratio of the interest to the principal, expressed as a percentage.

$$\text{rate of interest} = \frac{\text{interest}}{\text{principal}} \times 100$$

For example, if you borrow $500 for one year and you pay $60 interest, then the rate of interest on your loan is 12% per year. The rate of interest can be viewed as the price paid for the use of borrowed money.

Interest income depends on the amount of funds a factor owner has lent out and on the rate of interest. If I lend $1000 at an interest rate of 5% per year, my interest income will be $50 a year. If the interest rate were 10% a year, my interest income would be $100 a year. Clearly then, the rate of interest is important in determining the return on loans.

DETERMINATION OF THE RATE OF INTEREST

The rate of interest is determined by the demand for and supply of loanable funds.

Learning Objective 4:
interest and interest rate determination

Loanable funds theory of interest: the interest rate is determined by the demand for and supply of loanable funds.

The rate of interest is a price — the price of a loan. This price is determined in the market by the demand for and supply of borrowed funds or loanable funds. In Figure 14.3, the demand for loanable funds is shown by D. This demand is assumed to come from firms that want to borrow funds for investment purposes, from consumers who want to purchase certain consumer items, and from governments that want to spend more than their revenues, that is, to finance their deficits. The demand curve slopes downward, indicating that a greater amount of funds will be borrowed as the rate of interest falls. The supply of loanable funds comes from the savings of consumers, businesses, and governments in surplus positions. The demand and supply curves intersect at point A to give the equilibrium rate of interest, r, and the equilibrium quantity of loanable funds, LF. This model of interest rate determination is referred to as the **loanable funds theory of the rate of interest**.

Demand for and supply of loanable funds.

The intersection of the demand and supply curves for loanable funds determines the equilibrium rate of interest.

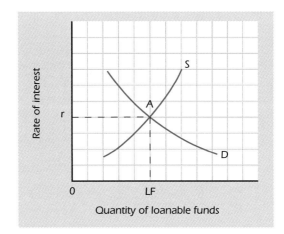

PROBLEM SOLVING 14-2

Canadians are big savers. How would interest rates be affected if Canadians were not such big savers?

INTEREST RATE DIFFERENTIALS

So far, we have talked about the rate of interest as if a single rate of interest existed for all types of credit instruments. (Credit instruments are written evidences that credit has been extended by the holder of the instrument.) In fact, interest rates vary according to the borrower and type of loan.

The risk premium is an addition to the interest rate to compensate for the risk of defaulting.

All loans carry a certain amount of risk, but the risks associated with different types of loans vary. One reason for differences in interest rates is differences in the degree of risk associated with loans. The probability of defaulting on a loan varies from borrower to borrower. Those borrowers likely to default will be charged a **risk premium**, an addition to the interest rate to compensate for the risk of defaulting. For example, the **prime lending rate** (the interest rate charged by banks to their most credit-worthy corporate customers) is lower than the rate charged to less credit-worthy borrowers. The greater the risk of default, other things being equal, the higher the risk premium will be.

The prime lending rate is the interest rate charged to the most credit-worthy customers.

A loan is paid off at maturity.

Another factor that contributes to interest rate differentials is maturity. **Maturity** is the length of time before the loan is paid off. Generally, the interest rate on a long-term loan is higher than that on a short-term loan. This conclusion is based on the assumption that people prefer to have their money now than later. In other words, people have a preference for liquidity; that is, they like to have ready access to their money. Since short-term loans are more liquid than long-term loans, lenders have to be induced to lend for longer periods by offering them higher interest rates.

A third factor that explains differences in interest rates is the stage of development of the market for the specific credit instrument. If the market for a specific credit instrument is well-developed, the transaction cost of buying or selling that instrument will be relatively low; hence the rate of interest will tend to be low. In places where financial markets are not well-developed, it is very difficult to negotiate loans, and often the very few lenders that operate in such places charge usurious interest rates.

REAL VERSUS NOMINAL INTEREST RATES

The nominal rate of interest is the real rate plus an adjustment for inflation.

Economists usually distinguish between the real rate of interest and the nominal rate of interest. The **real rate of interest** is the rate charged in the absence of inflation. The

nominal rate of interest is the rate quoted for a loan or a deposit, and includes a premium to compensate for the level of inflation. Let us illustrate the relation between the real and nominal rates of interest with the following example. Let us assume that the annual rate of inflation is 10%. This means that at the end of the year, a given sum of money will purchase only 90% of what it could purchase at the beginning of the year. If Mary Braley borrows $1000 for a year, when she repays the loan at the end of the year, the $1000 will purchase only $900. Without making any allowance for inflation, the lender would have lost 10% purchasing power over the year. An increase in prices lowers the value (purchasing power) of money. Thus, if lenders expect a rate of inflation of 10% per year, they will likely protect themselves from loss due to inflation by adding 10 percentage points to the real rate of interest. If lenders would normally have charged 7% interest in the absence of inflation, they would now charge 17% because of inflation. In the above example, the real rate is 7% while the nominal rate is 17%. The following equation expresses the relation between the nominal rate and the real rate:

$$NR = RR + e$$

where NR is the nominal rate, RR is the real rate, and e is the rate of inflation.

PROBLEM SOLVING 14-3
Is it always less costly to borrow money at a 4% interest rate than at a 17% interest rate?

PROFITS

In computing profits, economists consider all opportunity costs; accountants do not.

Learning Objective 5: profit and its economic significance

It is important for you to understand the difference between the accountant's notion of profits and the economist's concept of profits. Accounting profits refer to the excess of sales revenues from goods and services over the expenses incurred in producing the goods and services. Economic profits, on the other hand, refer to the excess of revenues from the sale of goods and services over the total cost, including opportunity cost, of producing the goods and services. The following example will help to illustrate the difference. The revenues and expenses of Joseph Seanan, the owner of a pine cabinet shop, are shown in Table 14.1. Such a statement is referred to as an **income statement**. Note that accounting profits are also referred to as **net income**.

TABLE 14.1

Revenues and expenses.

An income statement shows revenues, expenses, and net income.

Net income: revenue minus expenses.

Revenue:		
Sales..		$50 000
Expenses:		
Rent...	$ 2 500	
Utility	600	
Wages..	15 000	
Transportation	800	
Materials & supplies	10 000	
Miscellaneous................................	500	
TOTAL expenses......................................		$29 400
Net Income ($50 000 − $29 400)		$20 600

In order to calculate economic profits, however, we would need to know not just the expenses incurred by Joseph Seanan, but also how much Joseph could have earned in the next best alternative job. In other words, what is Joseph's opportunity cost? Let us assume that Joseph's opportunity cost is $20 600. Then we would have the following situation:

$$\text{Total revenue} \quad .... \quad \$50\ 000$$

$$\text{Total cost} = \$29\ 400 + \$20\ 600 = \$50\ 000$$

$$\text{Profits} (\$50\ 000 - \$50\ 000) \ .... \ = \qquad \$0$$

Normal profits are returns that just equal the opportunity costs of the resources.

In this case, Joseph is earning zero economic profits, or normal profits. If, however, Joseph can earn only $18 000 instead of operating his shop, then the situation would change as follows:

$$\text{Total revenue} \quad .... \quad \$50\ 000$$

$$\text{Total cost} = \$29\ 400 + \$18\ 000 = \$47\ 400$$

$$\text{Profits} (\$50\ 000 - \$47\ 400)...... = \ \$\ 2\ 600$$

He would then earn positive economic profits of $2600.

PROFIT AS A RETURN ON INNOVATION AND ENTREPRENEURIAL ABILITY

Why do people decide to own their own business enterprises rather than sell their factor services to others? One answer is the prospect of greater profits. Presumably, many people feel that they have better insight, more imagination, and are more adventurous than anyone they have worked for. If these people are indeed as innovative as they think and their innovations succeed, then they are compensated with profits. If they fail, they suffer losses.

PROFIT AS A RETURN FOR RISK-TAKING

Profits may be viewed as a return on innovation, a reward for risk-bearing, or the result of market power.

No matter how shrewd businesspeople may be, they must confront the risk involved in owning their own businesses. Profits are sometimes viewed as a reward for bearing the risks of business ownership — a sort of risk premium. In the absence of this risk premium, many people would not consider it worth their while to bear the risks associated with ownership.

PROFITS FROM MARKET POWER

We have already seen that a firm in pure competition may earn positive economic profits in the short run, but that in the long run, because of competition, such profits will dwindle away. A firm with significant market power may be able to earn positive economic profits even in the long run because of effective barriers to entry such as patent rights, economies of scale, and limit-pricing techniques.

THE ECONOMIC ROLE OF PROFITS

Profits serve as a signal for resource allocation, a motive for efficiency, and a reward for the enterprising.

Learning Objective 5: *profit and its economic significance*

Basically, profits perform three economic functions:

1. they serve as a signal to resource owners;

2. they provide a motive or incentive for efficiency;

3. they reward the resourceful.

Let us now briefly examine each of these economic functions of profits.

PROFITS AS A SIGNAL TO RESOURCE OWNERS

The existence of profits in any industry or sector of the economy is a clear signal that price exceeds average cost of production, and that resources should be shifted into that industry or sector. Likewise, the existence of losses in an industry is a loud and clear signal that resources should be shifted out of that industry and put to more productive uses.

PROFITS AS A MOTIVE FOR EFFICIENCY

The desire for profits serves as an incentive for producers to cut production costs where possible. In the face of competition, high-cost firms will lose their market shares to low-cost firms. Unless high-cost firms can increase their efficiency, they will ultimately be forced out of the market.

PROFITS AS REWARD

Profits serve as a reward for the resourceful, the imaginative, the innovative, and the enterprising. The prospect of earning profits is often the driving force behind the development and maintenance of special resources and talents.

PROBLEM SOLVING 14-4
What are the economic effects of taxation of excess profits?

APPLICATION

Understanding Income Inequality

Why is income unequally distributed in a market economy? People derive income from the resources at their disposal. Owners of labour of high quality in great demand will tend to earn high wages and salaries. Owners of prime land in great demand will receive huge payments in the form of rent. Owners of scarce capital will earn income in the form of interest and dividends, and people with entrepreneurial skills will receive profit income. Resources are unevenly distributed. Some individuals in our society, for a variety of reasons, do not own or have control over valuable resources, hence they receive relatively small incomes.

CHAPTER SUMMARY

1. About 25% of total income takes the form of rent, interest, and profits.
2. Pure economic rent is the return on a factor of production that is completely fixed in supply. The return on a factor that is fixed only in the short run, such as exceptional talent, is quasi rent.
3. Rent is determined in the market by demand and supply. Changes in demand explain changes in rent.
4. Rent differentials result mainly from differences in the demand for different parcels of land. Location is an important factor in rent differentials.
5. Rent serves as an incentive for the development and maintenance of certain types of resources.
6. Interest is income derived from loans. The loans may be made directly by the purchase of bonds or indirectly by deposits on financial institutions.
7. The demand for and supply of loanable funds determine the rate of interest. The demand for loanable funds comes from firms, consumers, and government. The supply of loanable funds comes from savers.

8. Profits may be viewed as a return on entrepreneurial ability or a reward for risk-taking.

9. Profits serve as a signal for resource movement, a motive for efficiency, and a reward for enterprise.

TERMS FOR REVIEW

rent (251)
pure economic rent (251)
transfer earnings (253)
quasi rent (253)
loanable funds theory of interest (254)
risk premium (255)

prime lending rate (255)
maturity (255)
real versus nominal rate of interest (255)
income statement (256)
net income (256)

QUESTIONS FOR REVIEW AND DISCUSSION

1. In what way does rent differ from other types of income? (L.O.1)
2. What are the main determinants of rent differentials? (L.O.3)
3. Justify the high salaries earned by superstars. (L.O.2,3)
4. Would you support a proposal to tax away the rent portion of income? Defend your position. (L.O.3)
5. Distinguish between interest and the rate of interest. (L.O.4)
6. How is the rate of interest determined in a purely competitive market for funds? (L.O.4)
7. How would an increase in government borrowing affect the rate of interest? (L.O.4)
8. Interest rates tend to be high during inflationary times. Explain why this is so. (L.O.4)
9. Why are some groups able to borrow at lower rates of interest than other groups? (L.O.4)
10. Differentiate between accounting profits and economic profits. (L.O.5)
11. Do profits perform any economic functions? (L.O.5)

PROBLEMS AND EXERCISES

1. Use diagrams to illustrate the difference in demand for a hectare of swamp land 60 km east of Blissfield, New Brunswick, and a hectare of commercial real estate in downtown Fredericton. Which piece of land would normally have the higher rental value and why? (L.O.2)
2. Buffy Fleetfoot plays lacrosse for the Winnipeg Wendigos and earns a salary of $175 000 per year. Outside of lacrosse, she could earn a maximum of $80 000 annually as the proprietor of a sporting goods store. Apart from the money, it makes no difference to Buffy whether she continues to play lacrosse or whether she assumes proprietorship of the store. What portion of Buffy's salary can be considered rent? (L.O.3)
3. Bab Rushdie earns $400 000 a year as an actor. He could have earned $60 000 at best as a consultant in the public relations department of TV Ontario. What part of his earnings is economic rent and what part is transfer earnings? (L.O.3)
4. How has the invention of television affected the rent portion of the earnings of sports and entertainment superstars? (L.O.3)

5. Your friend, Mei Ling, borrows $100 from you. Because she is your friend, you do not want to make a profit on the loan transaction. Therefore you do not charge her interest. Is this a rational decision? Explain. (L.O.4)

6. It has been said that one difference between profit and rent is that profit can be reduced by competition while rent cannot. Do you agree with this statement? Explain. (L.O.1,5)

7. Pierre Gunter is the proprietor of a photography studio. His typical monthly expenses are shown in Table 14.2. Pierre has been offered as much as $1500 per month to work for other companies. (L.O.5)

TABLE 14.2

Cost and revenue data for Pierre Gunter.

Revenue:
Sale of goods	$ 150
Sale of services	2 500
TOTAL	$2 650

Cost:
Rent	$ 200
Materials	50
Telephone	40
Utilities	30
Wages	500
Other expenses	25
TOTAL	$ 845

Compute:

(a) Pierre's monthly profit (in an accounting sense);

(b) Pierre's monthly profit (in an economic sense).

Internet Site

http://www.bmo.com
This site is the home page for the Bank of Montreal.

INTERNET EXERCISE

1. Go to the Bank of Montreal Web site.

2. Click on *Rates*.

3. List the different interest rates offered for prime, MasterCard, mortgages, RRSPs, GICs, Small Business, and Savings Accounts.

15

CHAPTER

INCOME DISTRIBUTION AND POVERTY

Learning Objectives

After studying this chapter, you will know about:

1 the criteria for income distribution

2 the size distribution of income

3 the dimensions of poverty

4 measures to alleviate poverty

5 aspects of the welfare system

6 the negative income tax (NIT)

7 Canada's income security program

For my own part, I believe that there is social and psychological justification for significant inequalities of incomes and wealth, but not for such large disparities as exist today.

J. M. Keynes, *The General Theory*

INTRODUCTION

In the two previous chapters, we looked at various sources of income, including wages, rent, interest, and profits. Each year, Canadians earn a considerable amount of income through the use or sale of the resources at their command. This income, however, is not distributed equally among Canadians. Some Canadians earn annual incomes in excess of $250 000, while others hardly earn enough for the bare necessities of life.

This apparent unfairness in the distribution of income is among the most hotly debated economic and social issues. In this chapter, we shall discuss income distribution in Canada. We shall also discuss the problem of poverty and look at some measures to deal with this great social problem. Finally, we shall look briefly at Canada's welfare system.

CRITERIA FOR INCOME DISTRIBUTION

Learning Objective 1:
the criteria for income distribution

Most people in our society seem to agree that income and wealth should be shared in some manner that is fair. There is no general agreement, however, about what constitutes fairness or equity, or how to distribute income equitably. We shall briefly examine three views about the equitable distribution of income.

DISTRIBUTION ACCORDING TO CONTRIBUTION

Three views on the equitable distribution of income: contribution, need, and equality.

According to this view, income should be distributed according to productivity. Supporters of this view claim that it is only fair to reward people according to their contribution to total output. They see certain advantages to this approach. First, it provides incentives for greater productivity. Second, the system works automatically through the market system.

DISTRIBUTION ACCORDING TO NEED

Another view of income distribution is based on the biblical model of Christian communism:

> For there was not a needy person among them, for all who were owners of land or houses would sell them and bring the proceeds of the sales, and lay them at the apostles' feet; and they would be distributed to each, as any had need.*

This idea has found subsequent expression in the popular saying of the early French revolutionary Louis Blanc: "From each according to his ability, to each according to needs." There are, however, obvious problems with this approach. First, how are needs to be determined? This, in itself, presents an almost insuperable problem. Second, if goods are distributed according to need, is there any incentive to work?

EQUAL DISTRIBUTION TO ALL

According to this view, income should be distributed equally to all. The simplicity of this procedure is appealing. To arrive at the amount to be distributed to each, we simply divide the total income by the population. The problem with this approach to income distribution is that it fails to provide incentives for economic activity; and if there is no incentive for economic activity, the level of economic activity will fall. Such a fall is undesirable.

THE SIZE DISTRIBUTION OF INCOME

Learning Objective 2:
the size distribution of income

The size distribution of income is the distribution of income according to the income groups of the households.

The distribution of income among individuals and households is referred to as the **size distribution of income**. It is a measure that is frequently used to determine how evenly total income is distributed in a given society. If 5% of the households controlled over 90% of the total income and wealth in a society, most people would conclude that the income disparity was too large, and would probably grumble about social injustice. Is income fairly evenly distributed in Canada? Let us consult Table 15.1 for the answer. It contains data on the size distribution of income in Canada in 1996.

*Acts of the Apostles 4:34–35.

	Income group	Percentage of families in group	Percentage of income received	Cumulative percentage of families	Cumulative percentage of income received
TABLE 15.1	**(1)**	**(2)**	**(3)**	**(4)**	**(5)**
Distribution of families and of aggregate income of families by income groups, 1996.	Under $10 000	2.3	0.2	2.3	0.2
	$ 10 000 – 14 999	4.2	0.9	6.5	1.1
	$ 15 000 – 19 999	5.5	1.7	12.0	2.8
	$ 20 000 – 24 999	7.0	2.8	19.0	5.6
	$ 25 000 – 29 999	6.5	3.2	25.5	8.8
	$ 30 000 – 34 999	6.2	3.6	31.7	12.4
	$ 35 000 – 39 999	6.6	4.4	38.3	16.8
	$ 40 000 – 44 999	6.4	4.8	44.7	21.6
	$ 45 000 – 49 999	6.0	5.0	50.7	26.6
	$ 50 000 – 54 999	6.3	5.8	57.0	32.4
	$ 55 000 – 59 999	5.3	5.4	62.3	37.8
	$ 60 000 – 64 999	5.2	5.8	67.5	43.6
	$ 65 000 – 69 999	4.4	5.3	71.9	48.9
	$ 70 000 – 74 999	4.2	5.4	76.1	54.3
	$ 75 000 – 79 999	3.7	5.0	79.8	59.3
	$ 80 000 – 89 999	6.1	9.1	85.9	68.4
	$ 90 000 – 99 999	3.9	6.6	89.8	75.0
	$100 000 and over	10.1	25.1	100.0	100.0

Source: Statistics Canada, Income Distribution by Size in Canada, 1996 (Cat. 13-207-XPB):100.

The table shows that in 1996, 2.3% of Canadian families had incomes under $10 000 per year. On the other hand, 10.1% of Canadian families received incomes of $100 000 and over. The information in columns four and five of Table 15.1 is useful in this discussion. About 19% of families received 6% of the total income, while about 90% of the total number of families received about 75% of the total income.

THE LORENZ CURVE

An important device for measuring income inequality is the **Lorenz curve**, named after a German economic statistician. The construction of a Lorenz curve is a relatively simple matter, and is illustrated in Figure 15.1. We are measuring the cumulative percent of income along the vertical axis and the cumulative percent of families along the horizontal axis. The diagonal straight line 0A in Figure 15.1 represents an equal distribution

The Lorenz curve is used to measure the degree of income inequality.

FIGURE 15.1

A Lorenz curve.

The shaded area in the diagram shows the extent of income inequality.

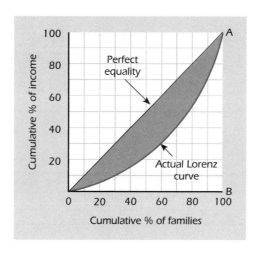

of income. If we were to plot the data contained in columns four and five on a graph, the resulting curve would resemble the actual Lorenz curve indicated in Figure 15.1. The shaded area in the diagram shows the degree of income inequality. The greater the shaded area, the greater the inequality in income distribution.

The Gini coefficient gives an even more precise measure of the extent of inequality in income distribution. The **Gini coefficient** is the area enclosed by the Lorenz curve and the line of perfect equality in income distribution (that is, the shaded area) expressed as a proportion of the area of triangle 0AB in Figure 15.1. For example, if the area of the shaded area is F and the area of the triangle is H, then the Gini coefficient is F/H. The larger the Gini coefficient, the greater the inequality in the distribution of income.

The Gini coefficient is a ratio that measures the degree of inequality in income distribution.

INCOME INEQUALITY BETWEEN THE SEXES

Even before the advent of feminism, there were cries against prejudicial treatment of women. It was claimed that income has always been distributed in favour of men. Figure 15.2 is a graphic presentation of the present-day distribution of income between males and females.

In 1996, about 15% of women but only about 8% of men had incomes under $5000 per year. At the other extreme, 23.3% of men had incomes of $45 000 or more per year, compared with only 7.6% of women. In fact, while the highest concentration of men was in the $50 000-and-over income bracket, the highest concentration of women was in the $10 000-$12 999 income group. We may note also that the average income for men in 1996 was $31 788, while the average for women was only $19 855. Hence, on average, men received more than one and a half times as much income as women did.

PROBLEM SOLVING 15-1

Should everyone in Canada receive the same income?

FIGURE 15.2

Income distribution by sex, 1996.

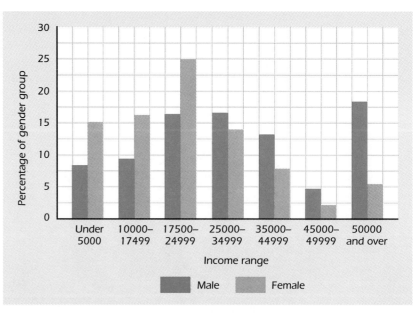

Source: Statistics Canada, *Income Distribution by Size in Canada, 1996* (Cat. 13–207-XPB): 136.

POVERTY

Canada is viewed as a wealthy country and Canadians enjoy a relatively high standard of living. These facts notwithstanding, many Canadians live in poverty. In this section, we shall attempt to define poverty and examine the incidence of poverty.

DEFINITION OF POVERTY

People are poor absolutely when their incomes are below the poverty line.

We can define poverty either in an absolute sense or in a relative sense. We say that a family is living in **absolute poverty** if its income is so low that it cannot afford the goods and services that most people in the society would consider to be just enough to enable the family to live in minimum comfort. There are obvious problems with this definition. How is minimum comfort defined? Who decides what is minimum comfort? Evidently, the amount required to achieve this minimum comfort will vary from family to family and from individual to individual. Despite these problems, it is clear that poverty is the condition of not having enough money to afford the basic needs as society views these needs.

The poverty line (low-income cut-off) is the income level below which a family cannot maintain a satisfactory standard of living.

Poverty is often discussed in terms of what has become known as the **poverty line**, an arbitrary measure of a level of income below which a family or an individual is unable to maintain a satisfactory standard of living.

Statistics Canada has established a **low-income cut-off** or *poverty line* based on the size of the area of residence and on the size of the family unit. For example, the poverty line for an unattached person living in a rural area will be much lower than the poverty line for a couple with three children living in a large urban area. This difference, of course, reflects the fact that the latter would require a larger sum of money to be able to afford the basic necessities of food, shelter, and clothing. According to this criterion, any family or unattached individual whose income is below the poverty line is considered to be living in poverty. Table 15.2 shows low income cut-offs for family units. Based on these low income cut-offs, approximately 1 207 000 families and 1 587 000 unattached individuals, totalling an estimated 5 million persons or about 17% of the Canadian population, were living below the poverty line in 1996. It is interesting to note that in 1991, the figure was 14%.

Another way of determining poverty is to consider the proportion of income spent on food, shelter, and clothing. Statistics Canada has established that families who on average spend 56.2% or more of their income on food, shelter, and clothing are considered to be in straitened circumstances.

TABLE 15.2

Low-income cut-offs of family units, 1996, in dollars.

| Size of family unit | Low income cut-offs, based on population of area of residence | | | | |
	500 000 and over	100 000– 499 999	30 000– 99 999	Less than 30 000	Rural areas
1 person	17 132	14 694	14 591	13 577	11 839
2 persons	21 414	18 367	18 239	16 971	14 799
3 persons	26 633	22 844	22 684	21 107	18 406
4 persons	32 238	27 651	27 459	25 551	22 279
5 persons	36 036	30 910	30 695	28 562	24 905
6 persons	39 835	34 168	33 930	31 571	27 530
7 or more persons	43 634	37 427	37 166	34 581	30 156

Source: Statistics Canada, *Income Distribution by Size in Canada, 1996* (Cat. 13-207-XPB): 51.

People are poor relatively if their incomes are far below the incomes of others.

A family is in **relative poverty** if its income forces it to accept a standard of living significantly below that enjoyed by other families in the society. Thus, an unattached individual with an annual income of $60 000 will be considered to be relatively poor if the majority of people in the society have annual incomes in excess of $250 000. If we define poverty in relative terms, then there is a great deal of truth in the biblical saying, "ye shall have the poor with you always." Viewed in this way, any substantial unequal distribution of income will give rise to poverty, regardless of the absolute size of the income shares.

DIMENSIONS OF POVERTY

Poverty hurts the society as well as the individual.

Poverty imposes severe hardships on individuals. The poor are barred from enjoying the good things in life that many people take for granted. They are deprived of good homes and good health, and their children may be deprived of a good education. As a result, they may turn to various forms of criminal activities. Thus, not only the individual but the society also suffers as a result of poverty.

Learning Objective 3: the dimensions of poverty

In addition to the loss of property (and possibly life) that may result from poverty, there are other economic disadvantages. Because the poor are likely to have low levels of education and skills, their productivity is likely to be low. This low productivity prevents the economy's output of goods and services from reaching its full potential. Hence, the population as a whole must accept a lower standard of living.

THE INCIDENCE OF POVERTY

The incidence of poverty refers to the chances or likelihood of being poor.

Poverty is not confined to any one region, age group, sex, or race. It is found among the young as well as the old, among rural areas as well as large urban centres, among men as well as women. The distribution of low income families and unattached individuals roughly follows the distribution of the population. Yet, in general, there are certain groups that are more likely to be poor than other groups. Below, we discuss the **incidence of poverty**, identifying groups with a high probability of being poor.

Families with many children

Families with a large number of young children have a high incidence of poverty. For example, the incidence of poverty for a family with three or more children under 16 is nearly one and a half times as high as for a family with one or two children under the age of 16.

Families in certain provinces

Certain groups have a higher incidence of poverty than others.

Families in the Atlantic provinces (particularly in Newfoundland and Nova Scotia) and Quebec are more likely to be poor than families in Ontario or B.C. This should not obscure the fact that most Canadians living in poverty are from Quebec and Ontario, the two provinces that comprise the country's largest population.

Families in rural areas

The incidence of poverty is also usually high among families in rural areas. Poverty in rural areas is usually less visible than in urban areas. For instance, the urban poor may live in run-down houses, while the rural poor may not. The prospects of finding jobs that offer high remuneration in rural areas are usually not very good, and in general, the incomes of farm operators and farm workers tend to be substantially below incomes earned by families in urban areas. Expectations of a better life in the city may attract some people (especially young adults) into the city, where they are only added to the list of the urban poor. This fact partly explains the high incidence of poverty in large urban areas.

Families headed by females
Poverty is widespread among families headed by females. A family headed by a female is over four times as likely to be poor as a family whose head is a male. Proportionally, the incidence of poverty is particularly high among families headed by single females. About 38% of all low-income families in Canada are headed by females. Fifty-eight percent of unattached females are poor.

Young families
The incidence of poverty is high among families whose heads are 24 years old or less. Such families are more than four times as likely to be poor as families whose heads are between 45 and 54 years old. One of the reasons for poverty among young families is that they often lack education, valuable skills, and working experience.

Elderly families
Female heads of families and unattached individuals who are over 70 years old have a high incidence of poverty. Just over 5% of all low-income families in Canada have heads who are 70 years old or older. These are mostly retired people who live on pension income.

Families headed by self-employed individuals
The incidence of poverty for families whose heads are self-employed is nearly twice as high as that for families whose heads are paid workers. About 10% of all low-income families in Canada have self-employed heads.

Families headed by individuals not in the labour force
Families whose heads are not in the labour force have a high incidence of poverty. The heads of such families are usually infirm or incapacitated, and must therefore look for ways of sustaining themselves other than employment income.

Unattached individuals
Those who are unattached, unemployed, self-employed, 70 years and older, female, or resident in the Atlantic provinces are most likely to be poor.

In general, the incidence of poverty among unattached individuals is about three times as high as that among families. The incidence of poverty is particularly high among unattached individuals who are not in the labour force, who are 70 years and older, who have low levels of education, who are self-employed, who live in the Atlantic Provinces, or who are females.

PROBLEM SOLVING 15-2
Can you account for the relatively large number of unattached individuals living below the poverty line in urban areas?

CAUSES OF POVERTY

It is impossible to identify any single cause of poverty or to attribute poverty to one major cause. The causes of poverty are numerous and no one cause can claim supremacy over the others. We can, however, discuss some of the prime causes of poverty.

Low productivity
Causes of poverty include low productivity, low economic growth, lack of resources, physical and mental disabilities, and discrimination.

One cause of poverty is low productivity. We know that in a purely competitive labour market, each worker will be paid the value of his or her marginal product. Even in an imperfect market setting, workers with high productivity tend to be paid higher wages than workers with low productivity. Workers with low productivity, then, will likely have low incomes.

Low economic growth

Poverty may be caused by the inability of the economy to expand fast enough to keep pace with a growing population. In such a situation, an increasing number of people will be numbered among the unemployed, and consequently among those considered to be in straitened circumstances.

Quantity and quality of resources

Individuals earn income from the resources at their command: rent from land, wages and salaries from labour, interest and dividends from capital, and profits from entrepreneurial services. One cause of poverty is lack of ownership of large quantities of valuable resources. Families with very small quantities and low quality of natural resources and physical and human capital will tend to have low incomes.

Physical and mental disabilities

Another cause of poverty is physical or mental disability. Individuals who are disabled may be unable to compete with others for a share of the output of the economy. They are quite often the victims of discrimination and may have to depend on government programs of assistance and various charities for their survival.

Discrimination

Economic discrimination occurs when workers are treated differently in the labour market, although there are no differences in their output. There are several forms of economic discrimination: employment discrimination, wage discrimination, and occupational discrimination. Let us briefly define each of these forms of economic discrimination.

Types of economic discrimination include employment discrimination, wage discrimination, and occupational discrimination.

> **Employment discrimination is a situation in which particular groups are denied employment.**
>
> **Wage discrimination is a situation in which particular groups are paid lower wages and salaries than others are paid for similar work.**
>
> **Occupational discrimination is a situation in which particular groups are prevented from entering certain occupations.**

Discrimination in its various forms is one of the major causes of poverty. Because of discrimination, certain groups may be prevented from taking advantage of opportunities that are open to others. They may be denied access to certain schools, or they may be prevented from entering certain occupations. Accounts abound of visible minorities being paid lower wages than whites, and women lower wages than men, not because of any difference in productivity among the groups, but because of prejudice against them. Numerous accounts also exist of promotions being given on the basis of race or sex rather than on the basis of merit as demonstrated by qualification, competence, or experience, or a combination of all three.

MEASURES TO ALLEVIATE POVERTY

Measures to alleviate poverty include productivity improvement, economic growth, anti-discrimination laws, subsidies, and special employment projects for the disabled.

Learning Objective 4: measures to alleviate poverty

The foregoing discussion of the causes of poverty points to some approaches whereby this problem may be alleviated. One approach is to increase the productivity of the working poor. This can be achieved by providing education and training so that workers can improve their skills. Second, an increase in the rate of economic growth and policies to promote employment will do much to reduce poverty. Third, legislation forbidding discrimination, though it will not eliminate discrimination, may help to lessen the misery of those who are victims of discriminatory practices. Fourth, the provision of certain goods and services free or at greatly reduced cost to the poor will help to reduce poverty. An example of this approach is the provision of subsidized housing to the poor. Finally, the government can provide employment for disabled persons in special government-operated workshops. In this way, the disabled will make a positive contribution to society's output of goods and services. The workshops will also provide on-the-job training and serve as transitions to regular work in the private or public sector.

CANADA'S INCOME SECURITY PROGRAMS

Learning Objective 5: aspects of the welfare system

In an attempt to alleviate the problems of low-income families and to provide income security for Canadians, the federal and provincial governments in Canada have instituted certain programs. Provincial and territorial governments have social assistance programs that provide minimum levels of income to those in need. The provincial and territorial governments are also responsible for Workers' Compensation plans that provide benefits to workers who sustain injury or death on the job. In this section, we look at a few of the programs of the federal government. Specifically, we shall discuss the Old Age Security (OAS) program, the Canada Pension Plan (CPP), and the Employment Insurance (EI) program.

Human Resources Development Canada (HRDC) administers the Old Age Security programs and the Canada Pension Plan, and through the Canada Employment Insurance Commission, it is responsible for the Employment Insurance program.

OLD AGE SECURITY PROGRAM

The Old Age Security (OAS) program incorporates three programs: Old Age Security Pension, Guaranteed Income Supplement (GIS), and Spouse's Allowance (SPA). The Old Age Security legislation which established the OAS program was enacted in 1952, and has seen many amendments since then. The OAS program is funded by the federal government, and benefits are indexed to the cost of living.

Old Age Security Pension

The Old Age Security Pension is paid monthly to eligible Canadian citizens or legal residents who have reached the age of 65 years. The pensioner's duration of residence in Canada determines the amount of OAS pension received, and OAS pension benefits are subject to federal and provincial income tax.

Guaranteed Income Supplement

The Guaranteed Income Supplement (GIS) is paid to recipients of OAS benefits who have little or no other income. Unlike the OAS benefits, GIS payments are made on the basis of need. Recipients must apply annually by filing an income statement, and the amount of GIS monthly payments varies with the applicant's annual income. Unlike the OAS pension, the GIS is not subject to federal or provincial income tax.

Spouse's Allowance

Many Canadians face difficult economic circumstances because they are widowed or because they are married and living on the pension of only one spouse. The spouse's allowance (SPA) is designed to provide assistance for such people. The SPA is a monthly payment made to the spouse of an OAS pensioner or to a widow or widower who is between the ages of 60 and 64 and who has lived in Canada for at least 10 years after the age of 18. Recipients of the SPA must apply annually, and in order to qualify for benefits under this scheme, the applicants' annual income cannot exceed certain limits. SPA benefits are not subject to income tax.

THE CANADA PENSION PLAN

The Canada Pension Plan (CPP) and its counterpart in Quebec, the Quebec Pension Plan (QPP), provide benefits to people who have contributed to the plan. Contributors are eligible to receive monthly retirement pension after their 60th birthday. Almost all employed and self-employed persons between the ages of 18 and 70 who earn more than a minimum yearly level of income are covered by the CPP/QPP. The plan is funded through contributions from employees, employers and self-employed persons, and from interest from the Canada Pension Plan Fund. The CPP and QPP are indexed to the cost of living.

EMPLOYMENT INSURANCE AND WORKERS' COMPENSATION

Established in 1940, the Unemployment Insurance program was intended to insure workers against loss of income during periods of unemployment. Employees contribute a certain percentage of their income to the plan while they are employed. Once they become unemployed and they qualify for benefits under the plan, they can draw benefits. This program was replaced by the new Employment Insurance system, the stated objective of which is to encourage people to return to the job market. In fact, the system emphasizes the merits of a rapid return to work. The Employment Insurance system extends temporary income support or income benefits to about three million people.

PROBLEM SOLVING 15-3
The depressing statistics on poverty seem to conflict with everyday observations of affluence. Why?

THE NEGATIVE INCOME TAX (NIT)

Negative income tax: a scheme whereby the government pays a subsidy to low-income people to provide a guaranteed minimum income.

Learning Objective 6:
the negative income tax (NIT)

Most people would probably agree that families ought to be guaranteed some minimum income. They would also agree that it is desirable to provide this minimum income without at the same time destroying the incentive to work. To accomplish both, however, is easier said than done. A negative income tax is one scheme proposed to deal with this question.

Under a **negative income tax** (NIT) system, an individual whose income is below a prescribed level need not pay income tax to the government: instead the government pays the individual. The amount of payment varies with the individual's income. There are many ways in which the payment by the government may vary with the individual's income. Table 15.3 illustrates one way in which an NIT program might work.

TABLE 15.3	Earned income	Government payment (a negative tax)	After-tax income
Operation of a negative income tax.	$ 0	$ 4 000	$4 000
	1 000	3 500	4 500
	2 000	3 000	5 000
	3 000	2 500	5 500
	4 000	2 000	6 000
	5 000	1 500	6 500
	6 000	1 000	7 000
	7 000	500	7 500
	8 000	0	8 000
	9 000	−500	8 500
	10 000	−1 000	9 000

Suppose the government decides to guarantee a minimum annual income of $4000 and that thereafter for every extra dollar earned up to say, $8000, the government subsidy will be reduced by $0.50. Thus, the government pays an individual who has earned no income for a year a subsidy — a negative income tax — of $4000. For an income of $1000, the subsidy of $4000 will be reduced by $500 ($0.50 for every dollar of income), so the individual receives a payment of $3500. If the individual earns $8000, the subsidy of $4000 is reduced by a half of that income (that is, by $4000) so no payment is received from the government. It is important to note that, under the NIT scheme, the income subsidy is reduced but not taken away entirely if the individual earns an income below $8000.

ADVANTAGES OF THE NIT

Proponents of the NIT claim for it the following advantages:

1. Under the NIT, the incentive to work is not destroyed. Under some welfare programs, the individual may be better off not working because the reduction in the subsidy may be greater than any extra income that could be earned by working. This is not the case with the NIT.

2. Individuals are left to spend their income as they see fit. They are not told how they should spend their income as is the case, for example, with subsidized housing. Thus, under the NIT, individuals have a greater freedom of choice.

3. The administration of an NIT program is relatively simple. It should require a smaller bureaucratic structure than that required for many other programs because for the most part, it would be administered by Revenue Canada personnel.

PROBLEMS WITH THE NIT

The above arguments in favour of the NIT have been countered by critics. The opponents of the NIT scheme advance the following arguments:

1. The NIT would not be less expensive than the programs now in existence, and the cost would also escalate.

2. The establishment of a national low-income cut-off is impractical. An established poverty line may be too low for Ontario but too high for Newfoundland. So it may be necessary to establish poverty lines on a regional or provincial basis.

3. The NIT is politically problematic, because many voters vehemently oppose the idea of making direct cash payments to people for staying at home and doing nothing.

CANADA'S EXPERIENCE WITH NIT

An experimental NIT program was introduced in Manitoba in the 1970s. As yet, no conclusive statement can be made about the effects of the NIT based on this experiment. However, evidence seems to suggest that less social stigma is attached to people who quit their jobs to accept an NIT than to those who quit to go on welfare as the term is traditionally understood. This implies that the NIT has an adverse effect on incentives to work. This view is supported by results from similar experiments in the United States where the NIT, aimed at encouraging people to work, seemed to have a disincentive effect on work effort.

CHAPTER SUMMARY

1. The unequal distribution of income among families and individuals is a hotly debated issue.

2. Three competing schools of thought about the equitable distribution of income

are: the productivity approach, the need approach, and the equality approach. The need and equality approaches may adversely affect work incentive.

3. The Lorenz curve is a useful graphic device for measuring and illustrating the degree of income inequality in income distribution.

4. The Gini coefficient expresses income inequality as a ratio. The larger the ratio, the greater the degree of income inequality.

5. Poverty, defined in an absolute sense, exists when families or individuals have such a low income that they cannot afford the goods and services necessary to maintain minimum comfort.

6. Poverty, defined in a relative sense, exists when a family or an individual has an income that is substantially lower than that of many other families or individuals.

7. Although poverty is not confined to any particular group, some groups are more likely to be poor than others. Groups with high incidence of poverty include families with many young children, families in the Atlantic provinces, families in rural areas, families with female heads, young families, elderly families, families with self-employed heads, families whose heads are not in the labour force, and unattached individuals.

8. Some of the causes of poverty are low productivity, low economic growth, lack of large quantities of valuable resources, physical and mental disabilities, and discrimination.

9. Suggestions to alleviate poverty include increasing the productivity of the working poor, accelerating the rate of economic growth, making laws forbidding discriminatory practices, assisting the poor, and providing employment for disabled persons in special government-operated workshops.

10. Through various income security programs, Canada offers assistance to people in difficult economic circumstances and provides income security for its citizens and legal residents.

11. A negative income tax, whereby instead of taxing people with low incomes, the government gives them subsidies, has been proposed as a means of dealing with the problem of poverty.

12. Supporters of the NIT claim that it does not destroy work incentive, that individuals are better off because they are left to decide how to spend their incomes, and that its administration is relatively simple. Arguments against the NIT are that it would be costly to operate, that it would be impractical to establish a national low-income cut-off, and that it is likely to encounter political resistance.

TERMS FOR REVIEW

size distribution of income (262)
Lorenz curve (263)
Gini coefficient (264)
absolute poverty (265)
poverty line (265)
low-income cut-off (265)

relative poverty (266)
incidence of poverty (266)
economic discrimination (employment, wage, and occupational discrimination) (268)
negative income tax (NIT) (270)

QUESTIONS FOR REVIEW AND DISCUSSION

1. What criteria have been suggested for an equitable distribution of income? (L.O.1)

2. Of the three criteria suggested for an equitable distribution of income, which do you consider to be the best? Support your choice. (L.O.1)

3. What problems could be expected from using the need approach to income distribution? (L.O.1)

4. What do you understand by the term size distribution of income ? (L.O.2)

5. What is the Lorenz curve? Is it of any practical importance? (L.O.2)

6. Write a short note on the incidence of poverty. (L.O.3)

7. What are some of the major causes of poverty? (L.O.3)

8. What are some of the measures that can be taken to alleviate poverty? (L.O.4)

9. What are the main issues in the NIT debate? (L.O.6)

10. Briefly describe the income security program. (L.O.7)

PROBLEMS AND EXERCISES

1. On the basis of Table 15.1, do you consider the size distribution of income in Canada to be unfair? Why or why not? (L.O.2)

2. On a graph, draw four Lorenz curves ranging from equal income distribution to most unequal distribution. Label the curves (L.O.2)

FIGURE 15.3

Lorenz curves.

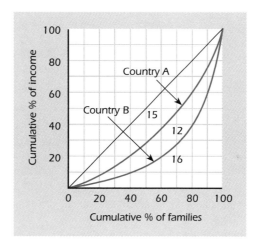

(a) equal distribution

(b) unequal distribution

(c) more unequal distribution

(d) most unequal distribution

3. Figure 15.3 shows Lorenz curves for two countries, A and B. The numbers in the diagram are for the areas indicated. (L.O.2)

    (a) Compute the Gini coefficient for countries A and B.

    (b) What do these coefficients tell you about income distribution in A relative to B?

4. "Poverty is not a serious problem in Canada because Canada is a rich country. Moreover, we have a welfare system that relieves the hardships that the poor would otherwise suffer." Discuss. (L.O.3)

5. "Poverty is a problem that will always exist." Discuss. (L.O.3)

6. The government establishes a guaranteed annual income of $2000 and decides to reduce the income subsidy (negative tax) by 40% of each extra dollar of earned income. Complete Table 15.4. (L.O.6)

TABLE 15.4	Earned income	NIT	Total income
Negative income tax.	$ 000	$2 000	$2 000
	1 000		
	2 000		
	3 000		
	4 000		
	5 000		

 7. Find out what social assistance or welfare programs are available from your provincial government and compile a list of those programs or services. (L.O.7)

VIDEO CASE

A UNION AT MCDONALD'S?

Introduction

Early Industrial-Revolution workers earned low wages for long hours of work in poor conditions. Groups of trade and craft workers tried to organize for better wages and working conditions but encountered severe problems, and union organizers experienced ugly incidents. Even the courts were unsympathetic to the labour union movement. Only in 1939 did it become illegal for employers to dismiss pro-union workers. Today, workers enjoy many advantages because of labour union activity.

A Brief Review of McDonald's

In 1948, Californian brothers Richard and Maurice McDonald opened the world's first McDonald's restaurant. In 1954, they granted exclusive U.S. franchising rights to 52-year-old salesman Ray Kroc, who in 1955 founded McDonald's Corporation.

In 1963, McDonald's was selling one million hamburgers a day. When Ray Kroc died in January 1984, McDonald's sales had reached over $10 billion, having sold over 50 billion hamburgers in 8300 restaurants across 36 countries. Over 24 500 McDonald's restaurants now exist in 114 countries. In 1997, sales totalled $33 638.3 billion.

McDonald's in Canada

On June 1, 1967, McDonald's opened in Richmond, B.C., its first non-American restaurant. In 1997, McDonald's Restaurants of Canada Limited had nearly 1000 outlets across Canada, employed more than 70 000 Canadians, and served on average two million customers daily.

The Labour Scene — The Context

McDonald's employs tens of thousands of high school and college students across Canada. McDonald's says it's a good place to work, offering employees exceptional training, specific skills, and important values like responsibility, self-esteem, punctuality and teamwork. Home Office employees enjoy educational assistance, excellent salary, life insurance, medical and dental benefits, and paid vacations and holidays. These benefits are not extended to the tens of thousands of employees who "sling burgers" at McDonald's, however. On March 5, 1997, employees of McDonald's in Montreal-suburb St. Hubert publicly complained of poor working conditions and low wages, and started a drive for unionization. The workers claimed that management made them work 30 minutes prior to their scheduled start time for free, and had them perform unsafe jobs apart from their assigned responsibilities. One employee alleged that after six years at McDonald's he was earning only $6.90/h—just $.20/h above minimum wage. Another claimed to be earning only $6.75 an hour after 15 months of employment. The powerful Teamsters union supported the unionization bid, and the organizers were optimistic that the union at McDonald's would be a reality. It did not happen. The restaurant closed its doors.

QUESTIONS

1. List the main points in this case.
2. Despite other attempts, no McDonald's restaurant in Canada has been unionized. Why do you think that management so resists unionization of McDonald's workers?
3. The St. Hubert outlet preferred to close rather than to allow unionization. What considerations might have led to that decision?
4. Find out from a McDonald's employee whether or not it is a good place to work.

C H A P T E R

THE ECONOMICS OF ENVIRONMENTAL PROTECTION

Learning Objectives

After studying this chapter, you should be able to:

1 discuss the main sources of market failure

2 understand the nature of economic externalities

3 discuss the concept of public good

4 evaluate the role of government in the light of market failure

5 explain how economic analysis can help to arrive at an appropriate level of pollution

6 discuss measures to deal with the problem of pollution

Nevertheless, there are responsible decisions to be made in this area, and these decisions are not reached wholly in the dark.

Kenneth E. Boulding, *Principles of Economic Policy*

INTRODUCTION

In our study of pure competition in Chapter 10, we observed that the purely competitive model resulted in the efficient allocation of resources. Under this hypothetical economic system, the economy produces what people want, and it does so efficiently, i.e., at the lowest cost. We showed that the purely competitive model achieves Pareto efficiency. We have also seen that when the assumptions of the purely competitive model are relaxed, as in the case of monopoly and imperfect competition, then the market fails to achieve efficient outcomes.

In this chapter, we study the problem of market failure, paying special attention to the economics of environmental protection. We shall also look at various responses (solutions) to market failure and examine the role of government.

SOURCES OF MARKET FAILURE

Learning Objective 1:
discuss the main sources of market failure

Economists use the term **market failure** to refer to malfunctions in the market mechanism that lead to inefficient outcomes. In this section, we examine four main causes of market failure. Market failure may result from imperfections in the market, lack of adequate information, the existence of externalities, or the existence of public goods. We shall discuss each cause in turn.

MARKET IMPERFECTION

Market failure is the inability of the price system to achieve an efficient allocation of resources.

Market imperfection is a source of market failure.

Product differentiation is when firms in an industry sell similar but not identical products.

A market is considered to be imperfect if individual buyers and sellers have so much power in the market that they can influence the prices of inputs and outputs. This is the situation described earlier as **imperfect competition.** Market imperfections lead to a misallocation of society's resources or to their unproductive use. The freedom of entry that is characteristic of a purely competitive industry ensures that other firms will enter the industry if there are profits to be gained in that industry. Their entry will reduce the price of the product to the point where economic profits are zero. In the case of a monopoly or oligopoly, effective barriers to entry prevent firms from entering the industry. Such firms will tend to set the prices of their products in order to earn maximum profits. Such firms may deliberately restrict output in order to keep price above average total cost.

In monopolistic competition, even though there is freedom of entry and exit, the firms acquire some degree of market power through **product differentiation**. In the long run, firms in monopolistic competition earn zero economic profit, but the price of the product is above the purely competitive price, and there is underproduction of the product. Allocative efficiency does not exist in this case.

INADEQUATE INFORMATION

Inadequate information causes market failure.

In the purely competitive model, buyers and sellers are assumed to have full knowledge of the market. In making their decisions in the market, they have full knowledge of the products and prices. Lack of adequate information may cause market players to make decisions that do not maximize their profits or their satisfaction.

Quite often, households may not have the expertise to be able to judge the quality of a product. The complexity of some products requires specific knowledge on the part of buyers if they are to be able to evaluate them — knowledge that many buyers just do not possess. We may conclude, erroneously, that a stereo system or a television set with a $1500 price tag is better than one with a price tag of $1000. But the price may not always send the right signal about quality. Also, buyers often purchase items on the basis of information contained in advertisements. If the advertisement lacks truth, then buyers' decisions will be based on false advertising, resulting in inefficient outcomes.

ECONOMIC EXTERNALITIES

Economic externalities are a major source of market failure.

Learning Objective 2: understand the nature of economic externalities

Private costs are borne solely by the individuals or firms directly involved.

The existence of external costs and benefits is another source of market failure. We can discuss the concept of economic externality by first introducing the concepts of private costs and social costs. When a firm decides to produce a product, the costs considered include such items as labour and raw materials. When an individual decides to take a vacation in a foreign country, the costs considered include items such as air fare, accommodation, and entertainment. Such costs are called **private costs,** borne solely by the firms or individuals directly involved in acquiring inputs or purchasing goods and services.

The social cost is the total cost to society of decisions made and actions taken by individuals or firms.

Some costs, however, are not borne solely by the individuals or by the firms, but by the society as a whole. Consider the case of a chemical manufacturer who dumps wastes into a river. The river becomes polluted, the fish population in the river is destroyed, and the river can no longer be used for swimming and recreation. Moreover, property values along the riverside decrease. These are costs that have to be borne, not only by the manufacturer, but by others as well. When these costs are added to private costs, we obtain what economists call *social costs.* **Social costs** are those costs that are borne, not just by private firms and households, but by society as a whole, in terms of the total sacrifice made when resources are used.

? PROBLEM SOLVING 16-1

We are a family living upstream of a pharmaceutical company on a certain river. Why should we, as members of society, concern ourselves with the fact that the company is using a part of the river to dispose of wastes? After all, we live upstream and the pollution is occurring downstream.

Economic externalities are costs (or benefits) that accrue to persons not directly involved in a firm's actions. An external economy is a benefit, and an external diseconomy is a cost.

Pollution is a good example of an external diseconomy.

Very often, we encounter situations in which private costs conflict with social costs. For example, a chemical manufacturer who pollutes the environment bears only a part of the cost of production: the private costs. The society as a whole bears the social costs. Such divergencies between private costs and social costs are called **economic externalities**. They are external because the firm or the individual does not take them into consideration when calculating costs. Society bears these costs in the form of a less healthy population, higher medical bills, the loss of animal life, the loss of good recreational areas, the loss of aesthetic value, and higher taxes to pay for the cleaning up of the environment.

An economic externality need not be a cost; it could also be an external benefit. For example, the development of a resort area will increase property values in that area. If the externality results in some benefit, we refer to it as an **external economy** or a **positive externality**. If it results in a cost, as in the case of pollution, we refer to it as an **external diseconomy** or a **negative externality**.

Throughout most of the 1980s, the big environmental issue was acid rain. Although the furor has died down somewhat, acid rain is still falling. Factories and power plants in the midwestern United States spew out dangerous amounts of sulphur compounds, which, when mixed with water, produce sulphuric acid. The acid then falls as acid rain in Canada and the northern United States. Acid rain is an example of a negative externality.

PUBLIC GOODS

We have seen that the unregulated market system may lead to the overproduction of some products that are harmful to society. It may also lead to the underproduction of some

Learning Objective 3:
discuss the concept of public good

A public good bestows collective benefits on society. Its consumption by one person does not diminish the amount available to others.

The existence of public goods is a source of market failure.

Learning Objective 4:
evaluate the role of government in the light of market failure

Merit goods are goods determined by governments to be necessary for society.

goods that society values, but that may not be produced by private, profit-seeking enterprise. Such goods are known as **public goods**, goods or services that bestow collective benefits on society. Once such a good or service is produced, it is generally impossible to exclude anyone from enjoying the benefits that it provides. Classic examples of public goods are police protection, public health services, national defence, and education.

The production of public goods presents a difficulty for the unregulated market mechanism. Private goods present no such difficulty. Automobile producers, for example, can earn a profit producing cars because people cannot obtain the services of these cars without purchasing them. But let us now consider the case of national defence. If a private firm were to provide this service, I would benefit from it, and so would every other person living in Canada. The firm, however, would not be in a position to enforce payment from me or from anyone else; hence, a private, profit-seeking firm is not likely to produce a public good. This explains why public goods are provided by the government and paid for collectively out of taxes.

The government may enact legislation making the consumption of certain goods mandatory. Education is a case in point. In Canada, children must attend school up to a certain age. Goods for which consumption is mandatory are referred to as **merit goods**, goods determined by the government to be good for people, regardless of how people evaluate these goods.

ENVIRONMENTAL PROTECTION

There can be no doubt that industrial nations such as Canada, the United States and Japan have made a significant amount of progress. Unfortunately, along with this progress comes a variety of problems: progress comes with a cost. In our attempt to maximize our total output of goods and services, we have seriously damaged our environment. For example, as the national output of goods and services rises, so does the national output of garbage. One of the questions that our society must answer is whether progress is worth the associated sacrifice. Since rapid economic progress is a major cause of environmental problems, should we not therefore have zero economic growth? This is exactly what some people have advocated. The fact is, however, that economic growth is essential in order that we can meet the challenges that face our economies and our societies.

Economic growth exacts a cost. Smog, water pollution, and acid rain threaten our environment. Greenhouse gases are causing global warming with potentially disastrous consequences. Our ecosystems are less productive and our health, our lifestyles, our economy and our society are all at risk because of pollution. We must protect our environment, and by doing so, we will be protecting ourselves.

THE APPROPRIATE LEVEL OF POLLUTION ABATEMENT

Learning Objective 5:
explain how economic analysis can help us to arrive at an appropriate level of pollution

We have seen that pollution imposes severe costs on society. Should we not therefore eliminate pollution altogether? If the cost of eliminating pollution were zero, the answer to this question would be emphatically yes! And perhaps the question would not even be asked. But the cost of achieving a zero level of pollution would be prohibitive. Economic analysis, however, can help us to determine what amount of pollution we should allow. If society considers the level of pollution to be sufficiently serious, then society should be willing to sacrifice some goods and services in order to attain a lower level of pollution. If the benefits derived from further pollution abatement exceed the costs, then additional funds should be spent on pollution abatement. On the other hand, if the costs of additional pollution abatement exceed the benefits, then the extra costs should not be incurred.

These tradeoffs are illustrated in Figure 16.1. As more and more abatement is undertaken, the extra benefit declines. Figure 16.1 shows this decline as a downward-sloping marginal benefit curve. On the other hand, as more pollution abatement is undertaken, the extra cost increases. The upward marginal cost curve depicts this increase. At a pollution abatement level of 0C, the extra benefits (0D) are less than the costs (0F). Therefore, there is too much abatement. At an abatement level of 0A, additional benefits (0G) exceed the extra costs (0D). Hence, more pollution abatement should be undertaken. At a level of 0B, the additional costs equal the additional benefits. Hence, 0B is considered to be the appropriate level of pollution abatement. Obviously, once the appropriate level of pollution abatement is determined, the appropriate level of pollution is also determined.

FIGURE 16.1

The appropriate level of pollution abatement.

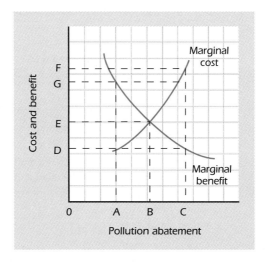

The appropriate level of pollution abatement is that level at which the marginal cost is equal to the marginal benefit.

MEASURES TO DEAL WITH THE PROBLEM OF POLLUTION

There are several ways of dealing with the problem of pollution. We may discuss these under the headings of direct regulation, effluent fees, tax incentives, property rights, and moral appeal.

DIRECT REGULATION

Learning Objective 6: discuss measures to deal with the problem of pollution

One way of dealing with the problem of pollution is for the government to prohibit the dumping of waste in certain areas, and to prohibit the use of certain chemicals. Regulations forbidding the use of DDT and the setting and enforcement of emission standards for automobiles and certain manufacturing plants that pollute the environment are examples of direct regulation.

One problem with direct regulation is the difficulty of enforcing it. For the regulation to be effective, an effort must be made to detect the offenders; and this involves a substantial cost. The offenders, if caught, must then be prosecuted. This can also be a costly process. The detection of an offence may be quite difficult. Some polluters, therefore, may find it less expensive to continue to pollute and pay the penalty (if caught) than to install expensive anti-pollution equipment.

Another problem with direct regulation is that of determining the permissible level of pollution for each polluter. If we aim to reduce pollution levels by say, 20%, should all polluters reduce their pollution levels by 20% regardless of cost and the amount of pollution caused? Or should pollution levels be reduced by more than 20% in some plants and by less than 20% in others? The decision is not an easy one.

EFFLUENT FEES

Effluent charges (fees) are part of an attempt to force polluters to internalize their costs.

Another way of dealing with the problem of pollution is to charge the polluter a fee for polluting the environment. This charge, known as an **effluent fee**, forces polluters to consider the social costs rather than just the private costs of their activities. In other words, they are forced to internalize their costs. The fee charged would vary directly with the level of pollution caused by each polluter. This approach to the problem of pollution has strong appeal among economists because it works through the market mechanism. Polluters are left free to pursue their objectives of profit maximization (in the case of firms) or utility maximization (in the case of consumers). Effluent fees provide polluters with an economic incentive not to pollute the environment. We can expect this method, therefore, to result in lower levels of pollution. The higher the level of the effluent fee, the lower the level of pollution.

TAX INCENTIVES

Tax incentives reduce pollution.

Anti-pollution devices impose a substantial cost on those who buy them. If tax relief is given to people who incur the cost of installing anti-pollution equipment, the level of pollution is likely to decrease as more and more of these anti-pollution devices are installed. One objection to tax incentives as a method of reducing pollution is that the practice of giving tax incentives may become widespread. If tax incentives are given for anti-pollution equipment, why not for other types of investment that may be considered by some groups to be equally important? We may find ourselves in a situation where tax incentives are given for just about anything.

Another problem with tax incentives is that there is a tendency to abuse them. For example, a producer could buy some equipment, state that it is to be used for pollution abatement, claim the tax credit, and then use the equipment for some other purpose.

PROPERTY RIGHTS

The establishment of property rights reduces pollution.

One reason that polluters abuse the environment is that nobody owns the environment. No one owns the air around us, so we can dump all kinds of poisonous gases into it without paying anything. Some people have suggested that the assignment of property rights to individuals and firms may lead to a reduction in the overall level of pollution. Let us suppose that there is a lake — Lake Blythe — owned by no one, and that the Morbus plant uses the lake for waste disposal. In the absence of government regulation forbidding the dumping of waste into the lake, the Morbus plant will use Lake Blythe for waste disposal. Let us now suppose that the government offers to sell Lake Blythe or to sell exclusive rights to use it for any purpose.

If there are individuals or groups of individuals who value the purity of Lake Blythe for recreation above the value placed on it by the Morbus plant for waste disposal, then they will be willing to buy the lake and keep it free from pollution. If the value of Lake Blythe to the Morbus plant as a place for waste disposal is greater than its value to those people who want to use it for recreation, then the Morbus plant will acquire the rights to the lake and use it for waste disposal. Note that the manufacturer will buy Lake Blythe for waste disposal only if the cost is lower than the cost of any alternative way of disposing of its waste.

MORAL APPEAL

Finally, an appeal to producers and consumers may help to reduce the level of pollution. Consumers can be persuaded to use public transportation and to organize car pools rather than to drive millions of air-polluting cars into the city every day. An appeal to firms to develop cleaner methods of production can also help to win the battle against pollution.

Moral appeal is most effective where polluters are convinced that a polluted environment is against their own interests.

PROBLEM SOLVING 16-2

Would you expect an individual producer voluntarily to take social costs into account in its production decisions?

ENVIRONMENTAL ROUND-UP

In this final section of this chapter, we take a close look at our environment, focusing on air pollution, water pollution, ecosystems and habitat, and climatic change. We shall examine the threats to our health, our economy and our lifestyles, and we shall pay some attention to efforts that are being made to deal with the problem. Let us begin with air pollution.

AIR POLLUTION

Air pollution: smog due mainly to burning fuels.

The importance of clean air is obvious. Without it, our environment and our health suffer. Because of the fuels we burn in our vehicles, in our homes and in our factories, the air is polluted. Smog signals the presence of air pollution. Ontario, the southern Atlantic region, and British Columbia are susceptible to smog. Vigourous economic activity in Ontario and air pollution from the United States account for almost all of the smog in Ontario. Much of the smog in parts of New Brunswick and Nova Scotia can be attributed to air pollution from the Eastern United States, while British Columbia itself generates the major part of its smog.

How serious is air pollution? It is claimed that thousands of Canadians die prematurely each year from air pollution as ground-level ozone (the major component of smog) and other pollutants are inhaled into the lungs. Because of air pollution, over 300 000 lakes are vulnerable and over 14 000 are acidified. It is estimated that damage to the ozone layer reduces the productivity of commercial crops in Ontario by $70 million annually. The benefit of reducing smog in our major cities is evaluated at about $10 billion annually. Thanks to government action, our cars are now equipped with catalytic converters, our gasoline is cleaner, and emissions from our factories are lower.

WATER POLLUTION

Water pollution: toxic waste, chemical spills, chemical production, municipal waste and acid rain.

Canada is blessed with an abundance of fresh water. Unfortunately however, some of the waters are polluted to the extent that they are unsafe for swimming, and the fish that they contain cannot be eaten. One of the main sources of water pollution is toxic waste from industrial, agricultural, and domestic activities. Chemical spills, chemical production, municipal waste and acid rain all contribute to water pollution.

Clearly, water pollution affects both our health and our economy. Toxic substances in our water are injurious to our health and are damaging our environment. Some are carcinogenic (cancer causing), and some are harmful to reproductive and immune systems. Toxic substances are adversely affecting beluga whales in the St. Lawrence River, and acid rain is threatening 15 000 lakes in eastern Canada.

Canada has made significant progress in reducing water pollution. Lake Erie, for example, which was considered dead about 30 years ago, now sustains commercial fishing. Tougher federal and provincial regulations have significantly reduced overall emissions of certain toxic substances. Reductions of pollution in the St. Lawrence River, the Great Lakes, and the Fraser River are success stories for Canada. Through a renewed and strengthened Canadian Environmental Protection Act, more success stories can be expected.

NATURE

Our activities are putting nature to the test. Many species of birds, mammals, and other creatures are disappearing or are threatened globally. In Canada, species of wildlife are being threatened or endangered. Rapid industrial and urban development are threatening and destroying habitat. Our ecosystems are under attack and their ability to maintain environmental balance is weakened. Urban development and resource-based industries such as mining and forestry have exerted severe strains on natural habitat.

We have much to gain by protecting nature. Nature provides many health benefits through the development of new sources of food and medicine. Many drugs used to treat diseases are derived from living organisms. Many economic benefits are also derived from nature. For example, agriculture, forestry and fishing provide employment for many Canadians and make significant contributions to the total value of goods and services produced in Canada annually.

Federal, provincial and community efforts and initiatives have reduced the threats to our ecosystems. The St. Lawrence Action Plan and the Fraser River Action Plan have protected over 70 000 hectares of wildlife habitat. Ecologically sensitive land has also been protected.

GLOBAL PERSPECTIVE

Environmental Protection: A Global Problem

Not too long ago, many people regarded pollution as a local problem. The pollution of a small lake, for example, was thought to affect only those people who lived in close proximity to the lake. It became clear, however, that a polluted river affects not only those who live close to the source of the pollution, but also people who live hundreds of kilometres from the source. The realization that pollution at a particular point is often spread throughout a wide area forced many people to adopt a regional or even a national perspective when thinking about pollution. Lately, it has become increasingly evident that pollution is a global problem.

It is now known, for example, that factories in the United States emit pollutants into the Canadian environment. Hence, even if Canada introduces legislation to reduce significantly the amount of pollutants that Canadian firms dump into the environment, unless Canada's initiative is matched by similar anti-pollution efforts in the U.S.A., our environment could still be very polluted.

In a more dramatic example of global pollution, the 1986 explosion of a nuclear power plant in Chernobyl, in the former U.S.S.R., was an environmental disaster of epic proportions. Radioactive material was spread over thousands of square kilometres. A dramatic increase in cancer in parts of the former Soviet Union and radioactive contamination in animals as far away as Sweden have been linked directly to this major environmental disaster.

The Exxon-Valdez catastrophe will also go down in history as one of the world's greatest environmental disasters. In 1989, an Exxon oil tanker spilled several million litres of oil in Prince William Sound, Alaska, the aftermath of which was the widespread destruction of fisheries, wildlife, and the environment. This was a global disaster.

There are many more ongoing environmental problems. A serious issue is the depletion of the ozone layer. The use of certain chemicals and gases has been found to destroy the ozone layer, which gives us some protection from cancer-causing radiation from the sun. Also of grave concern are global warming and the destruction of the Brazilian rain forests, which could have disastrous consequences for humanity.

Clearly, environmental protection is an issue that affects us all. International cooperation is required if we are to avert further disasters of this magnitude.

CLIMATIC CHANGE

Climate change is a pressing environmental problem. It can affect our economy and our way of life. The **greenhouse effect** regulates the earth's temperature. Greenhouse gases keep the earth's temperature at comfortable levels. Without them, the average temperature on earth would be −18°C, instead of the current 15°C. Human activities seem to be increasing the amount of greenhouse gases in the atmosphere, and hence global average temperature. An increase in global temperatures results in climatic change. The major causes of climatic change are the burning of fossil fuels and deforestation.

The consequences of climatic change for Canada are new infectious diseases, pollution, increased health problems from heat stress, reduced capability to grow crops, severe droughts, flooding, more frequent forest fires, and more severe weather disturbances. Climatic change could indeed have serious consequences for our environment, our economy, and our lifestyles.

How is Canada responding to climate change? In 1995, the federal, provincial and territorial governments approved a National Action Program on Climate Change (NAPCC). Through this initiative, many companies have developed action plans to reduce their greenhouse gas emissions, and many Canadian municipalities have joined the **20% Club** whose objective is to reduce local greenhouse gas emissions by 20% from 1990 levels. The various levels of government are involved in other programs to reduce greenhouse gas emissions.

Greenhouse effect: greenhouse gases maintaining the earth's temperature at comfortable levels.

20% Club: organizations which aim to reduce local greenhouse gas emissions by 20% from 1990 levels.

CHAPTER SUMMARY

1. Market failure refers to malfunctions in the market mechanism that result in inefficient outcomes or the unproductive use of resources.
2. Sources of market failure include market imperfection, lack of information, economic externalities, and the existence of public goods.
3. Private costs are costs borne solely by the firms or individuals who incur them. Social costs are borne by the whole society.
4. Economic externalities are the divergencies between private costs and social costs. If the economic externality results in some benefit, we call it an external economy. If it results in a cost, we call it an external diseconomy.
5. Pollution causes a variety of problems. It affects our health, our economy, and our way of life. There are numerous benefits to be derived from environmental protection.
6. Since pollution abatement involves substantial costs, the appropriate level of pollution abatement is not that which reduces the level of pollution to zero, but that level at which the marginal cost of pollution abatement equals the marginal benefit.
7. Measures to deal with the problem of pollution include direct regulation, charging effluent fees, providing tax incentives, selling property rights, and moral appeal.
8. Air pollution is a serious problem. It threatens the lives of many Canadians each year as they inhale ground-level ozone into their lungs. Government action has resulted in cleaner air as harmful emissions into the atmosphere are reduced.
9. Some of our waters are quite polluted as a result of toxic substances from industrial, agricultural and domestic activities. Tougher federal and provincial regulations have made our waters cleaner and safer.

10. Habitat and our ecosystems are threatened by rapid industrial expansion, rural development, and resource-based industries such as mining and forestry. Nature provides many benefits to us so when we protect nature, we also protect ourselves.

11. The greenhouse effect regulates the earth's temperature. It would be impossible for us to live without greenhouse gases. Our activities are increasing the amount of greenhouse gases in the atmosphere and causing climate changes which have severe consequences.

12. Cooperation between the various levels of government and various programs and initiatives have resulted in improvements in our environment.

TERMS FOR REVIEW

market failure (276)
imperfect competition (276)
product differentiation (276)
private cost (277)
social cost (277)
economic externality (277)
external economy
 (positive externality) (277)

external diseconomy
 (negative externality) (277)
public goods (278)
merit goods (278)
effluent charge (fee) (280)
air pollution (281)
water pollution (281)
greenhouse effect (283)
20% Club (283)

QUESTIONS FOR REVIEW AND DISCUSSION

1. What is market failure? What are some sources of market failure? (L.O.1)

2. Distinguish between private costs and social costs. (L.O.2)

3. What are economic externalities? How is the concept of economic externality related to environmental pollution? (L.O.2)

4. What is environmental pollution? Why is it considered such a serious problem? (General)

5. "Society should aim at a zero level of pollution." Discuss. (L.O.5)

6. Briefly discuss the measures that can be taken to reduce the level of pollution. (L.O.6)

7. Do you think that tax incentives are effective in reducing the level of pollution? Why or why not? (L.O.6)

8. What regions of Canada are most susceptible to smog, and what accounts for the smog in each of those regions? (L.O.6)

9. Give some indication of the seriousness of air pollution in Canada. (L.O.6)

10. What are some of the main sources of water pollution in Canada, and what progress has Canada made in dealing with water pollution? (L.O.6)

11. "We have much to gain by protecting nature." Discuss this statement. (L.O.6)

12. What are some of the consequences of climate change? How is Canada responding to climate change? (L.O.6)

PROBLEMS AND EXERCISES

1. The Campo Steel plant is situated upstream from the Clairview Recreation Park. Clairview has to clean up the water polluted by Campo Steel. Campo Steel decides to purchase Clairview. Will Campo Steel continue to dump the same amount of pollutants into the river? Explain. (L.O.7)

2. In the summer months, many of the beaches around Montreal have to be closed because of high levels of pollution. Do you think that private ownership of those beaches would solve the problem? Explain. (L.O.6)

3. Do you agree that we can reduce pollution only by reducing population? (L.O.6)

4. Why should we expect people in Toronto to be more concerned with air pollution than people in Twillingate, Newfoundland? (General)

5. Explain what has been done in your community to reduce pollution in any of its forms or to protect the environment. (General)

 6. Visit a manufacturing concern in your community and find out what steps it has taken to reduce pollution or to protect the environment. Write up a *brief* report on your findings.

Internet Site

http://www.doe.ca/envhome.html

This "Green Lane" home page is an Environment Canada site. It contains a great deal of useful information about climate change, clean air, clean water, and other important environmental issues.

INTERNET EXERCISE

Visit the Greenpeace Web site at **http://www.greenpeace.org** and read up on some of their activities.

17

THE AGRICULTURAL SECTOR

Learning Objectives

After studying this chapter, you should know about:

1 agriculture in the Canadian economy

2 some problems of agriculture

3 policies dealing with the problems of agriculture

4 the role of government in agriculture

We have therefore a strange paradox, that labour-saving techniques in agriculture are of supreme importance to society at large but are a distinct source of embarrassment to agriculture itself.

Kenneth E. Boulding, *Economic Analysis and Agricultural Policy*

INTRODUCTION

This chapter deals with a very important topic: agriculture. Although the structure of the Canadian economy has undergone considerable changes over the past several years, we still depend substantially on the agricultural sector. In 1996, our exports of wheat alone earned us $2.4 billion in terms of 1986 dollars; other agricultural products earned us a further $16 billion. First, we will pay some attention to the role of agriculture in the Canadian economy. Then we will study some of the special problems that farmers must face. Microeconomic concepts and tools will help us to explain these problems. Next, we will consider some policies to deal with the problems of agriculture, and finally, we will examine some government programs for assisting farmers.

AGRICULTURE IN THE CANADIAN ECONOMY

Learning Objective 1:
agriculture in the
Canadian economy

As an economy develops, the share of agriculture in total output tends to diminish.

Most countries single out the agricultural sector for special treatment. Canada is no exception. After all, this is the sector that produces food for the population. As the population grows, more food is needed. A country that relies very heavily on imported food is obviously in a very vulnerable position. It makes good economic sense, therefore, to allocate resources to the agricultural sector to ensure that food is available for Canadians. It can be stated as a general rule that, as an economy develops, the share of agriculture in the total output of the economy declines. This general principle applies to the Canadian economy. The share of agriculture in the total output of the Canadian economy fell from over 16% in 1931 to 0.2% in 1997. Figure 17.1 shows farm income as a percent of total income for selected years from 1965 to 1997.

FIGURE 17.1

Farm income as a percentage of total income

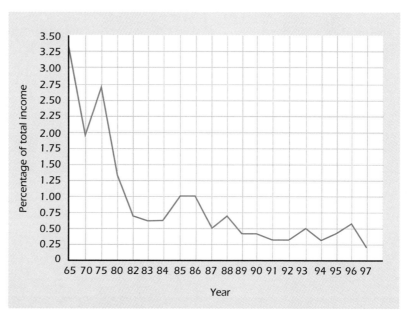

Source: Statistics Canada, *Canadian Economic Observer* (Cat. 11-210-XBP), 1997–98: 2

It has been observed also that as economic growth proceeds, the proportion of the labour force engaged in agriculture also declines. The Canadian economy exemplifies this fact. In 1950, the proportion of the labour force employed in agriculture was over 18%. By 1960, this figure had fallen to 10.7% and in 1997, it had reached 2.8%. Figure 17.2 shows the proportion of the labour force in agriculture from 1978 to 1997.

These facts notwithstanding, agriculture is still an important economic activity in the Canadian economy. It provides employment directly for about 450 000 people, and indirectly to several hundred thousand more who work in related fields such as transportation, marketing, and the processing of agricultural products. There are over 275 000 farms in Canada. Many of these farms are relatively small, with annual sales of less than $5000. On the other hand, some large farms average over $75 000 in annual sales. An important pattern can be observed in Canadian agriculture: the number of large farms has increased over the years while the number of small farms has decreased. Canadian farms, on average, are 22% larger today than they were 20 years ago. The average size of a farm in 1976 was 499 acres, while in 1996, the average size was 608 acres (1 acre = 0.4 hectares). In Canada, farm size varies from province to province. The average size of a farm in Newfoundland in 1996 was 146 acres, while in Saskatchewan it was 1152 acres. The tendency towards larger and fewer farms in Canada means that fewer farmers are producing more food than ever before, but it may also suggest that farming is becoming less competitive as an industry. These farms are of various types including dairy, cattle, wheat, field crops, and fruit and vegetable farms. The most common types of farms are cattle, wheat, small grains other than wheat, and dairy farms. Ontario, Saskatchewan, and Alberta are the provinces with the most farms in the country.

Canadian farmers produce a wide variety of agricultural products including milk and cream, maple sugar and maple syrup, eggs, and a variety of field crops. Table 17.1 contains data on some of Canada's agricultural products, with the cash receipts from each item.

Over time, the number of small farms has decreased while the number of large farms has increased.

Canadian farmers produce a wide variety of agricultural products.

FIGURE 17.2

Employment in agriculture in Canada, 1978–97.

As an economy develops, the proportion of the labour force engaged in agriculture tends to decline.

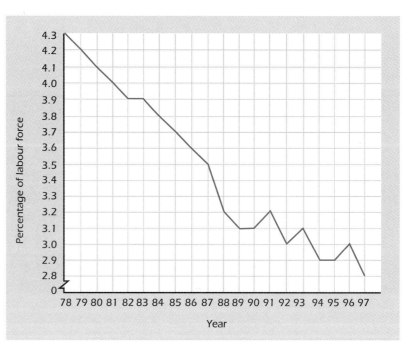

Source: Statistics Canada, *Canadian Economic Observer* (Cat. 11-210-XBP), 1997–98: 32, 33.

	Product	Cash receipts ($million)
TABLE 17.1	Wheat	3 626
Farm cash receipts, selected products, 1997.	Canola	1 999
	Livestock & products	14 539
	Vegetables	1 001

Source: Statistics Canada, *Canadian Economic Observer* (Cat. 11-010-XPB), July 1998: 41.

Canadian agricultural production can be arranged into five major agricultural sectors. In terms of cash receipts, the most important sector is the grains and oilseeds sector with 34% of total farm cash receipts. The other major sectors are red meats, dairy, horticulture, and poultry and eggs. The five major agricultural production sectors in Canada are shown in Figure 17.3.

FIGURE 17.3

Major agricultural production sectors.

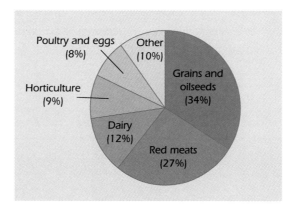

Source: Canadian Federation of Agriculture, *Commodities*, Ottawa, March 1998: 1

THE AGRI-FOOD INDUSTRY IN CANADA

So far, we have been focusing on agriculture specifically. However, in order to really appreciate the important role that agriculture plays in the economic life of the country, we need to pay some attention to the agri-food industry. The agri-food industry includes, in addition to primary agriculture, such activities as food processing, food services, beverage and processed exports and imports related to food. In 1996, the agri-food industry contributed in excess of $70 billion worth of goods and services to the Canadian economy, representing about 8.8% of the total value of all goods and services produced in the country. Of this $70 billion, primary agriculture accounted for over 24%. The rest was accounted for by food and beverage processing, retail, wholesale and food service industries.

The agri-food industry also contributes to the Canadian economy through employment. Approximately two million people were employed in food-related jobs in 1996, representing about 14% of the total number of people employed in Canada. The agri-food industry's greatest employers are hotels, restaurants and institutions. Other high employers are the wholesale and retail sectors and primary agriculture. Primary agriculture has traditionally been dominated by men, but the proportion of women has been increasing slowly, reaching 33% in 1996.

THE ROLE OF COOPERATIVES

Cooperatives are business organizations that are owned, financed, and controlled by their member-patrons, who share the risks and benefits in proportion to their patronage. In 1995, there were over 800 agriculture-based cooperatives in Canada, with membership totalling over 620 000 producers. The cooperatives play an important role, particularly in the marketing of certain products. With a combined volume of business exceeding $11.8 billion, agricultural marketing and processing cooperatives deserve some attention.

AGRICULTURAL TRADE

International trade is a vital part of the Canadian economy, and the Canadian agri-food industry is an important part of that trade. In 1996, we exported about 70% of the value of our total agricultural production and imported about 47% of our agricultural and food products. The dollar value of our agricultural exports, including food, feed, beverages and tobacco, amounted to approximately $19.9 billion and represented about 7.4% of total Canadian exports. At the same time, we imported about $13.2 billion worth of agricultural goods, representing about 5.7% of all goods and services imported into Canada. Thus, these trading activities resulted in a surplus in agricultural trade of $6.7 billion. As Figure 17.4 shows, the major purchasers of our agri-food exports are the United States (51.4%), Japan (10.5%), European Union (7.1%), and China (5.8%).

FIGURE 17.4

Destination of Canada's agricultural exports.

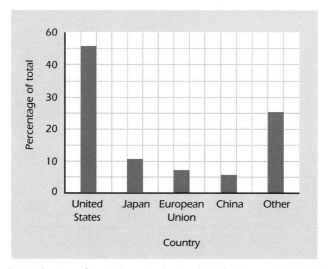

Source: The Canadian Federation of Agriculture, *Agricultural Trade*, Ottawa, March 1998: 2

SOME PROBLEMS OF AGRICULTURE

Learning Objective 2:
some problems of agriculture

The prices of farm products and farm incomes tend to fluctuate significantly because the demand for farm products is inelastic.

FLUCTUATIONS IN PRICES AND INCOME

One of the major problems facing agriculture is the wide fluctuation in the prices of farm products and in the incomes of farmers. Changes in total income and farm income are graphed in Figures 17.5A and 17.5B to demonstrate the difference in the degree of fluctuation between farm income and total income. Figure 17.5A shows total income while Figure 17.5B shows agricultural income.

It is not very difficult to find a reason for the fluctuations in farmers' incomes. A fall in the price of farm products does not cause people to increase their purchases of

FIGURE 17.5A

Farm income compared with total income.

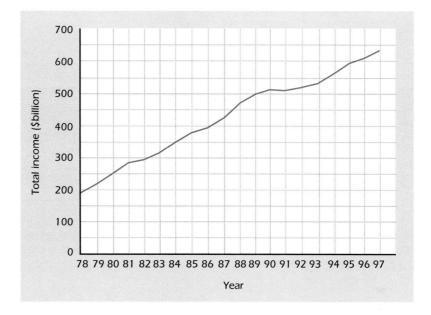

FIGURE 17.5B

Farm income compared with total income.

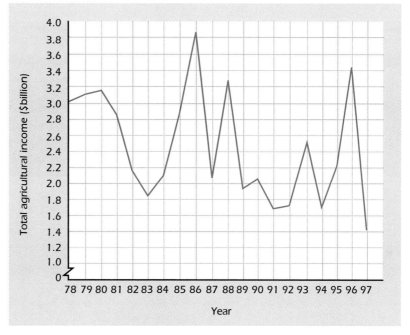

Source: Statistics Canada, Canadian Economic Observer (Cat. 11-210-XPB, 1997-98: 2

these products substantially. Similarly, an increase in the price of farm products does not cause people to reduce their purchases of these products substantially. In other words, the quantity demanded does not respond significantly to price changes: the demand for farm products is inelastic.

Consider Figure 17.6. The demand curve DD is relatively inelastic. If in a particular year farm production increases because of good weather or because of a significant

FIGURE 17.6

Effect of an increase in
supply when demand
is inelastic.

The inelastic demand
causes a substantial price
decrease when supply
increases.

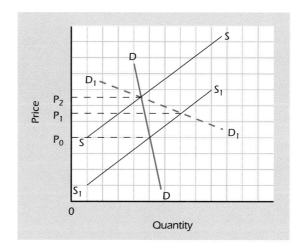

increase in the productivity of farmers, the supply curve shifts from SS to S_1S_1. This increase in supply causes price to fall from P_2 to P_0. Note that if the demand curve were more elastic, such as D_1D_1, the price would have fallen only to P_1. Thus, we see that because the demand for farm products is inelastic, an increase in supply results in substantial reductions in price. And since the lower prices do not stimulate corresponding increases in purchases, the incomes of farmers decline.

On the other hand, consider Figure 17.7. If supply falls from SS to S_0S_0, given demand DD, the price increases from P_0 to P_2. A more elastic demand such as D_1D_1 would have resulted in a smaller increase in price (P_1 instead of P_2). The increase in price from P_0 to P_2 does not lead to a corresponding fall in the quantity purchased. Hence, the income of farmers increases. It is well known that the supply of particular farm products is subject to severe fluctuations from year to year because of weather, diseases, insects, floods, and a host of other factors quite beyond the control of the farmer.

FIGURE 17.7

Effect of a fall in supply
when demand is
inelastic.

Because the demand is
inelastic, a decrease in
supply causes a substantial
increase in price.

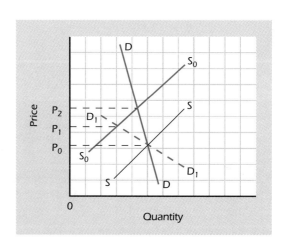

LOW INCOME ELASTICITY

Engel's Law states that as income rises, the percentage spent on food will diminish.

Another problem farmers face is that as total income in the economy increases, the demand for farm products does not increase as fast as the demand for other products. As income increases, a smaller proportion is spent on food — for there is obviously a limit to the amount of food that people can eat! The observation that the percentage of income spent on food declines as income increases has been called **Engel's Law**, named after statistician Ernst Engel. Engel's Law can be stated in terms of income elasticity of demand (introduced in Chapter 5). Because farm products have a low income elasticity of demand, income from farm operations does not increase as fast as total income does. Farm income fell in eight of the 20 years between 1978 and 1997, falling by as much as 59% in 1997. On the other hand, total income rose in every single year during the same period, except in 1991 when the economy experienced a recession. It is ironical that the agricultural sector has recorded the most spectacular increase in productivity, yet farmers have not really benefited from their fabulous performance.

PROBLEM SOLVING 17-1

The price elasticity of demand for farm products has been estimated to be about 0.2. What light does this information throw on the farm problem?

POLICIES TO DEAL WITH THE PROBLEMS OF AGRICULTURE

Learning Objective 3:
policies dealing with the problems of agriculture

Many solutions for the problems of agriculture have been suggested and many of these have been implemented by the government. Among policies dealing with the economic problems of agriculture are price support, deficiency payments, direct income subsidies, market quotas, easy credit to farmers, and various fiscal and monetary policies. Let us look at each of these in turn.

PRICE SUPPORTS (OFFERS TO PURCHASE)

Price supports (offers to purchase): a system of markets and prices that determines what to produce, how to produce, and for whom to produce.

A government may establish a **price-support** system to prevent the prices of certain farm products from falling below a certain level. Let us assume that the government wants to support the price of a certain agricultural product. You will recall from Chapter 4 that a price support will be effective only if the price floor is set above the market equilibrium price. Diagram A of Figure 17. 8 will help us to analyze a price-support program. The equilibrium price and quantity are $5 and 55 000 units respectively. Suppose now that the government sets a price of $8. At this price, consumers are willing to buy only 40 000 units of the product, while producers are willing to offer 80 000 units for sale. There will therefore be a surplus of 40 000 units (80 000 – 40 000). At a price of $8, the value of this surplus is $320 000, and is shown by the shaded rectangle in Diagram A.

One obvious result of the price-support program is that it results in a surplus of the product on the market. To maintain the artificially high price of $8, the government offers to purchase the surplus. This surplus tells us that more resources are put into the production of this product than society requires. Resources are misallocated. Furthermore the government-purchased surpluses must be stored, and this could result in high storage costs.

Let us now examine the effects of a price-support program on producers and consumers.

FIGURE 17.8

Price support and deficiency payment.

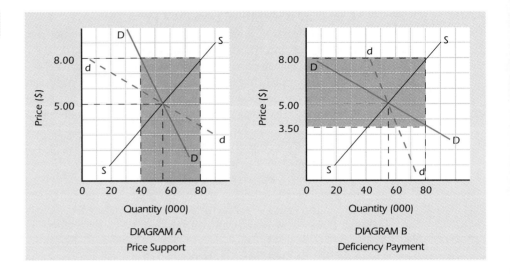

DIAGRAM A
Price Support

DIAGRAM B
Deficiency Payment

Producers

Clearly, if a program of price supports is initiated, the farmers gain. In the absence of the price-support program, they would produce 55 000 units at a price of $5, and receive a total revenue of $275 000, that is (55 000 × $5). With the price-support program, they produce 80 000 units at a price of $8, and receive a total revenue of $640 000, that is (80 000 × $8). The price support increases their revenue by $365 000 ($640 000 − $275 000).

Consumers

With the price-support program, consumers pay a price of $8 instead of the market equilibrium price of $5. Also, they consume a smaller quantity of the product (40 000 units instead of 55 000). On this count, they lose. Moreover, the surplus of 40 000 units, which the government must buy, will increase consumers' tax burden by the amount of the surplus ($320 000). And that is not all. Storage costs must be added to this amount.

ELASTICITY AND PRICE SUPPORT

The demand curve DD in Diagram A of Figure 17.8 is inelastic. Let us assume instead that the demand for the product is elastic, as shown by the demand curve dd in Diagram A. A price floor of $8 would result in a quantity of zero being demanded by consumers. In this case, the government would have to purchase the entire output of 80 000 and give it away to consumers. The following conclusion can be drawn:

> **A price-support program in which a price floor is set should not be used if the demand for the product is elastic with respect to the price.**

DEFICIENCY PAYMENTS

Deficiency payments: a subsidy to farmers given at a certain amount per unit.

Diagram B of Figure 17.8 will help us to analyze how **deficiency payments** work. The demand and supply curves are DD and SS respectively, and the equilibrium price and quantity are $5 and 55 000 units. Let us assume that the government, instead of setting a price of $8, allows the price to be determined by the market, but guarantees a price of $8 to farmers. At this price, farmers respond by moving up the supply curve and producing an output of 80 000 units. According to the demand curve, however, this quantity will be purchased only at a price of $3.50. The government therefore gives a deficiency payment (a subsidy) of $4.50 per unit — a total of $360 000, which is shown by the shaded area in Diagram B. How are producers and consumers affected by deficiency payments? Let us investigate.

Producers

Without the deficiency payment, farmers would have produced 55 000 units at a price of $5. Their total revenue would have been $275 000. The guaranteed price of $8 causes farmers to produce 80 000 units. Their total revenue is therefore $640 000. As in the case of a price support, farmers' gross receipts increase by $365 000.

Consumers

Without the deficiency payment, consumers would have purchased 55 000 units at a price of $5 per unit. With the deficiency payment, they purchase 80 000 units at a price of $3.50 per unit. In this sense, consumers gain. They get $1.50 out of the $4.50 deficiency payment. But let us dig a little deeper. The deficiency payment of $360 000 must be paid for out of taxes, so consumers must bear this tax burden. The total payment by consumers is therefore $640 000 ($280 000 + $360 000) — the same as in a price-support scheme.

ELASTICITY AND DEFICIENCY PAYMENTS

The demand curve DD in Diagram B is elastic. Suppose instead that the demand curve was inelastic as in dd. With a guaranteed price of $8, farmers produce 80 000 units, but consumers will not be willing to pay any positive price for this output. The government would therefore have to purchase the entire output of 80 000. Obviously, this does not make sense. We can therefore draw the following conclusion:

> **A deficiency-payment system should not be used if the demand for the product is inelastic with respect to price.**

EVALUATION OF PRICE SUPPORTS AND DEFICIENCY PAYMENTS

Our analysis shows that the benefits that farmers derive from price supports and deficiency payments are identical. In each example, they obtained a total revenue of $640 000. We have also seen that although consumers obtain a greater quantity of the product at a lower price under a deficiency-payment system than under a price-support system, when the tax burden is considered, they pay the same total amount under both schemes.

A price-support program results in a surplus, whereas a deficiency-payment program does not. In both cases, however, a greater amount of society's resources are channelled into the production of the product than society requires. Farmers produce more of the product than consumers want at the equilibrium market price. In this sense, both schemes result in a misallocation of resources.

Price supports and deficiency payments have another disadvantage in common. They benefit the larger commercial farmers. To see why this is so, let us take the case of a price support of $2 per unit. A farmer who sells 100 units receives $200 in support, while a farmer who sells 1000 units receives $2000 in support. If the larger commercial farmers have lower unit costs than the smaller farmers do (which is usually the case), then the system of price supports will benefit least those farmers who need it most. The same argument applies in the case of a deficiency payment. To conclude, both systems prevent the price system from doing its job efficiently. By artificially maintaining high prices for farmers, both systems prevent resources from moving out of agriculture and into other industries where they would be more efficient.

DIRECT INCOME SUBSIDIES

Another policy that may be used to improve the low incomes of farmers is the payment of direct income subsidies. Under this scheme, the determination of prices for agricultural products would be left entirely to the market. Referring to Figure 17.8, we see that under this system, the price would be $5 and the quantity would be 55 000 units. No surplus would exist.

Policies to assist agriculture include offers to purchase, deficiency payments, income subsidies, market quotas, easy credit, and general economic policies.

Two major criticisms have been levelled at this program of assistance. First, determining the criteria on which to base the income subsidy is likely to be difficult, and the program would likely be costly to administer. Second, if farmers are subsidized, why not some other groups as well? Thus, we could end up with a situation in which the government is subsidizing an unreasonably large number of industries, thus creating a huge tax burden for taxpayers.

MARKET QUOTAS

Producers in a market-quota system are permitted to sell only the amount of their quota.

Another solution to the agricultural problem is the use of **market quotas**. Under this system, producers would receive marketing quotas for each commodity. Each producer would receive a prescribed number of marketing certificates for each product. Thus, a producer who had fifty certificates for peas could sell only fifty units of peas. In this way, the supply of any particular farm product is controlled. Price fluctuations can therefore be greatly reduced. Two major problems are encountered with the use of this policy, however. First, the direct restriction of output in order to raise the price of the product may be socially undesirable. You may recall that this was precisely one of the problems we mentioned in our discussion of monopolistic firms. Second, farmers have shown a strong tendency to resist this type of control.

EASY CREDIT TO FARMERS

Another policy to deal with the problems of agriculture is the granting of loans to farmers on easy terms. This policy provides more funds to farmers and reduces their costs by reducing their interest payments.

FISCAL AND MONETARY POLICIES

A poor economic performance and an unstable economy may cause changes in demand for all products, including agricultural products. If total income in the economy falls, then the demand for agricultural products will also fall, and this fall in demand will result in a fall in agricultural prices, other things being equal. Lower agricultural prices will, in turn, result in lower incomes for farmers. It follows that government economic policies designed to promote a healthy economy will help to stabilize agricultural prices, and hence the incomes of farmers.

PROBLEM SOLVING 17-2

Which of these policies — price supports, income subsidies to farmers, or market quotas — is best from the consumers' point of view, assuming that the tax burden is equal in all cases?

THE ROLE OF GOVERNMENT IN AGRICULTURE

Learning Objective 4:
the role of government in agriculture

Through Agriculture and Agri-Food Canada (the federal department of agriculture and agri-food), and through its support of various programs and initiatives pertaining to agriculture, the federal government engages in research into various aspects of agriculture and agri-food, and offers various types of assistance to farmers. The following are just a few of the federal agencies that offer services to the agricultural and agri-food sector.

THE CANADIAN GRAIN COMMISSION

A number of federal agencies have been established to offer a variety of services to the agricultural sector.

The Board of Grain Commissioners, established in 1912, became the Canadian Grain Commission in April 1971. Its responsibilities include the weighing, inspection, and storage of grain, the establishment of grading standards, and the licensing of grain elevator operators. In addition, the Canadian Grain Commission conducts research relating to grains. Through its Grain Research Laboratory and Corporate Services, the Commission conducts economic studies and collects and publishes relevant statistics. The Commission employs about 700 people.

THE CANADIAN WHEAT BOARD (CWB)

Established in 1935, the Canadian Wheat Board (CWB) is the marketing agency for Western Canadian wheat and barley growers. Its role is to market Canadian wheat and barley at the best possible prices. The net proceeds from the marketing of wheat and barley are passed on to the farmers. With annual revenue of more than $6 billion, the CWB is one of the world's largest grain marketing organizations. The CWB has what is called a *single-desk policy,* which means essentially that the Board has a monopoly in the export of Western Canadian wheat and barley. The federal government guarantees the loans of the CWB, allowing it to finance its operations at lower rates of interest than would otherwise be the case. Thus, Canadian farmers realize significant savings.

THE CANADIAN DAIRY COMMISSION

The Canadian Dairy Commission (CDC) was established through the Canadian Dairy Commission Act of 1996. Funded partly by the federal government, the CDC promotes the interests of dairy producers, processors, exporters, the public, and governments. It administers the federal government's subsidy of about $145 million to dairy producers, and employs about 62 people. The stated objectives of the CDC are to provide an opportunity for efficient producers of milk and cream to obtain a fair return, and to ensure that consumers obtain an adequate supply of high quality dairy products. Among other activities, the CDC establishes support prices for butter and skim milk powder, and recommends the target level of national milk production for industrial milk.

THE CANADIAN FOOD INSPECTION AGENCY (CFIA)

Canada exports a good amount of food and food products. It is important for our customers around the world to be able to rely on the safety and high quality of our food exports. It is also important that the food and food products imported into Canada meet Canadian safety and quality standards. The Canadian Food Inspection Agency (CFIA) provides these assurances. The CFIA is a federal government agency with the objective of helping to build a thriving and competitive agri-food and seafood industry. Any farmer knows how devastating animal and plant diseases can be to agriculture. The Canadian Food Inspection Agency tries to prevent foreign diseases and pests from entering Canada, and to control or eradicate them if they do happen to enter. With over 4500 employees, the Agency works to help growers succeed and to ensure food safety for all consumers.

THE FARM CREDIT CORPORATION (FCC)

The Farm Credit Corporation (FCC), a federal Crown Corporation, was established in 1959, and is now Canada's largest agricultural lender. The Corporation employs about 900 people and provides services from over 100 offices in farming communities across Canada. The main focus of the FCC's lending operations is the family farm. The FCC makes loans for any agricultural or farm-related purpose, such as the purchase of land, equipment and livestock, the construction of farm buildings including houses, and improvement of land and buildings. In short, the FCC grants loans for any purpose that will help farm businesses to grow and prosper. Terms of payment can be arranged to suit the particular circumstances of the borrower, and may be made for as long as 29 years.

Note: The foregoing list of federal programs is representative rather than exhaustive. In addition, the provincial governments have introduced a number of programs to aid farmers and the agricultural sector.

CHAPTER SUMMARY

1. The Canadian economy exemplifies the general principle that, as an economy develops, the share of agriculture in total output declines. The proportion of the labour force engaged in agriculture in Canada has in fact declined.

2. Agriculture is an important sector of the economy, providing employment for nearly half a million people, adding over $18 billion to the country's output of goods and services, and providing food for the country's population.

3. Among the agricultural products produced in Canada are: livestock, wheat, corn, milk, cream, maple sugar and syrup, eggs, and a variety of field crops.

4. Wide fluctuations in the prices of farm products and in the incomes of farmers have created difficulties for farmers. This is due to the fact that the demand for farm products is inelastic, agricultural output is subject to a substantial degree of variation, and farm products have a low income elasticity of demand.

5. Solutions to the agricultural problem include price supports or offers to purchase, deficiency payments, direct income subsidies to farmers, market quotas, easy credit to farmers, and economic policies to enhance economic performance.

6. The federal and provincial governments have designed a variety of programs to assist the agricultural sector of the economy.

TERMS FOR REVIEW

Engel's Law (293)	deficiency payments (294)
price supports (offers to purchase) (293)	market quotas (296)

QUESTIONS FOR REVIEW AND DISCUSSION

1. Why has the share of agriculture in the total output of the Canadian economy declined over the years? (L.O.1)

2. Briefly discuss the importance of agriculture to the Canadian economy. (L.O.1)

3. What is the composition of Canada's agricultural output? (L.O.1)

4. What are the major problems faced by farmers? (L.O.2)

5. Explain why farm prices and incomes are subject to wide fluctuations. (L.O.2)

6. What arguments can you offer in support of government assistance to agriculture? (L.O.3)

7. Discuss some measures that deal with the problems of agriculture. (L.O.3)

8. What are the disadvantages of each of the following? (L.O.3,4)

   (a) price supports (offers to purchase)

   (b) deficiency payments

   (c) market quotas

9. Briefly discuss the role of the federal government in providing assistance to the agricultural sector. (L.O.4)

PROBLEMS AND EXERCISES

1. Technological advances have substantially increased the productivity of farmers. Use a graph to show the effect of this increase in productivity on the farm problem. (L.O.2)

2. The farm population has declined considerably over the years, both in absolute and relative terms. Would farmers have been better off if this decline had not occurred? (L.O.2)

3. Do you agree with the statement that everyone except farmers has benefited from the success of agriculture? Discuss. (L.O.2)

4. Figure 17.9 shows the market for a particular farm product. The government wants the price of the product to be $6. The government may use either offers to purchase or a deficiency-payment scheme. Assume that there is no storage cost. (L.O.3)

FIGURE 17.9

Demand and supply for a farm product.

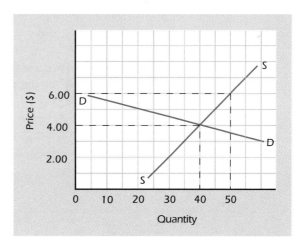

(a) What method should the government use to ensure a price of $6?

(b) How much would consumers spend in purchasing this product?

(c) Would a surplus exist in this case? If so, what would be its value?

(d) How much total revenue would producers receive?

(e) How much would this program cost the government?

5. Figure 17.10 shows the demand and supply for a particular farm product. The government wants the price of the product to be $6. There is no storage cost, and the government has the option of using either offers to purchase or deficiency payments. (L.O.3)

FIGURE 17.10

Demand and supply of a farm product.

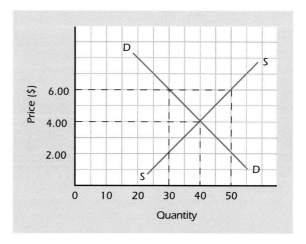

(a) What method should the government use to ensure a price of $6?

(b) How much would consumers spend in purchasing this product?

(c) Would a surplus exist in this case? If so, what would be its value?

(d) What would be the total revenue of farmers?

(e) How much would this program cost the government?

6. (a) "The agricultural and agri-food industry is the most important industry in Canada."

(b) "The agricultural and agri-food sector is not that important. If it were, agricultural product prices would be higher, more people would enter that industry, and there would be no need for government assistance to farmers."

Write down as many points as you can to support or defend each of the statements above.

Internet Site

http://www.agr.ca
This is the main site for Agriculture and Agri-Food Canada. It will expose you to a great deal of information about Canadian agriculture.

http://www.cfa-fca.ca
This site is filled with information about various aspects of agriculture in Canada. It is the home page for the Canadian Federation of Agriculture (CFA).

INTERNET EXERCISE

1. Go to the Canadian Federation of Agriculture (CFA) Web site indicated above, and write a brief description of the CFA, including its mission, its aims and objectives, and its membership.

2. Follow the link *Members of CFA* to *Chicken Farmers of Canada*, and write a paragraph or two about chicken farmers.

CHAPTER 18

PUBLIC FINANCE

Learning Objectives

After studying this chapter, you should be able to:

1 explain the growth in government expenditure

2 discuss the role of government in society

3 discuss the expenditures of various levels of government

4 discuss sources of government revenue

5 distinguish between different taxation systems

6 explain the Laffer curve

7 analyze the effects of taxes

Those who pay no taxes, disposing by their votes of other people's money, have every motive to be lavish and none to economise. As far as money matters are concerned, any power of voting possessed by them is a violation of the fundamental principle of free government....It amounts to allowing them to put their hands into other people's pockets for any purpose which they think fit to call a public one.

John Stuart Mill, *Considerations on Representative Government*

INTRODUCTION

Public finance is the study of the microeconomic aspects of government spending and taxation.

The study of government behaviour in the areas of spending and taxation is known as **public finance**. The first part of this chapter deals with government spending. Government spending has significant impact on the economic life of the country. You should, therefore, have at least a general idea of the spending activities of the government in order to understand certain aspects of the operation of the economy. One of the objectives of this chapter is to provide you with that general idea. The second part of the chapter deals with government revenues. Since taxes constitute the largest source of revenue for the government, we shall spend a great deal of time studying taxes. We shall look at various principles of taxation, and at different types of taxes. We shall also consider the effects of taxes. Finally, we shall study the revenues of the various levels of government.

Let us begin by looking at the magnitude of government expenditure. Major reasons for the growth of government spending will then be given, followed by a discussion of government responsibilities. All levels of government are considered collectively and individually.

THE GROWTH IN GOVERNMENT EXPENDITURE

Government expenditure has grown tremendously over the years.

Learning Objective 1:
explain the growth in government expenditure

Government expenditure increased from $14 million in 1870 to $385 275 million (i.e., $385.28 billion) in 1997. In 1926, total government expenditure accounted for about 13% of the Gross Domestic Product (GDP)— the market value of all goods and services produced in the country. By 1974, government spending climbed to about 33%. By 1997, it was 45% of Gross Domestic Product. Today, the government buys about 20% of everything that the economy produces. Figure 18.1 shows government expenditure as a percentage of Gross Domestic Product from 1978 to 1997.

The principal expenditure items are social services, interest on the public debt, health, and education. Expenditures on these four items alone in 1995 constituted over 69% of total consolidated government expenditure. Figure 18.2 gives a breakdown of total consolidated government expenditure by function for 1995.

FIGURE 18.1

Government expenditure as a percentage of Gross Domestic Product, 1978–97.

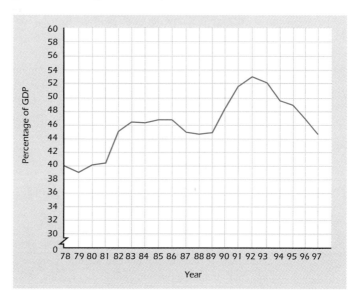

Source: Statistics Canada, *Canadian Economic Observer* (Cat. 11-210-XPB), 1997/98: 2, 15.

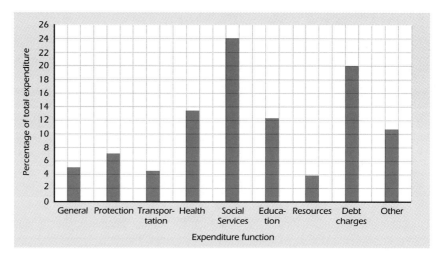

FIGURE 18.2

Consolidated government expenditure by major function, 1995.

Source: Statistics Canada, *Public Sector Finance* (Cat. 68–212-XPB), March 1996: 168.

GOVERNMENT PURCHASES OF GOODS AND SERVICES VERSUS TRANSFER PAYMENTS

A transfer payment is a payment representing a transfer of purchasing power from one individual or group to another.

Government purchases of goods and services, though they account for over 20% of total purchases, do not really tell the whole story of the magnitude of government expenditures. In addition to purchasing goods and services, government also spends a great deal of money in the form of **transfer payments**, which represent transfers of purchasing power from one group in the society to another. Examples of transfer payments are old age security payments, family allowances, and employment insurance benefits. These payments represent income to their recipients, but they do not represent payments for goods and services. The government also spends a large amount of money in interest payments on its debt. In 1997, interest on the public debt amounted to $74.9 billion, or 19.4% of total government expenditure. Government transfer payments and interest on the public debt together now account for about 50% of total government expenditure.

Figure 18.3 shows the share of government purchases of goods and services and government transfer payments to persons in total government expenditure for selected years from 1961 to 1997.

WAGNER'S LAW

Wagner's Law states that government spending will rise faster than total spending.

The German economist Adolf Wagner postulated over one hundred years ago that the rate of increase in government spending would eventually outrun the rate of growth of total spending on goods and services. This means that the government's share of the total output of the economy would increase. According to **Wagner's Law**, economic development would increase the complexity of government activity, thus making government more expensive.

To what extent does Wagner's Law apply to Canada? Total expenditure on goods and services from 1926 to 1997 increased by more than 13 000% while government expenditure during the same period increased by over 47 000%. On this basis alone, one could conclude that Wagner's Law does apply to Canada. But in order to see more clearly the relation between the growth rate of total spending and the growth rate of government spending, we can compare the annual percentage change in government expenditure with that of total spending. The necessary information is contained in Figure 18.4. In general, the growth rate of government spending has outstripped that of total spending.

FIGURE 18.3

Relation between government purchases of goods and services and transfer payments, 1961–97.

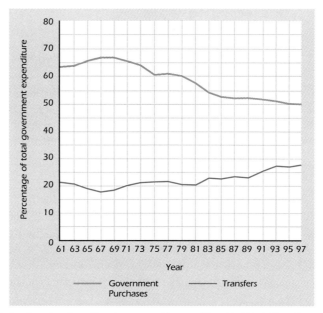

Source: Statistics Canada, *Canadian Economic Observer* (Cat. 11–210-XPB), 1997–98: 15.

FIGURE 18.4

Growth rates of government spending and total spending, 1978–97.

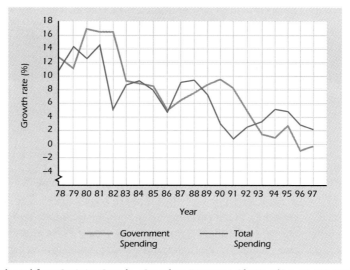

Source: Adapted from Statistics Canada, *Canadian Economic Observer* (Cat. 11–210-XPB), 1997–98: 5, 15.

REASONS FOR THE GROWTH IN GOVERNMENT SPENDING

Several factors are responsible for the growth of public sector expenditure over the years. Among them are increasing government responsibilities for certain services, inflation, and population growth. Let us discuss each of these in turn.

Greater responsibility

Factors responsible for the growth in government spending are increases in government responsibility, inflation, and population growth.

The government has assumed increasing responsibility for providing certain services such as health care, education, and social programs. Total expenditure on these three functions amounted to $7.8 billion in 1966. By 1995, the figure had reached $176.8 billion. The government's tax revenues have not been enough to cover its expenditures. The government until recently has been running its budget at a deficit. It has been borrowing money. And just like any other economic unit, when the government borrows money, it pays interest on its debt. In 1966, debt charges for all levels of government were only $1.7 billion. By 1995, these charges amounted to $71.3 billion. They have certainly added to the growth in government spending.

Inflation

Relatively rapid rates of price increases (inflation) over the years mean that the government has had to pay higher prices for the goods and services that it purchases. Between 1948 and 1995, prices rose above 8% annually in 1948, 1951, 1973–76, and 1979–82. The rate of inflation was particularly high in 1974, when a rate of over 14% was recorded. Also, wages and salaries have risen substantially over the years, and this means that the government must pay more to civil servants for their services.

Population growth

An important factor in the growth of government spending is the increase in population. Obviously, we can expect the government's budget to increase as population increases, because there will be a larger number of people for whom services must be provided. The population of Canada increased from 10 376 786 in 1931 to 27 000 400 in 1991 — an increase of approximately 160%. For the 1971–91 period alone, the increase was over 25%. The population now stands at about 30 million. Moreover, the Canadian population has been aging (that is, the proportion of elderly people in the population is increasing). This means that there are increasingly more people who depend on government for financial assistance, and this implies an increase in government spending.

THE ROLE OF GOVERNMENT

Learning Objective 2: discuss the role of government in society

Government should protect persons and property, provide education and health and social services, and adopt policies to improve the economy.

In Chapter 3, we discussed the role of government in a market economy. It would be a good idea for you to review that section now. It is generally agreed that it is the responsibility of the government to provide the services that would not be profitable for private individuals to provide but that are socially desirable. It is generally agreed also that the government should engage in those activities where government is more efficient than private individuals. Thus, the provision of law and order and the protection of persons and property are considered the province of government.

It is now an accepted view that education benefits the society and not just the individual who receives that education. Hence, most people would probably agree that the government should provide at least elementary and secondary education out of the public purse. The government pays for elementary and secondary education, and it subsidizes college and university education quite heavily. Whether education beyond the secondary level should be provided by the government without a direct charge is still much debated.

It is also considered desirable for the government to provide sanitation and health services. Another function generally considered essential for the government to undertake is the provision of social welfare services. Such services, it is felt, should not be left in the hands of private enterprise. It is also believed that it should be the responsibility of the government to build and maintain water supply systems, roads, and sewage systems.

Finally, it is believed that the government should play a role in the efficient operation of the economy. For example, most people would agree that the government should regulate certain industries. But just how active the government should be in these areas is still an unsettled issue. The generation of electrical energy in Quebec, for example, is undertaken by the government-owned Hydro-Quebec. Would the community benefit more if Hydro-Quebec were privately owned? Would Canadians get more efficient mail service if Canada Post Corporation were privately owned? There is no certain answer.

In the Canadian confederation, the federal government has the responsibility for certain functions, while the provincial and local governments have jurisdiction over certain other functions. In a political arrangement such as ours, a certain amount of duplication is inevitable. We can gain some insight into the distribution of responsibilities between the three levels of government by examining the expenditure pattern of each. Let us begin with the federal government.

FEDERAL GOVERNMENT EXPENDITURE

The largest share of government spending goes to social services.

As can be seen in Table 18.1, total federal government expenditure in 1995–96 was $177 billion. The three leading expenditure items of the federal government were social services (32.2%), debt charges (26.9%), and protection of persons and property (8.2%). Thus, these three functions alone accounted for 67% of the total expenditure of the federal government.

TABLE 18.1

Federal government expenditure by function, 1995–96.

Learning Objective 3: discuss the expenditures of various levels of government

Function	Amount ($million)	% of Total
General services	7 633	4.3
Protection of persons and property	14 642	8.2
Transportation and communications	3 258	1.8
Health	8 288	4.7
Social services	57 276	32.2
Education	5 129	2.9
Resource conservation and industrial development	8 128	4.6
Environment	915	0.5
Recreation and culture	780	0.4
Labour, employment, and immigration	1 632	0.9
Housing	2 026	1.1
Foreign affairs and international assistance	3 371	1.9
Regional planning and development	447	0.3
Research	1 284	0.7
General purpose transfers to other levels of government	10 606	6.0
Transfers to own enterprises	1 981	1.1
Debt charges	47 800	26.9
Other expenditures	2 509	1.4
TOTAL	177 705	100.0

Source: Statistics Canada, *Public Sector Finance* (Cat. 68-212-XPB), 1995-96: 114.

The largest expenditure item in the social services group was social security, which accounted for over 40% of the social service budget. Other important items in this group are unemployment insurance, social welfare, and family allowances. Interest on the public debt accounts for about 95% of total debt charges. The magnitude of the public debt has given rise to considerable controversy, which we shall examine in a later chapter.

PROBLEM SOLVING 18-1
It has been reported that the Canadian population is getting older. What effect can we expect this aging of the population to have on government expenditure?

PROVINCIAL GOVERNMENT EXPENDITURE

Health, education, and social services are important expenditure items for the provinces.

Turning now to the expenditures of the provincial governments, we see a somewhat different expenditure pattern. This pattern reveals the difference in the responsibilities of the federal government and those of the provincial governments. As Table 18.2 indicates, the largest expenditure items here are health (26.4%), education (17.9%), and social services (18.7%). Thus, these three items account for over 63% of the total expenditure of the provincial governments.

TABLE 18.2

Gross general expenditures of the provincial and territorial governments, 1995.

Learning Objective 3: discuss the expenditures of various levels of government

Function	Amount ($million)	% of total
General services	7 258.7	4.1
Protection of persons and property	5 004.0	2.9
Transportation and communications	7 343.7	4.2
Health	45 179.7	25.8
Social services	34 560.0	19.7
Education	32 017.4	18.3
Resource conservation and industrial development	7 417.8	4.2
Environment	1 973.2	1.1
Recreation and culture	1 632.0	0.9
Labour, employment, and immigration	825.5	0.5
Housing	1 281.4	0.7
Regional planning and development	692.8	0.4
Research establishments	513.3	0.3
General purpose transfers to other levels of government	2 034.0	1.2
Transfers to own enterprises	1 485.3	0.8
Debt charges	26 209.7	14.9
Other expenditures	6.0	0.0
TOTAL	175 434.5	100.0

Source: Statistics Canada, *Public Sector Finance* (Cat. 68-212-XPB), March 1996: 140.

Other provincial government expenditure items of significance are debt charges, which account for nearly 15% of the total provincial expenditure; transportation and communications, which use up 4.2% of the budget; and general services, which account for 4.1% of the total provincial government expenditure.

LOCAL GOVERNMENT EXPENDITURE

Expenditure on elementary and secondary education accounts for nearly 40% of the total expenditure of the local governments.

The expenditures of the local governments (municipalities) are shown in Table 18.3. Education (elementary and secondary) is the largest single expenditure item, accounting for about 39% of total general expenditures of local governments. Other heavy expenditure items for the local governments include transportation and communications, the environment, protection of persons and property, recreation and culture, and debt charges. And whereas expenditures on health and social services account for significant percentages of the total budget of the provinces, expenditures on these items represent only 5.0% and 7.7% respectively of local governments' budget.

TABLE 18.3	Function	Amount ($million)	% of total
	General services	3 701.3	5.1
	Protection of persons and property	5 750.4	8.0
	Transportation and communications	6 609.2	9.2
	Health	3 577.7	5.0
	Social services	5 570.7	7.7
	Education	28 341.0	39.4
	Resource conservation and industrial development	684.5	1.0
	Environment	6 181.4	8.6
	Recreation and culture	4 485.2	6.2
	Housing	655.5	0.9
	Regional planning and development	647.4	0.9
	Transfers to own enterprises	1 425.1	2.0
	Debt charges	4 222.6	5.9
	Other expenditures	134.8	0.2
	TOTAL	71 986.7	100.0

Gross general expenditures of local governments, 1994.

Learning Objective 3: discuss the expenditure of various levels of government

Source: Statistics Canada, *Public Sector Finance* (Cat. 68-212-XPB), 1995-96: 166.

TAXATION

Learning Objective 4: discuss sources of government revenue

Taxes are compulsory payments levied by governments.

The government must have funds in order to carry out the various functions that it has assumed. The main source of such funds is taxation. A **tax** is a compulsory payment levied by a government to pay for goods and services provided for the benefit of the community. Taxes obviously impose some degree of hardship on the taxpayer, yet they are necessary and will most likely continue to be the most important source of government revenue. Evidently, a great deal of truth lies in the time-honoured saying that if there are only two things that are certain, they are death and taxes!

DESIRABLE CHARACTERISTICS OF A TAX

To the taxpayer, there is probably no such thing as a good tax, but to the government that imposes the tax, it obviously has some merit. The resentment that many people feel about taxes notwithstanding, we can still discuss the essentials of a good tax.

It should yield adequate revenue

Generally, a tax is designed to produce revenue for the government. It follows that a tax should be such that it can be relied upon to supply a fairly adequate revenue. We should remember that some taxes are designed to achieve objectives other than raising revenue. The primary objective of some taxes may be to discourage the consumption of certain goods. For example, the government may impose a surtax on gasoline during a period of gas shortage to discourage consumption. In such cases, the revenue function will be subordinate to the primary function. As a general principle, however, we can say that the greater the revenue from the tax, the better the tax. It is not only the amount of revenue that the tax yields that is important. Significant consideration must also be given to the dependability of the revenue. The personal income tax is a steady revenue yielder. Tax on capital gains is a much less steady revenue yielder. Any tax that yields a fairly steady stream of revenue from year to year will be preferred to one that yields a widely fluctuating stream, other things being equal.

It should be fair

This principle is much easier to state than to achieve. While most people may agree that a tax should be equitable, they may disagree over what constitutes equity. One cri-

The benefit principle and the ability to pay principle are two standards by which equity may be judged.

terion by which equity may be judged is the **benefit principle**, which states that the tax paid should be proportional to the benefits received. This implies that if Conrad Small, say, benefits more than Marina Mendez from the provision of a certain service, then Conrad should be taxed more for that service. There are some problems associated with this criterion. How does one measure the amount of benefit received by each person from a certain service? Furthermore, it is often quite difficult to identify which groups benefit. For example, a playground or a park obviously benefits those who use the facilities, but it also benefits other residents who do not like the noise of children playing in the streets, or who have no patience for the accidents — like broken windows — caused by children playing in inappropriate places.

Another criterion for assessing equity is based on the principle that people in similar circumstances should be affected similarly by the tax. This criterion, known as the **ability to pay principle**, implies also that high-income earners should pay more than low-income earners. That is, taxpayers should be taxed according to their abilities to pay. Using this criterion, an income tax is equitable if people with similar incomes and exemptions are taxed similarly. This criterion does not work when it is impossible to determine whether or not people are in similar economic circumstances. For example, is it accurate to say that people with similar incomes and exemptions are in similar circumstances? Moreover, some forms of incomes are not easily identified. What may appear to be equal incomes, therefore, may turn out to be quite unequal. A further difficulty arises in deciding how much more should be paid in taxes as income rises. That is, how rapid should the graduation of the tax rate be?

A tax should not impede the operation of the market system

A tax should not, in general, impede the operation of the market system, and it should not discourage work effort. If additional income is taxed extremely heavily, individuals will have no incentive to earn extra income. Similarly, if profit taxes are exorbitant, businesspeople may lose their drive and initiative. Investment, then, will fall off. If a tax is generally considered to be unreasonable, attempts to evade it may become widespread.

A tax should be as convenient as possible

This means that taxpayers should not have to put themselves through too much trouble to pay their taxes. A sales tax is very convenient in this sense: the tax is simply included in the price of the product. A tax should also be easy to administer, and collection should not entail much difficulty.

A tax should be simple

A tax should not be so complicated as to make it impossible for all but a few experts to understand it. Although the actual computation of taxable income is apparently becoming more and more difficult, most taxpayers understand the basic idea that the amount of tax to be paid depends on the amount of income that they earn and the amount of tax deductions to which they are entitled.

Needless to say, it is difficult to find taxes that possess all of the desirable characteristics that we have mentioned. A tax that is considered good because it yields an adequate revenue may be bad because it is not equitable. And a tax that is considered good because it is equitable may be bad because it is undependable.

PROGRESSIVE, PROPORTIONAL, AND REGRESSIVE TAXES

A tax may be progressive, proportional, or regressive. In this section, we discuss each of these types of taxes.

Progressive tax

A **progressive tax** is one for which the percentage of income paid in taxes increases as income rises. Thus, a progressive tax claims a higher percentage from high-income earners.

Proportional tax

A **proportional tax** is one for which the percentage of income paid in taxes remains constant as income increases. An example of proportional tax is a property tax. If the property tax is 1.5% of the value of the property, then regardless of the value of the property, the tax rate will be the same. The tax on a property valued at $40 000 will be $600 while the tax on a property valued at $150 000 will be $2250. Taxable income in Canada, over a wide range of income up to $29 590, is taxed at a constant rate of 17% and is therefore a proportional tax. Beyond that level of taxable income, however, the tax becomes progressive.

Regressive tax

A tax is said to be **regressive** if the percentage of income paid in taxes decreases as income increases. A tax of $10 imposed on each passenger who boards an aircraft is regressive. For passengers with incomes of $100 per week, the tax represents 10% of their income. For passengers with incomes of $200 per week, the tax paid is only 5% of their income.

Examples of progressive, proportional, and regressive taxes are presented in Table 18.4 and illustrated graphically in Figure 18.5. We have defined progressive, proportional, and regressive taxes with respect to income. This kind of definition is common practice. But these terms can also be defined in terms of property value or some other magnitude.

TABLE 18.4

Progressive, proportional, and regressive taxes.

Income ($)	Progressive tax ($)	Progressive rate (%)	Proportional tax ($)	Proportional rate (%)	Regressive tax ($)	Regressive rate (%)
100	10	10	10	10	10	10.0
200	24	12	20	10	18	9.0
300	42	14	30	10	24	8.0
400	64	16	40	10	28	7.0
500	90	18	50	10	30	6.0
600	120	20	60	10	33	5.3
700	154	22	70	10	35	5.0

FIGURE 18.5

Progressive, proportional, and regressive taxes.

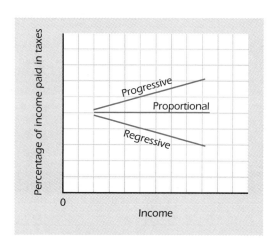

TAX RATES AND TAX REVENUE (THE LAFFER CURVE)

Learning Objective 6:
explain the Laffer curve

The Laffer curve shows that if tax rates are too high, total revenue may be reduced as a consequence.

Named after economist Arthur Laffer, the Laffer curve is a useful analytical device for illustrating the relation between tax rates and tax revenues. The **Laffer curve** is based on the view that as the tax rate increases, tax revenue will increase, but economic activity will decrease, thus lowering incomes and ultimately tax revenue. The Laffer curve depicted in Figure 18.6 shows that as the tax rate increases from 0 to *t*, tax revenue rises from 0 to R. But, as the tax rate rises beyond *t*, tax revenue declines. Note that a tax rate of 100% results in no tax revenue. Presumably, people will not work if the entire amount of their income is going to be taxed away.

FIGURE 18.6

The Laffer curve.

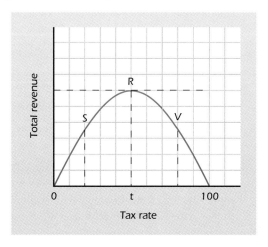

The optimum tax rate for a revenue tax is the rate that maximizes tax revenue.

The tax rate (*t* in our illustration) that maximizes tax revenue may be called the **optimum tax rate**, assuming that the tax is a revenue tax. The optimum tax rate for a revenue tax is the rate that maximizes tax revenue.

If the economy is at point S on the curve, then an increase in the tax rate will yield greater tax revenue. If, however, the economy is at point V, then an increase in tax revenues requires a reduction — not an increase — in the tax rate.

PROBLEM SOLVING 18-2

"A government can always raise additional tax revenues by simply raising the tax rate." Comment on this statement.

TYPES OF TAXES

There are many different types of taxes. There are personal income taxes, corporate income taxes, consumption taxes, and property taxes. We shall study each type in turn, beginning with the personal income tax.

THE PERSONAL INCOME TAX

Personal income tax: taxes, based on income, paid by individuals to federal and provincial governments.

The **personal income tax** has become the most important single source of revenue for the federal and provincial governments. Canadians pay personal income taxes to the federal government in addition to the personal income tax paid to the provinces. The federal government collects personal income taxes for all the provinces except Quebec, which collects its own personal income tax. Taxpayers are allowed to deduct certain amounts from their total income. The amount left after these deductions have been made is known as **taxable income**, and it is on this amount that income taxes are levied.

The personal income tax has certain obviously desirable characteristics. It produces a fairly adequate and dependable revenue. It is relatively fair (at least in principle) in the sense that people with equal incomes and deductions pay the same amount of tax. Tax deductions at source (that is, by the employer) make the personal income tax convenient. It is relatively easy to collect. And in most cases, even though the actual calculations may present some difficulty (extreme difficulty in some cases), it is sufficiently simple for most taxpayers to understand the basic principle.

Despite these desirable features, the personal income tax has certain defects. Various loopholes make tax evasion possible, and many people feel that high-income earners are most able to take advantage of tax evasion and tax avoidance. For example, contributions to a registered retirement savings plan (RRSP) are tax deductible. To take advantage of such a plan, however, you must be able to afford the contributions. A second criticism of the personal income tax is that it may be so progressive that it discourages individuals from earning extra income and so restricts economic activity. Actually, this criticism applies to the structure of the tax, rather than to the fact that personal income is taxed.

THE CORPORATE INCOME TAX

In addition to levying personal income taxes, the government also imposes a tax on the profits of corporations. The revenue from this tax represents approximately 5% of total public sector revenue. One of the criticisms made against the **corporate income tax** is that it discourages new investment by firms, and may thus slow down economic activity. Some people argue also that the corporate income tax represents a double taxation of income since the profit of the corporation is taxed and the income of the shareholders is taxed again when it is distributed to them as dividends. A third criticism that has been made against the corporate income tax is that it is passed on to consumers in the form of higher prices for goods and services. In other words, the **incidence** (burden) of the tax falls not on corporations but on consumers. The extent to which this criticism is justified is still being debated by economists.

THE CONSUMPTION TAX

Another source of tax revenue for the government is taxes on consumption. **Consumption taxes** include excise taxes and sales taxes. An **excise tax** is a tax levied on a specific commodity, while a **sales tax** is a tax levied on broad groups of goods and services. Excise taxes are levied, for example, on motive fuel (any fuel used to produce motion) and tobacco products. Sales taxes are levied on a large variety of goods and services. Since these taxes are added to the prices of the goods and services bought by the consumer, they are, in effect, taxes on consumption. As can be seen from Figure 18.7, consumption taxes account for approximately 20.3% of consolidated government revenue.

Sales taxes and excise taxes produce a dependable revenue. They are convenient and easy to collect (the consumer pays them at the time of purchase since they are added to the price of the product). And the only way for the taxpayer to evade these taxes is to refrain from purchasing the goods and services on which the tax is levied. The major disadvantage of these taxes is that they tend to be regressive. For example, although the sales tax is expressed as a given percentage of total purchases, high income earners will pay a smaller share of their income in sales taxes than low income earners will. An example of a consumption tax is the very controversial **Goods and Services Tax (GST)**. On

Taxable income is the gross income minus allowed deductions.

Major types of taxes are personal income taxes, corporation income taxes, and consumption taxes.

Corporate income tax: a tax on the profits of corporations.

The incidence of a tax is its burden.

An excise tax is a tax on the sale of a particular good. A sales tax is a tax on the sale of a broad group of goods and services. Both of these are consumption taxes.

The Goods and Services Tax is an example of a consumption tax.

FIGURE 18.7

Consolidated government revenue by major sources, 1995.

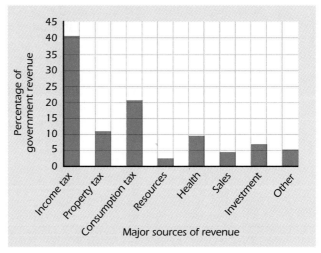

Source: Statistics Canada, *Public Sector Finance* (Cat. 68-212-XPB), March 1996: 167.

January 1, 1991, the GST replaced the manufacturers' sales tax (a tax on manufactured goods). The GST is a tax levied on almost all transactions and is applied to services as well as goods.

PROPERTY TAX

Property tax is levied mainly on real estate.

As the name implies, a **property tax** is a tax levied on property — mainly real estate (land and buildings). The revenue from property and related taxes accounts for over 11% of total consolidated government revenue. It will be seen that property taxes account for a substantial portion of the total revenues of the local governments.

EFFECTS OF TAXES

Learning Objective 7: analyze the effects of taxes

It is evident that the economic effects of a tax depend on the type of tax. Sales taxes and excise taxes tend to take a larger percentage of the incomes of low-income earners and hence tend to increase income inequality. Also, because these taxes are consumption taxes, they tend to reduce consumption (and hence production) of goods on which the taxes are levied. Resources will tend to shift away from industries producing the taxed goods and into other industries. Hence, these taxes affect resource allocation.

Sales and excise taxes definitely result in higher prices for the consumer. But there is little agreement on the extent to which firms are able to shift the incidence of corporate income taxes onto consumers in the form of higher prices. The effect of corporate income taxes on prices, however, is not expected to be significant. But high corporate income taxes do restrict business expansion, and impede economic growth.

If personal income tax is progressive, it will tend to reduce income inequality. This is so because, other things being equal, high-income groups are taxed more heavily than low-income groups. If the personal income tax rate is too steeply graduated, it will tend to reduce incentive. Individuals will be reluctant to expend effort to earn extra income if most of that extra income will be taxed away.

PROBLEM SOLVING 18-3

How can a consumption tax reduce production?

REVENUES OF VARIOUS LEVELS OF GOVERNMENT

Learning Objective 4:
discuss sources of government revenue

Figure 18.7 shows revenue sources for all levels of government (consolidated government revenue). The various revenue sources are not equally important to all levels of government. An important revenue source for one level of government may not be important at all for another level of government. For example, income tax is the major source of revenue for the federal and provincial governments, but it is not an important source of local government revenue. Let us now examine the revenues of each level of government.

FEDERAL GOVERNMENT REVENUE

Personal income tax is the main source of revenue for the federal government.

The major source of revenue for the federal government is personal income taxes. The revenue from this source accounts for over 45% of the total revenues of the federal government from all sources. Corporation taxes also provide a substantial portion of the revenues of the federal government. In fact, income taxes alone provide 56% of the federal government's total revenue. Other important tax revenue sources are general sales taxes, customs duties, unemployment insurance contributions, and universal pension plan levies. Approximately 90% of the total revenue of the federal government is derived from various types of taxes.

Other revenue sources besides taxes are sales of goods and services and return on investment. These two sources together provide just about 6% of the total revenue. Table 18.5 gives details on the revenues of the federal government.

TABLE 18.5

Federal government revenue, 1995–96.

Source	Amount ($ million)	% of total
Income taxes:		
Personal	65 602	45.1
Corporation	14 350	9.9
On payments to non-residents	1 523	1.0
TOTAL INCOME TAXES	81 475	56.0
Consumption taxes:		
General sales	22 130	15.2
Motive fuel	4 180	0.3
Alcoholic beverages and tobacco	2 892	2.0
Custom duties	3 270	2.2
Other consumption taxes	794	0.5
TOTAL CONSUMPTION TAXES	33 266	22.9
Health and social insurance levies	19 520	13.4
Miscellaneous taxes	504	0.3
Natural resource revenues	45	0.0
Privileges, licences, and permits	559	0.4
Sales of goods and services	3 523	2.4
Return on investments	4 952	3.4
Other revenue from own sources	1 530	1.1
Transfers from other levels of government	38	0.0
Transfers from government enterprises	41	0.0
TOTAL REVENUE	145 453	100.0

Source: Statistics Canada, *Public Sector Finance* (Cat. 68-212-XPB), 1995-96: 113.

PROVINCIAL GOVERNMENT REVENUE

Personal income tax and sales tax are the major sources of revenue for the provinces.

As in the case of the federal government, the main source of revenue for the provincial governments is personal income taxes, which account for 25.4% of total provincial revenue. The second most important tax source of revenue for the provincial governments is general sales taxes, which provide over 13% of the total revenue of the provinces. An examination of Table 18.6 reveals that corporation taxes, motive fuel taxes, and health insurance premiums and taxes are other important tax sources of revenue for the provinces.

TABLE 18.6	Source	Amount ($million)	% of total
Provincial and territorial government revenue, 1995.	Personal income taxes	40 479.7	25.4
	Corporate income taxes	6 575.9	4.1
	Property and related taxes	6 736.9	4.2
	General sales taxes	21 145.1	13.2
	Motive fuel taxes	6 197.8	3.9
	Alcoholic beverages and tobacco taxes	1 835.1	1.2
	Other consumption taxes	291.1	0.2
	Health and social insurance levies	10 434.4	6.5
	Miscellaneous taxes	4 676.4	3.0
	Natural resource revenues	7 562.4	4.7
	Privileges, licences, and permits	3 969.9	2.5
	Sales of goods and services	3 392.4	2.1
	Return on investments	14 578.3	9.1
	Other revenue from own sources	1 130.8	0.7
	Transfers from other levels of government	30 407.2	19.0
	Transfers from government enterprises	220.3	0.1
	TOTAL REVENUE	159 633.7	100.0

Source: Statistics Canada, *Public Sector Finance* (Cat. 68-212-XPB), March 1996: 127.

Important non-tax sources of revenue for the provincial governments include natural resource revenue, and general and specific purpose transfers from the federal government. Provincial government revenue may be divided into two categories: revenue from own sources, and transfers. Approximately 80% of the total revenue of the provincial governments is derived from their own sources. The remaining 20% takes the form of transfers from other levels of government. The most sizable transfers from the federal government to the provinces include equalization payments (transfers to the provinces to reduce income inequality among the provinces), social services, and other special purpose transfers.

LOCAL GOVERNMENT REVENUE

Property tax is the main revenue source for the local governments.

Table 18.7 shows that the largest single revenue item of the local governments (municipalities) is real property taxes, which account for over 37% of their total revenues and over 69% of revenues from their own sources. Local government revenues can be divided into revenues from own sources and transfers. Local governments raise about 54% of their total revenue from their own sources while the remaining 46% comes from transfers mainly from the provincial governments. Other important sources of revenue for local governments are sales of goods and services, business taxes, and return on investments.

TABLE 18.7	Source	Amount ($million)	% of total
Local government revenue, 1994.	Property and related taxes	26 731.7	37.9
	General sales taxes	44.3	0.1
	Other consumption taxes	3.1	0.0
	Miscellaneous taxes	124.7	0.2
	Privileges, licences, and permits	403.1	0.6
	Sales of goods and services	8 147.6	11.6
	Return on investments	1 664.5	2.4
	Other revenue from own sources	1 467.2	2.1
	Transfers from other levels of government	31 066.9	44.1
	Transfers from government enterprises	804.9	1.1
	TOTAL REVENUE	70 458.0	100.0

Source: Statistics Canada, *Public Sector Finance* (Cat. 68-212-XPB), 1995-96: 153.

GLOBAL PERSPECTIVE

International Comparisons of Total Government Expenditures

One important indicator of government involvement in an economy is the ratio of government expenditure to the value of goods and services produced in that economy. In this chapter, we have studied the expenditures of all levels of government. In this capsule, we now compare Canada with some other countries.

The accompanying graph shows that in 1998, Canada's expenditure as a percentage of the value of goods and services produced was fourth behind those of France, Italy, and Germany. The U.S. was the lowest, followed by Japan.

Almost everyone complains about high taxes in Canada. Does our government take a larger proportion of the value of total production of goods and services in taxes than do governments in other industrialized countries? The graph also shows that among the so-called G-7 countries, Canada took about 42.4% of the value of total production in taxes. Only France, Italy, and Germany took a larger share of the value of their countries' total production of goods and services.

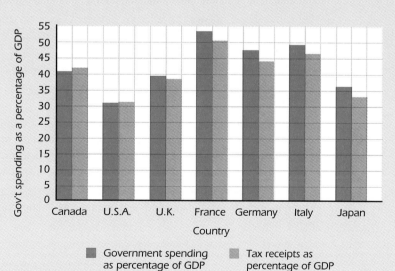

Source: OECD, *Economic Outlook*, December 1995: A31.

CHAPTER SUMMARY

1. Public finance deals with government taxation and spending behaviour.

2. Wagner's Law states that government spending will grow at a faster rate than total spending.

3. Government expenditure has increased substantially over the years mainly because of increasing government responsibilities, inflation, and population growth.

4. Because of different responsibilities, the patterns of expenditure for the various levels of government are different.

5. Social services, resource conservation and industrial development, debt charges, and protection of persons and property are chief items of federal government expenditure.

6. Health, education, and social services are among the chief expenditure items of the provincial governments, while elementary and secondary education, transportation and communications, the environment, and protection of persons and property are among the chief expenditure items of the municipalities.

7. It is generally agreed that government activity in certain areas is desirable. It is also generally agreed that the government should intervene to prevent widespread unemployment and rapid inflation.

8. A tax is a compulsory payment levied by a government to pay for goods and services provided for the benefit of the community.

9. A revenue tax should produce an adequate and dependable revenue. In general, a tax should be fair, it should not impede the operation of the market, it should not discourage work incentive, and it should be convenient, simple to collect, and easy to understand.

10. A progressive tax is one for which the percentage of income paid in taxes increases as income rises. A proportional tax is one for which the percentage of income paid in taxes remains constant as income rises, and a regressive tax is one for which the percentage of income paid in taxes falls as income rises.

11. The Laffer curve shows the relation between tax rates and tax revenues. Tax revenue increases as the tax rate rises. But after a point, further increases in the tax rate result in lower tax revenue.

12. Taxes levied by the federal and provincial governments include personal income taxes, corporate income taxes, and consumption taxes. The property tax is the major tax levied by the municipal governments.

13. The economic effects of taxes include changes in income distribution, consumption, production, and resource allocation. Some taxes also result in higher prices for consumers, and may dampen individual and business incentive to earn extra income.

14. Other sources of revenue include licences and permits, the sale of goods and services, and investment. Transfers from the federal government to the provincial governments, and from the provincial governments to the municipalities are important revenue sources.

TERMS FOR REVIEW

public finance (303)	optimum tax rate (312)
transfer payments (304)	personal income tax (312)
Wagner's Law (304)	taxable income (313)
tax (309)	corporate income tax (313)
benefit principle (310)	incidence of tax (313)
ability to pay principle (310)	consumption tax (313)
progressive tax (311)	excise tax (313)
proportional tax (311)	sales tax (313)
regressive tax (311)	Goods and Services Tax (GST) (313)
Laffer curve (312)	property tax (314)

QUESTIONS FOR REVIEW AND DISCUSSION

1. What are some of the major functions performed by our governments in Canada? (L.O.2)

2. What are the major factors responsible for the growth in government expenditure? (L.O.2)

3. What is Wagner's Law? Does it apply to Canada? (L.O.2)

4. It is sometimes said that government expenditure could be reduced if the government left certain functions to private enterprise. What functions do you think could effectively be carried out by private enterprise? (L.O.2)

5. Explain the difference in the expenditure patterns of the different levels of government. (L.O.3)

6. Identify the level of government that has jurisdiction over the following: (L.O.3)

    (a) primary and secondary education

    (b) national defence

    (c) hospitals

7. Do you believe that the public sector in Canada is too large? (L.O.2)

8. In what way(s) is a school tax of $300 a year different from a tuition fee of $300 a year? (L.O.4)

9. What are the essentials of a good tax? Do you consider the personal income tax to be a good tax? (L.O.4)

10. On what criteria can the fairness of a tax be judged? (General)

11. Give one example each of: (L.O.5)

    (a) a progressive tax

    (b) a proportional tax

    (c) a regressive tax

12. "A sales tax is progressive because it is expressed as a given percentage of total purchases, which means that the more you buy, the more you pay." Do you agree with this statement? Defend your position. (L.O.5)

13. List the major sources of revenue for: (L.O.4)

    (a) the federal government

    (b) the provincial governments

    (c) the local governments

14. Discuss the effects of taxes on prices, income, income distribution, and resource allocation. (L.O.7)

PROBLEMS AND EXERCISES

1. Complete Table 18.8 from data contained in the chapter. (L.O.3)

TABLE 18.8	Level of government	Total expenditure	% of total
Government expenditures.	Federal		
	Provincial		
	Local		
	TOTAL (all levels)		100

2. Study the federal government expenditure by function. Then explain why it is difficult for the federal government to reduce its spending. (L.O.2)

3. How does an income tax based on the benefit principle affect low-income earners? (General)

4. Give an example of each of the following: (General)
   (a) a tax yielding dependable revenue
   (b) a tax which may discourage consumption
   (c) a tax based on the ability to pay principle
   (d) a tax based on the benefit principle

5. Construct arithmetic examples of: (L.O.5)
   (a) a progressive tax
   (b) a proportional tax
   (c) a regressive tax

6. Describe a situation in which a regressive income tax system may benefit an economy. (L.O.5)

7. Construct an arithmetic example showing that sales taxes are regressive. (L.O.5)

8. Table 18.9 shows tax rates and the tax revenue associated with each rate. (L.O.6)
   (a) Plot the information on a graph.
   (b) On your graph, indicate the optimum tax rate.
   (c) Indicate the maximum revenue.
   (d) What is the name of the curve that you have plotted?

9. Taxes in Canada are based on income, wealth, and expenditure. Give an example of a tax that is based on: (General)
   (a) income
   (b) wealth
   (c) expenditure

TABLE 18.9	Tax rate (%)	Tax revenue ($million)
Tax rate and tax revenue.	8	150
	9	200
	10	260
	11	310
	12	350
	13	380
	14	400
	15	410
	16	400
	17	370
	18	320
	19	260
	20	180

10. Health care has become a major issue in Canada. Governments have reduced expenditures on health care and many people have to wait for a very long time (sometimes months) to obtain certain medical services. The federal government has announced that it will make health care a priority. Do you agree that user fees (some kind of direct payment by those who use medical services) should be introduced into the health care system? Why or why not?

Internet Site

http://www.rc.gc.ca
This is the Web site of Revenue Canada. It contains useful information about tax collection and it has links to other useful sites. It also has a *search* option.

INTERNET EXERCISE

1. Go to the Revenue Canada Web site.
2. Click on the *About Revenue Canada* button.
3. Click on the *README: About Revenue Canada* button.
4. Jot down some points about Revenue Canada.
5. Click on the *back* button.
6. Click on the *Revenue Canada's Collection Policies* button.
7. Click on the *T4060 Revenue Canada's Collection Policies* button.
8. Click on the *Your Obligations as a Tax Debtor* button.
9. Write down in point form:
   a) your obligations as a taxpayer
   b) your rights as a taxpayer.

19

C H A P T E R

INTERNATIONAL
TRADE

Learning Objectives

After studying this chapter, you should know about:

1 the basis for international trade

2 the gains from trade

3 the principle of comparative advantage

4 Canada's exports

5 Canada's imports

Each individual is better off if he receives more of every commodity while rendering less of every productive device.

Paul A. Samuelson, *The Gains from International Trade*

INTRODUCTION

International trade is the exchange of goods and services between nations.

Each year, Canadians consume a huge amount of goods and services not produced in Canada. Coffee, tea, and cane sugar are common items of consumption for many of us. Oranges, bananas, and other tropical fruits are other common items of consumption. We consume these items, but we do not produce them. On the other hand, consumers in other countries enjoy a host of goods and services produced in Canada. All this is made possible through **international trade**.

The Canadian economy depends greatly on international trade. Our exports play a major role in our country's economic growth and development. Among other things, international trade deals with the import and export of goods and services, and with the effects of these flows on the economy. The theory of international trade is quite involved. In this chapter, you will study the reasons for trade between nations, and the sources of gains from international trade. You will also have an opportunity to look at Canada's trade statistics, which teach us something about Canada's international economic activity.

THE BASIS FOR INTERNATIONAL TRADE

The basis for international trade is that different countries are differently endowed with resources. This is called regional specialization.

Learning Objective 1: the basis for international trade

In Chapter 7, we noted that certain advantages resulted from the specialization of labour. These advantages are not limited to labour specialization, however. They extend equally to **regional specialization**, which is the basis for international trade. The main reason for regional specialization is that different regions are differently endowed with resources and technical know-how. Some regions, for instance, are heavily endowed with natural resources. Others are less favourably endowed. Some regions (or nations) are rich in capital. Others suffer from a lack of capital relative to other resources. And human resources vary among regions. Some countries have more highly skilled labour forces than others. Some regions have larger populations than others. Moreover, technological capabilities are not evenly distributed across nations. Country A may have a technological edge over country B in the production of telecommunication equipment while country B may have a technological advantage over country A in the production of books.

A country well endowed with labour can be expected to have lower wage rates than a country with scarce labour resources. Consequently, we can expect the cost of manufacturing a product requiring a large amount of labour to be lower in a labour-abundant country than in a labour-scarce country. Similarly, we would expect the cost of growing tropical fruits such as oranges and bananas in a tropical climate to be much lower than it would be in a temperate climate. Consider the amount of resources that would have to be used to grow citrus fruits in northern Canada!

THE GAINS FROM TRADE

Learning Objective 2: the gains from trade

There are some obvious gains from trade. For example, Canadians can enjoy tropical fruits at relatively low prices, and people in tropical countries can enjoy McIntosh apples grown in Canada at relatively low costs. But some gains from trade are not quite so obvious. Let us now look at two fundamental principles that explain why countries benefit from international trade.

THE PRINCIPLE OF ABSOLUTE ADVANTAGE

A country has an absolute advantage if it can produce a commodity at lower cost, in terms of resources, than another country.

A country is said to have an **absolute advantage** over another country in the production of a commodity if it can produce the commodity more efficiently, that is, with fewer resources, than the other country can. In other words, if country A is more efficient than country B in the production of a certain commodity, country A has an absolute advantage in the production of that commodity. The following numerical example will help to illustrate the concept of absolute advantage.

Suppose that a Canadian worker can produce five cars per year while a worker in Labouria (a fictitious country) can produce only two cars per year. Suppose also that a Labourian worker can produce ten tonnes of grain per year, while a Canadian worker can produce only eight tonnes of grain per year. Table 19.1 contains the relevant data. A Canadian worker is 2.5 times as efficient as a Labourian worker in car production, but a Labourian worker is 1.25 times as efficient as a Canadian worker in grain production. In this case, Canada has an absolute advantage in the production of cars, while Labouria has an absolute advantage in the production of grain.

TABLE 19.1		Cars (units)	Grain (tonnes)
Hypothetical output per worker in Canada and Labouria.	Canada	5	8
	Labouria	2	10

The following example illustrates that the combined output of cars and grain in both countries will increase if Canada specializes in the production of cars and Labouria specializes in the production of grain. Suppose a Canadian worker is transferred from grain production into car production. The output of cars in Canada would increase by five while the output of grain would fall by eight tonnes. If, at the same time, a Labourian worker is transferred from car production into grain production, the output of cars in Labouria would fall by two, but the output of grain would increase by 10 tonnes. The net effect then would be that car production would increase by three while grain production would increase by two tonnes.

The existence of absolute advantage makes trade beneficial to both trading partners.

> **If each country has an absolute advantage in the production of a commodity, both countries can benefit if each specializes in the production of the commodity in which it has an absolute advantage, and trades with the other.**

Learning Objective 3: the principle of comparative advantage

If one country is more efficient than another in the production of two goods, and its efficiency is greater in the production of one commodity, it has a comparative advantage in that commodity.

THE PRINCIPLE OF COMPARATIVE ADVANTAGE

The previous section showed that two countries can gain by trading if each specializes in the production of the commodity in which it has an absolute advantage. But what if one country has an absolute advantage in the production of both commodities? Will trade still benefit both countries? The **principle of comparative advantage** provides the answer.

Let us assume that a Canadian worker can produce either 10 cars or five tonnes of grain per year, while a Labourian worker can produce either three cars or three tonnes of grain per year (see Table 19.2). A Canadian worker is therefore more efficient than a Labourian worker in the production of both commodities. Canada has an absolute advantage in the production of cars and in the production of grain.

TABLE 19.2		Cars (units)	Grain (tonnes)
Hypothetical output per worker in Canada and Labouria.	Canada	10	5
	Labouria	3	3

Instead of producing 10 cars, a Canadian worker could have produced five tonnes of grain. Hence, the opportunity cost of a car in Canada is 0.5 tonnes of grain. That is, in order to produce one car, Canada must sacrifice 0.5 tonnes of grain. On the other hand, instead of producing three cars, a Labourian worker could have produced three tonnes of grain. Hence, the opportunity cost of a car in Labouria is one tonne of grain. Since the opportunity cost of a car in Canada is less than the opportunity cost of a car in Labouria, Canada is said to have a comparative advantage in the production of cars.

The opportunity cost of a tonne of grain in Canada is two cars, while the opportunity cost of a tonne of grain in Labouria is one car. Since the opportunity cost of grain in Labouria is less than the opportunity cost of grain in Canada, Labouria has a comparative advantage in the production of grain.

A country has a comparative advantage in the production of a commodity if it can produce that commodity at a lower opportunity cost than another country.

We are now in a position to demonstrate the mutual gain from trade with comparative advantage. In the absence of trade, Canada must give up 0.5 tonnes of grain for one car while Labouria must give up one tonne of grain for a car. Let us assume that Canada and Labouria can exchange cars for grain at a rate somewhere between the ratio 1:0.5 and 1:1; let us say one car for 0.75 tonnes of grain (1:0.75). The actual rate at which cars will exchange for grain (called the **terms of trade**) is determined by cost and by demand for these two commodities in both countries.

For every worker transferred from grain production into car production in Canada, the output of grain falls by five tonnes, but the output of cars rises by 10. Each of those cars can now be exported to Labouria for 0.75 tonnes of grain, resulting in a net gain of $(0.75 - 0.5) = 0.25$ tonnes of grain per car for Canada. Does Labouria also gain from this transaction? Let us investigate. To produce one car, Labouria would have to give up one tonne of grain. By trading with Canada, Labouria obtains the car for only 0.75 tonnes of grain — a clear gain of 0.25 tonnes of grain.

If each country has a comparative advantage in the production of a commodity, both countries will benefit if each specializes in the production of the commodity in which it has a comparative advantage, and trades with the other.

Note that trade between the two countries is mutually beneficial only because of a difference in opportunity cost between the two countries. If the opportunity cost were identical in both countries, there would be no comparative advantage and therefore no gain from trade.

GRAPHICAL ILLUSTRATION OF COMPARATIVE ADVANTAGE

The principle of comparative advantage and the gains from trade can also be illustrated graphically. For simplicity, let us assume that Canada and Labouria each has only one worker, and that production in both nations takes place under conditions of constant opportunity cost, so that the production possibility curves are linear, as shown in Figure 19.1.

Canada's production possibility curve shows that if Canada uses all of its resources to produce grain, it can produce five tonnes of grain. Alternatively, if it uses all its resources to produce only cars, it can produce 10 cars. On the other hand, with full utilization of all its resources, Labouria can produce six cars or six tonnes of grain. Note that as before, Canada has a comparative advantage in the production of cars while Labouria has a comparative advantage in the production of grain.

Terms of trade are the rates at which a country's exports are exchanged for its imports.

Output will increase if each country specializes in the production of the commodity in which it has a comparative advantage.

FIGURE 19.1

Comparative
advantage.

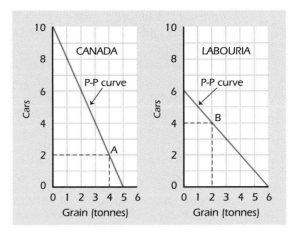

Let us assume that both countries want both grain and cars. In the absence of international trade, each country would have to produce some quantities of both goods. Suppose that Canada decides to produce two cars and four tonnes of grain, thus operating at point A on its production possibility curve. Suppose also that Labouria decides to produce four cars and two tonnes of grain, thus operating at point B on its production possibility curve. The total output of both countries is six cars and six tonnes of grain. Note that each country is operating efficiently because each is operating on its production possibility curve.

Now, let us introduce specialization and trade. Suppose that Canada specializes in the production of cars (in which it has a comparative advantage), and Labouria specializes in the production of grain (in which it has a comparative advantage). With Canada producing only cars, and Labouria producing only grain, the combined output of both countries would be 10 cars and six tonnes of grain. Because of specialization, the output of cars increases from six to 10 while the output of grain remains unchanged at six tonnes. But Canada has only cars, and Labouria has only grain. Here, trade can be beneficial to both countries.

Recall that in the absence of trade, Canada would operate at point A on its production possibility curve (Figure 19.1), producing two cars and four tonnes of grain. Labouria on the other hand, would operate at point B on its production possibility curve, producing four cars and two tonnes of grain. Note that Canada must sacrifice one tonne of grain in order to produce two cars. For Canada, one tonne of grain costs two cars. However, Canada would like to obtain one tonne of grain for less than two cars.

Recall that for Labouria, one car costs one tonne of grain. Therefore two cars cost two tonnes of grain. Suppose Canada offers to pay Labouria one car for 0.75 tonnes of grain (that is, two cars for 1.5 tonnes of grain) and Labouria accepts the offer. The terms of trade (one car for 0.75 tonnes of grain) would mean that Canada would obtain a tonne of grain more cheaply (for 1.33 cars instead of two cars), and Labouria would obtain a car more cheaply (for 0.75 tonnes instead of one tonne of grain). Figure 19.2 shows the gain from specialization and trade.

The production possibility curves for Canada and Labouria are the same as in Figure 19.1. With trade and specialization, Canada can specialize in car production, but now it can trade 10 cars, at the terms of trade, for 7.5 tonnes of grain. Canada's **trading curve** is illustrated in Figure 19.2. Labouria can specialize in grain production, but now it can trade six tonnes of grain, at the terms of trade, for eight cars. Labouria's trading curve is

The trading curve shows all
combinations of goods and
services available through
specialization and trade.

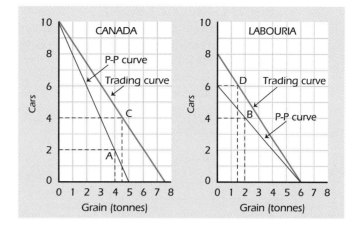

also shown in Figure 19.2. Note that because the trading curve is above the production possibility curve, any point on the trading curve is preferable to any point on the production possibility curve.

It would be inefficient for Canada and Labouria to remain on their production possibility curves when trade is possible. Canada can produce 10 cars and then trade (export) six cars to Labouria for 4.5 tonnes of grain, thus moving to point C on its trading curve. Canada is unambiguously better off at C than at A. But what about Labouria? If Labouria specializes in the production of grain, it can sell 4.5 tonnes of grain to Canada for six cars, thus moving to point D on its trading curve. Labouria is better off at point D than at point B.

PROBLEM SOLVING 19-1
What items of trade would you expect between Canada and Japan?

DETERMINANTS OF COMPARATIVE ADVANTAGE

NATURAL ENDOWMENT

The Caribbean islands have numerous white sandy beaches and a warm (sometimes hot) climate all year round, naturally. They therefore are a natural attraction for tourists who want to get away for a week or two between December and March, when it is cold and snowing in Canada. The comparative advantage enjoyed by the Caribbean islands in this field is a matter of natural endowment. In this case, the comparative advantage is geographically determined — hence the concept of **geographical determinism**, the theory that comparative advantage is determined by natural endowment. This theory has been around for a long time, but, despite its age, it still has relevance in explaining comparative advantage in some instances.

The theory of geographical determinism suggests that comparative advantage is determined by natural endowments.

ACQUIRED ADVANTAGE

In the same way that some individuals work hard to develop and improve whatever abilities may have been bestowed on them, so too can nations, by their own efforts, acquire comparative advantage in certain lines of production. Japan is often cited as the classic example of a nation that has compensated for its lack of natural endowments by saving and by making huge investment in capital, both physical and human.

SPECIAL KNOWLEDGE

Whether by accident or design, some countries have special knowledge that gives them a comparative advantage in the production of certain products. A country that comes to mind in this regard is Switzerland, with its reputation for watch-making. There is little doubt that Switzerland's expertise in watch-making is partly a result of many years of concentration on that activity.

FURTHER GAINS FROM TRADE

Learning Objective 2:
the gains from trade

In addition to the gains described above, gains can come from two other sources: greater efficiency and economies of scale. Let us examine each of these in turn.

Increased efficiency

Further gains from trade may result from increased efficiency.

We can reasonably assume that, as Canada specializes in the production of cars and Labouria specializes in the production of grain, Canadian workers will acquire greater skills and expertise in the production of cars. Labourians will likewise acquire greater skills and expertise in the production of grain. Thus, each country, by specializing, will experience an increase in worker productivity.

Economies of scale

Further gains may result from economies of scale made possible through trade.

Production costs may fall as the volume of output increases. If this is the case, then the average cost of producing cars in Canada will fall, because specialization in car manufacturing will have increased the volume of output. Similarly, the average cost of producing grain will fall in Labouria, because specialization in grain manufacturing will have increased the volume of output.

Canada has comparative advantage in a number of economic activities. Among these are the production of electricity, certain agricultural items, forestry items, certain minerals, and certain kinds of high technology such as communication. Canada's large supply of electric power attracts industries that require large amounts of electricity. Table 19.3 cites some products whose manufacture requires high and average levels of electricity.

TABLE 19.3	High	Medium
Products requiring high and medium levels of electricity.	Newsprint	Other pulp and paper
	Aluminum	Titanium
	Magnesium	Steel works
	Zinc and cadmium	Carbon steel mill
	Silicon carbide	Copper
	Chlorine & sodium hydroxide	Glass
	Phosphorus	Melted alumina — 95%

PROBLEM SOLVING 19-2
Why would you expect Quebec to be an exporter of newsprint?

CANADA'S EXPORTS

Learning Objective 4:
Canada's exports

Trade is very important to the Canadian economy. In 1997, exports of goods and services from Canada amounted to $343.5 billion, accounting for approximately 40% of the total amount of goods and services produced in Canada. Major export items include motor vehicles and parts, wheat, petroleum, natural gas, lumber, minerals, wood pulp, newsprint, chemicals, various metals, and transportation and communications equipment. Note that

Canada exports a wide variety of products.

a significant part of Canada's exports consists of raw materials and that only a few items — such as paper, automobiles, and communications equipment — undergo extensive processing before being exported. However, the largest single export item (motor vehicles and parts) undergoes complete processing in Canada. Table 19.4 shows the value and percentage of Canadian export items in 1996. The values are in 1986 dollars.

TABLE 19.4

Value and percentage of export items, 1996.

Item	Value ($million)	%
Food:		
Wheat	2 421	1.0
Other farm and fish products	15 962	6.5
Energy materials:		
Crude petroleum	7 264	3.0
Natural gas	9 433	3.8
Other energy products	7 351	3.0
Other (natural resource) materials:		
Lumber and sawmill products	9 390	3.8
Pulp and paper	14 695	6.0
Other metals and minerals	24 359	9.9
Chemicals and fertilizers	13 419	5.4
Motor vehicles and parts	57 867	23.6
Other manufactured goods	83 406	34.0
TOTAL	245 567	100.0

Source: *Bank of Canada Review*, Summer 1998: s105.

Canada's largest export market is the United States. In 1995, over 80% of Canada's merchandise exports went to that country. Other important export markets are Japan, Great Britain, Germany, the Netherlands, the People's Republic of China, and France. Figure 19.3 shows Canada's leading export markets along with the percentage of total exports destined for each.

In 1997, Canadian merchandise exports to the European Union amounted to $16.7 billion or over 5% of our total merchandise exports. There is also a lively trade between Canada and Japan. Our exports of goods to Japan in 1997 totaled $12.1 billion, accounting for 4% of our total merchandise exports. We sold $4.4 billion worth of goods to the United Kingdom and $7.9 billion to other countries of the Organization for Economic Cooperation and Development (OECD).

FIGURE 19.3

Canada's major export markets, 1997.

The United States is the main buyer of Canada's exports.

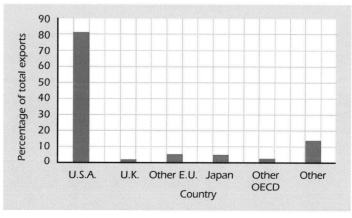

Source: Statistics Canada, *Canadian Economic Observer* (Cat. 11–010–XPB), July 1998: 31.

Canada's merchandise exports are grouped into several broad categories. Data on the value of merchandise exports in each category are shown in Table 19.5.

TABLE 19.5

Classification of Canada's merchandise exports, 1997.

Category	Value ($million)	% of total
Agricultural and fish products	24 705	8.5
Energy products	26 820	9.2
Forest products	34 896	12.0
Industrial goods	55 602	19.1
Machines and equipment	67 983	23.4
Automobile products	70 057	24.1
Consumer goods	10 650	3.7
TOTAL	290 703	100.0

Source: Statistics Canada, *Canadian Economic Observer* (Cat. 11-010-XPB), July 1998: 31.

CANADA'S IMPORTS

Learning Objective 5:
Canada's imports

The United States is the main supplier of Canada's imports.

To get a general overall picture of our international trade, we should really have some idea of Canada's imports. In 1997, Canada imported a total of $329.2 billion worth of goods and services, and its merchandise imports alone amounted to $276.8 billion. Table 19.6 provides information on Canada's imports. The values are in 1986 dollars.

Most of Canada's imports come from the United States. In 1997, imports from that country accounted for over 76% of our total merchandise imports. Figure 19.4 shows the major countries that supply Canada's imports.

In 1997, Canada purchased $6.1 billion worth of goods from the United Kingdom. Our imports from Japan were valued at over $8 billion — about 3% of our merchandise imports. Imports from other countries in the European Union amounted to $18 billion, or over 6.5% of imports from all countries. Other OECD countries supplied us with over $11 billion worth of goods.

TABLE 19.6

Value and percentage of import items, 1996.

Item	Value ($million)	%
Food	12 692	5.4
Energy materials:		
Crude petroleum	5 267	2.3
Other energy products	2 505	1.1
Other (natural resource) materials:		
Construction materials	2 683	1.1
Industrial materials	37 582	16.1
Motor vehicles and parts	54 657	23.4
Other manufactured goods	98 490	42.2
Other consumer goods	19 735	8.4
TOTAL	233 611	100.0

Source: *Bank of Canada Review*, Summer 1998: s106.

Just as we have categorized Canada's exports, so too can we categorize our imports. The value of imports in each category is shown in Table 19.7.

FIGURE 19.4

Major suppliers of Canada's imports, 1997.

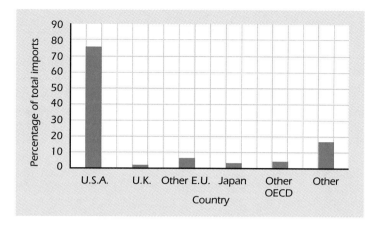

Source: Statistics Canada, *Canadian Economic Observer* (Cat. 11–010–XPB), July 1998: 32.

TABLE 19.7

Classification of Canada's merchandise imports, 1997.

Category	Value ($million)	% of total
Agricultural and fish products	15 579	5.9
Energy products	10 603	4.0
Forest products	2 373	0.9
Industrial goods	54 370	20.6
Machines and equipment	91 203	34.5
Automobile products	60 630	22.9
Consumer goods	29 588	11.2
TOTAL	264 345	100.0

Source: Statistics Canada, *Canadian Economic Observer* (Cat. 11-010-XPB), Summer 1998: 32.

CHAPTER SUMMARY

1. International trade concerns the import and export of goods and services and their effects on the economy.

2. The advantages derived from labour specialization apply also to regional specialization. Trade can mutually benefit two or more trading partners if each specializes in the production of the commodity in which it has an absolute advantage.

3. Trade will also mutually benefit trading partners if each specializes in the production of the commodity in which it has a comparative advantage. Thus, trade can benefit partners even in cases where one trading partner has an absolute advantage in the production of all goods.

4. Comparative advantage may result from natural endowment, acquired advantage, or from special knowledge.

5. Canada's major export items include motor vehicles and parts, newsprint paper, wood pulp, communications and electronic equipment, lumber, and wheat.

6. Canada's largest export market is the United States, which buys over 80% of Canada's merchandise exports.

7. Canada imports a wide variety of products, including motor vehicles and parts,

GLOBAL   PERSPECTIVE

Export Growth in Seven Countries

The growth of a country's exports measures its sales of goods and services to other countries over time. The economic fortunes of many countries are directly linked to the growth of their export sectors. In this capsule, we compare the growth of Canada's export sector with that of some other industrial countries.

The accompanying graph shows the average rate of growth of exports from 1990 to 1999. As can be seen from the graph, the U.S.A. led the pack with an annual average growth rate of 6.7% in exports. C anada

was second with its exports growing at an annual average of 6.3%. Japan was third, with an annual average of 5.6%, followed in order by Germany (5.4%), Italy (4.6%), and France (4.5%). Over the same period, the United Kingdom managed to increase its exports by an annual average of just 4.1%.

Caveat: Students are warned that conclusions about comparative overall economic performance cannot be drawn on the basis of the performance of any one sector of the economy.

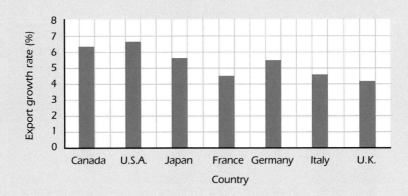

Source: International Monetary Fund, *World Economic Outlook*, May 1998: 176.

industrial machinery, chemicals and plastics, communications and electronic equipment, and crude petroleum.

8. The United States is our largest supplier of imports. Japan, Great Britain, and Germany are also important suppliers of our imports.

TERMS FOR REVIEW
international trade (323)
regional specialization (323)
absolute advantage (323)
principle of comparative advantage (324)

terms of trade (325)
trading curve (326)
geographical determinism (327)

QUESTIONS FOR REVIEW AND DISCUSSION

1. What is the importance of international trade to the Canadian economy? (General)

2. How would you respond to the question, "Why do nations trade?" (L.O.1,2)

3. Assume that Canada is the most efficient country in the world in the production of agricultural goods. Could Canada still benefit by importing food? Explain. (L.O.3)

4. Use an arithmetic example to explain the principle of comparative advantage. (L.O.3)

5. Explain why wheat and newsprint paper are among the leading products exported from Canada. (L.O.3)

6. Discuss the major determinants of comparative advantage. (L.O.3)

7. Name the major countries to which Canada exports goods. Which of these is the main buyer of Canadian exports? (L.O.4)

8. Name the major countries from which Canada imports goods. Which of these is the main supplier of Canadian imports? (L.O.5)

PROBLEMS AND EXERCISES

1. The country of Keylandia (a fictitious country) can produce a typewriter or 20 pairs of shoes. The country of Cloggon (another fictitious country) can produce a similar typewriter or 80 pairs of shoes. (L.O.1,2,3)

   (a) Which of these two countries has an advantage in the production of typewriters?

   (b) Is this advantage absolute or comparative?

   (c) Which country has an advantage in the production of shoes?

   (d) Is this advantage absolute or comparative?

   (e) Would trade benefit these two countries?

2. Suppose Keylandia can produce 75 000 typewriters and 100 000 pairs of shoes per year, while Cloggon can produce 1500 typewriters and 500 000 pairs of shoes per year. (L.O.2)

   (a) On the basis of this information, complete Table 19.8.

TABLE 19.8

Production of type-writers and shoes in Keylandia and Cloggon.

Country	Typewriters	Pairs of shoes
Keylandia		
Cloggon		
TOTAL		

   (b) Now, suppose that Keylandia specializes in the production of typewriters while Cloggon specializes in the production of shoes. Use the figures in Exercise 1 to complete post-specialization Table 19.9.

TABLE 19.9

Production of type-writers and shoes in Keylandia and Cloggon.

Country	Typewriters	Pairs of shoes
Keylandia		0
Cloggon	0	
TOTAL		

3. Economia and Simpletonia are neighbouring countries. A worker in Economia can produce either six units of clothing or three units of food. A worker in Simpletonia can produce either four units of clothing or one unit of food. (L.O.2,3)

   (a) Does either country have an absolute advantage in the production of both products? If so, which country?

   (b) Fill in the blanks.

_____ has a comparative advantage in the production of clothing while _____ has a comparative advantage in the production of food.

(c) The production of clothing and food in Economia and Simpletonia is shown in Table 19.10.

TABLE 19.10	Country	Clothing	Food
Production of clothing and food in Economia and Simpletonia.	Economia	5000 units	15 000 units
	Simpletonia	50 units	10 000 units
	TOTAL	5050 units	25 000 units

If Economia specializes in the production of clothing while Simpletonia specializes in the production of food, use the opportunity cost figures given above to complete post-specialization Table 19.11.

TABLE 19.11	Country	Clothing	Food
Production of clothing and food in Economia and Simpletonia.	Economia		0
	Simpletonia	0	
	TOTAL		

4. "Canada is much too dependent on foreign trade. We depend on foreigners to buy 40% of our goods and services and we buy 38% of our goods and services from foreigners. Canada should be more self-sufficient." Discuss.

Internet Site

http://www.dfait-maeci.gc.ca
This site is for the Department of Foreign Affairs and International Trade. It is a great source of information about Canada's foreign affairs and international trade.

INTERNET EXERCISE

1. Go to **http://www.infoexport.gc.ca/menu-e.asp**.
2. Click on *Canada's Trade Development Agenda*.
3. Click on *Team Canada Trade Mission*.
4. Click on *What is Team Canada?*
   Answer the following questions:
   a) What is Team Canada?
   b) What is the main function of Team Canada?
   c) Write down some trade facts from the 1998 Trade Mission to Latin America.

CHAPTER 20

TARIFFS AND TRADE POLICY ISSUES

Learning Objectives

After studying this chapter, you should understand:

1 the reasons for tariffs

2 classification of tariffs

3 tariff structure

4 arguments in favour of tariffs

5 arguments against tariffs

6 the optimum tariff

7 other restrictive and control devices

8 economic integration

9 an analysis of Separatism

10 the great free-trade debate

11 views on the North American Free Trade Agreement

The degree of protection should be roughly equal to the advantage of foreign producers in this market as a result of their lower labour standards, modified by relative productivity.

The National Labor-Management Council on Foreign Trade Policy.

INTRODUCTION

In the Canadian confederation, certain powers are given to the federal government and certain powers to the provinces. One of the areas over which the federal government has jurisdiction is the imposition of tariffs. As is to be expected, the tariff policies of the federal government affect economic activity all over the country.

We have seen that, through trade and specialization, countries can increase their well-being both individually and collectively. Despite the obvious advantages of free trade, we live not in a world of free trade but in a world with numerous restrictions on trade. The tariff is the most widely used of these restrictions. In this chapter, you will study some of the issues surrounding tariffs.

This chapter will also introduce you to various forms of economic integration. Economic integration is practised among many countries of the world. In 1987, Canada and the United States signed a free-trade agreement. In the summer of 1992, Canada, the United States, and Mexico reached a preliminary agreement on free trade between the three countries which is now in effect. Indeed, tariffs and trade policies are very topical issues.

WHY TARIFFS?

A tariff makes the imported good more expensive.

Learning Objective 1:
the reasons for tariffs

A tariff is a tax imposed on imported goods.

When we import goods from Japan or another country, we pay a tax or **duty** on those goods. Similarly, when Canadian exporters sell their goods to foreign countries, those countries impose a tax or duty on our goods. This duty, or **tariff** as it is called, raises the price of the product to the buyer.

A question well worth asking is "Why do nations impose tariffs?" There are many reasons. Nations may impose tariffs:

1. as a device for redistributing income from one group to another;

2. as a means of raising revenue for the government;

3. as a means of improving the country's balance-of-payments position;

4. as a means of dealing with the unemployment problem in the country;

5. as a means of restricting the consumption of certain goods that may be considered socially or economically undesirable;

6. as a means of improving the country's terms of trade, and thus increasing its share of the gains from trade;

7. as a means of protecting certain industries from the full force of international competition;

8. as a means of encouraging certain industries considered to be vital from an economic, military, or political point of view.

From the above list, it is clear that there is no shortage of reasons for imposing tariffs. A tariff can usually be defended (rightly or wrongly) on one or more of the grounds listed above.

CLASSIFICATION OF TARIFFS

Learning Objective 2:
classification of tariffs

Tariffs can be classified according to their main objectives. If the main objective of the tariff is to raise revenue for the government, than the tariff is called a **revenue tariff**. If the objective is to protect domestic producers, then the tariff is called a **protective tariff**. Protective tariffs are much more common in Canada than revenue tariffs. In

Revenue tariffs raise revenue for the government.

Protective tariffs protect domestic producers. Canadian tariffs are mainly protective.

A specific tariff is an amount per unit of the imported item.

An ad valorem tariff is a fixed percentage of the value of the imported item.

A compound tariff is a combination of specific and ad valorem tariffs.

Learning Objective 3: tariff structure

Canada, customs duties account for less than 5% of the total revenue of the federal government.

Tariffs can also be classified as specific, ad valorem, or compound. A **specific tariff** is expressed as so much per unit of the imported item. Thus, a tariff of $0.40 imposed on each 100-g bottle of hot sauce imported would be a specific tariff. An **ad valorem tariff** is expressed as a fixed percentage of the value of the imported item. Thus, a tariff of 35% of the value of textiles imported into Canada would be an ad valorem tariff. A **compound tariff** is a combination of specific and ad valorem tariffs. A tariff expressed as $0.25 per kilogram for the first 50 kg and 10% of the value of any amount over 50 kg is an example of a compound tariff. We shall examine arguments for and against tariffs in subsequent sections of this chapter.

TARIFF STRUCTURE

Four main categories of tariff rates apply to goods imported into Canada. These are: British preferential, most-favoured-nation, general, and general preferential.

British preferential

This rate applies to goods imported from British commonwealth countries, which enjoy the benefits of the British Commonwealth preferential tariff.

Most-favoured-nation

This rate is usually higher than the British preferential rate but lower than the general tariff rate, and applies to goods imported from countries with which Canada has trade agreements, such as the General Agreement of Tariffs and Trade (GATT).

General

This rate applies to goods imported from those countries with which Canada has no trade agreements.

General preferential

On July 1, 1974, Canada agreed to a generalized system of preferences designed to allow lower rates on goods imported from developing countries. This rate generally consists of the British preferential rate or the most-favoured-nation rate minus one third, whichever is less.

ARGUMENTS IN FAVOUR OF TARIFFS

Learning Objective 4: arguments in favour of tariffs

Several arguments have been advanced in favour of tariffs. These include both economic and non-economic arguments. In this section, we shall discuss some popular economic arguments in support of tariffs.

THE INFANT INDUSTRY ARGUMENT

Tariffs protect infant industries.

One argument put forward by supporters of tariffs is the **infant industry argument**. The argument is as follows. New domestic industries cannot compete with older and better established industries in foreign countries; hence, new domestic industries need to be protected by tariffs. New domestic industries, moreover, may have the potential to develop a comparative advantage. This potential may never be realized unless such industries are allowed to grow to maturity with the assistance of tariffs. In order for this argument to carry much weight, the tariff would have to be temporary — in place only until the industry matured. In practice, however, an industry is often protected for such a long time that we begin to wonder whether or not the infant will ever grow up! Moreover, protection is valid only if the gains from such protection cannot be claimed exclusively by the firms' owners in the form of eventual profits. In other words, the infant industry argument is significantly strengthened when external economies, in the form of benefits to the society, are present.

THE EMPLOYMENT ARGUMENT

Another argument often used to support the use of tariffs is that they help to create jobs. The imposition of tariffs, it is argued, keeps out foreign goods and thus increases domestic production. The increase in employment in domestic industries competing with the imported goods will spread to other industries. For example, increased employment in the communications industry will increase total income in that industry. This increase in income will increase demand for goods produced by other industries and thus increase employment in those industries. Additional investment may also be undertaken to produce domestic substitutes. When considering this argument, it is important to realize that the reduction of our imports due to tariffs means a reduction of exports from our trading partners, which may result in unemployment, falling incomes, and reduced imports abroad. Our exports will then also be reduced, and we, too, may suffer unemployment and falling incomes.

Tariffs create and protect jobs.

THE TERMS OF TRADE ARGUMENT

A third argument in favour of tariffs is that a country can improve its terms of trade by imposing tariffs on goods imported from other countries. Recall that the phrase **terms of trade** refers to the rate at which a country's exports can be exchanged for its imports. The imposition of a tariff means that a larger quantity of imports will be required for any given quantity of exports. Improvement in a country's terms of trade can make the country better off, but this is not a necessary consequence of higher tariffs. If the tariff is so high that it reduces imports to zero, then the country may be worse off than if the tariff had not been imposed. There is therefore some level of tariff that is optimal in terms of increasing the benefits derived from the terms of trade. The concept of an optimum tariff will be discussed below.

Tariffs can improve the terms of trade.

DIVERSIFICATION AND INDUSTRIALIZATION

It is often argued that protection of domestic industries by tariffs is necessary in order to promote diversification and industrialization. This argument seems to rest on the assumption that industrialization and diversification are desirable because they result in an increase in real income. If industrialization and diversification are desirable for their own sake, then protection by tariffs is one way (though not necessarily the most efficient way) of achieving these ends. We must understand, however, that diversification and industrialization do not necessarily lead to an increase in real income or purchasing power. Indeed, the pursuit of industrialization and diversification may lead to severe misallocation of resources and, consequently, to a reduction in real income. Of course, non-economic arguments exist in support of tariffs, but, as indicated earlier, we are concerned here only with the economic arguments.

Tariffs promote industrialization and diversification.

ARGUMENTS AGAINST TARIFFS

COMPARATIVE ADVANTAGE

The main economic argument against tariffs is that they interfere with the principle of comparative advantage. Thus, they reduce or negate the gains from specialization and trade.

Tariffs interfere with the principle of comparative advantage.

Learning Objective 5:
arguments against tariffs

We have seen that international trade benefits each trading partner and increases total production. The imposition of tariffs, on the other hand, can result in each trading partner being worse off.

EFFICIENCY

Tariffs are inefficient.

Another argument against tariffs is that the objectives that they are designed to achieve can, in most cases, be achieved by other, more efficient means. For example, the objective of industrialization can be achieved more efficiently by subsidization than by the imposition of tariffs. Also, in cases where a temporary tariff may achieve a specific objective, it becomes extremely difficult to remove the tariff once the objective has been achieved; tariffs tend to become permanent once they are imposed.

PROBLEM SOLVING 20-1
Could Canadian consumers benefit from a gradual elimination of the tariff on shoes?

THE OPTIMUM TARIFF

If a country's terms of trade improve, it will secure a larger share of the gains from trade and specialization. The imposition of a tariff is one way of improving a country's terms of trade. As a country raises its tariffs (assuming that other countries do not retaliate), its terms of trade increase, but its volume of trade decreases. The benefits from the improvement in the terms of trade, however, are likely to more than compensate for the loss resulting from the reduction in trade volume. Hence, the country obtains a net gain.

Learning Objective 6:
the optimum tariff

The optimum tariff is the tariff that maximizes the country's welfare.

After a point, however, the loss resulting from the reduction in the volume of trade will begin to outweigh the benefits from the improvement in the terms of trade. It follows that a tariff exists that maximizes the benefits to the country. Such a tariff is called an **optimum tariff**. Figure 20.1 shows that as the tariff increases from 0 to *t*, community welfare increases. Beyond *t*, however, the tariff chokes off trade so much that community welfare declines. The optimum tariff *t* maximizes community welfare.

FIGURE 20.1

The optimum tariff.

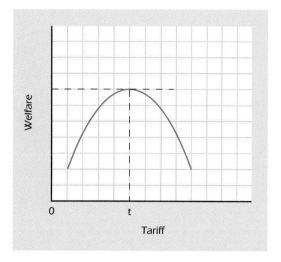

APPLICATION

The Effects of Tariffs

Let us use simple demand and supply graphs to help us to analyze the effects of a tariff. To avoid unnecessary complications, we assume that there are only two countries in the world: Canada and Rest of the World (ROW). For simplicity also, we assume that Canada and ROW use a common currency called the dollar ($). Diagram A shows the demand and supply curves for wheat in Canada while Diagram B shows the demand and supply curves for wheat in ROW. The world price of wheat is P. At that price, Canadian wheat producers supply X units to the Canadian market, but the quantity demanded at that price is X_2. At the world price, there is a shortage of X_2 - X units of wheat in Canada.

What about ROW? Let's take a look. The quantity demanded at the world price is Y, while the quantity supplied by ROW producers is Y_2 units. There is therefore a surplus of Y_2 – Y in ROW. This surplus is exactly equal to the shortage in Canada. Is this a coincidence? Not really. The total quantity of wheat demanded in both countries must be equal to the total quantity supplied at the world price. If Canada and ROW are allowed to trade freely, Canada will import X_2 – X units of wheat from ROW, and ROW will export Y_2 - Y units to Canada.

Let's assume now that Canada imposes a tariff of 50% on wheat imported from ROW. The Canadian price of wheat is now P_t. Canadian wheat growers increase the quantity supplied from X to X_1 units, and consumers reduce the quantity demanded from X_2 to X_1. ROW has lost its export market. This loss of the Canadian market forces the ROW price down from P to P_0 in Diagram B. ROW wheat growers reduce the quantity supplied from Y_2 to Y_1 while ROW consumers increase their purchases of ROW wheat from Y to Y_1.

What has the tariff done? Canadian consumers are paying a higher price and getting a smaller quantity of wheat. But Canadian wheat farmers are happy. They are getting a great deal more money — P_t . X_1 instead of P.X in Diagram A. And what has happened in ROW? Wheat farmers there must be a sorrowful group. They are hurting. They are selling less wheat at a lower price.

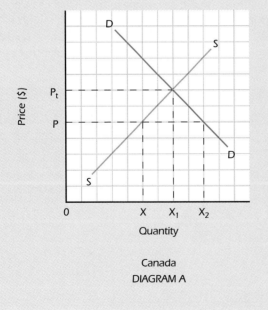

Canada

DIAGRAM A

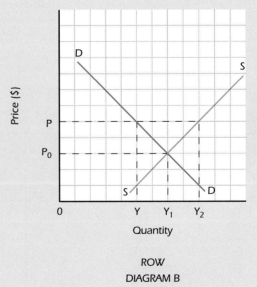

ROW

DIAGRAM B

OTHER RESTRICTIVE AND CONTROL DEVICES

Learning Objective 7: other restrictive and control devices

The tariff is not the only device that restricts and controls the volume of trade between countries. Other such devices include import quotas, export subsidies, and voluntary restrictions.

Import quotas

An import quota restricts trade. It is the maximum amount of a good permitted to enter the country.

An **import quota** is the maximum amount of a commodity that may be permitted to enter the country during a given period of time. To ensure that the quota is not exceeded, the government requires each importer to obtain an import licence for the amount to be imported.

Export subsidies

Export subsidies assist exporters. They are paid by the government to the exporter.

A government may offer assistance to its exporters by paying them a subsidy. Such **export subsidies** reduce the exporters' costs, thus enabling them to reduce their prices and so compete more effectively with foreign producers. Some countries use export subsidies rather liberally to promote their industries.

Voluntary restrictions

Voluntary restrictions impede trade.

Imports from a certain country may adversely affect a domestic industry. In this case, a government may ask the exporting country to cooperate by voluntarily restricting its exports. An example of voluntary restrictions has occurred between Canada and Japan. Canada has asked Japan to restrict its exports of radios and cars to Canada, and this has prevented a flood of low-priced goods on the market, enabling Canadian manufacturers to compete.

TARIFFS VERSUS QUOTAS

Both tariffs and quotas raise the domestic price of the product and reduce the volume of trade. There are, however, differences in the effects of tariffs and quotas.

First, import quotas are likely to be more effective than tariffs in limiting the quantity of imports entering a country. If the preference for an imported good is very strong, some amount of that good is likely to be imported in spite of a high tariff. Some consumers may be willing and able to pay the price. But in the case of an import quota, the quota establishes the limit and it cannot be exceeded. The government may even ban the importation of certain goods.

Tariffs and quotas differ in their effects.

Second, a tariff, as we have seen, raises the price of the imported product and thus reduces the quantity demanded of that product. The proceeds from the tariff accrue to the government as added tax revenues. The tax burden is borne by Canadian consumers of the imported product in the form of increased prices, and also by the foreign exporters in the form of reduced quantities demanded. Domestic producers of the product are thus at an advantage, because the tariff does not apply to their product. A quota, on the other hand, reduces the supply of the product on the domestic market, and hence pushes its price up. The higher prices are paid to foreign exporters of the product and also to domestic producers. They do not accrue to the government as tax revenues as in the case of a tariff.

Finally, a tariff is non-discriminatory in the sense that it applies equally to all foreign exporters. Thus, all domestic importers of the product pay the same tariff. On the other hand, import licences may be awarded on the basis of criteria that have nothing to do with efficiency. For example, import licences may be granted to some importers for political reasons, while more efficient importers may be denied import licences. In such cases, the consumers will be the main losers.

ECONOMIC INTEGRATION

The economic analysis of economic associations among sovereign states belongs to the theory of economic integration. We shall discuss, at a very elementary level, the major forms of economic integration. The objective is to provide you with an inkling of the concepts so that you will not be entirely lost in discussions of the issues relating to economic association.

Economic integration is an arrangement between two or more countries to *abolish* certain discriminatory practices between them. But let us not confuse economic integration with economic cooperation. **Economic cooperation** is an arrangement between two or more countries to *reduce* certain forms of discrimination among them. An example of economic integration is an agreement between Canada and the United States to abolish trade barriers between the two countries. An example of economic cooperation is an agreement to reduce tariffs.

FORMS OF ECONOMIC INTEGRATION

Integration arrangements can take various forms. These forms depend on the degree of integration involved. It is now customary to distinguish five major forms of economic integration. These are:

1. free-trade area
2. customs union
3. common market
4. economic union
5. complete economic integration

Each of these forms of economic integration will be discussed in turn.

Free-trade area

A **free-trade area** agreement entails the lowest degree of economic integration. It involves an agreement whereby goods and services flow freely (without tariffs) between the member countries. Each participating country, however, retains its own tariffs against the rest of the world.

Two main problems surround this form of economic integration: tariff evasion and industrial distribution. **Tariff evasion** is an attempt to avoid a tariff by rerouting imports. This may occur in the following manner. Let us suppose that two countries, A and B, agree to form a free-trade area. Let us assume also that countries A and B impose tariffs of 20% and 30% respectively on the value of goods imported from a third country, C. An importer in country B who wishes to import a product from country C can arrange for the imported product to enter the free-trade area at A, where the tariff is lower than at B. The importer can then transport the product to B and thus avoid B's higher tariff. Such an arrangement will benefit the importer only if transportation costs from A to B are sufficiently low to make the arrangement worthwhile. In any case, the possibility of such tariff evasions in a free-trade area presents a threat to the objectives of B's tariff, and imposes severe strains on the free-trade area agreement.

The problem of *industrial distribution* is actually a byproduct of tariff evasion. To understand this, let us return to our three-country example. If producers want to establish industries within the free-trade area, they must consider the sources of their inputs and the cost of obtaining those inputs. Let us assume that most of their inputs will be imported from country C, which is outside the free-trade area. Given the different tariff rates in A and B, these producers are likely to set up the industries in country A, where the tariff is lower, other things being equal.

We noted earlier that tariffs are used as a device to protect domestic industries. This being the case, a number of industries will tend to be established in the member country whose tariff policies offer greatest protection. Thus, we can see that as long as each member country is allowed to pursue its own tariff policies with the rest of the world, there will be unfavourable consequences. This partly explains why free-trade areas tend to be relatively short-lived and serve mainly as stepping grounds for higher levels of economic integration.

Customs union

A customs union is a form of economic integration in which member countries remove all tariffs among themselves, but erect a common tariff against the rest of the world.

A customs union is a higher form of integration than a free-trade area.

The problems inherent in the free-trade area arrangement have led countries to favour a higher level of economic integration. The problems mentioned above in connection with a free-trade area stem from the fact that member countries do not have a common tariff on trade with the rest of the world. A level of economic integration higher than the free-trade area is a **customs union**, in which a common tariff is levied on goods imported from outside the customs union. In a customs union, an agreement must be reached on how to distribute customs revenues among the members of the customs union.

Although this form of economic integration avoids the problems associated with a free-trade area, it has problems of its own. One such problem is the levying of a common tariff against the rest of the world. Let us assume that each country's tariff structure is consistent with its own interests. Negotiations for a common tariff, then, are likely to be quite difficult. Each participating country will try to secure a tariff that protects its own industries.

A second problem with this form of economic integration is that agreeing on how to distribute joint customs revenues among the participating countries can be very difficult. At first glance, an obvious solution appears to be to divide the proceeds proportionately according to each member country's volume of imports. But the formation of the customs union is likely to affect the volume of imports of each member of the union. We must take this fact into account.

A third problem with customs unions is the difficulty of ensuring that the rules of the common tariff structure are interpreted and applied in the same manner in each member country. If countries interpret and administer the customs laws differently, then the problem of tariff evasion discussed in connection with a free-trade area will certainly resurface in a customs union arrangement.

Common market

A common market is a form of economic integration in which goods flow freely between member countries, a common tariff exists with non-member countries, and there are no restrictions on the movement of labour and capital between the members.

A common market is a higher form of integration than a customs union.

In a **common market**, not only is there free movement of goods between the member countries, but there is no restriction on the free movement of the factors of production. Thus, in a common market, capital and labour move freely between the member countries.

This greater degree of integration requires a greater coordination of policies among the independent member countries. Their economies are united. They must therefore act in concert on a number of important issues. For example, widespread unemployment in one of the member countries will result in an exodus of people from that country to another member country where there are better job prospects. This labour mobility may be economically desirable, but undesirable politically. Since economic and political considerations are fused in a common market, a central body must coordinate the policies of the member states.

Economic union

An economic union includes the harmonization of economic policies.

An **economic union** is an even more highly integrated form of association than the common market. It permits not only free movement of goods and factors of production, but a greater degree of harmonization of national economic policies than a common market does.

Complete economic integration

The most highly integrated form of economic association is complete economic integration. At this level of integration, a supra-national authority is responsible for the monetary, fiscal, and social policies of the integrated group. Decisions taken by this authority are binding on the participating members.

SOME EFFECTS OF ECONOMIC INTEGRATION

Economic integration is extremely popular in many parts of the world today. Although the idea is not new, it has certainly picked up momentum in recent years in both developed and underdeveloped countries. We can reasonably assume that countries agree to enter into the various forms of economic integration because they expect to obtain some benefits. Conventional analysis of the benefits of economic integration concerns trade creation and trade diversion.

In trade creation, trade is shifted from a higher cost supplier to a lower cost supplier. It is an advantage.

Trade creation results from a shift from high-cost domestic production to low-cost production due to economic integration in a member country. Thus, if country A is a high-cost producer of a certain product and country B is a low-cost producer of the same product, country A may produce the product under tariff protection. If these two countries now decide to eliminate tariffs between them, country A will find it more economical to import supplies of the product from country B. This is trade creation.

In trade diversion, trade is shifted from a lower cost supplier to a higher cost supplier. It is a disadvantage.

Trade diversion, on the other hand, results from a shift from the lowest-cost external producer to a higher-cost member producer due to economic integration. Trade creation is felt to be beneficial since it involves shifting resources into more efficient uses. Trade diversion, on the other hand, is felt to be harmful if it shifts resources into less efficient uses.

Economic integration may favourably affect the terms of trade.

Economic integration appears to be advantageous because of its effect on the terms of trade. A group of countries bargaining as a unit can win trade concessions from the rest of the world — concessions that probably could not be won if each country bargained individually. These concessions contribute to improved terms of trade.

It can also increase competition.

Another argument in favour of economic integration is that it increases competition. Sometimes, industries are established by erecting high tariff walls. Because of the high degree of protection for these industries, they do not have to compete with similar industries in other countries. This can result in high-cost, inefficient production. Competition forces industries either to seek more efficient methods of production or to leave the market. Lack of competition allows industries to produce inefficiently and at high cost. Now, suppose some countries agree to integrate. This will jeopardize the high-cost inefficient firms because imports can now come from member countries without a tariff. The increase in competition among member countries will result in a more efficient use of resources. Costs and prices will then tend to decrease.

Economic integration may promote technological change.

Another advantage of economic integration is that it promotes technological change. Limited domestic markets, on the other hand, impede technological change. In response to the larger market, existing firms will tend to expand. Resources may then flow into research and development. Possibly, latent comparative advantage may also be realized, and the area could become an exporter to non-member countries. All in all, technological change is a positive force, because it promotes economic growth.

Economic integration also dispels fears that markets may disappear due to changes in tariffs, quotas, and other forms of trade restrictions. The market stability ensured by economic integration reduces risk and uncertainty, and promotes a more favourable climate for domestic investment. Foreign investment may also increase as a result of economic integration.

Economic integration may lead to the realization of economies of scale.

Finally, economic integration provides an opportunity to take advantage of economies of scale. Economic integration promotes the development of a larger domestic market. This larger domestic market encourages firms to set up plants and equipment that facilitate economies of scale, since these firms will be supplying a larger regional market.

PROBLEM SOLVING 20-2

Claude Depapier operates a paper mill in Quebec. Is Claude likely to favour free trade between Canada and the United States?

SEPARATISM: AN ECONOMIC VIEW

A SOVEREIGN QUEBEC

On October 30, 1995, Quebecers went to the polls to vote on the question of separation from Canada. The majority of Quebecers voted in favour of remaining in Canada, but the threat of separation in Quebec is a real and powerful force. Premier Lucien Bouchard has made no secret of the fact that his intention is sovereignty for Quebec. He has promised that another referendum on separation will not be held until after the next provincial election.

Learning Objective 9: an analysis of Separatism

The question of the unilateral declaration of independence by Quebec was brought before the Supreme Court of Canada, and the Court's ruling was handed down on August 20, 1998. The gist of the judgment is that if a "clear majority" of Quebecers, on a "clear" question vote to secede from Canada, then Canada would be obliged to *negotiate* the terms of separation with Quebec. Clearly, the issue is far from settled.

The seriousness of the threat of Quebec separating from Canada has sparked serious discussions about the divisibility of Quebec. As the saying goes, "If Canada is divisible, then so is Quebec." The partition of Quebec, in whatever form it may take, has far reaching economic consequences for both Quebec and Canada. The issues are quite complicated and need not detain us here. Instead, let us turn our attention to an analysis of the consequences of Quebec's secession from Canada.

Let us suppose that Quebec did indeed become a sovereign state. Presumably, it would proceed to negotiate some type of agreement with the rest of Canada — probably an economic union. It could be, however, that so much hostility might result from Quebec's secession, that any meaningful negotiations would be impossible. Quebec would therefore find itself as an independent sovereign state with no economic association with Canada. Canada would then impose tariffs on goods imported from Quebec, and Quebec too would impose tariffs on goods imported from Canada. Depending on the height of the tariff walls, both Quebec and Canada could end up getting supplies from a third country. In other words, Quebec could end up losing its Canadian market and Canada could end up losing its Quebec market. Needless to say, this loss of markets could result in unemployment in both Quebec and Canada. To deal with this problem, still higher tariffs might be imposed to protect domestic producers in Canada and Quebec. These tariffs would result in higher domestic prices, a reduction in the volume of trade, and a misallocation of resources. The standard of living would then fall in both Canada and Quebec.

Let us now suppose that Canada would be willing to negotiate an association with a sovereign Quebec. Let us assume further that the type of association to be negotiated would be a customs union. The decision to negotiate implies an acknowledgement of potential benefits from the association. One major problem would be to agree on how to distribute the benefits from the union among the member states. Conceivably, a union could also result in gains for one state and losses for the other, even though a net gain might be realized by the union as a whole. The country that gained would then have to compensate the country that lost. Agreement on compensatory transfers is one of the major problems of economic integration.

A matter often discussed is how secession might affect manufacturing establishments in Canada and in Quebec. Let us examine this issue briefly. Again, we shall consider two cases: Quebec as a sovereign state with no association with Canada, and a sovereign Quebec in a customs union with Canada. In a sovereign-state Quebec, Quebec industries catering to the large Quebec-Canada market would tend to move out of Quebec and re-establish elsewhere in Canada, assuming that the move was economically feasible. Quebec industries that catered mainly to the Quebec market would tend to remain in Quebec. Quebec industries supplying the American market (these account for about 60% of Quebec's total exports) would also tend to remain in Quebec. In a sovereign-associate Quebec, no logical economic reason would exist to expect an exodus of firms from Quebec or Canada. What is likely to affect investment in Canada and in Quebec is the great uncertainty caused by the threat of secession. This is so because investment does not thrive well in a climate of uncertainty.

THE GREAT FREE-TRADE DEBATE

HISTORICAL BACKGROUND

Several attempts have been made to establish free trade between Canada and the United States.

Learning Objective 10: the great free-trade debate

Notions of free trade between Canada and the United States are not new. On the basis of the gains from trade discussed earlier, proposals for free trade between the two countries can be traced as far back as pre-Confederation Canada. In 1854, a free-trade agreement was signed between Britain and the United States, ensuring the removal of artificial barriers to trade between Canada and the United States. This agreement lasted until 1866. Successive attempts were made in the three decades following 1866 to return to the 1854 protocol, but each attempt failed.

An agreement of sorts was reached in 1911, but lack of enthusiasm for the agreement both in Canada and in the United States, coupled with the defeat of the government of Sir Wilfrid Laurier in the same year, sounded the death knell of the 1911 accord. It was not until 1935 that another trade agreement was negotiated by the two countries. The 1935 agreement marked the beginning of trade liberalization between Canada and the United States.

In October 1947, the General Agreement on Tariffs and Trade (GATT) was signed at Geneva. The objective of the GATT was to increase trade flows between the countries of the world by tariff reduction. Under the GATT, Canada and the United States negotiated further tariff reductions. In 1953, President Eisenhower showed interest in a more comprehensive trade agreement, but the Canadian government was content with the GATT. But two accords merit our attention. In 1941, an agreement between Canada and the United States made free trade in defence equipment a virtual reality; and in 1965, the Auto Pact brought free trade between the two countries into the auto industry.

In 1985, then-President Ronald Reagan and then-Prime Minister Brian Mulroney met in Quebec City on March 17 (St. Patrick's Day). This so-called "Shamrock Summit" involv-

The most comprehensive trade agreement between Canada and the U.S. was signed in 1987.

ing the two leaders paved the way for a comprehensive trade agreement between Canada and the United States, which was signed in 1987. This Canada–U.S. trade agreement is by far the most important trade agreement that Canada has ever negotiated. Table 20.1 is a summary of the history of free trade between Canada and the United States.

TABLE 20.1

Summary of historical background of Canada-U.S. free trade, 1854–1987.

1854	Free-trade agreement signed between the United States and Britain.
1870–1890	Several abortive attempts made at free trade.
1911	Short-lived trade agreement reached between Canada and the U.S.
1935	Trade agreement reached. This was the beginning of significant tariff reductions on trade between the two countries.
1941	Free trade in defence equipment.
1947	The establishment of the GATT. Further tariff reductions negotiated.
1953	U.S. expressed interest in more comprehensive trade agreement; Canada preferred to stay with the GATT.
1965	The Auto Pact: free trade in the auto industry.
1985	Commitment to free trade at the Shamrock Summit.
1987	Comprehensive trade agreement signed.

THE GREAT 1988 DEBATE

The trade agreement between Canada and the United States, signed on October 4, 1987, produced one of the biggest debates in recent Canadian history. It was the main issue in the 1988 federal election. The liberals, led by John Turner, and the New Democratic Party, led by Ed Broadbent, opposed the trade deal. The Conservatives, on the other hand, led by Brian Mulroney, argued in favour of the deal. By returning the Conservatives to power, Canadian voters knew that they were accepting a free-trade arrangement with the United States.

The trade agreement between Canada and the United States is a rather complex document. We can, however, point out some of the possible consequences of such an arrangement.

POSSIBLE BENEFITS FOR CANADA

Increased income

The trade agreement could lead to increased income for Canada.

The removal of tariffs on goods flowing between Canada and the United States means that the tariff previously paid to the U.S. government by Canadian exporters now reverts to the Canadian producers and ultimately to Canadian factor owners. Thus domestic income is likely to increase.

Economies of scale

It could lead to economies of scale.

The trade agreement with the United States will likely benefit Canadian manufacturers who are able to take advantage of economies of scale. To help you to understand this point, let us assume that tariffs are imposed on goods flowing between the two countries. Consider a small Canadian firm producing a relatively small quantity of some product for a small domestic market. Because of the small size of the market, the Canadian producer operates at a relatively high average cost. On the other hand, an American firm producing a similar product for a much larger U.S. market operates at a much lower average cost. The Canadian producer will find it extremely difficult, if not impossible, to compete with the American producer in the U.S. market. The U.S. firm, however, may be able to compete in the Canadian market because its lower unit cost may more than offset the Canadian tariff. The elimination of tariffs between the two countries will give the Canadian firm easier access to the huge U.S. market, enabling it to take advantage of economies of scale, and compete effectively with the U.S. producer.

Lower-priced imports

The free-trade agreement will benefit Canadian consumers by reducing prices.

The removal of tariffs on imports into Canada from the United States will cause the prices of such imported goods to fall, resulting in an increase in the quantity of imported goods demanded. Canadian consumers will benefit as they replace high-cost (inefficient) domestic production with low-cost imports.

POSSIBLE COSTS TO CANADA

Unemployment

The free-trade agreement may cause unemployment in Canada.

One possible effect of the trade agreement between Canada and the United States is that American firms with subsidiaries established in Canada (to cater to the Canadian market without having to face high tariffs) will close the Canadian subsidiaries and concentrate production in the United States. This, of course, will result in the loss of many jobs in Canada. It may also be argued that the removal of tariffs on U.S. imports will make it impossible for Canadian firms to compete with low-cost imports from the United States. Canadian firms will be forced to close, thus causing unemployment. Another argument related to the unemployment issue is that with the trade agreement, Canadian industries will be forced to reorganize into larger firms to be able to compete with U.S. firms. This so-called "rationalization" of Canadian industries will be the cause of many lost jobs.

Loss of independence

The free-trade agreement could lead to a loss of independence.

Another possible effect of the Canada–U.S. trade agreement is greater reliance on the U.S. market. Once Canadian industries have adjusted to the new trade arrangements, many of our industries will be supplying the U.S. market, thus our industries will be heavily dependent on that market. Knowing that Canadian industries are so heavily dependent on the U.S. market, the United States could conceivably use this heavy reliance as a tool to influence decisions in Canada, even though such decisions may not be in the best interest of Canada. For example, the United States could threaten to dissolve the trade agreement in order to gain certain political concessions. Although there are good reasons for believing that the United States would not resort to this type of tactic, this possible loss of political independence is a cost that should not be ignored.

NORTH AMERICAN FREE TRADE AGREEMENT

Learning Objective 11:
views on the North American Free Trade Agreement

While the merits and drawbacks of the free-trade arrangement between Canada and the United States are still being debated, an even wider free-trade area including Mexico has been negotiated. A preliminary North American Free Trade Agreement (NAFTA) between Canada, the United States, and Mexico, reached in the summer of 1992, is now in effect. Supporters of NAFTA argue that such an agreement will open up new opportunities for Canadian firms to penetrate the huge Mexican market. Opponents of NAFTA, on the other hand, claim that free trade between Canada, the United States, and Mexico will be disastrous for Canada.

Two main arguments are presented in support of this pessimistic view. First, opponents claim that firms will relocate to Mexico, where the wage rate is substantially below the Canadian average and pollution standards are almost non-existent. This movement of firms out of Canada will result in a tremendous loss of jobs. Second, opponents of NAFTA argue that because of the huge wage discrepancy between Canada and Mexico, it will be virtually impossible for Canadian products to compete with products made with Mexican cheap labour. In reply to this last argument, supporters of free trade point out that Canada has a comparative advantage over Mexico in the production of many goods, and will therefore benefit from trade. As is usually the case in these matters, the truth probably lies somewhere between these two positions.

NAFTA has been in effect since January 1, 1994. The trade agreement between Canada, the United States, and Mexico calls for tariff reductions between the three countries. By the year 2009, 15 years after NAFTA came into effect, all tariffs between Canada, the United States, and Mexico will be eliminated. Is Canada benefiting from NAFTA? Will Canada benefit from NAFTA? Are some members of NAFTA benefiting at Canada's expense? There is still much debate on these issues. Some are extolling the virtues of NAFTA while others are condemning it.

In April 1998, the NAFTA Commission, in Paris at its fifth meeting, stressed the importance of NAFTA in promoting trade, investment, economic growth and jobs in the three member countries. The commission pointed out that since NAFTA came into effect, trade within North America has grown by nearly 65%. In 1993, trade between Canada, the United States, and Mexico was under U.S. $300 billion. By 1997, trade between the three countries had reached almost U.S. $500 billion. The commission hailed these figures as constituting a clear indication of NAFTA's success in its first four years of implementation. Could this be a case of the *post hoc, ergo propter hoc* fallacy? In addition, Sergio Marchi, the International Trade Minister, said in 1998 that NAFTA has been a tremendous benefit to Canadians of all walks of life. These are powerful claims.

These pronouncements notwithstanding, the Economic Policy Institute (EPI), a Washington-based think tank, has argued that NAFTA has been a failure and should be repealed or drastically revised. The EPI and other organizations including the Institute for Policy Studies, the International Labour Rights Fund, Public Citizen's Global Trade Watch, the Sierra Club, and the U.S. Business Industrial Council Educational Foundation, claimed that NAFTA has, among other things, displaced more than 400 000 jobs in the United States, eliminated more than 2 million jobs and caused the failure of more than 28 000 small businesses. And what damage has NAFTA done to Canada? Well, according to the CPI, NAFTA has increased unemployment in Canada and forced Canada to begin to dismantle its long-standing social safety net, resulting in falling standards of living for the average Canadian. If this is food for thought, perhaps it should be taken with a grain of salt.

CHAPTER SUMMARY

1. A tariff or import duty is a tax imposed on goods from foreign countries. A revenue tariff is designed mainly to raise revenue for the government, while a protective tariff is designed to protect domestic industries from foreign competition.

2. A specific tariff is stated as a given amount per unit of the imported item. An ad valorem tariff is a percentage of the value of the imported item. A compound tariff is a combination of a specific and an ad valorem tariff.

GLOBAL PERSPECTIVE

The European Union and the World Trade Organization

NAFTA is not an isolated case of a free trade agreement. Free-trade areas have been formed all over the world. For example, free-trade areas have been formed between groups of developing countries, and a free-trade area has been established between Australia and New Zealand. These agreements among nations to reduce or eliminate trade barriers between themselves are not limited to countries in close proximity. For example, a free-trade area has been established between the United States and Israel. Our concern here, however, is with two organizations — one regional (the European Union), the other global (the World Trade Organization) — whose objectives include the promotion of free trade and international cooperation.

The European Union (EU) is a group of 15 countries — Austria, Belgium, Denmark, Finland, France, Germany, Greece, Ireland, Italy, Luxembourg, The Netherlands, Portugal, Spain, Sweden, and the United Kingdom — that have agreed to form a trading bloc, and to create by this union a stable and predictable environment with the certainty that the rules of the game will not be changed by capricious government behaviour.

One of the main objectives of the EU is to promote free trade. With a population of 370 million, the EU is indeed a force to be reckoned with. It accounts for one-fifth of the total global trade in goods. The EU is much more tightly integrated than NAFTA. It has its own flag, its own anthem, its own 626-member parliament, its own budget, and a single currency. Thus, the EU is more than a free-trade area. It is a political entity.

A look at some statistics might help to place the EU in some perspective. The 15 member countries cover a total area of 1 249 000 square miles. The GDP of the EU is U.S. $8093.4 billion, and it has an unemployment rate of 10.7%. It exports 9.1% of its GDP (the value of all goods and services produced), and its imports account for 9.4% of its GDP. It is interesting to note that the EU and the United States, though economic competitors, have agreed on a plan to promote cooperation, partnership and joint action in areas ranging from trade liberalization to security. They have agreed to contribute to the expansion of world trade and closer economic relations.

The World Trade Organization (WTO), with its headquarters in Geneva, Switzerland, was established on January 1, 1995, following the Uruguay Round of negotiations (1986-94). The WTO was preceded by the General Agreement on Tariffs and Trade (GATT), which is now part of the WTO agreements. Whereas the GATT was established as a *provisional* body, the WTO is a permanent organization with the same legal foundation and legitimate status as the International Monetary Fund (IMF). The GATT dealt only with trade in goods, but the WTO deals with trade in goods and services, and with issues such as copyright, trademarks, and patents — the so-called intellectual property.

The WTO consists of 132 countries and its secretariat employs a staff of 500. The functions of the WTO include administering WTO trade agreements, providing a forum for trade negotiations, handling trade disputes among member countries, monitoring national trade policies to ensure that they do not violate the terms of the WTO agreements, providing technical assistance and training for developing countries, and cooperation with other international organizations. The work of the WTO is conducted by its committees and councils.

3. Economic arguments in favour of tariffs include the infant industry argument, the employment argument, the terms of trade argument, and the diversification and industrialization argument. The main anti-tariff argument is that tariffs interfere with the operation of the principle of comparative advantage.

4. Other devices (besides tariffs) used to control trade flows include import quotas, export subsidies, and voluntary restrictions. Import quotas are often more restrictive than tariffs.

5. Economic integration is an agreement between two or more countries to abolish certain discriminatory practices among them.

6. Economic integration may take the form of a free-trade area, a customs union, a common market, an economic union, or complete economic integration.

7. An economic integration that causes a participating country to shift from high-cost domestic production to lower-cost production results in trade creation.

8. An economic integration that causes a shift from the lowest-cost external producer to a higher-cost member producer results in trade diversion.

9. Economic integration is beneficial because it improves the terms of trade of the integrated group. Other advantages of economic integration include increased competition, technological change, and investment.

10. A sovereign Quebec with no economic association with the rest of Canada would result in tariffs between the two countries. These tariffs could result in a lower standard of living in both countries.

11. An economic union between Canada and a sovereign Quebec would face the problem of agreeing how to distribute benefits and costs resulting from the union.

12. Possible benefits to Canada from the Canada–U.S. trade agreement include increased income, gains from economies of scale, and lower-priced imports. Possible costs include unemployment and loss of independence.

13. The North American Free Trade Agreement brings certain benefits to Canada, but there are some costs as well.

TERMS FOR REVIEW

tariff or import duty (336)
revenue tariff (336)
protective tariff (336)
specific tariff (337)
ad valorem tariff (337)
compound tariff (337)
infant industry argument (337)
terms of trade (338)
optimum tariff (339)
import quota (341)

export subsidies (341)
economic integration (342)
economic cooperation (342)
free-trade area (342)
tariff evasion (342)
customs union (343)
common market (343)
economic union (344)
trade creation (344)
trade diversion (344)

QUESTIONS FOR REVIEW AND DISCUSSION

1. What is the difference between a revenue tariff and a protective tariff? What kind of tariffs does Canada usually impose? (L.O.2)

2. Name some techniques used by Canada to restrict its imports. Do these restrictions benefit Canadian industries? If so, how? (L.O.1,7)

3. List the main features of the infant industry argument in favour of tariffs. Is there a problem with this argument? If so, what is it? (L.O.4)

4. State the employment argument in favour of tariffs. Is it a valid argument? Discuss. (L.O.4)

5. What is meant by terms of trade? Does an improvement in a country's terms of trade necessarily result in an improvement in the country's economic well-being? (L.O.6)

6. List the arguments against restricting trade through tariffs. (L.O.5)

7. Compare tariffs and quotas as restrictive devices. (L.O.7)

8. What is the difference between economic integration and economic cooperation? (L.O.8)

9. List the major forms of economic integration. (L.O.8)

10. Briefly explain how tariff evasion may occur by the formation of a free-trade area. (L.O.8)

11. What problems are likely to result from a customs union arrangement? (L.O.8)

12. Name some advantages of economic integration. (L.O.8)

13. What is the difference between trade creation and trade diversion? (L.O.8)

14. We often hear that if Quebec secedes from Canada, a large-scale exodus of firms from Quebec will result. Do you agree? Why or why not? (L.O.9)

15. "The secession of Quebec from Canada, with no economic association with Canada, is likely to result in lower living standards in both Canada and Quebec." Discuss. (L.O.9)

16. Provide a historical background to the Canada–U.S. free-trade agreement. (L.O.10)

17. What are the possible benefits to Canada from the trade agreement with the United States? (L.O.10)

18. What are the possible costs to Canada from the Canada–U.S. trade agreement? (L.O.10)

19. Discuss the benefits and costs to Canada of NAFTA. (L.O.11)

PROBLEMS AND EXERCISES

1. Do you support a gradual elimination of the tariff on shoes imported into Canada? Why or why not? (L.O.1,4,5)

2. Let us suppose that Canada and the United States agree to trade freely in all goods. Let us suppose also that Quebec decides to opt out of the free-trade agreement. Explain how a Quebec importer can import goods from the United States and thus avoid the tariff. (L.O.8)

3. You are a low-cost producer of forestry products in British Columbia. Do you favour free trade with the United States? (L.O.10)

4. Why would many Canadian producers favour import quotas over tariffs? (L.O.7)

5. Table 20.2 contains data on the various quantities of picture frames demanded (Q_d) in Canada at various prices. The various quantities supplied by Canadian producers ($Q_s c$) and by foreign producers ($Q_s f$) are also shown. (General)

TABLE 20.2	Price ($)	Q_d	$Q_s c$	$Q_s f$	Q_s	$Q_{st} f$	Q_{st}
Demand and supply for picture frames.	10.00	800	1150	650			
	9.60	900	1100	600			
	9.20	1000	1050	550			
	8.80	1100	1000	500			
	8.40	1200	950	450			
	8.00	1300	900	400			
	7.60	1400	850	350			
	7.20	1500	800	300			
	6.80	1600	750	250			
	6.40	1700	700	200			
	6.00	1800	650	150			

(a) Fill in the total quantity supplied (Q_s) column.

(b) At what price would the market be in equilibrium?

(c) What quantity would be exchanged at that price?

(d) Given a tariff imposed by Canada of $1.20 per frame, compute the new quantities that would be supplied by foreign producers after the tariff ($Q_{st}f$). Then fill in the ($Q_{st}f$) column.

(e) Fill in the column showing the total quantity supplied after the tariff (Q_{st}).

(f) Estimate the new equilibrium price and the new equilibrium quantity.

 6. "When we buy from others, we send money out of the country. When we buy from ourselves, the money stays in the country. By extension, when province A buys from another province, money leaves province A. Therefore, by eliminating interprovincial trade in Canada, each province will keep its money and the entire country will be better off." Discuss.

Internet Site

http://europa.eu.int
This is a good starting place for general information on the European Union. The site explains the mission and operation of the European Union.

http://www.wto.org
This is the Web site for the World Trade Organization. Information on the WTO can be obtained here.

INTERNET EXERCISE

1. Go to **http://www.eurunion.org.**

2. Click on *Information Resources* .

3. Click on *General information about the EU.*

4. Click on *Facts and Figures on the EU and the U.S.*

5. Compare the EU with the U.S. in terms of:

   a) Area (sq. miles);

   b) Population;

   c) Unemployment;

   d) GDP;

   e) Trade (imports and exports) as a percentage of GDP.

VIDEO CASE

Environmental Threat to Salmon

How far must suffering and misery go before we see that even in the day of vast cities and powerful machines, the good earth is our mother and that if we destroy her, we destroy ourselves.

(Paul Bingelow Sears)

Introduction

The market mechanism does many things well, but it does not do all things well; the forces of demand and supply don't take care of everything. A serious problem that our price system does not take care of is pollution. After many years of trying to cope with this mammoth environmental problem, we are still faced with many and varied forms of pollution. Four years ago, it was reported that some of our rivers and lakes were polluted to the extent that they could no longer sustain life. Environment Canada reported that many lakes and rivers in Ontario and Nova Scotia could no longer support salmon fry or trout. Pollution was threatening the salmon industry.

International conflict

Canada and the United States have generally enjoyed a relatively peaceful coexistence, however some issues have caused conflict between the two normally friendly neighbours. The Canadian-American Pacific Salmon Conflict is one such issue.

At the heart of the conflict is each country's contention that the other is intercepting too many of its fish, with disastrous economic and environmental consequences — reduced revenue and overfishing that will seriously deplete fish stocks. The annual catch of Pacific salmon is valued at $300 million. In 1985, the Pacific Salmon Treaty was signed by Canada and the United States, with the intent of equity in sharing the catch, while conserving dwindling stocks. Each country would limit its catch on the basis of estimates of how many salmon originate in its rivers. Negotiations have failed to establish agreeable limits however, and since 1993,

each country has attempted to establish its own limits.

In 1997, Canadians accused Americans of catching five to six million more salmon annually than they were entitled to. On the other hand, Americans have accused Canadians of overfishing salmon headed for rivers in Washington and Oregon states. The conflict is clearly not one that can be easily resolved.

An equally serious problem

A problem as serious as the Canada-United States Pacific salmon conflict is the shortage of salmon from British Columbia. The problem of overfishing mentioned earlier is compounded by the destruction of salmon habitat due to pollution, particularly from an old copper mine that has poisoned a British Columbian salmon lake. If that type of pollution continues, the conflict over who is catching whose fish will be a moot point, because there will be no salmon to catch. The situation is critical, and the governments on both sides must take decisive action to end the pollution of our waters and the destruction of salmon and other habitat.

QUESTIONS

1. Itemize the main points in this case.

2. In what sense would you consider the issue raised in this case a matter of market failure?

3. Canada and the United States agreed to limit their catch of salmon by negotiating quotas based on estimates of how many salmon originate in each country's rivers. What problem or problems do you see arising out of this agreement?

4. Paint a word picture of the seriousness of the Pacific salmon issue discussed in this case.

Video Resource: "Salmon Pak," *National Magazine* (June 1998).

APPENDIX I: STATISTICAL TABLES

		TABLE S1						

CANADA'S GDP BY EXPENDITURE — Current (nominal) $million

Year	Consumption	Investment	Government purchases	Exports	Imports	Statistical discrepancy	GDP	Percentage Change
1952	15 282	5 823	3 620	5 373	4 862	−66	25 170	13.0
1953	16 296	6 583	3 824	5 174	5 311	−171	26 395	4.9
1954	17 078	5 773	3 825	4 944	5 023	−66	26 531	0.5
1955	18 543	7 047	4 036	5 536	5 804	−108	29 250	10.2
1956	20 273	9 379	4 426	6 141	7 007	−310	32 902	12.5
1957	21 699	9 228	4 573	6 158	6 996	−195	34 467	4.8
1958	23 064	8 584	4 854	6 072	6 558	−327	35 689	3.5
1959	24 643	9 421	4 976	6 403	7 168	−398	37 877	6.1
1960	25 780	9 253	5 281	6 728	7 222	−372	39 448	4.1
1961	26 240	8 870	6 166	7 296	7 450	−236	40 886	3.6
1962	27 985	9 928	6 567	7 939	7 977	−34	44 408	8.6
1963	29 846	10 673	6 923	8 748	8 398	−114	47 678	7.4
1964	32 042	12 260	7 526	10 067	9 565	−139	52 191	9.5
1965	34 714	14 960	8 269	10 719	10 832	−307	57 523	10.2
1966	37 952	17 200	9 643	12 564	12 584	−387	64 388	11.9
1967	41 068	16 453	11 092	14 161	13 461	−249	69 064	7.3
1968	44 842	17 229	12 685	16 166	15 186	−318	75 418	9.2
1969	49 093	19 621	14 186	17 844	17 705	−13	83 026	10.1
1970	51 853	19 250	16 448	20 078	17 830	−683	89 116	7.3
1971	56 271	21 941	18 228	21 173	19 531	−792	97 290	9.2
1972	63 021	24 660	20 136	23 737	22 779	−146	108 629	11.7
1973	72 069	30 722	22 851	29 767	28 024	−13	127 372	17.3
1974	84 231	39 372	27 480	37 805	37 366	590	152 111	19.4
1975	97 566	43 213	33 266	38 954	41 362	−97	171 540	12.8
1976	111 500	49 037	38 274	44 252	45 279	140	197 924	15.4
1977	123 555	52 090	43 411	51 183	51 252	−1 108	217 879	10.1
1978	137 427	55 632	47 386	61 152	60 052	59	241 604	10.9
1979	153 390	68 428	52 288	75 073	73 279	198	276 096	14.3
1980	172 416	72 624	59 250	87 579	81 933	−45	309 891	12.2
1981	196 191	87 305	68 792	96 880	93 001	−173	355 994	14.9
1982	210 509	71 574	78 655	96 651	82 598	−349	374 442	5.2
1983	231 452	78 329	84 571	103 444	89 832	−2 247	405 717	8.4
1984	251 645	89 460	89 089	126 035	110 632	−862	444 735	9.6
1985	274 503	96 479	95 519	134 919	123 388	−44	477 988	7.5
1986	297 478	104 117	100 129	138 119	133 369	−808	505 666	5.8
1987	322 769	119 788	105 836	145 416	140 502	−1 710	551 597	9.1
1988	349 937	136 585	114 472	159 309	156 384	1 987	605 906	9.8
1989	378 933	149 682	124 108	163 903	166 079	201	650 748	7.4
1990	399 319	138 541	135 157	168 917	171 223	−1 244	669 467	2.9
1991	411 960	128 766	144 885	164 849	172 805	−1 178	676 477	1.0
1992	422 515	125 164	150 390	181 189	187 254	−1 882	690 122	2.0
1993	436 542	129 987	152 158	209 370	212 534	−2 668	712 855	3.3
1994	452 859	142 014	150 758	249 371	243 756	−1 193	750 053	5.2
1995	466 313	144 452	150 158	288 543	269 223	−216	780 027	4.0
1996	477 927	142 223	168 965	320 739	289 319	−210	820 323	2.7
1997	505 896	165 822	168 459	343 536	329 193	583	855 103	4.2

TABLE S2

CANADA'S GDP BY EXPENDITURE — Constant (real) 1986 $million to 1960, and (real) 1992 $million since 1961

Year	Consump-tion	Invest-ment	Government purchases	Exports	Imports	Statistical discrepancy	GDP	Percentage Change
1952	66 842	21 274	30 676	20 140	17 650	−317	118 627	8.3
1953	71 420	24 295	31 610	19 873	19 247	−860	124 526	5.0
1954	73 994	21 823	30 378	19 166	18 140	−311	123 163	−1.1
1955	80 277	25 815	31 045	20 607	20 652	−519	134 889	9.5
1956	86 413	31 886	31 774	22 259	24 115	−1 471	146 523	8.6
1957	89 538	31 486	31 261	22 445	23 396	−915	150 179	2.5
1958	92 779	29 924	32 205	22 248	21 578	−1 518	153 439	2.2
1959	97 943	31 771	31 931	23 086	23 795	−1 811	159 484	3.9
1960	101 455	31 276	32 703	24 114	23 738	−1 673	164 126	2.9
1961	134 009	31 628	36 968	27 532	23 931	−485	220 816	3.1
1962	140 860	34 601	53 923	28 775	24 460	264	235 900	6.8
1963	146 731	36 031	55 760	31 347	24 874	−232	247 944	5.1
1964	154 507	39 707	58 702	35 648	28 038	−496	264 174	6.5
1965	163 548	46 215	61 356	37 253	31 820	−604	281 249	6.5
1966	171 654	50 722	66 789	42 333	36 099	−1 154	299 689	6.6
1967	178 057	47 540	72 649	46 762	38 070	−550	308 639	3.0
1968	185 983	49 407	77 397	52 736	42 014	−383	325 147	5.3
1969	195 023	54 079	80 760	56 984	47 446	906	342 468	5.3
1970	198 364	50 644	87 850	62 317	46 595	−1 845	351 434	2.6
1971	210 322	54 953	91 485	65 349	49 957	−2 325	370 859	5.5
1972	224 819	58 097	94 346	70 971	57 145	49	390 702	5.4
1973	240 443	65 584	98 782	78 534	65 509	1 073	418 797	7.2
1974	252 874	73 293	105 059	76 487	72 716	3 009	436 151	4.1
1975	263 377	71 541	112 092	71 547	71 168	1 758	445 813	2.2
1976	277 572	76 452	114 247	79 193	76 830	2 340	470 291	5.5
1977	285 897	76 552	119 590	85 363	77 599	−902	486 562	3.5
1978	295 598	78 027	121 700	94 616	82 016	426	506 413	4.1
1979	303 855	90 386	122 979	98 092	88 772	540	527 703	4.2
1980	309 935	90 197	127 172	99 897	93 296	1 442	535 007	1.4
1981	314 720	103 137	129 157	103 568	103 147	2 481	551 305	3.0
1982	306 931	78 790	131 901	102 305	86 865	1 108	535 113	−2.9
1983	315 693	87 266	134 119	108 822	96 247	−1 154	549 843	2.8
1984	329 926	96 598	135 654	129 078	113 709	−997	581 038	5.7
1985	346 955	106 433	141 501	136 229	123 759	123	612 416	5.4
1986	360 738	110 329	144 166	143 359	134 335	−709	628 575	2.6
1987	375 678	122 040	146 180	148 093	141 920	−1 546	654 360	4.1
1988	392 093	133 110	152 897	162 162	161 382	2 036	686 176	4.9
1989	406 034	142 813	157 195	164 103	171 580	479	703 577	2.5
1990	411 343	131 466	162 937	171 977	175 482	52	705 464	0.3
1991	405 783	122 876	167 541	175 926	181 120	11	692 247	−1.9
1992	412 940	120 483	169 262	189 784	192 393	−1 532	698 544	0.9
1993	420 595	123 857	168 864	212 603	208 046	−1 750	716 123	2.5
1994	433 812	135 045	165 888	237 684	227 054	−1 155	744 220	3.9
1995	441 263	135 860	165 244	259 695	242 306	553	760 309	2.2
1996	451 682	135 534	163 164	274 456	254 908	−198	769 730	1.2
1997	470 177	156 877	162 988	296 534	288 933	540	798 183	3.7

TABLE S3

LABOUR FORCE STATISTICS

Year	Labour Force (000)	Employed (000)	Unemployed (000)	Unemployment rate (%)	Participation rate (%)
1978	11 265	10 320	945	8.4	63.1
1979	11 630	10 761	870	7.5	64.0
1980	11 983	11 082	900	7.5	64.6
1981	12 332	11 398	934	7.6	65.3
1982	12 398	11 035	1 363	11.0	64.7
1983	12 610	11 106	1 504	11.9	64.9
1984	12 853	11 402	1 450	11.3	65.3
1985	13 123	11 742	1 381	10.5	65.8
1986	13 378	12 095	1 283	9.6	66.3
1987	13 631	12 422	1 208	8.9	66.7
1988	13 900	12 819	1 082	7.8	67.2
1989	14 151	13 086	1 065	7.5	67.5
1990	14 329	13 165	1 164	8.1	67.3
1991	14 408	12 916	1 492	10.4	66.7
1992	14 482	12 842	1 640	11.3	65.9
1993	14 663	13 015	1 649	11.2	65.5
1994	14 832	13 292	1 541	10.4	65.3
1995	14 928	13 506	1 422	9.5	64.8
1996	15 145	13 676	1 469	9.7	64.9
1997	15 354	13 941	1 414	9.2	64.8

TABLE S4

MONEY SUPPLY — (Monetary Aggregates)

Year	M1 ($000 000)	M2 ($000 000)	M3 ($000 000)
1973	13 525	41 678	52 069
1974	14 788	50 386	65 377
1975	16 808	57 777	75 155
1976	18 157	65 574	89 154
1977	19 710	75 266	104 059
1978	21 848	84 469	119 534
1979	23 439	98 016	143 069
1980	25 092	116 535	166 908
1981	25 886	134 170	189 344
1982	25 848	146 317	197 844
1983	28 678	155 627	201 023
1984	29 772	164 244	207 295
1985	31 198	180 612	220 921
1986	33 187	198 450	238 040
1987	37 918	223 694	264 222
1988	39 941	242 779	287 154
1989	41 497	275 815	321 340
1990	41 188	306 450	354 668
1991	43 074	327 341	377 662
1992	45 444	339 379	396 935
1993	50 352	372 043	438 752
1994	56 181	379 977	457 258
1995	58 992	394 966	479 477
1996	65 511	407 149	506 554
1997	76 039	406 229	533 469

TABLE S5

INTEREST RATES, EXCHANGE RATES, AND PRICE INDEXES

Year	Interest rates Bank rate	Prime rate	Exchange rates $Cdn per $US	Price indexes (1992 = 100) GDP deflator	% Change	CPI
1961	3.06	5.60	1.013	24.2	0.8	23.9
1963	3.88	5.75	1.079	19.4	2.2	19.2
1964	4.04	5.75	1.079	19.9	2.8	19.6
1965	4.29	5.77	1.078	20.6	3.6	20.0
1966	5.17	6.00	1.077	21.7	5.0	20.8
1967	4.98	5.92	1.079	22.6	4.4	21.5
1968	6.79	6.92	1.077	23.5	3.7	22.4
1969	7.46	7.96	1.077	24.5	4.6	23.4
1970	7.13	8.17	1.044	25.7	4.8	24.2
1971	5.19	6.48	1.010	26.6	3.4	24.9
1972	4.75	6.00	0.991	28.2	6.0	26.1
1973	6.13	7.65	1.000	30.8	9.4	28.1
1974	8.50	10.75	0.978	35.4	14.7	31.1
1975	8.50	9.42	1.017	39.0	10.3	34.5
1976	9.29	10.04	0.986	42.6	9.2	37.1
1977	7.71	8.50	1.063	45.5	6.8	40.0
1978	8.98	9.69	1.141	48.5	6.6	43.6
1979	12.10	12.90	1.171	53.1	9.6	47.6
1980	12.89	14.25	1.169	58.9	10.9	52.4
1981	17.93	19.29	1.199	65.4	11.0	58.9
1982	13.96	15.81	1.234	71.0	8.5	65.3
1983	9.55	11.17	1.232	74.8	5.4	69.1
1984	11.31	12.06	1.295	77.3	3.4	72.1
1985	9.65	10.58	1.366	79.2	2.5	75.0
1986	9.21	10.52	1.389	81.4	2.8	78.1
1987	8.40	9.52	1.326	85.3	4.8	81.5
1988	9.69	10.83	1.231	89.2	4.5	84.8
1989	12.29	13.33	1.184	93.3	4.6	89.0
1990	13.05	14.06	1.167	96.1	3.1	93.3
1991	9.03	9.94	1.146	98.7	2.7	98.5
1992	6.78	7.48	1.209	100.0	1.3	100.0
1993	5.09	5.94	1.290	101.2	1.2	101.8
1994	5.77	6.88	1.366	102.4	1.2	102.0
1995	7.31	8.65	1.372	105.1	2.6	104.2
1996	4.53	6.06	1.364	106.6	1.4	105.9
1997	3.52	4.96	1.385	107.1	0.5	107.6

? APPENDIX II:
SOLUTIONS TO PROBLEM SOLVING EXERCISES

1-1 Solution: There are probably a few people in the world who can have anything they want. It is tempting to think that scarcity (lack of resources) is not a problem for such people. But as soon as we consider time as a resource, then it becomes quite obvious that they have to decide whether to spend an afternoon shopping in Paris, or entertaining friends. Every individual is subject to the problem of scarcity.

1-2 Solution: Although economics is not fundamentally a vocational subject, it help us to solve a great number of problems that affect us personally. Moreover, economics help us to develop the skill of logical thinking which is useful in many real-life situations. Many people are concerned with basic economic issues such as, Will I be able to find a job after graduation from school? Will I be able to repay my student loan? Will I be able to finance my car if interest rates rise? What is the opportunity cost of going to college or university? Economics, therefore, is of great practical value.

1-3 Solution: There is a fair amount of disagreement among economists, but there is also considerable agreement among them. In fact, there is much more agreement than disagreement on the positive aspects of economics. But economists, like ordinary human beings, do have different values and opinions on many issues. It is natural, therefore, that they would disagree on normative issues.

Note: Disagreement within any field of inquiry is not a measure of the extent to which it is "scientific." After all, physicists and chemists do sometimes disagree among themselves. For example, there has been disagreement recently about the future of nuclear fusion.

1-4 Solution: In this model, the endogenous variables are consumption, income, and the rate of interest. These variables will be determined within the model. The exogenous variables, i.e., the "givens" of the model, are wealth and income distribution. The values of these variables are predetermined.

1-5 Solution: Economists are well aware that other things are not equal, but without that assumption, it would be extremely difficult to isolate the effect of one variable on another. The assumption greatly simplifies the thinking process.

2-1 Solution:
1. $g = g(h)$
2. $H = H(a)$
3. $M = M(Y)$
4. $S = S(r,Y)$

2-2 Solution:

FIGURE 2.A

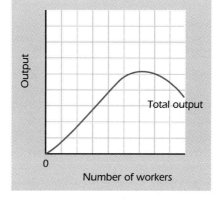

2-3 Solution: We can put interest rates on the vertical axis and the amount of loans on the horizontal axis. Since these two variables move in opposite directions, the resulting curve will be downward sloping as shown in Figure 2.B

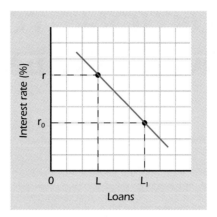

FIGURE 2.B

Relation between the rate of interest and the amount of money borrowed.

As the rate of interest falls from r to r_0, the amount of money borrowed rises from L to L_1.

3-1 Solution: Whether or not a car is a capital good depends on the purpose for which the car is used. If the car is for personal use, it is not a capital good but a consumer good. If, however, it is used as a taxi, or as a delivery vehicle for a firm, then it is a capital good.

3-2 Solution: There is no income the source of which is not a resource. On the surface, it may appear that government welfare payments do not originate from resources. However, upon careful reflection, we find that tax dollars pay for welfare programs, and that those tax dollars are derived from some kind of income whose source is either land, labour, capital, or entrepreneurial services.

3-3 Solution: 1. The opportunity cost of watching the hockey game is probably a better score on the test. The opportunity cost of studying for the economics test is the thrill of seeing Gretzky and company do battle against the Canadiens. You have to evaluate each of these opportunity costs subjectively. If the opportunity cost of watching the game outweighs the opportunity cost of studying economics, then you should study for the test. If, on the other hand, the opportunity cost of studying for the test outweighs the opportunity cost of watching the game, then you should watch the hockey game.

3-3 Solution: 2. The production of anti-pollution equipment would cause resources to be diverted from other uses. The opportunity cost would be the goods and services that the economy could not produce because it decided to use some resources to produce anti-pollution equipment.

3-4 Solution: Since the carpenters were unemployed, output would not fall in any sector of the economy by hiring them. Regardless of what they are paid by Antigonish Construction, society does not make any sacrifice in terms of lost output or anything else. Thus the opportunity cost of employing the carpenters for a week is zero.

Note: If the carpenters were employed in pulp and paper at the time they were hired by Antigonish Construction, the opportunity cost would be the fall in output in pulp and paper resulting from transferring them from that industry.

3-5 Solution: A shift in the p-p curve implies a change in the economy's productive capacity. This will happen only if there is a change in technology or in resources. Since the computer programmers already existed, their employment does not affect the economy's productive capacity. Thus, the p-p curve would not shift.

Note: The presence of unemployed computer programmers represents unemployment of resources. This would be illustrated by a production possibility point below the p-p curve. The employment of the programmers would move the economy closer to the p-p curve but the curve would not shift.

3-6 Solution: If we accept the view that the main objective of business firms is to maximize profits, then businesses in Canada are likely to favour capitalism or free enterprise over other economic systems. Businesses would generally prefer government to leave them alone to pursue their own interests. They would tend to favour the system with the least amount of government involvement in the economy. This system is the free enterprise system.

3-7 Solution: We rely on the market mechanism. Authors know that students are willing to buy books, so they write books in the hope of finding publishers who are willing to publish them and pay royalties to the authors. The publishers, on the other hand, publish the books in the hope of making a profit in the process. Although there is no direct command to the authors or the publishers to produce books, they respond to market signals, which indicate to them that writing and publishing textbooks can be a profitable undertaking.

3-8 Solution: Education provides benefits not only to the recipient directly, but also to society. A better-educated population implies a better-educated labour force and a more productive economy. Hence, the entire society benefits and should help to defray the costs. This is done out of tax dollars.

4-1 Solution: It is obvious that a price of $5 is too high for Roisin to be able to sell her entire stock by the end of the day. By lowering her price, Roisin will be able to increase the quantity sold. She may even be able to sell her entire stock if she lowers the price sufficiently. Businesses use the same strategy to increase their sales. Think of designated "sales days" at department stores.

4-2 Solution: 1. Crayons and colouring books are complementary goods. The bookstore can charge a relatively low price for its crayons, because it can obtain them at a relatively low cost. Other things being equal, this will result in an increase in the quantity of crayons that will be bought. As people buy more crayons, however, they will also buy more colouring books since one is used in conjunction with the other.

4-2 Solution: 2. The fact that people buy more gold when the price rises does not refute the law of demand. The law states that less will be bought at higher prices than at lower prices, <u>other things being equal.</u> People may buy more gold when gold prices rise because they expect the price to rise even higher. If their expectations are correct, they make a capital gain. Their behaviour can be explained by changing expectations; other things are not equal.

4-3 Solution: An increase in the quantity of typewriters bought might be a response to falling prices of typewriters and not to an increase in the demand for typewriters. If that is the case, then Vinud would be making a mistake to think that the demand for typewriters was increasing. An increase in quantity demanded may not signify any increase in demand.

Note: Vinud found this out after he took his first course in economics.

4-4 Solution: An increase in wages in the shoe industry will increase the cost of producing shoes, and will therefore reduce the supply of shoes.

4-5 Solution: The following is a plausible explanation. As the price of gold rises, people buy less gold. They substitute silver for gold in their investment portfolios. This increase in demand for silver (an upward shift in the demand curve) results in an increase in the price of silver.

5-1 Solution: A price elasticity of demand of 2.8 means that a certain percentage increase in price causes quantity demanded to fall by 2.8 times the percentage increase in price. Since the increase in price is 15%, the quantity demanded falls by $2.8 \times 15 = 42\%$.

5-2 Solution: 1. When people are ill, medical attention becomes a necessity. Therefore, the demand for the services of medical doctors is likely to be inelastic.

2. The demand for toilet paper is likely to be inelastic for two main reasons. First, this product has no close substitutes. Second, the fraction of the budget spent on it is relatively small.

3. There are many substitutes for diamond necklaces. Moreover, many people would consider them to be luxuries. Therefore, the demand for diamond necklaces is likely to be elastic.

4. Telephone services are essential. A small change in price is unlikely to cause any significant change in the quantity demanded. In other words, the demand is inelastic.

5-3 Solution: 1. Since the income elasticity of demand for beef is 2.2, then an increase in income of 10% causes the demand for beef to increase by 22% (10 × 2.2). Beef farmers should therefore increase their production of beef by 22%.

5-3 Solution: 2. Because tea and coffee are substitutes, we know that an increase in the price of tea leads to an increase in the demand for coffee, other things being equal. Since the cross elasticity of demand between coffee and tea is 2.5, then a 6% increase in the price of tea causes the demand for coffee to rise by 6 × 2.5 = 15%.

5-4 Solution: Andrei has incurred a cost of $10 on each unit produced. His minimum acceptable profit is 10%. His reservation price is therefore $11. He will withdraw his glasses from the market unless the price is at least $11. For (a), (b), and (c), the market price is above his reservation price, so he will sell. But a market price of $10 is below his reservation price, so he will withdraw his product from the market.

6-1 Solution: Provided that the marginal utility is positive, additional Cherry Coke consumption will increase your total satisfaction. This is so whether the marginal utility is increasing or decreasing. Since the marginal utility is positive after the third bottle is consumed, you should continue to drink Cherry Coke.

6-2 Solution: With $14, Yuki will now buy $6 worth of A and $8 worth of B in order to maximize her satisfaction. The marginal utility of the last dollar spent on each will be equal at 30.

7-1 Solution: In a partnership, each partner is fully liable, not only for debts resulting from his own actions, but also for those resulting from the actions of the other partners. If one lawyer in the firm bungles a case, it exposes the other lawyers as well to any unfavourable consequences. This is a sort of safety net that ensures that each lawyer in the firm will do his or her best to see that the best decisions are made. It provides an incentive for consultation among the lawyers, which is definitely a great advantage to the firm's clients.

7-2 Solution: 1. The most effective form of business organization, from the capital-raising perspective, is the corporation. The corporation provides limited liability to its shareholders. Potential investors who are unwilling to invest in an enterprise that does not have limited liabilty can safely do so in a corporation. Should the business go bankrupt, the personal assets of the investors are protected. Therefore, Hitchcock, James, and Chill Filmmakers might be able to raise sufficient capital to expand their operation if they were to form a corporation.

7-2 Solution: 2. The profits of a corporation are taxed twice: first as corporation income and again as dividend income paid out to shareholders. Thus, governments generally favour the formation of corporations. But a government may lose this tax revenue advantage since the maximum tax rate on corporate profits is lower than that on income from other forms of business organizations. The one source of taxation must be weighed.

7-3 Solution: Under the circumstances, it appears that a single proprietorship is the most appropriate form of organization for this business. The organization of a sole proprietorship entails no legal red tape and is relatively inexpensive. Once the experimental state is over and the idea proves to be good, then some other form of business organization should be considered.

7-4 Solution: Labour costs are an important factor in the decision regarding the location or the establishment of firms. Other things being equal, firms will tend to locate in areas where labour costs are lowest. Industries that use a large quantity of workers who are paid minimum wages will tend to shy away from the province with the highest minimum wage, provided that other factors do not outweigh the labour cost factor.

8-1 Solution: A firm seeking to maximize its profits will be cost conscious. It will tend to hire workers on the basis of their ability to contribute to the output of the firm, and not on the basis of sex or race. In fact, to the extent that workers of a certain sex or race (for example, women and blacks) are skilled and relatively inexpensive, the profit motive dictates that they will be hired in preference to more expensive groups. Discrimination in hiring will not be in the best interest of the firm seeking to maximize its profits.

8-2 Solution: The choice between methods 1 and 2 will be made on the basis of their relative economic efficiency. Using method 1, the value of the inputs is $(10 \times \$5) + (6 \times \$6) = \$86$. The value of the output is $(24 \times \$10) = \$240$. Therefore, the economic efficiency ratio is $240/86 = 2.79$. Using method 2, the value of the inputs is $(15 \times \$5) + (2 \times \$6) = \$87$. The value of the output is $(25 \times \$10) = \$250$. Therefore, the economic efficiency ratio is $250/87 = 2.87$. Method 2 should be chosen, since it is more efficient.

9-1 Solution: Your total revenue is $2000. From this, you must deduct $50 for the advertisement, $550 for paint, brushes, etc. This leaves you with $1400. Is this all profit? Remember, you used your own car to get from one job to the next, so you must deduct something for gas, oil, and wear and tear — let's say $200. This still leaves you with $1200. To determine whether or not you have made a profit, you must estimate the opportunity cost of your time. If you could have earned more than $1200 elsewhere, you have actually incurred a loss. If you could have earned only $800 elsewhere, then you have made a profit of $400.

Note: This problem illustrates the importance of not neglecting implicit costs — in this case, depreciation, your time, and the income you could have made by leasing your car for the summer.

10-1 Solution: No. By definition, a purely competitive firm can sell as much as it can produce at the existing price. Advertising involves a cost. For the purely competitive firm, this cost does not result in any direct benefit to the firm incurring the cost. That being the case, a firm in a purely competitive industry will not advertise its product.

Note: While advertising by a purely competitive <u>firm</u> will not be beneficial to that firm, the <u>industry</u> as a whole may attempt to increase the demand for the product by advertising.

10-2 Solution: Provided that a firm is maximizing its profits, it must be equating its marginal revenue with its marginal cost. This is so whether the firm's manager knows it or not. The economic analyst can examine a firm's operations and advise the firm's managers on adjustments that it may make in order to increase its profits, but if the firm happens to attain the maximum profit position, then its marginal revenue will equal its marginal cost.

10-3 Solution: In certain circumstances, the firm may do better to operate at a loss, in the short run, than to cease operating. This is the case if the firm is in a position where the price of its product is below its average total cost but above its average variable cost. If the firm suspends its operation temporarily, it still has fixed costs but earns nothing to help to defray these costs. If it continues to operate, any earnings above its variable costs can be used to help to pay its fixed costs. If it seems that the firm will continue to incur losses in the long run, it should close its plant.

11-1 Solution: This is one of the popular misconceptions about the monopolistic firm. While the firm in a monopoly situation can manipulate market supply by virtue of being the only firm in the industry, remember that demand plays an important role in price determination. If the monopolistic firm decides to put a certain quantity on the market, the market demand will establish the price. If the monopolistic firm decides to charge a certain price, the quantity that it can sell at that price will be determined by the demand for its product. Except for the exceptional case where the demand for the product is perfectly inelastic, the monopolistic firm cannot charge <u>any</u> price and at the same time sell any quantity at that price. The statement is therefore false.

11-2 Solution: The notion that a monopolistic firm can always increase its profits by raising its price is utterly false. If the firm is charging a price that is less than that at which marginal revenue equals marginal cost, then an increase in price will raise its profits. If it is charging a price higher than that at which marginal revenue equals marginal cost, then an increase in price will reduce its profits. If the firm is charging a price consistent with the MR = MC condition for profit maximization, then any change in its price will result in lower — not higher — profits.

11-3 Solution: The monopolistic firm maximizes its profits when it produces at the point where marginal revenue equals marginal cost. If marginal cost equals zero, then the profit-maximizing monopolist will produce where marginal revenue equals zero. But when marginal revenue is zero, demand is unitary elastic. Hence, it is shown that if marginal cost equals zero, the monopolist will maximize profits by producing where the price elasticity of demand is one.

11-4 Solution: The general conclusion that pure competition results in a lower price and larger quantity than monopoly does is valid, provided that the monopolistic firm faces cost conditions similar to those confronting the purely competitive firm. However, if substantial economies of scale are present, then the general conclusion may no longer hold. A single firm in a purely competitive market may be quite incapable of taking advantage of economies of scale, while a firm in a monopolistic situation may have such a large output that its unit cost may be relatively low. In such a case, the price of the product may be lower in a monopolized market and output may be greater than in a purely competitive market.

12-1 Solution: A pharmacy is a good example of a firm that operates in a monopolistically competitive market structure. Prices could successfully be set slightly above those in other pharmacies if, by product differentiation, you were able to increase demand for your products. However, it would be unwise to charge significantly higher prices. After all, your products may be different, but not that different. And a significantly higher price will result in a significant reduction in your share of the market.

12-2 Solution: The installation of the air-conditioner by the competitor is an example of a type of non-price competition known as quality competition. Other things being equal, patrons will prefer to have coffee in an air-conditioned café. In order to avoid losing customers to your competitor, and perhaps to attract some of his customers to your café, you might try installing an air-conditioner in your café, cutting your price, or advertising.

12-3 Solution: On the surface, price cutting may appear to be a good strategy. But let us not be too hasty; let us analyze the situation. If you cut your prices, your competitors are likely to retaliate with price cuts of their own. They may even undercut your prices. Before you know it, you may be involved in a vicious price war. And what are the likely results? They are lower profits, lower prices, and hardly any change in market shares.

13-1 Solution: The institution of minimum wage laws is actually a type of price control, the price being the price of labour. To see how this type of price control may affect employment, let us study Figure 13.8. DD and SS are the demand and supply curves of labour respectively. The equilibrium wage rate is 0W, and at that wage rate, the number of workers employed is 0L. Now, suppose the government legislates a minimum wage of $0W_1$. Firms can no longer legally pay workers a wage rate of 0W. The quantity of labour demanded at $0W_1$ has fallen to $0L_0$, while the quantity supplied has risen to $0L_1$. A surplus of labour $(0L_1 - 0L_0 = L_0L_1)$ has resulted. Thus, the effect of the minimum wage law is to increase unemployment.

FIGURE 13.A

Effect of minimum wage on employment.

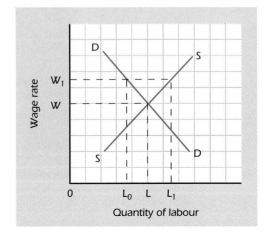

13-2 Solution: A closed shop, though obviously benefiting the union, may also benefit the employer. The closed shop serves as a central employment agency for the employer, from which a pool of workers can be drawn when required. Thus, a closed shop arrangement may reduce the cost to the employer of searching for an employee with the requisite skills. The employer may also benefit from greater industrial peace and harmony resulting from the fact that all of the employees are union members — a fact that will eliminate any conflict between union and non-union members.

13-3 Solution: Many strikes do result in a loss in total output as plants close, but not all strikes do. A strike in a certain factory at a certain time may mean simply that the factory has to work harder and longer at the end of the strike to compensate for the loss of production during the strike. In this case, the strike results in a shifting of the timing of production rather than in the volume of output.

13-4 Solution: If Canadian economists were subjected to a licensing procedure, we could expect some of them to fail the licensing requirements. The total supply of practising economists would therefore decline. Then, assuming no change in the demand for the services of economists, we could expect the average salaries of economists to increase.

Note: This would be a case of an association limiting the number of entrants into a profession and thus shifting the supply curve to the left.

14-1 Solution: The demand for land in the business section of the city is high relative to the demand for land in outlying areas. Consequently, the rental value of land in the downtown area is high relative to the rental value of land in outlying areas. To overcome problems of scarce space and hence high rent, we erect high-rise buildings. In the absence of high-rise buildings, we would have to use a considerable amount of land to obtain the space that is now provided by high-rise buildings. The cost would be astronomical. The abundance of high-rise buildings in many business districts results largely from the high rental value of land in those areas.

14-2 Solution: If Canadians were not such big savers, a smaller amount of loanable funds would be available at any given rate of interest. Figure 14.4 will help to explain how this would affect the rate of interest. D is the original demand curve and S is the original supply curve for loanable funds.

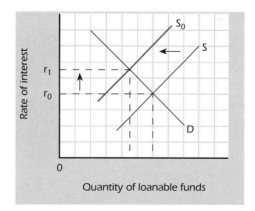

FIGURE 14.A

Demand for and supply of loanable funds

A fall in saving increases the rate of interest.

The corresponding equilibrium rate of interest is r_0. A smaller amount of saving by Canadians would cause the supply of loanable funds to fall, other things being equal. (The supply curve will shift from S to S_0.) This results in an increase in the rate of interest from r_0 to r_1.

14-3 Solution: On the surface, the answer to this question seems quite obvious. After all, if you borrow $100 for a year at a 4% interest rate, your interest cost is $4, while at an interest rate of 17%, your interest cost is $17. But let us not be too hasty to jump to any conclusions. Suppose the rate of inflation is only 1% when the rate of interest is 4%. The real interest cost is $3; and if the rate of inflation is 15% when the interest rate is 17%, then the real interest cost is only $2. Clearly, in some circumstances, it is more costly to borrow at 4% than at 17%.

14-4 Solution: A tax levied on the excess profits of a firm may cause the firm to forgo certain economic activities that could earn extra profits. The tax may also weaken the incentive to keep cost down. The firm may then engage in certain programs and projects that could not be justified were it not for the excess-profits tax. For example, excess-profits taxes have resulted in the increased padding of expense accounts.

15-1 Solution: If everyone in Canada were to receive the same income, regardless of contribution to the total output of goods and services in the economy, certain consequences could be expected. Many people have exerted themselves and have taken risks in the pursuit of an income above the average. If income were distributed equally, then the prospect of earning above-average incomes would disappear. Consequently, the incentive to take risks and to work hard would be greatly reduced. Total output would then fall. Additional reward in the form of income for extra effort is an important motivator for economic activity.

15-2 Solution: The prospects of young people finding worthwhile jobs in rural areas are quite limited. Also, for young people, city life is often more exciting than country life. Entertaining hopes of a more appropriate job and greater excitement, unattached individuals may migrate from the rural areas to the urban areas where they may end up being numbered among those living in poverty.

15-3 Solution: Most Canadians do not see poverty to the same extent as the statistics reveal because poverty in Canada is, to a significant degree, invisible; it is hidden. In many cases, the poor live in city slums, which we do not see from the highways and the subways. They also live in rural areas, which many of us hardly ever see. Moreover, many of the poor are old and infirm and remain indoors for much of the time. For all these reasons, the statistics on poverty seem more horrible than our everyday experiences would lead us to believe.

16-1 Solution: Pollution, in its various forms, imposes a cost on society. In the case of a pharmaceutical company that pollutes a river, the society is being robbed of a better environment, of the use of the river for recreational purposes, and of the fish population. All these are costs that we, as members of society, will be forced to bear whether we live upstream or not. Moreover, any tax dollars that may be used to clean up the river represent additional costs. These costs are sufficient reasons for us to concern ourselves about the pollution of the river by the company.

16-2 Solution: It is quite unlikely that an individual producer would voluntarily internalize all its costs. The objective of the producer is to maximize profits. If one producer internalizes all costs, then that producer voluntarily incurs a cost disadvantage vis-à-vis other producers. Thus, the producer's profitability relative to that of competitors would decline.

17-1 Solution: We have stated that the demand for farm products is price inelastic. Now, we know that the elasticity coefficient is 0.2. This means that a 10% fall in the prices of farm products results in only a 2% increase in the quantity of farm products demanded. In order to induce a 10% increase in consumer purchases of farm products, the prices of farm products would have to fall by 50%. Clearly, this is a colossal problem for farmers.

17-2 Solution: Let us examine the effect of each of these policies on consumers. Price supports result in higher prices for consumers. Market quotas result in both fewer farm products and higher unit prices. Subsidies, on the other hand, allow consumers to have more agricultural products at lower unit prices. Therefore, from the consumers' point of view, subsidies to farmers are better than either of the other two policies.

18-1 Solution: A significant portion of government spending is allocated to social service programs, including old age security payments. As the population ages, one expects expenditure for this function to increase. The Canada Pension Plan and the Quebec Pension Plan also provide benefits to persons who have reached the age of 65 years. In addition, expenditure on health services is likely to rise with an aging population.

18-2 Solution: The effect of increasing the tax rate depends on the effect of the higher tax rate on economic activity and hence on income. If the increase in the tax rate does not result in a corresponding decrease in economic activity and income, then tax revenues will increase. If, however, the increase in the tax rate acts as a disincentive to work, then total income may fall to the extent that the higher rate yields a lower — rather than a higher — tax revenue.

18-3 Solution: A tax imposed on a commodity will tend to reduce the quantity of that commodity that will be bought. If producers continue to produce the same quantity as they did before the imposition of the tax, they will notice that their stocks (inventories) will begin to pile up as consumers reduce their purchases of the commodity. In response to this situation, producers will reduce their level of production.

19-1 Solution: Canada is well endowed with fertile agricultural land. Japan, on the other hand, is well endowed with the kind of labour and technology that allows it to produce electronic items cheaply. Hence, we can reasonably expect Canada to export agricultural products to Japan and to import electronic items from Japan.

Note: This is not to suggest that Canada is mainly an agricultural country. Although we have a very strong agricultural sector, we are also well endowed with many high technology industries.

19-2 Solution: Newsprint is an output of the forest industry and Quebec is well endowed with forest resources. Also, the newsprint industry uses a lot of electricity, and Quebec is well endowed with electricity. Consequently, Quebec enjoys a cost advantage in the production of newsprint. We can therefore reasonably expect Quebec to export newsprint.

20-1 Solution: A gradual reduction and ultimate elimination of the tariff on shoes will lead to the importation of relatively inexpensive shoes. Canadian producers, in order to compete with foreign producers, will have to be more efficient and reduce their prices. This means that Canadian consumers will benefit from a reduction in the price of shoes. If Canadian producers cannot compete with foreign manufacturers in the shoe industry, then they will gradually shift resources out of the shoe industry into some other industry where they will be more efficient. This more efficient allocation of resources will also benefit Canadian consumers.

20-2 Solution: Quebec is well endowed with water, electricity, and forest resources. These resources are important inputs in paper production. Claude Depapier is likely to enjoy a comparative cost advantage in the production of paper. Free trade with the United States will extend Claude's market. He may also benefit from economies of scale. It seems to be in Claude's interest to support free trade between Canada and the United States.

GLOSSARY

A

Ability-to-pay principle: The idea that people should be taxed according to their ability to pay. The rich should pay more in taxes than the poor.

Absolute advantage: One country is said to have an absolute advantage over another country in the production of a commodity if it can produce the commodity with fewer resources than the other country can.

Absolute price: The monetary price of a good or service. The amount of money that must be spent to obtain one unit of a good or service.

Acceleration principle: The hypothesis that the level of investment is proportional to the rate of change of output (income).

Accelerationists: Economists who claim that attempts to keep unemployment below its natural level will simply accelerate inflation.

Actual output: The level of output actually produced by the economy.

Actual rate of inflation: The percentage rate at which the price level moves upward annually.

Ad valorem tariff: A tariff expressed as a fixed percentage of the value of the imported item.

Adaptive expectations: The hypothesis that people form their expectations solely on the basis of the experience of the recent past. For example, the expected rate of inflation for 1998 is based on the actual rate of inflation in 1997.

Administered price: A price that is controlled rather than determined exclusively by demand and supply.

Aggregate: Total.

Aggregate demand: The total amounts of all goods and services that will be bought at various price levels.

Aggregate demand curve: The curve showing the relation between the total amount of all goods and services that will be purchased and the price level.

Aggregate expenditure: Total spending in an economy, consisting of consumption spending, investment spending, government spending, and net exports.

Aggregate expenditure curve: The curve showing the relation between total spending and total income.

Aggregate output: A measure of the total production of all goods and services.

Aggregate supply: The levels of output supplied at various price levels.

Aggregate supply curve: The curve showing the relation between the total output of all goods and services that will be produced and the average level of prices.

Aggregation problem: The problem encountered in adding up individual units in order to arrive at a single total.

Air pollution: smog mainly due to burning fuels.

Allocative efficiency: A situation in which it is impossible to make someone better off without making someone else worse off by a change in production or consumption.

Appreciation (of exchange rate): A market determined increase in the value of a country's currency in terms of another country's currency.

Arbitrage dealing: Buying in a lower price market in order to resell in a higher price market.

Arbitration: A mechanism for settling disputes in the collective bargaining process whereby a decision is made by an independent person or persons.

Arc elasticity (of demand): A measure of elasticity for a segment of the demand curve.

Asset: Anything that is owned by an economic unit.

Assumptions: Statements about the conditions under which a model operates.

Automatic fiscal policy: Fiscal policy tools built into the system. They automatically help to stabilize the economy. Also called automatic (built-in) stabilizers.

Automatic stabilizers: Built-in measures that increase the budget surplus during inflationary periods and increase the budget deficit during periods of recession.

Automatic teller machines (ATMs): Machines that allow clients to make certain banking transactions without the aid of a bank teller/clerk.

Autonomous investment: Investment that is independent of any other variable.

Average cost (AC): Total cost divided by the number of units produced. Also known as average total cost (ATC) or unit cost.

Average cost pricing: A pricing strategy in which price and average cost are equated. Often used by regulatory agencies in regulating monopolies.

Average fixed cost (AFC): Total fixed cost divided by the number of units produced.

Average product (AP): Total product divided by the quantity of the variable factor employed.

Average propensity to consume (APC): The proportion of total income that goes into consumption. (APC = C/Y).

Average propensity to save (APS): The proportion of total income that is saved. (APS = S/Y).

Average revenue (AR): Total revenue divided by the number of units sold.

Average total cost (ATC): See average cost.

Average variable cost (AVC): Total variable cost divided by the number of units produced.

B

Backward-bending labour supply curve: Illustrates that higher wages may result in a decrease in the number of hours worked.

Bad money: Money whose face value is less than the value of the commodity from which it is made.

Balance of merchandise (visible) trade: Total goods exported minus total goods imported.

Balance of payments: A record of a country's economic transactions with the rest of the world.

Balance of trade: The difference between the value of a country's exports and the value of its imports.

Balance of trade deficit: The excess of imports over exports.

Balance of trade surplus: The excess of exports over imports.

Balance sheet: A statement of assets, liabilities, and owners' equity.

Balanced budget: A situation in which government spending equals tax receipts.

Balanced budget change in spending: A situation involving an equivalent change in government spending and taxes.

Balanced budget multiplier: The number which, when multiplied by the change in government spending, yields the change in equilibrium income when G = T.

Balanced budget theorem: The hypothesis that, in the simple Keynesian model, the balanced budget multiplier equals 1.

Bank Act: Federal legislation that governs the chartered banks.

Bank of Canada Act: Federal legislation enacted in 1934 to establish the Bank of Canada.

Bank rate: The rate of interest the central bank charges on loans to members of the Canadian Payments Association.

Banking system: The network of the central bank and chartered banks.

Barriers to entry: Obstacles preventing firms from entering an industry.

Barter: The direct exchange of goods and services for other goods and services (without the use of money).

Base year: A year chosen as a reference point when comparing price level changes from period to period. Current values are expressed as constant values with reference to a base year.

Basic economic problem: The scarcity of resources relative to wants.

Basic sectors of the economy: Household sector, producing sector, and government sector.

Beggar-thy-neighbour policy: A policy of trade protectionism that restricts the flow of imports.

Benefit principle (of taxation): The idea that people should be taxed in proportion to the benefits received from goods and services provided by the government.

Better measure of economic well-being (BMEW): GDP plus non-marketed goods and services plus under-the-table transactions minus environmental damage.

Black market: A market in which goods and services are sold illegally above the legal maximum price.

Bond: A written evidence of debt issued by a borrower, which pays interest to the lender for a specified period and the principal when the loan matures.

Boycott: An effort to persuade consumers not to purchase certain goods and/or services, or not to deal with certain firms.

Branch banking system: A banking system having few banks with many branches.

Break-even level of income: The level of income at which consumption equals income.

Break-even level of output: That output level at which the firm's total cost is equal to its total revenue.

Break-even point: The output level at which total revenue equals total cost; profits are 0.

Budget deficit: The excess of government spending over government revenue.

Budget deficit theory of inflation: Theory that government deficit spending causes inflation.

Budget philosophy: A general view concerning budget policies.

Budget surplus: The excess of government revenue over government spending.

Built-in stabilizers: See automatic fiscal policy.

Business cycles: Alternating periods of ups and downs in economic activity.

Business sector: See firm.

C

Caisse populaire: See credit union.

Canada Deposit Insurance Corporation (CDIC): Government agency that insures deposits in chartered banks, trust companies, and loan companies up to a maximum of $60 000 per depositor.

Canadian International Development Agency (CIDA): Government agency that dispenses foreign aid to less-developed countries.

Canadian Payments Association (CPA): An industry association that facilitates transfers between financial institutions.

Capital: The productive factor defined as all man-made means of production. It includes the stock of machinery, equipment, buildings, etc.

Capital account: The part of the balance of payments that contains long-term and short-term capital flows.

Capital consumption allowance: The allowance made for the depreciation of capital stock during production.

Capital flows: Movement of capital, usually between international economic entities.

Capital-output ratio: The ratio of the value of capital stock to the value of annual output.

Capitalism: An economic system characterized by free enterprise and which emphasizes private ownership of resources.

Cartel: An organization of firms whose objective is to act jointly to control price and output in the market for a particular product.

Cash reserve ratio: The ratio of a bank's cash to its deposits.

Central bank: An institution whose function is to act as banker to the commercial banks and the government, and to ensure the efficient working of the country's monetary system.

Central planning: The mechanism whereby decisions about what to produce, how to produce it, and for whom to produce are made by central authorities in a command economy.

Ceteris paribus: A Latin phrase meaning "other things being equal."

Chartered bank: A financial institution operating under federal charter. It accepts deposits, including those transferable by cheques, and makes loans and investments. Also called commercial bank.

Choice: The need to choose between one thing and another when the means to obtain both is not available.

Circular flow: The flow of income, resources, goods, and services between economic sectors.

Classical economics: The body of pre-Keynesian economic knowledge based on the assumption of flexible wages and prices, and leading to the conclusion of automatic full employment.

Classical range: The vertical range of an AS curve, in which output is at a maximum.

Clearing house system: The mechanism through which the net indebtedness between financial institutions is determined.

Closed economy: An economy that does not engage in foreign trade.

Closed shop: An arrangement in which jobs are given only to union members.

Coefficient of elasticity: The number derived from the calculation of the elasticity measure.

Coincidental indicators: Indicators that coincide exactly with the business cycle.

COLA clause: Cost-of-living-adjustment clause often found in labour agreements.

Collective bargaining: The process by which wages and other working conditions are negotiated between a union and an employer.

Collusion: An agreement among firms not to compete against one another.

Command economy: An economy in which economic decisions are made mainly by central authorities.

Commercial bank: See chartered bank.

Commodities: Goods and services that satisfy wants.

Common market: An arrangement between nations to allow the free movement of goods and factors between them.

Comparative advantage: If a country is more efficient than another country in the production of two commodities, but its efficiency is greater in the production of one commodity, then it has a comparative advantage in the production of that commodity.

Competitive capitalism: The free enterprise economic system.

Complementary goods: Goods that are consumed together. Examples are tennis racquets and tennis balls, and coffee and cream.

Compound tariff: A combination of specific and ad valorem tariffs.

Compulsory arbitration: An arrangement whereby the parties to a dispute are forced to submit their dispute to an arbitrator, whose decision is binding.

Concentration ratio: The proportion of the total market output produced by a few (usually four or eight) of the largest firms in an industry.

Conciliation: The process of submitting a dispute to a mediator for suggestions for settlement.

Constant: Anything that does not vary.

Constant-cost industry: Costs remain unchanged as the industry expands.

Constant prices: Values expressed in terms of the prices existing in a given (base) year.

Constant returns (to scale): A situation in which output increases in proportion to the increase in all inputs.

Consumer durables: Consumer goods intended to last for a long period of time (arbitrarily, more than a year).

Consumer price index (CPI): An index that measures the changes in the prices of consumer goods and services over time.

Consumer sovereignty: The notion that consumers have the power to decide, by their expenditures, what goods and services will be produced.

Consumer surplus: The difference between what consumers would be willing to pay and what they actually pay.

Consumption: The use (or purchase) of consumer goods and services to satisfy wants.

Consumption curve: A curve that illustrates a consumption schedule of current income and consumption.

Consumption function: The functional relation between consumption expenditure and its determinants. Often, a relation between consumption and income.

Consumption schedule: Relates total income and total consumption.

Consumption tax: Taxes on goods and/or services, such as sales tax and excise tax.

Contestable markets: Markets characterized by easy entry.

Contractionary fiscal policy: Any change in government spending and/or taxes designed to reduce total spending.

Cooperative: A special type of corporation in which benefits are distributed according to member patronage. Each member has only one vote, regardless of the number of shares owned.

Corporate income tax: A tax on the profits of corporations.

Corporation: A form of business organization that is a legal entity apart from its owners, and enjoys limited liability.

Correlation: A relationship between variables. Variables are correlated if they change together.

Cost function: The relation between cost and output.

Cost-push inflation: Inflation resulting from increases in wages and the cost of other factor inputs.

Cost-plus (mark-up) pricing: Price equals cost plus a percent mark-up.

Craft union: A union whose membership consists of workers in a single occupation. Also called trade union.

Credit union: A financial institution organized on the principle of the cooperative. Also called a caisse populaire.

Creeping inflation: inflation that creeps at a rate lower than 10%.

Cross elasticity of demand: A measure of the degree of responsiveness of the quantity of a commodity purchased to a change in the price of some other commodity.

Crowding-out effect: The concept that increases in government spending lead to a reduction in private sector spending.

Crown corporation: A corporation owned by the government.

Currency: The notes and coins which serve as a country's medium of exchange.

Current account: The section of the balance of payments that contains exports and imports of goods and services, investment income, and transfers.

Current account balance: Total current receipts from foreigners minus total current payments to foreigners.

Current GDP: Gross domestic product measured in current (as opposed to constant) dollars.

Current income hypothesis: The proposition that consumption depends on current income.

Customs union: An arrangement between nations to eliminate tariffs on goods traded between them, and to maintain a common tariff with the rest of the world.

Cyclical unemployment: Unemployment that results from cyclical fluctuations in economic activity.

D

Debentures: Bonds secured by the credit-worthiness of the borrower rather than by specific assets.

Debit (payment) cards: Similar to a credit card, except the money is transferred from the consumer's bank account to the merchant's account immediately.

Debt capital: Capital (funds) raised by selling bonds or by using bank credit.

Decision lag: The time that elapses from the recognition of a problem to the implementation of a policy to deal with the problem.

Decreasing returns (to scale): A situation in which output increases less than in proportion to the increase in all inputs.

Deficiency payments: A subsidy to farmers given at a certain amount per unit.

Deficit: Occurs when spending exceeds income.

Deficit financing: The methods used to finance a budget deficit.

Definitions: Identify the variables of the model so that measurement can be facilitated.

Deflationary gap: The amount by which aggregate expenditure falls short of aggregate output at full employment. Also called recessionary gap.

Demand: The various quantities of a good or service that people are willing to buy at various prices.

Demand curve: The curve showing the relation between price and quantity demanded.

Demand deposit: A bank deposit that can be withdrawn on demand and is transferable by cheque.

Demand-pull inflation: Inflation resulting from excess aggregate demand. Also called excess demand inflation.

Demand schedule: A table showing the relation between quantity demanded and price.

Demand shifters: Non-price determinants of quantity demanded that cause the demand curve to shift.

Dependent variable: The variable to be explained.

Deposit switching (drawdowns and redeposits): Switching of federal government deposits between the central bank and the chartered banks.

Depreciation (in national income accounting): The wear and tear of the capital stock during production. Also called capital consumption.

Depreciation (of exchange rate): A market-determined decrease in the value of a country's currency in terms of another country's currency.

Depression: A period characterized by low economic activity and high unemployment.

Derived demand: The demand for a productive factor that exists because of the demand for the output produced by the factor.

Devaluation (of exchange rate): The lowering of the value of a country's currency in terms of another country's currency.

Differentiated oligopoly: A market with few firms selling differentiated products.

Differentiated products: Products that are similar in many respects yet sufficiently different that the sellers are able to charge prices different from those charged by their competitors.

Diminishing marginal utility: The decrease in satisfaction experienced as additional units of a commodity are consumed.

Diminishing returns: A situation in which output increases less than the increase in the variable factor when at least one factor remains constant.

Direct demand: The demand for final goods and services as opposed to the demand for inputs.

Direct foreign investment: Investment in a foreign country that involves ownership or control of a firm.

Direct relation: The relation that exists between variables that increase or decrease together.

Dirty float: See managed flexible exchange rate.

Discomfort index: The rate of inflation plus the rate of unemployment.

Discouraged workers: Workers who have given up looking for work because they think there is none.

Discretionary fiscal policy: Deliberate changes in government spending and taxes in an effort to promote economic stability. **Diseconomies of scale:** A situation in which long-run cost rises as output increases.

Disposable income: After-tax income available to households to spend or save or both.

Dissaving: Negative saving. A situation where current consumption exceeds current income.

Dividends: Payments made to shareholders of corporations. The reward for capital.

Division of labour: A situation in which a task is broken up into a number of operations, each of which is performed by a different worker.

Double coincidence of wants: Required for successful bartering: each party wants what the other can provide.

Double counting: Counting an item more than once when calculating the GDP.

Drawdown: See deposit switching.

Dual economy: The coexistence of an advanced sector and an underdeveloped sector in the same economy. Found in many less-developed countries.

Dumping: The act of selling a good in the export market at a price below the domestic price.

Duopoly: An industry consisting of only two firms.

Durable good: A good that is intended to last for a long period of time (arbitrarily, more than a year).

E

EB curve: Curve showing equilibrium in the foreign exchange market.

Econometrics: The branch of economics that uses statistics to test economic theories.

Economic cooperation: An arrangement between two or more countries to reduce certain forms of trade discrimination among them.

Economic discrimination: A situation in which certain groups are treated differently in the labour market.

Economic efficiency: A situation in which the least costly method of production is attained.

Economic efficiency ratio: The value of output divided by the cost of the input.

Economic externality: The social costs or benefits of an economic decision.

Economic forecast: A statement giving specific values predicted for particular variables.

Economic growth: An increase in real per capita output.

Economic integration: An arrangement between two or more countries to abolish certain trade-discriminatory practices among them.

Economic policy: A course of action designed to achieve some economic objective.

Economic prediction: A conditional statement about the general direction of economic events or situations.

Economic profits: The difference between total revenue and the opportunity cost of the factor inputs.

Economic rent: A payment to a factor input in excess of what is required to supply the factor.

Economic system: A set of mechanisms by which a society accomplishes the task of producing goods and services to satisfy its wants.

Economic union: An arrangement between two or more countries to abolish restrictions on the free movement of goods and factor inputs and to harmonize economic policies.

Economies of scale: A situation in which long-run average cost decreases as output increases.

Economies of scope: Cost reduction derived from producing products together rather than producing each separately.

Economy: An entity within which production, consumption, and exchange take place.

Effluent charge (fee): A fee imposed on a producer for polluting the environment.

Elasticity: A measure of the degree of responsiveness of quantity to changes in some variable.

Electronic funds transfer system (EFTS): Transfers funds instantly between bank accounts.

Empirical: Descriptive; as in observed, measured, and recorded.

Endogenous variable: A variable whose value is determined within a model.

Engel's Law: As income rises, the percentage spent on food will diminish.

Entrepreneurship (entrepreneurial services): The services provided by the organizer of land, labour, and capital in the process of production.

Envelope curve: See long-run average cost curve.

Equalization payments: Transfer payments from the federal government to the provinces to reduce economic inequality among the provinces.

Equation of exchange: The quantity of money times the velocity at which it turns over is equal to the quantity of output produced times the average price per unit ($MV = PQ$, where M is the money supply, V is the velocity of circulation, P is price level, and Q is the quantity of output).

Equilibrium: A situation in which change is unlikely to occur. A state of balance.

Equilibrium income: Income is at its equilibrium level when aggregate expenditure equals aggregate output.

Equilibrium price: The price at which quantity demanded equals quantity supplied.

Equilibrium quantity: The quantity traded at the equilibrium price.

Equimarginal principle: Equates marginal values to maximize or minimize a variable.

Equity capital: Funds raised by selling stocks (shares).

Escalator clause: A stipulation in a labour contract that future wages and salaries will be adjusted to reflect changes in the price level.

Ex ante, ex post: Before the fact, after the fact.

Excess capacity theorem: The hypothesis that firms in monopolistic competition will have excess capacity when they are in equilibrium.

Excess demand inflation: See demand-pull inflation.

Excess quantity demanded: The amount by which quantity demanded, at a given price, exceeds quantity supplied at that price. Also called shortage.

Excess quantity supplied: The amount by which quantity supplied, at a given price, exceeds quantity demanded at that price. Also called surplus.

Excess reserves: Any reserves in excess of desired reserves.

Exchange rate: The value of a country's currency in terms of another country's currency.

Excise tax: A tax imposed on a specific commodity.

Exogenous variable: A variable whose value is determined by factors outside the model being considered, but which affects the variables in the model.

Expansion: The phase of the business cycle characterized by an increase in employment, income, and economic activity in general. Also called recovery.

Expansionary fiscal policy: Changes in government spending and taxes designed to increase total spending.

Expectational inflation: Inflation believed to be caused by the behaviour of buyers and sellers responding to expectations of inflation.

Expenditure approach: Measures the total amount spent on the total output.

Explicit costs: Payments to parties that are external to the producer. Examples are wages, rent, and utility bills.

Export subsidies: Assistance offered to exporters by the government to help them compete in world markets.

Exports: Goods and services sold to foreign countries.

External balance: Equilibrium in the foreign exchange market.

External debt: A debt owed to a foreign entity.

Externalities: Costs or benefits that accrue to persons not directly involved in the production or consumption of a commodity.

F

Factor market: A market in which factors of production are sold.

Factors of production: Resources used to produce goods and services.

Fallacy of composition: The assumption that what is true of the part is also true of the whole.

Featherbedding: Providing workers with unnecessary work in order to keep them on the payroll.

Federation (of unions): An association of national unions.

Fiat money: Legal tender money that is not backed by gold or any other precious metal.

Final products: Products intended for final use and not to be subjected to further processing.

Financial market: The market in which funds are lent and borrowed.

Fine tuning: Controlling some of the ups and downs of the economy by minor adjustments in government spending and/or taxes.

Firm: The economic unit within which production takes place. The firm buys inputs and converts them into output.

Fiscal drag: Automatic stabilization that prevents the economy from recovering from a recession.

Fiscal policy: Changes in government spending and taxes designed to promote economic stability.

Fixed costs: Costs that do not vary with the volume of output; they exist even when output is zero.

Fixed exchange rate: An exchange rate that is fixed by the government at some specified level.

Fixed factor: A factor of production whose quantity does not vary with the volume of output.

Flexible exchange rate: An exchange rate determined by market forces.

Flow variables: Income, consumption, and interest earned.

Fractional reserve banking system: A banking system in which banks are required to hold only a fraction of their deposit liabilities as cash reserves.

Franchise: An exclusive right given to a firm to provide a good or service in a certain area.

Free enterprise system: See capitalism.

Free good: A good that is so plentiful that even at a price of zero, the quantity available exceeds the quantity demanded.

Free trade: Trade between countries that is unimpeded by tariffs or other trade restrictions.

Free trade area: An arrangement between two or more countries to eliminate tariffs between them. Each member, however, maintains its own tariffs on goods from non-member countries.

Frictional unemployment: The unemployment of people who are between jobs or are new entrants into the labour market.

Full-employment budget: The position of the budget if the economy were at full employment.

Full-employment surplus: The difference between government revenues and expenditures at the full-employment level of income.

Function: The expression of a relation between two variables.

Functional distribution of income: Income distribution according to the ownership of the factors of production.

Functional finance: Using government spending and taxes as a tool of economic stability.

Functional notation: A mathematical tool that uses functions to show relations between variables.

Functional relationships: Cause-effect relationships among variables.

Fundamental psychological law: People increase consumption as their income increases, but by less than the increase in income.

G

Galloping inflation: Inflation that gallops at a rate between about 10% and 1000%.

GDP per capita: The GDP divided by the population.

General equilibrium analysis: A method of analysis that studies the effects of a variable in different markets.

Generalized multiplier: The multiplier that results from considering all withdrawals. It is the reciprocal of the marginal propensity to withdraw.

Gentlemen's agreement: Informal business agreement, often concluded with a handshake.

Geographical determinism: The theory that comparative advantage is determined by natural endowments.

Gini coefficient: A ratio that measures the degree of inequality in income distribution.

Good: Anything that is tangible and satisfies a want.

Good money: The face value of good money is equal to the value of the commodity it is made from.

Goods and Services Tax (GST): A consumption tax imposed on the final sale of goods and services.

Government sector: [definition to come—two lines left]

Government spending multiplier: The ratio of the change in income to the change in government spending that causes it.

Government transfer payments: Payments that do not represent payments for production.

Graph: A geometric (diagrammatic) representation of information.

Great Depression: A period in the 1930s during which many people were unemployed. Economists had to revise their thinking.

Greenhouse effect: Greenhouse gases maintaining the earth's temperature at comfortable levels.

Green revolution: The tremendous increases in agricultural yields.

Gresham's Law: The proposition that bad money will drive good money out of circulation.

Gross domestic product: The market value of all final goods and services produced within the borders of a country during a period of time.

Gross domestic product (GDP) deflator: The price index used to deflate the gross domestic product (to express current or nominal GDP as real GDP). Also called the implicit price deflator.

Gross investment: The total expenditure on investment goods. The sum of net investment and replacement investment.

Gross national product (GNP): The market value of all final goods and services produced by a country's nationals and their resources during a period of time.

Growth rate: The rate of change of a variable.

H

Homogeneous product: Products that are so similar that no one firm can profitably charge a different price from that charged by other sellers.

Household sector: The unit that makes decisions about the sale of factor services and the purchase of consumer goods and services.

Human capital: The education, training, skills, and health possessed by individuals.

Hyperinflation: An excessively high rate of inflation.

Hypothesis: An expression of the relation among variables.

I

IB curve: Curve showing equilibrium in the domestic economy.

Impact lag: The time required for decisions to take effect.

Imperfect competition: A market structure other than pure or perfect competition, particularly monopolistic competition and oligopoly.

Implementation lag: The time required for decisions to be implemented.

Implicit cost: The opportunity cost of using factors already owned by the producer. Also called imputed cost.

Implicit price deflator: See gross domestic product deflator.

Import quotas: Restrictions on the quantity of a good that may be imported.

Imported inflation: Inflation caused by increases in the prices of imported inputs.

Imports: Goods and services bought from foreign countries.

Imputed cost: See implicit cost.

Incidence of poverty: The probability of being poor.

Incidence of tax: The burden of the tax.

Income approach: Measures the total income of those involved in production.

Income effect: The effect on real income or purchasing power of a change in price.

Income elasticity of demand: A measure of the degree of responsiveness of quantity demanded to changes in income.

Income (output) gap: The difference between full-employment output and actual output.

Income statement: A statement showing revenues and expenses.

Incomes policies: A whole set of policies ranging from wage-price guidelines to wage and price controls designed to curb inflation.

Increasing-cost industry: Costs increase as the industry expands.

Increasing returns (to scale): A situation in which output increases more than in proportion to the increase in all inputs.

Independent good: Goods for which the demands are not related.

Independent variable: The variable that explains the dependent variable.

Index numbers: Numbers that measure changes in variables from one time period to another.

Indexation clause: In a labour contract, adjusts wages as prices rise.

Indirect business taxes: Taxes other than income tax, imposed on businesses, such as property taxes and sales taxes.

Induced investment: Investment that depends on changes in income.

Industrial union: A union whose membership comprises workers in a given industry.

Industry: A group of firms producing similar products.

Industry equilibrium: A situation in which all firms in the industry are in equilibrium. Industry output remains stable.

Inertial inflation: See expectational inflation.

Infant industry argument (for tariffs): The notion that new domestic industries need protection from foreign competition so that they can develop their potential.

Inflation: A sustained increase in the average level of prices over time.

Inflationary gap: The amount by which desired aggregate expenditure exceeds full-employment income or output.

Inheritance (bequest) saving: Saving motivated by the desire to leave an inheritance to children or grandchildren.

Injections: Any income injected into the income-expenditure stream.

Innovation: The introduction of new techniques of production.

Input: Anything used in the process of production.

Institution of private property: The right of individuals to own things.

Interest: The reward for capital; the payment for borrowed money.

Interest rate: The ratio of the interest to the amount borrowed.

Intermediate product: An output of one firm that is to be used as an input of another firm.

Intermediate range: The upward sloping range of an AS curve, in which real output and price level are related.

Internal balance: A situation in which aggregate expenditure equals aggregate output at full employment.

Internal debt: A debt that a nation owes to its citizens.

Internalize: To take a previously external effect into account.

International economy: The economy viewed from a global or international perspective.

International trade: The exchange of goods and services between nations.

International union: A union whose membership consists of local unions in different countries.

Inventories: Stocks of finished and semi-finished goods and raw materials kept by a firm.

Inventory cycles: Economic fluctuations caused by changes in inventory.

Inverse relation: As one variable increases, a related variable decreases.

Investment: Expenditure on capital goods.

Investment function: The relation between investment spending and its determining factors.

Invisible hand: The term given by Adam Smith to the market mechanism.

J

Joint products: Complements in production, produced together. One may be a byproduct of the other.

K

Keynesian cross: The 45-degree diagram showing aggregate expenditure and aggregate output.

Keynesian economics: Economics based on the premise that total output is determined by total spending. The demand side of the economy is emphasized.

Keynesian model: A model of the economy that emphasizes demand-side factors as determinants of output and employment, and the importance of fiscal policy as a means of stimulating the economy.

Keynesian range: The horizontal section of an AS curve that represents high unemployment.

Kinked demand curve: A demand curve with a kink, used to explain price rigidity in oligopoly markets. The upper portion of the curve is relatively flat while the lower portion is relatively steep.

L

Labour force: The number of people employed plus the number unemployed.

Labour: The factor of production defined as human effort.

Labour force participation rate: The labour force as a percentage of the adult population.

Labour market: The market in which labour is traded.

Labour mobility program: Program designed to reduce unemployment by encouraging movement of labour.

Labour union: See union.

Laffer curve: A graph showing that revenues increase as the tax rate rises, but after a while, further increases in the tax rate cause revenues to fall.

Lagging indicators: Indicators that turn downward after the cycle peaks and upward after the trough.

Land: The factor of production defined to include all natural resources.

Law of demand: The hypothesis that the higher the price of a commodity, the smaller the quantity demanded, other things being equal.

Law of diminishing marginal utility: The hypothesis that, as more and more of a commodity is consumed, extra satisfaction diminishes.

Law of diminishing returns: The hypothesis that as increasing quantities of a variable factor are added to a fixed factor, after a point, the increase in the total product will diminish.

Law of supply: The price of a product and the quantity offered for sale are directly related, all other things being equal.

Law of variable proportions: See the law of diminishing returns.

Leading indicators: Indicators that turn downward before the cycle peaks and upward before the trough.

Leakage: See withdrawal.

Legal tender (money): Anything that must, by law, be accepted as payment for goods and services or in settlement of a debt.

Lender of last resort: The central bank's function of advancing loans to financial institutions.

Less-developed country (LDC): A country with a relatively low per capita income.

Liability: Debt. The amount owed to a creditor.

Life-cycle saving: Saving that is motivated by the desire to maintain a certain level of consumption during retirement.

Limit pricing: A strategy of setting price low enough to prevent entry of new firms into the industry. Also called predatory pricing.

Limited liability: Liability limited to the amount of money invested in a business.

Limited partnership: A partnership in which one or more partners have limited liability. There must be at least one partner without limited liability.

Liquidity: The ease with which an asset can be converted into cash without much loss.

Liquidity preference: The total demand for money.

Liquidity preference schedule: A schedule showing the relation between the quantity of money demanded and the rate of interest.

Liquidity trap: A situation in which the liquidity preference curve becomes perfectly flat so that increases in the money supply have no effect on the rate of interest.

Loanable funds theory of interest: The interest rate is determined by the demand for and supply of loanable funds.

Local union: The lowest level of a union, to which a worker belongs directly.

Lockout: A temporary closing of a plant by the employer, in order to win or end a dispute.

Long run: A situation in which the firm is able to vary all its factors of production.

Long-run average cost curve: The curve showing the minimum average cost of producing each level of output in a situation where all inputs are variable.

Long-run supply curve: Curve showing supply conditions after the economy has adjusted to change.

Lorenz curve: A curve showing the degree of inequality that exists in the distribution of income.

Low-income cut-off: See poverty line.

Lump-sum tax: A fixed tax, independent of income level.

M

M1: A measure of the money supply consisting of currency and demand deposits.

M1A: A measure of the money supply consisting of M1 plus daily interest chequable and non-personal notice deposits.

M2: A measure of the money supply consisting of M1A, other notice deposits, and personal term deposits.

M2+: A measure of the money supply consisting of M2, deposits at trust and mortgage loan companies, credit unions and caisses populaires; life insurance company individual annuities; personal deposits at government-owned savings institutions; and money market mutual funds.

M3: A measure of the money supply consisting of M2, other non-personal fixed-term deposits, and foreign currency deposits of residents of Canada.

Macroeconomic policy: Deliberate government action taken to achieve certain economic objectives.

Macroeconomics: The branch of economics that studies the behaviour of aggregate economic variables such as national income, employment, and the price level. Also referred to as income and employment theory.

Managed flexible exchange rate: An exchange rate that is neither fixed nor flexible. Also called dirty float.

Marginal cost: The extra cost incurred in producing an additional unit of output.

Marginal cost pricing: A pricing strategy that involves setting price equal to marginal cost.

Marginal efficiency of investment (MEI) schedule: The schedule showing the relation between the rate of interest and the level of investment.

Marginal (physical) product (MPP or MP): The extra output produced by employing one more unit of a variable factor.

Marginal product (MP): See marginal physical product.

Marginal productivity theory (of wages): The notion that the employment of labour should be carried to the point where the marginal revenue product equals the wage rate.

Marginal propensity to consume (MPC): The change in consumption resulting from a change in income. (MPC = C/Y). Mathematically, it is the slope of the consumption function.

Marginal propensity to save (MPS): The change in saving resulting from a change in income. (MPS = S/Y). Mathematically, it is the slope of the saving function.

Marginal propensity to withdraw (MPW): The change in total withdrawals resulting from a change in income.

Marginal revenue: The extra revenue received from selling an additional unit of output.

Marginal revenue product: The additional revenue contributed by the last unit of a variable factor.

Marginal tax rate: The fraction of extra income that is paid in taxes. (MTR = T/Y).

Marginal utility: The extra satisfaction derived from consuming an additional unit of a commodity.

Market: A point of contact between buyers and sellers.

Market economy: An economy in which the market forces of demand and supply play a prominent role.

Market failure: The inability of the price system to achieve an efficient allocation of resources because of externalities or market imperfections.

Market mechanism: The complicated network of markets and prices found in most western countries.

Market period: A situation in which supply is perfectly inelastic.

Market power: The extent to which a firm or a group of firms can influence the price of a product.

Market quotas: Limits placed upon the amount of a product that producers may market.

Market share: The fraction of the total output of goods accounted for by a firm or a group of firms.

Market size effect: Demand increases when the market size increases.

Market structure: Market features that affect pricing and output decisions: pure competition, monopoly, monopolistic competition, and oligopoly.

Maturity: The date at which a loan becomes due.

Medium of exchange: Anything that is generally accepted as payment for goods and services.

Menu costs: Costs incurred when changing prices, such as updating catalogues and labels.

Merit goods: Goods determined by the government to be good for people, regardless of people's evaluation of these goods.

Microeconomics: The branch of economics that deals with the behaviour of the individual units of the economy, allocation of resources, and price and output determination of individual commodities. Also called price theory.

Minimum efficient scale: The level of output at which economies of scale end and constant returns to scale begin.

Misery index: See discomfort index.

Mixed economy: An economy in which there is a mixture of free enterprise and central decision-making.

Mixed private enterprise economy: A free enterprise economic system with some government intervention.

Model: A simplified version of a more complex system of relationships. See theory.

Monetarism: The school of thought that claims that changes in the money supply are the major cause of economic fluctuations, and that macroeconomic stability can be achieved by a steady increase in the money supply.

Monetary policy: Action taken by the central bank to change the money supply and the rate of interest in order to achieve a high level of employment and relative price stability.

Monetary theory: The study of the demand for and supply of money and their effects on the economy.

Monetary theory of inflation: The proposition that inflation is caused by increases in the money supply.

Money: Anything that is generally accepted as payment for goods and services.

Money (deposit) expansion multiplier (bank multiplier): Reciprocal of the reserve ratio.

Money multiplier: The number that, when multiplied by a change in reserves, gives the potential change in the money supply.

Money supply: The total quantity of money.

Monopolistic competition: A market structure characterized by a large number of firms selling a differentiated product.

Monopolized market: A market in which sellers have significant control over price or output.

Monopoly: A market structure in which there is only one seller of a commodity that has no close substitutes.

Monopoly power: The ability to control price or output, but not both, in an industry.

Moral suasion: An appeal by the central bank for the support of the commercial banks in achieving certain economic objectives.

Multiplier: The ratio of the change in income to the change in autonomous spending which generates the change in income.

Multiplier effect: The result that the ultimate change is greater than the initial change by some multiple.

N

National debt: The amount the government owes its creditors. Also called the public debt.

National energy policy: The federal government's program for energy self-sufficiency.

National income: The total income earned for factor services by the owners of the factors of production.

National income accounting: The process of measuring and recording various economic aggregates which describe the economic health of a country over time.

National union: A national association of local unions, which usually sets policy and does the bargaining for the associated unions.

Natural monopoly: A situation in which one firm can supply the entire market most efficiently.

Natural rate of unemployment: The rate of unemployment that is consistent with price stability.

Near bank: A financial institution such as a credit union, trust company, or mortgage loan company.

Near money: Assets that can be easily converted into the medium of exchange without any appreciable loss of value.

Negative income tax: A system whereby payments are made by the government to persons whose incomes are below the taxable level.

Negative slope: The slope of a declining curve.

Net capital formation (net investment): The difference between total (gross) investment and replacement investment. Net investment increases the capital stock.

Net domestic income at factor cost: The total income earned by the factors of production.

Net income: Revenue minus expenses.

Net investment: The difference between gross investment and depreciation; investment that increases the capital stock.

Net national income at factor cost: The total income earned by a country's factors of production.

Net national product (NNP): Gross national product minus depreciation.

New classical economists: Economists who emphasize rapid macroeconomic adjustment.

New Keynesian economists: Economists who hold that there are factors that prevent the economy from adjusting rapidly to full employment equilibrium.

Nominal income: Income expressed in current dollars.

Non-merchandise transactions (invisibles): Services, investments, and transfers, as noted on the current account.

Normal profit: Income that is just sufficient to make production worthwhile to the entrepreneur.

Normative economics: The study of what the economic situation ought to be.

Normative statement: A statement that expresses what ought to be as opposed to what is.

Notice deposits: Interest-earning deposits subject to notice before withdrawal.

O

Offers to purchase: See price supports.

Official Development Assistance (ODA): Foreign developmental aid channelled through CIDA.

Official reserves: Reserves held by a central bank to make international payments.

Okun's law: The observation that for a given percentage rise in unemployment, output falls by a greater percentage.

Oligopoly: A market structure in which there are only a few sellers. They recognize their interdependence.

Open economy: An economy that engages in international trade.

Open-market operations: The buying and selling of securities (bonds) by the central bank.

Open shop: An arrangement in a work situation whereby union membership is not a prerequisite for employment.

Opportunity cost: The alternative that is sacrificed in order to obtain something else.

Optimal labour force: The labour force that produces maximum real output per worker.

Optimum tariff: The tariff that maximizes the country's welfare.

Optimum tax rate: For a revenue tax, the rate that maximizes tax revenue.

Origin: The intersection of the x-axis and the y-axis, (0,0), on a graph.

Output (income) gap: The potential GDP minus the actual output.

Outputs: The goods and services produced by the factors of production.

Overall balance: This is achieved where the IB and EB curves intersect.

P

Paradox of thrift (saving): The apparent contradiction in the fact that an increase in intended aggregate saving results in a decrease in actual saving.

Paradox of value: The apparent contradiction in the fact that an absolute necessity like water has a lower value than a luxury item such as diamonds. Also called the water-diamond paradox.

Pareto optimality: A situation in which it is impossible to make someone better off without at the same time making someone else worse off. Also called Pareto efficiency.

Partial equilibrium analysis: A method of analysis that studies the behaviour of variables in individual markets in isolation from other markets.

Participation rate: The labour force expressed as a percentage of the adult population.

Partnership: A nonincorporated business formed by two or more partners.

Patent: A legal right given to a producer to produce a good or service and not extended to any other producer for the duration of the patent. It is therefore a barrier to entry.

Payments system: The mechanism by which exchange of goods and services is effected in non-barter situations.

Peak: The phase of the business cycle when economic activity has reached its highest point.

Per capita income: Total income divided by total population.

Perfect competition: A market structure characterized by a large number of firms selling an identical product. None of the firms has the ability to influence the price of the product it sells, and there is freedom of entry and exit. Also called pure competition.

Permanent income hypothesis: The hypothesis that current consumption depends significantly on permanent (average longterm) income.

Personal disposable income: Personal income minus personal taxes and personal transfers to the government.

Personal income: Total income of an individual before personal income taxes are paid.

Personal income tax: Taxes, based on income, paid by individuals to federal and provincial governments.

Personal saving: The part of the disposable income not spent on consumer goods and services.

Phillips curve: The curve showing the trade-off between inflation and unemployment.

Political business cycle: Economic fluctuations caused by government spending policies timed to create a favourable economic climate prior to an election.

Population explosion: Rapid population growth.

Portfolio investment: The purchase of securities whose term to maturity is more than one year.

Positive economics: The descriptive study of the behaviour of economic units and the operation of the economic system.

Positive slope: The slope of a rising curve.

Positive statement: A statement about what is. It can be verified by looking at the facts.

Post hoc, ergo propter hoc fallacy: The common error in thinking that A causes B just because A precedes B.

Potential gross domestic product: The level of gross domestic product that an economy could produce if full employment existed. Also called full-employment income or full-employment gross domestic product.

Poverty line: The level of income below which a family is considered to be poor.

Precautionary demand for money: The desire to hold money for unexpected contingencies.

Precautionary saving motive: The notion that people save in order to provide for illness and emergencies.

Predatory pricing: See limit pricing.

Price: Value expressed in terms of money. The amount of money paid for a unit of a commodity.

Price ceiling: A maximum price at which a commodity may be sold.

Price discrimination: The sale of a commodity at different prices to different customers for reasons unrelated to cost differentials.

Price elasticity of demand: The percentage change in quantity demanded as a result of a small change in price.

Price elasticity of supply: The percentage change in quantity supplied as a result of a small change in price.

Price floor: A minimum price at which a commodity may be sold.

Price indexes: Numbers that show changes in prices over a period of time.

Price leadership: A situation in which one firm (the leader) sets the price, and the other firms (the followers) simply follow.

Price level: The average level of prices as measured by an appropriate price index.

Price line: See budget line.

Price supports: A system established by government to prevent the prices of certain farm products from falling below a certain level.

Price system: A system of markets and prices that determines what to produce, how to produce, and for whom to produce.

Price taker: A firm that cannot, by itself, affect the market price of its product by varying its production. A firm in pure competition is a price taker.

Price theory: See microeconomics.

Primary reserves: Cash reserves held by banks.

Prime (lending) rate: The rate of interest that banks charge their most credit-worthy customers.

Principal: The amount lent (or borrowed) upon which interest is normally paid.

Principle of substitution: The hypothesis that a firm will use less of a more-expensive factor and more of a less-expensive factor.

Private costs: Costs that are borne solely by the individuals or firms making the decision.

Private debt: A debt owed by households or firms to other households or firms.

Private sector: The household sector and the private business sector. The non-public sector.

Private transfer payments: Payments by individuals and firms that do not represent payments for production.

Producer: See firm.

Producer sovereignty: The concept that producers decide what to produce and then convince consumers to buy it.

Product differentiation: A situation in which the firms in an industry sell similar but not identical products.

Product market: A market in which firms sell their products.

Production: The process of converting or transforming inputs into outputs.

Production function: The relation between a firm's inputs and its output.

Production possibility curve: A curve showing the various combinations of commodities that can be produced if all resources are fully employed and technology is constant.

Production possibility point: A combination of goods or services that an economy can produce.

Production possibility schedule: A table showing the different combinations of goods that an economy can produce if it uses all its resources.

Profit: The difference between total revenue and total cost. The reward for risk taking.

Progressive tax system: A system in which the tax rate increases as income increases.

Property tax: A tax levied on property, usually on real estate.

Proportional tax system: A system in which the tax rate remains constant as income increases.

Protective tariff: A tariff whose main objective is to protect domestic producers.

Psychic income: Non-monetary rewards, such as satisfaction, derived from a job.

Public debt: See national debt.

Public finance: The study of the microeconomic aspects of government spending and taxing.

Public good: A good or service for which the consumption by one person does not diminish the amount available to others. Once the good or service is produced, it is often impossible to prevent anyone from consuming it. An example is national defence.

Public investment: The purchase of new capital or the production of capital goods by the government.

Public sector: The sector of the economy where production decisions are made by government or government agencies. Also called the government sector.

Pure competition: See perfect competition.

Pure economic rent: The income earned from a factor of production whose supply is completely price inelastic.

Q

Quality competition: Competition by a firm attempting to make its products superior to the competitors'.

Quantity demanded: The amount of a commodity that households are willing to buy at some given price.

Quantity supplied: The amount of a commodity that firms are willing to sell at some given price.

Quantity theory of money: The theory that states that the money supply is directly proportional to the price level. A modified version states that the money supply is directly proportional to nominal income.

Quasi rent: The income from a factor whose supply is fixed only in the short run.

R

Rand Formula: Legislation that made it compulsory for a worker to pay union dues even if not a union member.

Rational expectations: The theory that people are aware of all the factors that determine a given event and that they base their expectations on this knowledge.

Real business cycle: The theory that the main causes of business cycles are shifts in the aggregate supply curve.

Real capital: Capital items such as buildings, tools, and equipment.

Real gross domestic product: Gross domestic product adjusted for price level changes.

Real income (constant prices): Income expressed in constant dollars.

Real output per capita: Real GDP divided by the population.

Real rate of interest: The rate of interest adjusted for inflation.

Recession: A phase of the business cycle characterized by a general downswing in economic activity.

Recessionary gap: See deflationary gap.

Recognition lag: The time required to recognize a problem.

Recovery: See expansion.

Redeposit: See deposit switching.

Regional specialization: A situation in which different regions of a country concentrate on the economic activity in which they have an advantage.

Regressive tax system: A system in which the tax rate decreases as income increases.

Regulated monopoly: Monopolies controlled by government legislation.

Relative price: The ratio of two absolute prices. The price of one good expressed in terms of the price of another good.

Rent: Payment for the services of land.

Reservation price: The lowest price a seller is willing to accept for a good or service.

Reserve requirement: The amount the commercial banks were legally obliged to keep in cash or as deposits at the central bank. No longer in effect.

Resources: See factors of production.

Retained earnings: Profits of a firm that are not distributed to shareholders. Also called undistributed profits.

Revaluation (of exchange rates): The raising of the value of a country's currency in terms of another country's currency.

Revenue tariff: A tariff with the main objective of raising revenue for the government.

Risk premium: An extra charge that reflects the degree of risk involved in a transaction.

Robin Hood effect: The redistribution of income from high-income earners to low-income earners, thereby increasing consumer spending.

Rule of 70: A formula that allows quick calculation of the time required for the price level to double, given the rate of inflation. The time required is 70 divided by the rate of inflation.

S

Sales tax: A percentage tax imposed on the selling price of a wide range of commodities.

Saving: That part of disposable income that is not spent on consumer goods and services.

Say's Law: The proposition that the very act of production indicates the presence of an equivalent demand: that is, supply creates its own demand.

Scarcity: Limited resources in the face of unlimited wants.

Schedule A banks: Canadian-owned banks.

Schedule B banks: Foreign-owned banks.

Scientific method: A method of inquiry stressing the formulation and testing of hypotheses.

Seasonal unemployment: Unemployment caused by seasonal variations.

Secondary reserves: Excess cash reserves, treasury bills, and day-to-day loans held by banks.

Selective controls: Controls that affect certain industries or sectors of the economy, but not the whole economy directly.

Sellers' inflation: Inflation caused by price increases by firms due to increases in production costs. See cost-push inflation.

Services: Intangible things that satisfy a want. Examples are banking services and transportation services.

Short run: A situation in which the firm is unable to vary all its inputs.

Short-run shutdown point: The price-output combination at which price just equals average variable cost.

Short-run supply curve: That portion of the MC curve that lies above the AVC curve.

Short-term capital flows: Movements of financial assets whose term to maturity is less than one year.

Shortage (excess quantity demanded): Quantity demanded exceeds quantity supplied at a given price.

Single proprietorship: A form of business organization in which there is a single owner who is responsible for all actions taken by the firm. A single proprietor does not enjoy limited liability.

Size distribution of income: The distribution of income according to households in various income groups.

Slope of a linear curve: The slope is constant.

Slope of a non-linear curve: The slope at any point on the curve is the tangent to that point; the slope varies from point to point on the curve.

Social cost: The total cost to society as a whole of decisions made, and actions taken, by individuals and firms.

Social science: The study of aspects of behaviour of human society.

Socialism: The state owns and controls the economy's resources.

Socialistic system: See command economy.

Sole proprietorship: See single proprietorship.

Specialization: Concentration on a particular occupation or task to become proficient at that task.

Specific tariff: A tariff expressed as a certain amount per unit of the imported item.

Speculative demand for money: The desire to hold money in anticipation of the movement of the prices of financial assets.

Stabilization policies: Actions taken to promote economic stability.

Stagflation: The simultaneous occurrence of high rates of inflation and high rates of unemployment.

Stock variable: The amount existing at a point in time.

Stocks (shares): Evidence of ownership in a company.

Store of value: Money or other valuables put away for future use.

Strike: Work stoppage by a union in an attempt to put pressure on the employer.

Structural unemployment: Unemployment that results when workers do not possess the skills required for various job opportunities.

Substitutes: Goods that can be used in place of other goods. Examples are tea and coffee, pens and pencils.

Substitution effect: The effect on the demand for a product when the price of a substitute changes.

Supply: The various quantities of a commodity that will be offered for sale at various possible prices.

Supply curve: The curve showing the relation between price and quantity supplied.

Supply schedule: A table showing the relation between price and quantity supplied.

Supply shifters: Factors that cause the supply curve to shift.

Supply side: the production side of the economy.

Supply-side economics: An approach to economics that stresses supply factors such as incentives to work, save, and invest.

Surplus: See excess quantity supplied.

T

Target saving: Saving for a specific purpose, such as the purchase of a car or house.

Tariff: A tax imposed on imported goods.

Tariff evasion: Avoiding tariffs by rerouting goods through other countries.

Tax: A compulsory payment imposed by a government.

Tax-based incomes policies (TIPS): The use of tax incentives to encourage compliance with wage and price controls.

Taxable income: The portion of income on which income tax payable is calculated.

Technological efficiency: Efficiency measured in terms of the use of inputs in physical terms. Also called technical efficiency.

Technological unemployment: A type of structural employment caused by the introduction of labour-saving equipment or methods.

Terms of trade: The rate at which a country's exports exchange for its imports.

Theory: A testable hypothesis about the way in which variables are related.

Total cost (TC): The sum of all costs incurred in producing a given output of goods or services. The sum of total fixed cost and total variable cost.

Total product (TP): The total output of goods and services produced during a period of time.

Total revenue (TR): The total amount received from the sale of goods and services. It equals the product of price and quantity sold.

Total utility: The total satisfaction derived from consuming a commodity.

Trade creation: A situation in which economic integration leads to a change in the direction of trade from a higher cost supplier to a lower cost supplier.

Trade deficit: See balance of trade deficit.

Trade diversion: A situation in which economic integration leads to a change in the direction of trade from a lower cost supplier to a higher cost supplier.

Trade surplus: See balance of trade surplus.

Trade union: See craft union.

Transactions demand for money: The desire to hold money for transactions purposes.

Transfer earnings: The minimum payment required to attract resources away from other uses.

Transfer payments (transfers): Payments that do not represent a reward for productive services.

Treasury bill (T-bill): A security sold by the government with a promise to pay a certain amount within a short time, usually from 30 to 90 days.

Trough: The phase of the business cycle when economic activity is at its lowest level for that cycle.

20% Club: organizations which aim to reduce local greenhouse gas emissions by 20% from 1990 levels.

U

Underground economy: Includes all economic activities and transactions that are not recorded by national income statisticians and on which no taxes are paid.

Undistributed profits: See retained earnings.

Unemployment: A situation in which people are unable to find jobs.

Unemployment rate: The number of people unemployed expressed as a percentage of the labour force.

Union: An association of workers organized to negotiate the terms and conditions of their employment with their employer.

Union shop: An arrangement whereby workers who are not union members may be hired provided that they become union members within a specified period of time.

Unit banking system: A banking system with many independent banks.

Unit of account (measure of value): The unit for expressing the value of goods and services; in Canada, the dollar is the usual unit of account.

Util: The unit of satisfaction derived from consuming goods and services.

Utility: Satisfaction derived from consuming goods and services.

V

Value-added: The difference between the value of a firm's output and the value of its inputs purchased from other firms.

Variable: Anything that can assume different values.

Variable cost: Any cost that varies with the level of output.

Variable factor: Any factor whose quantity can be varied in the short run.

Velocity of circulation (of money): The number of times, on average, that a unit of money is spent during a period of time.

Very short period (market period): A situation in which sellers are unable to vary their output.

Voluntary arbitration: Each party in a labour dispute submits its case to an arbitrator and agrees to abide by the decision.

Voluntary restrictions: One government may ask another to restrict its exports to that country.

W

Wage and price controls (incomes policies): Imposed by the government to limit increases in both wages and prices.

Wage-price spiral: Increases in wages followed by increases in prices followed by increases in wages and so on.

Wage rate: The price of labour per unit of time.

Wage transfer mechanism: The process by which wage changes in one industry are transmitted to other industries.

Wages: Payment for labour services.

Wagner's Law: The statement that government spending will grow at a faster rate than the rate of increase in output.

Water-diamond paradox: See paradox of value.

Water pollution: Toxic waste, chemical spills, chemical production, municipal waste and acid rain.

Wealth: The value of one's assets.

Wholesale price index: A price index that measures price changes in primary goods.

Withdrawal: Any income taken out of the income-expenditure stream, including savings, taxes, and imports.

Workable competition: Under workable competition, an industry is competitive enough to maintain output and keep profits at reasonable levels.

X

X-inefficiency: Failure to use resources in a manner that results in the lowest cost of producing any given level of output.

INDEX